Digital Transformation, Perspective Development, and Value Creation

This edited collection aims to provide relevant theoretical frameworks and the latest empirical research findings in the area of business management. It covers case studies provided by teachers visiting the University of Economics in Katowice, Poland, within Erasmus and CEEPUS programs. Over 12 years, approximately 25 teachers have been coming year by year to Katowice, presenting their monographic lectures and participating in seminars on their research results and educational achievements. This book contains descriptions of case studies, elaborated by Erasmus and CEEPUS teachers, illustrating that the case study is a method of research as well as a method applied in education and emphasizing the value of qualitative methods by example of case studies.

The key benefit of qualitative research is that it allows a researcher to perceive and understand context within which decisions and actions take place. Hence, to understand peoples' motivations, their reasons, their actions, and the context for their beliefs and actions, qualitative research is the best route. Assuming that business organizations as well as individuals are entirely linked together via the Internet, a new approach to business communication and marketing, business modeling and management are developed to reveal an increase of business synergy effects, the alignment of information and communication technologies (ICT) and business and social value creation, as well as sustainability and environment protection. Through this book, readers have an opportunity to learn about relevance and rigor in qualitative research and how the case study can be applied in various organizational contexts.

Małgorzata Pańkowska, PhD, is a professor of social science, and chair of the Department of Informatics at the University of Economics in Katowice, Poland.

Routledge Advances in Management and Business Studies

Human Resource Management and Internal Marketing
Teena Mishra

Human Resources Management in Multinational Companies
A Central European Perspective
Marzena Stor

Corporate Culture and Globalization
Ideology and Identity in a Global Fashion Retailer
Yi Zhu

Corporate Compliance and Conformity
A Convenience Theory Approach to Executive Deviance
Petter Gottschalk

CSR Reporting and the Belt and Road Initiative
Implementation by Chinese Multinational Enterprises?
Ruopiao Zhang, Carlos Noronha and Jieqi Guan

Corporate Social Hypocrisy
CSR in the Era of Global Crises
Dalia Streimikiene, Asta Mikalauskiene and Gabija Stanislovaityte

Information, Security and Society in the COVID-19 Pandemic
Edited by Natalia Moch, Wioletta Wereda and Jerzy Stańczyk

Technologies and Trends in the Halal Industry
Edited by Nor Aida Abdul Rahman, Kamran Mahroof and Azizul Hassan

Digital Transformation, Perspective Development, and Value Creation
Research Case Studies
Edited by Małgorzata Pańkowska

For more information about this series, please visit: www.routledge.com/
Routledge-Advances-in-Management-and-Business-Studies/book-series/SE0305

Digital Transformation, Perspective Development, and Value Creation
Research Case Studies

Edited by Małgorzata Pańkowska

Routledge
Taylor & Francis Group
NEW YORK AND LONDON

First published 2024
by Routledge
605 Third Avenue, New York, NY 10158

and by Routledge
4 Park Square, Milton Park, Abingdon, Oxon, OX14 4RN

Routledge is an imprint of the Taylor & Francis Group, an informa business

© 2024 selection and editorial matter, Małgorzata Pańkowska; individual chapters, the contributors

The right of Małgorzata Pańkowska to be identified as the author of the editorial material, and of the authors for their individual chapters, has been asserted in accordance with sections 77 and 78 of the Copyright, Designs and Patents Act 1988.

All rights reserved. No part of this book may be reprinted or reproduced or utilised in any form or by any electronic, mechanical, or other means, now known or hereafter invented, including photocopying and recording, or in any information storage or retrieval system, without permission in writing from the publishers.

Trademark notice: Product or corporate names may be trademarks or registered trademarks, and are used only for identification and explanation without intent to infringe.

Library of Congress Cataloguing-in-Publication Data
Names: Pańkowska, Małgorzata, editor.
Title: Digital transformation, perspective development, and value creation : research case studies / edited by Małgorzata Pańkowska.
Description: New York, NY : Routledge, 2024. | Series: Routledge advances in management and business studies | Includes bibliographical references and index.
Identifiers: LCCN 2023018669 | ISBN 9781032453408 (hardback) | ISBN 9781032453569 (paperback) | ISBN 9781003376583 (ebook)
Subjects: LCSH: Technological innovations--Economic aspects. | Information technology--Economic aspects.
Classification: LCC HC79.T4 D544 2024 | DDC 658/.05--dc23/eng/ 20230421
LC record available at https://lccn.loc.gov/2023018669

ISBN: 978-1-032-45340-8 (hbk)
ISBN: 978-1-032-45356-9 (pbk)
ISBN: 978-1-003-37658-3 (ebk)

DOI: 10.4324/9781003376583

Typeset in Times New Roman
by MPS Limited, Dehradun

Contents

List of Figures	*viii*
List of Tables	*ix*
List of Contributors	*xi*
Forewords by John Traxler and Vera G. Meister	*xx*
Preface by Małgorzata Pańkowska	*xxiv*
Acknowledgments	*xxxi*

PART 1
Digital Transformation and Development of High
Education Institutions   1

1   Innovations in a CEEPUS Academic Network and
Their Impact on Management Effectiveness and
Research Achievements   3
GALIA MARINOVA AND KRISEL TOLA

2   The Effect of Ethical Leadership and Leadership
Effectiveness on Employees' Turnover Intention in
High Education Institutions: A Case Study of Ibagué
University   23
CESAR AUGUSTO DÍAZ MOYA AND
PAULA LORENA RODRÍGUEZ FERRO

3   Digital Transformation in Education: A Case Study
of Teacher Information Network (TIN) in Turkey   43
EMRAH TOSUN, HÜSEYIN CAN BARUTCU, SUAT ŞAHİN,
ZÜMRÜT ECEVİT SATI, AND SEVİNÇ GÜLSEÇEN

vi *Contents*

4 Ambient, Guerilla, and Event Marketing in
Education of Marketers, and Development of
Creative Abilities: A Case Study 64
KATARÍNA FICHNOVÁ, ŁUKASZ P. WOJCIECHOWSKI, AND
EDITA ŠTRBOVÁ

PART 2
Digital Transformation and Perspective Development at
Business Organizations 83

5 Testing and Certification of New Product
Development in the Electronics Industry: Case Studies 85
DARIUSZ MEISER AND MACIEJ NOWAK

6 Role of Information System Support in Project
Management: Case of Companies Competing at
Publicly Funded Calls for Projects 103
JERNEJA ŠAVRIČ AND BLAŽ RODIČ

7 Comparison of Multi-Criteria Decision
Methodologies: Case of Water Management
Investment Project 118
MARJAN BRELIH AND BLAŽ RODIČ

8 Augmented Reality in Medical Training of Patient
Referrals: A Nursing Case Study of Children's
Hospital in Taiwan 137
SHU RU UEN AND YUH WEN CHEN

9 The Use of Blockchain Technology in the Sports
Sector: The Case of AC Milan Football (Soccer)
Team 159
KACPER ZAGAŁA AND MARIO NICOLIELLO

PART 3
Value Creation at Business Organizations 175

10 "Pacto pela Industria": Reindustrialization
Opportunities in the Great ABC Region, Brazil 177
CRISTINA FRÓES DE BORJA REIS, AROALDO OLIVEIRA SANTOS,
SHEILA RIBEIRO MARQUES, AND AMANDA COLOMBO

Contents vii

11 Auditing Human Resource Management Practices:
A Case Study in the Egyptian Hospitality Industry 193
HAZEM TAWFIK HALIM, YASSER HALIM, HAZEM ABDELHADY,
AND KARIM SALEM

12 Organization and Incentivization of Risk
Management: An Agency Theory Case Study 219
MARTA MICHAELIS

13 Embracing CSR as an Essential Part of Business:
The Case of Viking by Raja Group, Cluj-Napoca 251
ZENOVIA-CRISTIANA POP

Index *265*

Figures

1.1	Dashboard of IMA-NET platform	13
1.2	The fulfillment as a measure of effectiveness in the CEEPUS network BG-1103 (obtained in MATLAB)	17
1.3	Local, CEEPUS, and total students at summer schools and academia	17
2.1	Management and economics school structure	26
2.2	Adopted research model	30
2.3	New model in Ibagué University case study	37
3.1	Scopus database – digital transformation studies by year	44
4.1	Holistic model of creativity development	67
4.2	Examples of TTCT solutions in both groups of subjects: irrelevant (a), relevant low creativity (b), and relevant high creativity (c)	72
7.1	Overview of the top-level criteria in the proposed hierarchical multi-criteria decision-making model	125
7.2	The tree of criteria with definitions and value domains	126
7.3	Graphical representation of projects ranked by selected criteria	130
8.1	The organization of NTUCH referral team	140
8.2	The clinical situation for patient referral of NTUCH	141
8.3	Framework of TAM	144
8.4	Research framework	147
8.5	AR system of patient referrals in children hospital by HMT-1 and Webex	149
8.6	Calibrated results of final model	152
11.1	The accountability HR measurement trends	197
12.1	Research methodology of an agency theoretical case study	222
12.2	Core results in centralization and decentralization, depending on RM's risk aversion	238
12.3	Core results in centralization and decentralization, depending on the BUM's risk aversion	239

Tables

1.1	Participants in the CEEPUS network events	9
1.2	Measures of the research activities in the CEEPUS network BG-1103	19
2.1	Measures in factor analysis	31
2.2	Mean scores, validity, and reliability of research model	33
2.3	SEM results	36
3.1	Main elements of digital transformation	45
3.2	Demographics of participants	50
3.3	Codes obtained from the dimension of scope and content	51
3.4	Codes obtained from the dimension of technical and design features	53
3.5	Codes obtained from the dimension of teacher competencies	55
3.6	Codes obtained from the dimension of motivation	57
4.1	Scores of the pretest and retest of the investigated groups in dimensions of creativity and the standard deviation	73
4.2	Results of statistic confrontation of dimension of creativity between the control group and the experimental group, ante, and post	73
7.1	Basic criteria values for options P1, P2, P3, and P4	128
7.2	Simple if-then rules for the criterion "external"	129
7.3	Evaluations of projects for aggregated criteria	130
8.1	Questionnaire design	148
8.2	Path analysis	151
10.1	Summary profile of the seven cities in the Greater ABC region	179
10.2	SDG achievement indicators in the ABC municipalities	180
10.3	Participation of the sectors of activity in formal jobs in the Greater ABC Paulista Region, 1989–2020	183

x *Tables*

12.1	Overview of the core contributions of the chapter	221
12.2	Overview of the symbols used in the case study	225
12.3	Summary of the exercises, their results, conclusions, and practical value	245

Contributors

Hazem Abdelhady is Raya Holding's chief human resources officer. Abdelhady joined Raya Holding in 2012 with 20 years of experience across the banking and hospitality sectors with a knowledge, experience, and exposure spanning Egypt and Africa. In 2005, amid the start of the banking sector reform, Abdelhady managed the Central Bank of Egypt and the United Bank Human Resources modernization initiative. Prior to that, Abdelhady's work experience includes serving as the human resources director of Four Seasons Hotels & Resorts in Egypt, regional director of Training at Accor Hotels in Egypt, and as director of the Hilton Africa Training Center in Kenya. Abdelhady holds a bachelor's of science (BSc) in hotel management and a master's in public administration (MPA) from the American University in Cairo.

Hüseyin Can Barutcu, who was born in Antakya/Turkey in 1990, completed his high school education at Bursa Erkek Lisesi. He received a bachelor of business administration education and completed his master's degree studies in the field of Industry 4.0 and Digital Transformation. Currently, he is carrying out his doctoral studies in the field of expert systems, machine learning, and data science in the Department of Informatics at Istanbul University, and also gives lectures in the Department of Management Information Systems at Haliç University.

Marjan Brelih completed the doctoral study program Organization and Management of Information Systems at the Faculty of Organizational Sciences in Kranj, Slovenia. During his 15-year career, he was involved in the planning, development, implementation, and maintenance of software and information systems in the field of reducing energy consumption and environmental burdens. He works in the field of energy retrofit, renewable sources, industry, public lighting, water cycle, and decarbonization. He deals with PLC automation, IIoT, SCADA, EMS, technical and economic optimization, Carbon Audit, and predictive data analytics. The solutions, which were developed or co-developed by him, are implemented in the following countries: Austria, BIH, Bulgaria, Croatia, Czech Republic, Italy, Montenegro, Romania, Serbia, and Slovenia.

Yuh Wen Chen, PhD, is a professor, now the dean of academic affairs at Da Yeh University, Taiwan. His main interests and specialties are the Internet of Things, optimization methods, multiple criteria decision-making, and artificial intelligence. Some of his research is available at ResearchGate: https://www.researchgate.net/profile/Yuh-Wen-Chen.

Amanda Colombo graduated in law and postgraduated in public and constitutional law. She has specialization in real estate business law. Currently, she is legal coordinator of the Greater ABC Economic Development Agency, Brazil.

Cesar Augusto Díaz Moya was born in Colombia in 1982, graduated in foreign languages and international business, specialist in strategic marketing and international business, and master in innovation for business development from ITESM-México. He has 18 years of experience in university teaching. He has worked as advisor and business consultant in internationalization processes, supply chain logistics management, international physical distribution logistics, and technological innovation projects. He is a researcher, director, and jury of degree projects related to business diagnoses, internationalization plans, and intra-company projects of logistics management, business innovation, and corporate social responsibility. He is a lecturer with experience in international teaching and active participation in academic networks in Europe and Latin America.

Katarína Fichnová is a professor, PhD, and a university pedagogue in the Department of Mass Media Communication and Advertising at the Faculty of Arts of the Constantine the Philosopher's University in Nitra, Slovak Republic. She is a long-term researcher focused on the topics of creativity and its effectivity, creative potential of marketing-communication agencies, creative process, social-psychological phenomenon, and their application in mass media and marketing, and on new trends in media and marketing communication. She is a laureate of several accolades (rectors' honors, deans' honors, the deans' bronze medal, and others).

Cristina Fróes de Borja Reis is PhD in economics, and adjunct professor at the Center of Engineering, Modeling and Applied Social Sciences/ Federal University of ABC, Brazil. She is director of the Centre of Strategical Studies on Democracy, Development and Sustainability (NEEDDS), UFABC Vice-Coordinator of the Global Value Chains Research Group, UFABC. She is board member also of the Sao Paulo Regional Council of Economists.

Sevinç Gülseçen, PhD, completed her doctoral degree in MIS. Within the scope of Erasmus and bilateral agreements, she carried out research and lecture activities and took part in projects in Lithuania, France, Scotland, Slovakia, Bulgaria, Italy, and Poland. She worked as a visiting scholar at Dell TECH (Delaware, USA) in 1987–1988 within the scope of Higher Education Council of Turkey-World Bank Project, NOAO (Arizona, USA) in 2000 and Ball State University (Indiana, USA) in 2008 and 2011, respectively. She is the founder of Istanbul University Human-Computer Interaction (HCI) Laboratory. Dr. Gulsecen is the chief editor of *Acta INFOLOGICA*, a scientific peer-reviewed journal, published by Istanbul University Press, Turkey. She continues her administrative duties as Head of Informatics Department at Istanbul University.

Hazem Tawfik Halim is a professor of human resource management, director of the MBA program, the Faculty of Business Administration, Economics and Political Science, the British University in Egypt. Hazem studied hotel management in Helwan University before commencing a research and teaching career in this area. He graduated in 1991 with excellent honors. In 1997, he obtained his MSc in the field of education and training from the same university and then completed his PhD in human resource management from the Manchester Metropolitan University, England, in 2002. Hazem is a senior fellow in the Higher Education Academy, UK (SFHEA). He assumed an academic career at the Department of Hotel Management, the Faculty of Tourism and Hotel Management, Suez Canal University, in 1995. He was promoted to the post of associate professor in 2008, then to a full professor of human resource management at the same university in 2013. In 2010, he joined the Business Administration Department at the British University in Egypt, and then assumed the role of the acting head of department from 2011 to 2013. Hazem is an expert in the preparation and execution of educational and training programs. His industrial and unique academic experience has helped him to devise and conduct numerous undergraduate, postgraduate, professional educational, and training programs; both inside and outside Egypt. He also executed auditing programs to few hotels in Cairo. Hazem has worked in a teaching and consulting capacity in many different universities, institutions, and academic bodies in Egypt and abroad. He also had a wide number of research responsibilities in the Suez Canal University. He supervised a number of MSc and PhD students involved in projects on human resource management practices. Hazem has published several research studies in the area of performance management, employee resourcing, employee development, employee minimum wage, psychometric analysis, and emotional intelligence. In addition, he is currently a research associate at

xiv *Contributors*

the center of hospitality and employment research (CHER), England, and a member of the Egyptian Society of Scientific Experts on Tourism "ESSET", Egypt. Moreover, Hazem is a certified behavior and attitude assessor from TTI Insight, USA. Hazem also worked as an organizational development and human resource management consultant for distinguished consultancy companies in the past 14 years. He utilized his concepts and academic methodologies to successfully accomplish many assignments both in the public and private sectors. Hazem has successfully completed projects of the following nature: full re-structuring process, performance management, and performance measurement.

Yasser Halim is a professor; he obtained his PhD in the specialization in marketing. He is currently working at MSA University as the vice dean of Environmental Affairs and Community Service and also head of Marketing and International Business Department. Besides, he is currently the Quality Consultant of the Faculty of Management Sciences, MSA University, Egypt. Prof. Yasser's work has enabled him to gain experience in many fields such as education, human resource management, organizational behavior, organizational change, marketing management, sales, service marketing, social marketing, consumer behavior, and others. During his work in several universities, research centers, and other organizations, he has enriched his capabilities in consultancy and training in different management and marketing fields. Prof. Yasser has published several books and research studies in different areas. In addition, he is a fellow in the Higher Education Academy in the UK.

Galia Marinova graduated and postgraduated in electronics in 1988 from the Technical University of Sofia (TUS), Bulgaria. She received a PhD degree in 1994 from TUS. Since 2011, she's an associate professor in the Faculty of Telecommunications at TUS. G. Marinova did one-year post-doctoral research in CNAM-Paris, France, in 1999–2000. She has ten doctoral students, three of them graduated. She is author and co-author of more than 100 scientific papers. She was the general chair of IWSSIP'2022 conference. She's coordinator of the CEEPUS network project: CIII-BG-1103-07-2223: Modeling, Simulation and Computer-Aided Design in Engineering and Management. She is IEEE CAS and WIE senior member, vice-chair of IEEE CAS/SSC Chapter, and chair of the IEEE WIE affinity group in Bulgaria.

Dariusz Meiser is a PhD student at the University of Economics in Katowice, Poland. He received a master of science degree in electronics engineering from Silesian Technical University in Gliwice, Poland, and master of business administration (MBA) degree from the University of Gdansk, Business Centre Club in Warsaw, Poland, and Erasmus University in

Rotterdam, Netherlands. He has 25 years of managerial experience in the electronics industry. He was, among others, the founder and long-term manager of the Electromagnetic Compatibility (EMC) laboratory. He currently works as the director of Development in Dysten Ltd. in Zabrze, Poland. His research interests focus on the project management, risk management in New Product Development (NPD) projects, quality management systems, and EMC issues in electronic manufacturing industry.

Marta Michaelis obtained her bachelor's degree from the University of Economics in Katowice, Poland, in 2012. Afterward, she obtained her master's degree (2015) and her PhD (2022) from the Faculty of Business and Economics, University of Goettingen, Germany. In years 2015–2022, she has been a research associate at the Chair of Finance and Control at the same university. Currently, she works in a private sector. Her research focuses on game theory and agency theory. Her special interests lie in the didactic excellence in higher education.

Mario Nicoliello is currently a researcher in business administration at the University of Brescia, Italy, where he teaches accounting and financial reporting. After the PhD at the University of Brescia – with a dissertation about the history of accounting studies in Italy – he taught at the University of Pisa and the University of Genoa. His research interests focus on accounting history, accounting education, and economics of sports, particularly the annual accounts of football clubs and the management of sports events. He is a visiting professor at Nuertingen-Geisslingen University in Germany and Haaga Helia University in Finland, and he collaborates with the King's College Business School in London.

Maciej Nowak is a professor at the University of Economics in Katowice in Poland, Faculty of Informatics and Communication, Department of Operations Research. His research interests include decision theory, operations research, multiple criteria decision making, simulation, project management, operations management, and logistics. His most important scientific achievements include new methods for multiple criteria decision making under risk. He is an author and co-author of 12 books and over 90 scientific articles. His papers appeared in leading operations research journals, including *European Journal of Operational Research, Journal of Global Optimization, Control & Cybernetics, Journal of Business Economics and Management*, and *Technological and Economic Development of Economy*. He participated in international research projects in collaboration with colleagues from Spain, Canada, Taiwan, Lithuania, and Czech Republic.

xvi *Contributors*

Małgorzata Pańkowska, PhD, is a professor of social science and chair of the Department of Informatics at the University of Economics in Katowice, Poland. She received the qualification in econometrics and statistics from the University of Economics in Katowice, the PhD and the Doctor Habilitatus degree from the University of Economics in Katowice. She was a visiting professor at ISLA Braganca, Portugal; Trier University, Germany; ICHEC in Brussels, Belgium; Istanbul University, Turkey; Ionian University in Corfu, Greece; Lapland University in Finland; Universidad de Ibague, Ibague-Tolima, Colombia; USEK, Lebanon. She is the Vice-President in the Board of Information System Audit and Control Association (ISACA) Katowice Chapter. She is a Program Committee member of the following conferences: Perspectives in Business Informatics Research (BIR), International Conference on Digital Economy (ICDEc), and Information Systems Development (ISD).

Zenovia-Cristiana Pop is an assistant professor at the Faculty of Economics and Business Administration of the Babeş-Bolyai University of Cluj-Napoca, Romania. Her research interests include strategic management, entrepreneurship, and business ethics. Currently, her work focuses on topics related to entrepreneurial intentions, gender roles, and SMEs. She is the author and co-author of numerous scientific articles and books in the field of management and trade relations. She has carried out extensive research in countries such as Austria, Germany, and Poland.

Sheila Ribeiro Marques graduated in financial management. She is executive MBA in financial administration. Currently, she is administrative and financial coordinator of the Economic Development Agency of Greater ABC, Brazil.

Blaž Rodič is an associate professor of information studies at the Faculty of Information Sciences in Novo mesto, Slovenia. He holds a PhD degree in organizational sciences – information systems management and a BSc degree in electrical engineering. He has been a visiting scholar at the Waterford Institute of Technology, Ireland, and at the University of Houston, among others. His research interests include development of decision support systems using multicriteria decision analysis and optimization solutions for manufacturing, transport/logistics, and service systems using system dynamics, discrete event simulation, and agent-based modeling of societal and organizational systems. He has published over 100 works, including WoS/SCOPUS indexed papers and an international patent.

Paula Lorena Rodríguez Ferro was born in Colombia in 1984. She graduated as a financial manager, then became specialist in strategic marketing and international business, and got a master's degree in administration with an emphasis on prospective from Externado University in Colombia. She has 16 years of experience in university teaching, and is curriculum and academic director of International Business Administration and Economics programs, researcher, director and jury of degree projects related to business plans, entrepreneurship projects, and project formulation and evaluation.

Suat Şahin is a PhD student in Informatics Department from Istanbul University. He is currently working as an IT teacher at Tuzla Dede Korkut Secondary School in Istanbul, Turkey. He studies in the fields of computer science, artificial intelligence, machine learning, and educational data mining.

Karim Salem is an associate professor at the School of Business Administration, Economics, and Political Science at the British University in Egypt and a former member of the Egyptian Parliament. Dr. Salem holds doctorate from the Faculty of Economics and Political Sciences at Cairo University. His bachelor's and master's degrees, in business and public administration, were received from the American University in Cairo, Egypt. Dr. Salem has also served on the Faculty of Foreign Trade at the Helwan University, on the Faculty of the Arab Academy for Science, Technology, and Maritime Transport, and was a visiting faculty member at the National University of Public Service in Hungary. He has served as an instructor at the American University in Cairo, the Egyptian Police Academy, and at the Anti-corruption Academy of the Administrative Control Authority. Representing Heliopolis in the Egyptian Parliament from January 2016 until January 2021, Dr. Salem served on the Education and Scientific Research Committee. Additionally, he served on the Planning and Budgeting, Culture and Media, and on the General Parliamentary Committees. While serving on these committees, he contributed to legislation regarding education, as well as civil service reform, public finance, local government, social empowerment, public enterprise, and economic development. Dr. Salem has a keen interest in public policy, education and education reform, and governance. He has contributed to numerous publications, including the *Journal of Business Studies*, *Arab Journal of Political Sciences*, *International Journal of Business and Public Administration*, *Journal of US-China Public Administration*, and the *Scientific Journal of Economics and Commerce*. Dr. Salem has been contracted as a strategic development consultant by several Egyptian government institutions from 1997 through 2016, as well as several international development organizations, including the World Bank, the United Nations Development Programme, the United States Agency for International Development, and the Canadian Agency for International Development Agency.

Zümrüt Ecevit Sati graduated from Dokuz Eylül University, Turkey, Faculty of Economics and Administrative Sciences. He completed his master's and doctorate degrees in business management. His PhD thesis topic is "The Impact of Supply Chain Management on the Competitiveness of Companies". He worked at Michigan State University's Business College-CIBER between 2004 and 2005. Dr. Ecevit Sati has done various researches in the fields of innovation management, logistics management, supply chain management, digital transformation, and new technologies. In addition to these studies, he works in various industrial organizations for the purpose of university-industry cooperation and contributes to this effort with training seminars and scientific research.

Jerneja Šavrič is a project manager at the Faculty of Tourism, University of Maribor, Slovenia, where her work is directed in facilitating the preparation of project proposals and management of ongoing research projects. She has a law degree from the Faculty of Law, University of Ljubljana, Slovenia, and PhD from the School of Advanced Social Studies. In her dissertation, she has studied the EU cohesion policy financial instruments absorption capacity of the EU member states and strategies of companies competing for the public research grants. Her current research interests include the development of tourism strategies and sustainable tourism.

Aroaldo Oliveira Da Silva graduated in social sciences. He got extension in Defense Resources Management. He has worked as the director of the ABC Metalworkers Union. Currently, he is the president of Industriall Brazil and president of the Director Council of the Economic Development Agency of the Great ABC region.

Edita Štrbová is an associate professor, PhD, and a university pedagogue in the Department of Mass Media Communication and Advertising at the Faculty of Arts of the Constantine the Philosopher's University in Nitra, Slovak Republic. Her work focuses on event marketing, experiential marketing, art marketing, and digital marketing communication. In her pedagogical activities she applies knowledge of general, developmental, and social psychology within marketing and media communication. Since 2013, she has been the editor-in-chief of *Dot.comm* journal aimed at the theory, research, and practice of media and marketing communication.

Krisel Tola is a lecturer in the Department of Computer Sciences, Faculty of Information Technology at the Aleksandër Moisiu University of Durrës, Albania. He postgraduated from the Aleksandër Moisiu University of Durrës as MSc in applied computer sciences. Besides working as a lecturer, he is also pursuing his PhD from the Faculty of Telecommunications at the Technical University of Sofia, Bulgaria. Furthermore, he is the founder and CEO of KTSoftware Solutions, a software house company based in Tirana, Albania. Tola has authored or co-authored several publications in peer-reviewed journals and regional, national, and international conferences in the framework of information technology.

Emrah Tosun, who worked as an information technologies teacher at the Ministry of National Education in Turkey, was born in Isparta in 1986. He completed his primary and high school education here. He completed his undergraduate education at Kahramanmaraş Sütçü İmam University and his master's degree at Süleyman Demirel University. He is currently a PhD student at Istanbul University in Turkey, Department of Informatics.

Shu Ru Uen is the head of nursing in the children's intensive care unit (ICU) of National Taiwan University Children's Hospital, acting as a team manager for the transfer/referral of children with acute illnesses to an external support. The duty of a team manager for children in critical care is to arrange the team's human resources, coordinate the personnel transfer, plan the education and training of the nurses, and maintain the related equipment.

Łukasz P. Wojciechowski is an associate professor, PhD, and a university pedagogue in the Department of Mass Media Communication at the Faculty of Mass Media Communication of the University of Ss. Cyril and Methodius in Trnava, Slovak Republic. His work focuses on guerilla marketing, ambient marketing communication and on new trends, questions in necro-marketing, semiotics, and the history of film and photography. He has practical experience in film production as director assistant and producer assistant at international projects. He is a laureate of the Grand Prix of theatrical photography and an author of photography expositions, book covers, and posters.

Kacper Zagała is currently an assistant in the Department of Informatics at the University of Economics in Katowice, Poland. He teaches students operating systems and also computer systems and networks. He is a former student of UE Katowice, where he did both bachelor's and master's theses. During his studies, he worked as a project manager in an IT startup company, and he spent one semester on the exchange at the Faculty of Business and Economics in Zagreb, Croatia. He is a PhD candidate, and his research interests cover gaming culture, esports, startups, and technology usage in sports and business.

Forewords

I am delighted to be able to contribute this foreword to *Digital Transformation, Perspective Development, and Value Creation: Research Case Studies*. It is a valuable contribution to the literature of economics in times of digital transformation. It has developed out the mobility that is vital to the strategic development of higher education institutions and addresses current work in the area of business management grounded in methodologically diverse case studies. The authors are drawn from more than a decade of European exchange and mobility based at the University of Economics in Katowice, Poland.

I was one of the participants in the first iteration of the mobility program. My work is mostly research focused on the impact of universal, ubiquitous, pervasive and intrusive connectedness and mobility, afforded across many countries and communities by personal mobile phones.

It is obviously different in different countries, in different communities, and across different age groups and demographics. Consequently, it was very exciting and informative to have the opportunity to spend a week in the University of Katowice working with young people from a different culture and country to my own. It was very rewarding to be able to test my thinking and my theories against their experiences and expectations. I took away valuable insights and idea that enriched my subsequent work, and reminded me of the rewards of teaching.

It was also fascinating to see much of the city, both the social and cultural life and the commercial and industrial activity. It is clearly an area very similar to that of my own university, facing big challenges with a declining industrial base and the opportunities to develop IT industries and different forms of tourism. It was instructive to see how different communities address these challenges and to explore the contribution and the synergy of economics, the digital and international mobility.

This is clearly a strong endorsement of the ideal of the internationalization of university education and also a fabulously stimulating chance to work with colleagues from other environments. Internationalization is an aspect of

Foreword xxi

mobility, and mobility is at the heart of my work; mobility is increasingly apparent in the mobility of the goods, services, assets, transactions, and organizations that constitute economic life; mobility is also apparent in the mobility of people and ideas.

Mobility is also at the core of the European ideal, the mobility of people, the mobility of resources, the mobility of services and the mobility of ideas, and these are especially important now in times when freedom and democracy are under such obvious threats. This book, addressing digital transformation perspective development and value creation, is an important contribution to all of these different and interlocking concerns.

Robust competitiveness, sustainable development, and democratic capitalism are central to the contemporary philosophies and objectives; they are the subjects of an evolving curriculum, but new technologies, including the Internet and mobile communication, have transformed many aspects of delivering the curriculum as well as its subject matter.

The book highlights emerging research and practice at the increasingly dynamic intersection of these fields, where participants in the mobility program have used cased studies to show how they harnessed creativity and invention to achieve and sustain growth. The book has a specific modern and European focus exploring cases studies from around the world.

John Traxler, FRSA, MBCS, MIET, AFIMA
UNESCO Chair & Professor of Digital Learning
Institute of Education
University of Wolverhampton

Forewords (cont.)

It is my pleasure to introduce to the scientific community the book *Digital Transformation, Perspective Development, and Value Creation: Research Case Studies* authored by participants of the International Week at the University of Economics in Katowice. This book is a valuable addition to the literature on digital transformation, which has become a critical area of study and research in recent times.

The authors have skillfully submitted research case studies that present the theoretical background and the practical applications of digital transformation in different industries and social sectors. These case studies offer insights into the challenges faced by organizations in adapting to digital transformation and the strategies they have implemented to achieve success.

The book includes 13 chapters, each of which focuses on a specific aspect of digital transformation, such as innovation, value creation, and customer experience. The preface by the editor Małgorzata Pańkowska opens the field with a sophisticated glance at properties and implications of research case studies. The authors have brought together their expertise and diverse perspectives to provide a comprehensive and insightful analysis of these topics.

Moreover, the book highlights the importance of collaboration and knowledge sharing in the field of digital transformation. The annual International Week at the University of Economics in Katowice provides a unique opportunity for scholars and lecturers from different countries and backgrounds to come together and exchange ideas and experiences.

In today's rapidly changing and complex world, the case study method has become an essential tool for conducting research and education in a wide range of disciplines, including business, management, social sciences, and engineering. This method allows researchers to investigate complex phenomena in their natural context, providing a deeper understanding of the issues under investigation. For teaching, case studies are an excellent way to engage students and provide them with a practical and relevant learning experience. By using real-life examples, case studies help students

Foreword xxiii

to develop critical thinking skills, problem-solving abilities, and a deeper understanding of the complexities of the world around them.

I would like to express my appreciation for the international character of the network of authors and their heterogeneous research experiences that they bring to this book. As a multiple International Week participant myself, I'm acquainted with the value of this highly productive atmosphere. The authors come from different countries and cultural backgrounds, which enriches the perspectives and insights presented in this book. This diversity not only provides readers with a profound understanding of digital transformation but also showcases the global impact of this phenomenon.

In conclusion, *Digital Transformation, Perspective Development, and Value Creation: Research Case Studies* is an outstanding contribution to the field of digital transformation research and education. The book offers a valuable collection of case studies that provide insights into the challenges and opportunities of digital transformation in different industries and social sectors. I highly recommend this book to researchers, educators, students, and practitioners who are interested in understanding the theoretical clues and the practical implications of digital transformation in today's world.

Vera G. Meister

University of Applied Sciences Brandenburg, Germany

Preface

The various cases presented in this book reflect the concerns on strategic, functional, and operational management in business organization, human behavior, technology, and business processes. The cases presented in this book are not only from business units, but also from non-profit institutions. They showcase the situation in a given industry or country. Authors' challenge of this monograph was to present a high level of multi-nationality to achieve a comprehensive view of the various topics addressed. This approach enables readers to transfer, through cases, experiences and observations to different countries, recognize culture diversification and specific local realities. In this book, the organizational dimension also varies from small companies to large units of national or multinational scale.

This book is designed for managers, executives, business strategists, industry professionals, students, researchers, and academicians browsing current research on key business strategies. The type of audience the authors are writing for determines how they present the study findings, in terms of style, length, language, content, and the key messages they convey. Therefore, in this book, authors focus on writing for an academic audience and they typically give greater emphasis to the review of academic literature, the theoretical framework, and methodological procedures. This book began with the conference panel on University Research Work Methods during the Smart Technology and Smart Research conference, within the Erasmus Programme 11th International Week at University of Economics in Katowice in 2022. The central issue of this book is research case study development. Evidently, this issue is not novel; however, authors propose their unique considerations. Authors argue that case study is a research method in social and technical sciences and as such is applicable for studying organizational management, business communication, decision making, data analytics, value chain creation, etc.

The fundamental question is what a case is. According to Perri 6 and Bellamy (2012), case is a unit, which is defined by the researches to answer a particular phenomenon, either empirically and inductively, or theoretically

Preface xxv

and deductively. Therefore, a case can be considered as a certain whole. Cases are context-dependent. They are established by authors and enable studying various factors and variables, and relationships among them. Context of cases does not have an unambiguous interpretation. Case context is determined by human understanding of concepts, by their motivations, and actions. Context means situations where various factors enable or disable a research phenomenon development, increase or decrease the impact on the outcome of research. Cases use a wide range of available data and methods to capture and analyze it. Fitzgerald and Dopson (2011) identified data used in case study research, i.e., factual data on the context of the case, data from stakeholders in the investigated organization, and data from several sources utilized in a triangulation process. On the one hand, data is collected in questionnaires, through standardized interviews. Researchers use well-structured observation, documents, experiments, randomized controlled trials, and statistical analyses. On the other hand, qualitative research requires non-standardized interviews, participant observation and fieldwork, analyses of documents, diaries, photographs, and graphic materials. Researchers provide thematic or constant comparative analyses, and description of narrative analyses (Daymon & Holloway, 2011). Researchers must ensure trustworthiness, authenticity, and validity of research data and results.

Triangulation of research methods within a case study is permitted. It has been considered as a process of using multiple perceptions to clarify meaning and to verify the repeatability of an observation or interpretation (Stake, 2000). Triangulation is an excellent applicable idea if the researcher wants to look at the same topic in different aspects. It allows to combine data from interviews with data from documents, or data from two different research methods, i.e., qualitative and quantitative. Cases may cover social systems such as software projects, teams, or business organizations, or technical systems such as a complex software systems, hardware or networks (Wieringa, 2014). In case study research, qualitative and quantitative methods cannot be mistakenly perceived as competing types of research. That said, the qualitative research aims for the exploration, understanding, and description of participants' experiences, while quantitative researchers search for causal explanations, testing hypotheses, prediction, and control. In the first group of methods, informants and sampling units such as place, time, and concepts are deeply described. Sampling is purposive and non-random. In quantitative studies, samples are fixed before the research starts, and researchers apply randomized sampling. According to Hennink et al. (2011), qualitative research covers a wide range of techniques and philosophies to examine human experiences and competencies in detail, by using a specific set of research techniques, i.e., in-depth interviews, focus group discussions, observation, content analysis, visual methods, and life histories.

xxvi *Preface*

The most distinctive feature of qualitative methods, i.e., case study, ethnographic research, or autoethnography is that the approach allows to identify research phenomena from the perspective of researchers and to understand their meanings and interpretations and event social values and cultural norms. Qualitative researchers are able to study people in their natural settings, which are also the settings of these researchers. They are able to correctly recognize the experiences and behavior shaped by the context of their lives, such as the social, economic, technology, culture, or physical context. The strength of case study research is its ability to capture the full significance of a complex data set. Through the case studies, researchers answer the questions of why people act as they do, and how they understand and motivate their actions. Smith (2014) argues that case study is a very pragmatic approach, which treats social research as a problem solving activity closely related to social life. Case studies are mainly used in inductive reasoning, however, they can also be used deductively to develop theory, by moving forward and back between theory and an empirical investigation of hypotheses deduced from that theory (Perry 6 and Bellamy, 2012). De Vaus (2014) explained that social researchers ask two fundamental questions:

- In descriptive research: What is going on?
- In explanatory research: Why is it going on?

Answers can be very concrete or abstract. Myers (2014) adds that case study is a research strategy developed for understanding the dynamics within a case setting. Case study is analytic and linear, and includes its division into sections or chronological and presenting the history of phenomena (Hennink et al., 2011). A case study uses both qualitative and quantitative data and utilizes various types of data-collecting methods. Case studies allow to study things in their context and consider the subjective meanings that people bring to their situation (De Vaus, 2014). Myers (2014) argues that case study research uses empirical evidence from one or more sources and most of the evidence comes from interviews and documents. Yin (2009) believes that case study should include multiple methods of data collection to investigate specific phenomena in their natural setting. He argues that case study reflects quasi-experimental research through identifying critical contrasts and comparing selected cases to verify them.

Stake (2000) notices that case study is a part of scientific methodology and it focuses on the choice of what is under investigation. In this book, the case study is defined by interest of an individual researcher, not by the methods of investigation used. Authors want to reveal what is particular in each case study. They portray something of the uncommon, something particular in a concrete context. Each case has important characteristics, situations, actors, actions, and relationships. The purpose of each case is not to represent the world, but to represent the case in real world. Each case should be different from the others, with its own features and human involvement. Although famous case studies have been published by Harvard Business School, authors of this book made the decision to share their own experiences. In contrast to research case studies, universities widely recommend teaching case studies usage. Teaching cases are written primarily for students. They are designed to illustrate an existing theory and real business objects, processes, people, and principles. In contrast to them, research cases are written primarily for researchers, they are designed to contribute to a new theory or explore contemporary business organizations. Research case studies are expected to provide empirical evidence to convince readers as professionals of the applicability of a particular proposition. These case studies provide arguments pro the theory. They are expected to contribute to knowledge in a particular field. Presented in this book research case studies are descriptive, explanatory as well as exploratory. They discover the relevant features, factors, and issues that might be applied in other similar situations. Although generalization is difficult, what authors can do is to propose best practices for business and socio-technical solutions for the next implementations, following those presented in this book.

Yin (2009) argues that understanding the differences between the analytic generalization and statistical generalization is an important challenge in case study research process. A case study can be used to develop, support, or falsify a theory. Multiple case studies may resemble multiple experiments. In case study research process, the generalization is analytical, and a previously developed theory is used as a template to compare the empirical results of the case study. In case study research, the use of theory aids in defining the appropriate research design, data collection, and conclusions. In case studies, the results' trustworthiness, credibility, confirmability, and data dependability are used to estimate the quality of research (Suddaby & Greenwood, 2011). Case studies are believed to be valuable for refining theory and suggesting problems and complexities for further investigations, or even to establish the limits of generalizability (Stake, 2000). Case study authors believe that readers can draw their own conclusions and make their own comparisons. The case study research allows readers to learn and recognize trustworthy phenomena, to provide critical discourse analysis, as well as historical analyses, to study social issues in digital transformation and for value creation. The case studies are expected to help readers understand complex and emergent processes. The book should give readers insights into how information communication technologies influence the processes, cultures, human behaviors, and organizational communication.

xxviii *Preface*

In terms of layout, this book divides the research work into specific parts and is structured accordingly, although, in each chapter, data collection, analysis, and writing often occur simultaneously rather than in discrete stages. The conceptual part of the book deals with three notions, i.e., digital transformation, perspective development, and value creation. The volume is structured in three parts.

The first one is designated to digital transformation and development of high education institutions and cooperation among them. This section covers four chapters.

Chapter 1 "Innovations in a CEEPUS Academic Network and Their Impact on Management Effectiveness and Research Achievements" describes a network of universities involved in teaching staff exchange, provides quantitative and qualitative measure of network effectiveness. Authors believe that case is a good base for the development of the university alliance program in the future.

Chapter 2 "The Effect of Ethical Leadership and Leadership Effectiveness on Employees' Turnover Intention in High Education Institutions: Case Ibagué University" covers a qualitative approach including data triangulation for testing, in Ibague University, Colombia, a previously proposed research model.

Chapter 3 "Digital Transformation in Education: A Case Study of Teacher Information Network (TIN) in Turkey" presents the distance learning activities becoming increasingly widespread within the scope of Education 4.0.

Chapter 4 "Ambient, Guerilla, and Event Marketing in Education of Marketers, and Development of creative abilities: A Case Study" concerns the possibilities of targeted stimulation of creativity in the creation of marketing communication campaigns and soft skills of university course participants.

The second part concerns digital transformation and value creation at business organizations. This part consists of five chapters.

Chapter 5 "Testing and Certification of New Product Development in Electronics Industry: Case Studies" reveals problems related to the implementation of production projects, risk management, formal testing, and compliance in the electronics industry in Polish companies.

Chapter 6 "Role of Information System Support in Project Management: Case of Companies Competing at Publicly Funded Calls for Projects" focuses on the development of science, technology, and society (STS) projects, reveals conflicts and dilemmas, and finally presents project management models successfully applied in Slovenia.

Chapter 7 "Comparison of Multi-Criteria Decision Methodologies: Case of Water Management Investment Project" presents the case of a

Preface xxix

decision support system development in the context of the design science research framework.

Chapter 8 "Augmented Reality in Medical Training of Patient Referrals: A Nursing Case Study of Children's Hospital in Taiwan" considers impacts of new technologies. Hence, authors use the technology acceptance model (TAM) to evaluate the nurses' responses and attitudes toward augmented reality technology.

Chapter 9 "The Use of Blockchain Technology in the Sports Sector: The Case of AC Milan Football (Soccer) Team" examines how tokenization is used in sports and particularly by football clubs.

The third part consists of chapters considering value creation at business organizations.

Chapter 10 "'Pacto pela Industria': Reindustrialization Opportunities in the Great ABC Region, Brazil" focuses on problems in global value chains during the pandemic, in the context of climate change, new technology impact, and geopolitical conflicts.

Chapter 11 "Auditing Human Resource Management Practices: A Case Study in the Egyptian Hospitality Industry" aims to explain how state-owned and private Egyptian hotels audit their human resources management practices to improve organizational performance, and ensure standard compliance, risk mitigation, and financial effectiveness.

Chapter 12 "Organization and Incentivization of Risk Management: An Agency Theory Case Study" explores the organization's risk management and supports a better understanding of scientific research outcomes for organizational design.

Chapter 13 "Embracing CSR as an Essential Part of Business: The Case of Viking by Raja Group, Cluj-Napoca" presents that large companies use the chance to transform society through appropriate reflection, discourse, and corporate social responsibility actions in Cluj-Napoca, Romania.

Małgorzata Pańkowska

References

Daymon, Ch., & Holloway, I. (2011). *Qualitative Research Methods in Public Relations and Marketing Communications.* London, New York: Routledge Taylor & Francis.

De Vaus, D. (2014). The Context of Design. In M. Frenz, K. Nielsen, & G. Walters (Eds.), *Research Methods in Management* (pp. 3–18). Los Angeles: SAGE Publications.

Fitzgerald, L., & Dopson, S. (2011). Comparative Case Study Designs: Their Utility and Development in Organizational Research. In D.A. Buchanan & A. Bryman (Eds.), *The SAGE Handbook of Organizational Research Methods* (pp. 465–483). Los Angeles: SAGE Publications.

xxx *Preface*

Hennink, M., Hutter, I., & Bailey, A. (2011). *Qualitative Research Methods*. Los Angeles: SAGE Publications.

Myers, M.D. (2014). Case Study Research. In M. Frenz, K. Nielsen, & G. Walters (Eds.), *Research Methods in Management* (pp. 235–256). Los Angeles: SAGE Publications.

Perri, 6, & Bellamy, Ch. (2012). *Principles of Methodology, Research Design in Social Science*. Los Angeles: SAGE Publications.

Smith, P.K. (2014). Philosophy of Science and Its Relevance for the Social Sciences. In M. Frenz, K. Nielsen, & G. Walters (Eds.), *Research Methods in Management* (pp. 315–326). Los Angeles: SAGE Publications.

Stake, R.E. (2000). Case Studies. In N.K. Denzin & Y.S. Lincoln (Eds.), *Handbook of Qualitative Research* (pp. 435–454). Thousand Oaks, London: SAGE Publications.

Suddaby, R., & Greenwood, R. (2011). Methodological Issues in Researching Institutional Change. In D.A. Buchanan & A. Bryman (Eds.), *The SAGE Handbook of Organizational Research Methods* (pp. 176–195). Los Angeles: SAGE Publications.

Wieringa, R.J. (2014). *Design Science Methodology for Information Systems and Software Engineering*. Berin: Springer-Verlag, Berlin.

Yin, R. (2009). Designing Case Studies: Identifying Your Case(s) and Establishing the Logic of Your Case Study. In M. Frenz, K. Nielsen, & G. Walters (Eds.), *Research Methods in Management* (pp. 272–312). Los Angeles: SAGE Publications.

Acknowledgments

Hereby, we would like to thank the contributors for their dedication and patience during the various commenting and editing stages.

There are many people who have offered their support, creativeness, and contributions to the idea of Erasmus and CEEPUS Program cooperation, named International Week at University of Economics in Katowice, Poland. At first, we would like to thank Professor Sławomir Smyczek, Rector of University of Economics in Katowice, Poland, for the inspiration to elaborate the monograph on research case study application in various countries involved in Erasmus and CEEPUS program cooperation. Further, we thank all that programs' supporters: Edyta Gałecka, Patrycja Macioł from International Relations Office, as well as Agnieszka Put from Marketing Centre at University of Economics in Katowice. We thank academicians from the Department of Informatics at University of Economics in Katowice: Anna Sołtysik-Piorunkiewicz, Artur Strzelecki, Joanna Palonka, Mariusz Żytniewski, Mariia Rizun, Artur Machura, Andrzej Sołtysik, Edyta Abramek, Wiesław Wolny, Patryk Morawiec, Paulina Rutecka, and Kacper Zagała.

We thank our publisher, Routledge, and especially the editors Jessica and Brianna for picking up on this important topic, their patience with us, and the production work that went into this book, as well as copyeditors for their exhaustive work.

Editor
Małgorzata Pańkowska
University of Economics in Katowice, Poland

Part 1

Digital Transformation and Development of High Education Institutions

1 Innovations in a CEEPUS Academic Network and Their Impact on Management Effectiveness and Research Achievements

Galia Marinova and Krisel Tola

Review on CEEPUS and Other Academic Networking Programs

A literature review on existing academic network programs shows that the oldest one is COST established in 1971 (Kostelidou et al., 2010). Its focus is research and development cooperation. The Central European Exchange Program for University Studies (CEEPUS) established in 1995 is a regional program aiming at the origin to prepare the founding countries to participate in Erasmus and other European research programs (Sorantin, 2020). The practice proved that the program largely overpassed the original aim. Detailed information about CEEPUS program can be found at the program site (website of the CEEPUS program www.ceepus.info). An evaluation of the program is presented by Scheck (2015) and its remarkable viability is confirmed later by Klaus (2019); the connection between CEEPUS and other programs such as ERASMUS +, Horizon 2020, Marie Skłodowska-Curie Actions (MSCA), and COST is studied. Contributions of CEEPUS to specific countries such as Hungary (Holicza, 2020) and Czech Republic (Jonsta et al., 2004) are discussed in these chapters. Besides regions and countries, the academic networks influence individuals also, for example, they have positive impact on successful career (Heffernan, 2020). Some criticism to academic network programs in Europe can also be found in the publication of Johnston (2020).

Most of the authors agree that CEEPUS has great impact on development and integration of the Central European region, it has the advantage of flexibility, supports joint programs and doctoral student's co-supervision, is complimentary to other EU academic and research programs, and supports the research and development potential in the region, which is basically with low capacity to lead and even to participate in bigger European research projects. Authors also underline some drawbacks: insufficient amount of the grants in some partner countries; need to support management and traveling expenses. Some risks of misuse of grants are also mentioned by Scheck

DOI: 10.4324/9781003376583-2

4   *Galia Marinova and Krisel Tola*

(2015) but the administrative measures taken in some national CEEPUS offices (NCO) were not really efficient and created some new problems rather than solving the existing ones. As mentioned in Master Academia, shared activities are a good means to activate an academic network. Nevertheless, the analysis shows that CEEPUS program should be prolonged after 2025 with some improvements and be transformed into "CEEPUS IV incubator" (Sorantin, 2020). The innovations described in the next sections are an attempt to support the development and improvement of CEEPUS and other networking programs.

CEEPUS Network BG-1103

The CEEPUS supports around 80 networks that apply annually for prolonging the support, together with about 40–50 new candidates. The CEEPUS region is specific with a complicated history, it includes all seven ex-Yugoslavia countries, including Kosovo* (*All references to Kosovo, whether the territory, institutions, or population, in this text, shall be understood in full compliance with United Nations' Security Council Resolution 1244 and without prejudice to the status of Kosovo.), ex-socialist countries such as Bulgaria, Romania, Hungary, Czech Republic, Slovakia, Albania, Poland, and Moldova, which were part of Soviet Union and Austria. Cooperation is of great importance in this region in transition and it contributes to its development and European integration (Marinova, 2019).

The CEEPUS network BG-11-3 was created in 2016 and it is coordinated by the Department of "Technologies and Management of Communication Systems" at Technical University-Sofia, Bulgaria. The distribution of the 36 partner institutions, the six silent business partners, and the partners involved in the joint doctoral program developed in the network, in the 16 eligible countries forming the CEEPUS region (website of the CEEPUS program), is as follows:

- Albania – two universities from the cities of Tirana and Durres; two business partners and nine doctoral students enrolled in the joint doctoral program. The first enrolled student received the doctoral diploma in 2022.
- Austria – two universities from the cities of Vienna and Graz; one business partner from Vienna.
- Bosnia and Herzegovina – three universities from the cities of Bihac, East Sarajevo, and Sarajevo.
- Bulgaria – three partner institutions from the city of Sofia, both involved in the joint doctoral program, coordinator of the network.
- Croatia – four universities from the cities of Rijeka, Slavonski Brod, Varazdin, and Zagreb.
- Czech Republic – one university from the city of Olomouc.

- Hungary – two universities from the cities of Pecs and Veszprem.
- Moldova – one university.
- Montenegro – one university.
- North Macedonia – four partners from the cities of Skopje and Tetovo; one business partner.
- Poland – two universities from the cities of Gliwice and Katowice, involved in the development of the joint doctoral program.
- Romania – two universities from the cities of Brasov and Bucharest.
- Serbia – three universities from the cities of Kragujevac, Nis, and Novi Sad; one business partner is also involved.
- Slovakia – two partners from the cities of Bratislava and Trnava.
- Slovenia – three universities from the cities of Ljubljana, Novo Mesto, and Maribor; one business partner is involved.
- Kosovo* – one university from Pristina; involved in the joint doctoral program; three students enrolled in it.

The contact persons of 12 partner universities are female and those of the other 24 institutions are male, which makes a ratio of 1/3 to 2/3.

The resources of a CEEPUS network come from the grants awarded annually by the NCO, usually related to the Ministries of education and research in the countries. The amounts of the grants differ strongly from one country to another, up to 11 times and the effectiveness of the network is measured in terms of the percentage of fulfillment of the mobilities awarded to the network. It's the main factor evaluated for prolonging or not the support for a network.

With the objective to be successful, the CEEPUS network BG-1103 adopted the event-based approach and implemented three innovations to achieve higher effectiveness. Additionally, the coordinator of the network realized the so-called coordinator's tour in all partner countries in the network, meeting with representatives from all partner universities, to motivate their activities and involvement in the network. Although the CEEPUS exchange is basically academic, research is also the focus, especially through the highly prioritized joint doctoral programs.

Further, the chapter describes the event-based approach, the coordinator's tour, and the three innovations implemented in BG-1103 and considers their impact on management optimization and effectiveness as well as on the research achievements in the network.

Event-based Approach and Implementation of the Innovative Flexible Course

The CEEPUS network adopted the event-based approach and created the innovative Flexible course as a kind of joint program for increasing the use of students' and teachers' mobilities awarded by NCO to the network each year. They are influencing both academic and research activities in the network.

Three kinds of CEEPUS events are organized:

- Summer/Winter/Doctoral schools or academia;
- CEEPUS involvement in International Weeks;
- Workshops or Special sessions at International Conferences organized by network partners.

The program of the Summer/Winter schools is defined based on the needs and requests of students expressed in the surveys performed by the E-management platform of the network IMA-NET, described by Marinova and Tola (2020) and further in the chapter. The program of the Doctoral Schools is defined based on the individual plans of study of the doctoral students and offers courses developed by the network program for the joint doctoral program. Students' academies are organized mainly for training students in leadership, soft skills, and green transformation. During these sessions, students' vision, needs, desires, and expectations of the network are also discussed.

The Summer/Winter/Doctoral schools or academia organized in the CEEPUS network BG-1103 are:

- Summer School in University of Ljubljana, Slovenia, 2017;
- Students' Leadership Academia in University of Maribor, Maribor, Slovenia, 2018;
- Summer School on autonomous vehicles in University of Maribor, Maribor, Slovenia, Joint with CEEPUS network CIII-SI-1313-01-1819, 2019;
- CEEPUS Summer School, University of Maribor and TU-Graz, Slovenia, Austria, 2021;
- CEEPUS Doctoral School, UBT, Pristina, Kosovo*, 2023;
- CEEPUS Summer School "Advanced Communications and global impact" in TU-Graz, Graz, Austria, 2023 (in preparation).

Involvement of the CEEPUS network BG-1103 with teachers and students in International weeks was established as a good practice and was realized as follows:

- International Weeks in the University of Economics in Katowice, Katowice, Poland – 2017, 2018, 2019, 2021 (virtual), 2022;
- International Weeks in Palacký University Olomouc, Czech Republic, 2019, 2020;
- International Weeks in TU-Sofia, Sofia, Bulgaria, 2021, 2022.

Innovations in a CEEPUS Academic Network 7

CEEPUS workshops or special sessions at International Conferences organized by network partners gave the opportunity to teachers, researchers, and doctoral students in the CEEPUS network to present joint papers. Several CEEPUS events and coordination meetings were realized in parallel with the CEEPUS workshops and special sessions. The list of these events follows bellow:

- 14th PhD and DLA Symposium 2018 hosted by the University of Pecs, Pecs, Hungary – Two joint papers were published and a CEEPUS Workshop on the joint doctoral program in the network was organized with attendees from Albania, Bulgaria, Hungary, and North Macedonia.
- ICEST'2018, Sozopol, Bulgaria – The International Scientific Conference on Information, Communication and Energy Systems and Technologies is organized annually and consecutively in Bulgaria, North Macedonia, and Serbia. The Special CEEPUS Session organized within 53rd International Scientific Conference on Information, Communication and Energy Systems and Technologies – ICEST'2018 included nine joint papers from teachers, students, and Ph.D. students from the CEEPUS network. The best paper award for young scientist at ICEST'2018 was won by a doctoral student from the CEEPUS network BG-1103 for her paper on Electromagnetic pollution estimation in a communications laboratory. The paper was co-authored by Serbian and Bulgarian researchers cooperating within the network (Joint Papers – CEEPUSMODCAD (ubt-uni.net)).
- COMETA-2018, Jahorina, Bosnia and Herzegovina, Conference on Mechanical Engineering. Technologies and Applications. A joint paper was published; besides, a CEEPUS Workshop on the Flexible course was organized. Attendees from Bulgaria, Serbia and Bosnia and Herzegovina developed the concept of the Flexible course in the CEEPUS network BG-1103. The new Joint program Flexible course was later introduced in the network.
- TELSIKS-2019, Nis, Serbia, International Conference on Advanced Technologies, Systems and Services in Telecommunications. A CEEPUS workshop and a coordination meeting with attendees from six partner countries of the CEEPUS network was organized within TELSIKS-2019, where the new partners in the network from North Macedonia, Austria, and Romania presented their institutions and five joint papers were presented.
- CoBCoM'2020, Graz, Austria – International Conference on Broadband Communications for Next Generation Networks and Multimedia Applications. A CEEPUS session was organized where two joint papers with authors from Austria, Bulgaria, and Slovenia were presented.

- CONTEL'2021, Zagreb, Croatia – International Conference on Telecommunications, Two joint CEEPUS papers were presented at CONTEL'2021 with authors from Austria, Bulgaria, and Slovenia.
- TELSIKS-2021, Nis, Serbia; A Special CEEPUS session was organized with participants from Albania, Bulgaria, Serbia, Slovenia, where three joint papers were published.
- UBT (University for Business and technology) International Conference'2021, Pristina, Kosovo*. A Special CEEPUS session within the UBT International Conference'2021 was organized – three CEEPUS teachers, four doctoral students, and four students from Albania, Bulgaria, and Kosovo* presented six joint papers.
- IWSSIP'2022, Sofia, Bulgaria – International Conference on Systems, Signals and Image Processing. A CEEPUS workshop and coordination meeting with attendees from 13 network partners attended and presented the recent development in the institutions were presented. Ten joint papers were presented and published. Two doctoral students received awards for their papers. Additionally a CEEPUS Flexible course on Academic English with two CEEPUS teachers from North Macedonia and Bosnia and Herzegovina was organized. Sixteen students from CEEPUS and non-CEEPUS countries attended the Flexible course and obtained certificates generated by the IMA-NET platform and signed by the coordinator of the CEEPUS network and the dean of the Faculty of Telecommunications in Technical University of Sofia. All students-attendees of the Flexible course obtained three ECTS (European Credit Transfer System).
- CoBCoM'2022, Graz, Austria, an Invited lecture on the innovations in CEEPUS network was presented by the network coordinator. Two joint papers were presented and published.
- CONTEL'2023, Graz, Austria (in process), A CEEPUS Summer School on Advanced Communications and global impact is planned in parallel with CONTEL'2023. Ten teachers from the partner countries are involved with courses, a business partner of the network is organizing one-day training and 40 students from 13 CEEPUS countries submitted their applications to attend the event. Technical University of Graz is hosting the event and included it in the electronic system for the academic activities of the university. This contributes to the visibility and the institutional recognition of the activities of the network.

The number of participants in the enumerated events is presented in Table 1.1.

The Flexible courses, each of them composed of three 6-hour modules and 2 hours assessments and presented by two or more CEEPUS teachers, were introduced as an innovation in the CEEPUS network BG-1103 and realized as follows:

Table 1.1 Participants in the CEEPUS network events

Event	Type	Incoming CEEPUS teachers	Local teachers	Incoming CEEPUS students	Local students	Business partners/ NGOs
Ljubljana, Slovenia, 2017	Summer School	6	4	1	10	–
Maribor, Slovenia, 2018	Students' academia	4	2	5	5	2 NGOs
Maribor, Slovenia, 2019	Summer School Joint	5	1	15	–	2 BP
Maribor, Slovenia and Graz, Austria, 2021	Summer School	3	1	2	10	2 NGOs
UBT, Pristina, Kosovo*, 2023	Doctoral School/ Flexible course	3	1	3	3	–
Graz, Austria, 2023	Summer School	5	5	39	6	4 BP
Katowice, Poland, 2017, 2018, 2019, 2021 (virtual), 2022	Int. week	1, 2, 4, 4, 4	–	–, 3, –, –, –	60	BPs
Olomouc, Czech Republic, 2019, 2020	Int. week	1, 2	1	2,–	10	–
Pristina, Kosovo, 2019	Flexible course	2	1	–	12	–
Pristina, Kosovo, 2021	Flexible course	3	–	–	10	–
TU-Sofia, Sofia, Bulgaria, 2021	Flexible course	1	1	7	1	–
TU-Sofia, Sofia, Bulgaria, 2022	Flexible course	2	–	13	2	–

- Flexible course "Edge technologies and challenges to management" in UBT, Pristina, Kosovo*, 2019;
- Flexible course "Advanced technologies in computer-aided design and e-learning, and implementation of advanced optimization methods" in UBT, Pristina, Kosovo*, 2021; In the framework of this event the students from UBT* organized a course on Basic Albanian which was very interesting for the incoming students and teachers;
- Flexible course "Academic English and Literacy" in Technical University of Sofia, Sofia, Bulgaria, 2021;
- Flexible course "Academic English and Literacy, and English for Engineers" in TU-Sofia, Sofia, Bulgaria, 2022;
- Flexible course "CEEPUS Doctoral School" in UBT, Pristina, Kosovo*, 2023.

Information about past, current, and planned events in BG-11-03 can be found on the network website (website of the CEEPUS network BG-1103).

Coordinator's Tour and Its Role

The number of the partners in a CEEPUS network is growing each year and very small is known about the new partners and their potential. The risk in a big network with more than 30 partners is that some of the partners stay inactive. In order to avoid this risk and to offer all partners equal opportunities to participate and/or organize events a coordinator's tour was organized. The goal was to visit all 16 partner countries and to meet representatives of all partner institutions. The meetings of the coordinator in the partner institutions allowed:

- To present the network activities and the planned activities in the current year.
- To find out the area of expertise of the partner countries, the events that they organize, the conditions that they offer to incoming students.
- To meet students in the partner institutions, to register them in the IMA-NET platform, to invite them to fill the surveys, to get familiar with their interests, desires and needs.
- To collect courses and modules from the teachers in the partner institutions and to include them in the IMA-NET platform.
- To encourage the partner institution to organize a CEEPUS event, to attend current events, to involve more teachers and students in using the CEEPUS grants awarded to attend events mobilities.
- To train the partner institution staff and students to work with the CEEPUS platform and with the platform IMA-NET.

Innovations in a CEEPUS Academic Network 11

- To introduce the joint doctoral program to the Partner institution, to acquire information about the legal and administrative norms concerning joint doctoral programs in the partner countries and universities and to motivate them to consider their participation.
- Organize discussion with students, staff, and teachers in the partner institutions, answer questions, and collect recommendations.
- The Coordinator's tour took six years, as follows:
- In 2018 were visited Albania, Austria, Hungary, Kosovo*, Bosnia and Herzegovina and Croatia;
- In 2019 – Serbia, Czech Republic, Poland, and Moldova;
- In 2020 – the coordinator's tour was interrupted by COVID-19;
- In 2021 – Montenegro (virtually), Slovakia, and Romania;
- In 2022 – not any new country was visited;
- In 2023 – North Macedonia.

It became visible that the activity and the involvement of the partners increased visibly (in terms of events proposed and organized, in terms of incoming and outgoing mobilities after the visit of the coordinator). The CEEPUS program and its potential were not very well known locally and the visit of the coordinator increased the interest to it.

After the Coordinator's tour was recently completed in all 16 countries involved in the CEEPUS network, there are no more marginalized partners and activity is observable in all partner institutions.

Joint Doctoral Program with an Innovative Network-wide Joint Co-tutorship and Co-supervision

The countries involved in the development of the joint doctoral program in CEEPUS network BG-1103 are Bulgaria, Kosovo*, Poland, Slovenia, and Albania. The joint doctoral students in the network come from Albania and Kosovo*. Recently universities from Moldova and Romania expressed their interest to become part of the joint doctoral program of the network.

The research areas for doctoral research, identified and proposed in the CEEPUS network BG-1103, are:

- Business models of Electronic Design Automation (EDA);
- Study of the dynamics of EDA companies;
- FPGA-based low-power design;
- Hardware security;
- E-management tools;
- E-learning and multimedia tools for Computer-aided design;
- Automation and control;

12   *Galia Marinova and Krisel Tola*

- Internet of Things (IoT) for green transformation – virtual models for ports and university campuses;
- Artificial Intelligence and Human Resources;
- Classification, decision-making, and artificial intelligence with health and medicine information systems;
- Diversity and inclusion.

The courses developed (20 hours, 5 ECTS) for the joint doctoral program are:

- Advanced Computer-aided design tools in telecommunications;
- Quantitative and qualitative modeling;
- Advanced optimization methods in management;
- Advanced optimization methods in engineering;
- Advanced modeling methods in management;
- Modeling and Simulation in Automatic Control;
- Virtual leadership in research projects;
- Modeling, Simulation, and Computer-aided design on the Internet of Things (IoT) and Internet of Everything (IoE) environment;
- Web and Cloud Programming. Cloud computing.

Additional courses offered to doctoral students in the framework of Flexible courses, International weeks, or Doctoral schools are:

- Design Science Research Paradigm;
- Academic English and Literacy;
- English for Engineers;
- Introduction to Cybersecurity.

These courses were realized both on-site and virtually during the COVID-19 pandemic.

The research achievement in the joint doctoral program obtained so far are:

- Innovative e-management platform for academic network IMA-NET;
- Experimental setup for studying logical encryption;
- Multimedia assistant for learning communication circuits – direct digital synthesis, power consumption of logically encrypted circuits;
- Database for the business models of EDA companies;
- Tool for studying the dynamics of EDA companies;
- Online platform to assist Computer-aided design in communications.

The number of published papers with authorship or co-authorship of the doctoral in the joint doctoral program is 30, which already have more than 20 citations.

Innovative Platform for E-management of the Academic Network IMA-NET

The complexity of the management in a CEEPUS network and the desire of the network to achieve effectiveness, higher mobility fulfillment, and to respond better to teachers' and students' expectations has led to the search for a tool to support the process. The study on e-management has shown that there is not a specific tool oriented to networks that could be directly implemented for managing a network (Tola & Marinova, 2022). An innovative e-management platform for academic network management IMA-NET was designed and developed. The dashboard of IMA-NET is presented in Figure 1.1.

The main resources organized in IMA-NET are:

- Database with courses proposed by network teachers;
- Database with 6-hour modules proposed by network teachers;
- Database with students' feedback or survey results.

The main features of IMA-NET are:

- Survey of students' interest chosen from a list of topics proposed in the network;
- Statistics obtained from the survey;

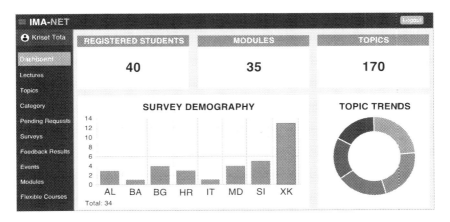

Figure 1.1 Dashboard of IMA-NET platform.

- Creation of different 20-hours Flexible courses composed of three 6-hour; modules and 2 hours for assessment and giving 3ECTS;
- Managing students' registration on different available Flexible courses;
- Event management;
- Certificate generation for the students and teachers involved in a Flexible course or event;
- Feedback module for evaluation of the Flexible courses and events from attendees – students and teachers;
- Statistics obtained from feedback.

The features of the platform IMA-NET are presented in detail in (Marinova & Tola, 2020).

The platform IMA-NET was probated at different events and with different Flexible courses. Some of the results from probation are presented by Tola et al. (2021).

The feedback results obtained in IMA-NET are analyzed by the network management in order to improve the event and Flexible course organization.

The platform IMA-NET is accessible at Website of the IMA-NET platform.

Detailed Feedback results from the Flexible course "Academic English and Literacy, and English for Engineers" in TU-Sofia, Sofia, Bulgaria, 2022, obtained in the IMA-NET platform, Flexible course "Academic English and Literacy, and English for Engineers" in TU-Sofia, Sofia, Bulgaria, 30.05.2022–03.06.2022, are presented below:

1 Would you recommend a similar event to other teachers and students?

a Two out of two or 100% choose Very high

2 How do you estimate the lectures?

a Fourteen out of fourteen or 100% choose Very good

3 Would you recommend a similar event to other students?

a Fourteen out of sixteen which means 87.5% choose Very high
b Two out of sixteen which means 12.5% choose High

4 What is the overall estimation of the event?

a Seventeen out of eighteen which means 94.4% choose Very good
b One out of eighteen which means 5.6% choose Bad

5 How do you estimate the study program of the event?

a Eleven out of fourteen which means 78.6% choose Very good

b Three out of fourteen which means 21.4% choose Good

6 How do you estimate students' interest, participation, and achievements?

a Two out of two or 100% choose very Good

7 How do you estimate the organization of the event?

a Eighteen out of eighteen which means 100% choose Very good

8 How do you estimate the location of the event?

a Fourteen out of eighteen which means 77.8% choose Very good
b Three out of eighteen which means 16.7% choose Good
c One out of eighteen which means 5.6% choose Average

9 How do you estimate the networking and social aspects of the event?

a Thirteen out of eighteen which means 72.2% choose Very good
b Three out of eighteen which means 16.7% choose Good
c Two out of eighteen which means 11.1% choose Average

10 Would you be interested to attend other events of the CEEPUS network?

a Seventeen out of eighteen which means 94.4% choose Very high
b One out of eighteen which means 5.6% choose Average

The feedback form was filled out by 18 participants – two teachers and 16 students. All teachers and students obtained certificates with three ECTS generated by the platform IMA-NET.

Teachers have profiles and can add or edit their courses and modules. The results from student surveys help to define better the program of Flexible courses and Summer Schools to respond to students' expectations.

During the COVID-19 period, some events were performed virtually.

Innovative Ways of Cooperation with Business Partners of the Network

In the CEEPUS program business partners are classified into the group of silent partners. The CEEPUS network BG-1103 management makes efforts to activate the involvement of the business partners, starting with making them speak. The first meeting with the business partners was online because it took place during the COVID-19 pandemic. At this meeting, the companies presented their activities and expressed their interest to be better presented on the network website, propose modules for Flexible courses, and defined their own interests. The network management developed a special webpage on the network website wall requested information and links to company websites were added.

The business partners of the network offered training and courses at:

- Flexible courses;
- Summer schools;
- Small projects distributed to students' teams;
- Companies' presentations and demonstrations;
- Visits to companies;
- Internships.

Business partners were consulted for the doctoral study on EDA companies – for data collection, interviews, meetings, probation, and refining of the business models and optimization methods with realistic data from companies.

Impact of the Innovations in the Network BG-1103 on the Effectiveness and Research Achievements

The innovations adopted in the CEEPUS network BG-1103 aimed to improve both its management effectiveness and its research achievements.

The effectiveness in the management of a CEEPUS network is measured through the so-called fulfillment. In CEEPUS program it is a term indicating the percentage of grants awarded annually by NCO to the network partners, which are used by teachers and students to perform teaching or study in a partner higher education institution. The process is organized fully online – teachers and students apply in the online CEEPUS platform, they are approved by the contact person of the home institution and the NCO in the home country, then by the contact person of the host institution, and finally the NCO of the host country awards a CEEPUS grant to the applicant. He or she accepts it, realizes the teaching or study, receives a grant, fills reports, and uploads them signed and stamped to the same platform. Usually not all awarded grants are used and the annual fulfillment is one of the indicators evaluated by NCO for prolonging or not the network for the next academic year. Figure 1.2 presents the fulfillment as a measure of effectiveness in the CEEPUS network BG-1103.

The numbers in Figure 1.2 show that even in the COVID-19 years, the network could maintain its dynamics. After the completion of the COVID-19 period, fulfillment raises to the highest numbers.

Figure 1.3 presents the participation of students at summer schools and academia; local students and students with CEEPUS grants attending the events are also shown.

The increase of attending students with CEEPUS grants after the end of COVID-19 period is visibly in the figure. These two figures are an

Innovations in a CEEPUS Academic Network 17

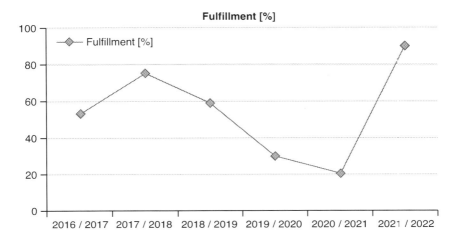

Figure 1.2 The fulfillment as a measure of effectiveness in the CEEPUS network BG-1103 (obtained in MATLAB).

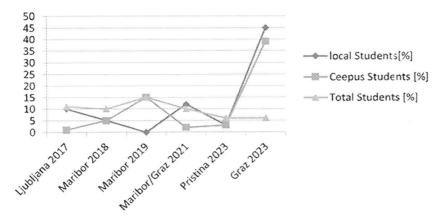

Figure 1.3 Local, CEEPUS, and total students at summer schools and academia.

illustration of the improved mobility fulfillment and network effectiveness thanks to the approach adopted and innovations implemented.

The objectives of the CEEPUS network in the area of research are:

- Identification of common or complementary research areas by the partners in the CEEPUS network and preparation and publication of common research papers.

- Definition of interdisciplinary research topics by the partners involved in the joint doctoral program of the network.
- Enrolment of doctoral students in the joint doctoral program "Thèse en cotutelle" under co-supervision from different partner institutions.
- Use of the resources in terms of know-how and research equipment, distributed in the network partners, to achieve research results. The instrument of network mobilities is used for this purpose.
- Joint research papers of doctoral students, supervisors, and other contributing researchers from the network.
- Involvement of business partners of the network in data collection or the research probation.
- Preparation and application for EU projects by Consortiums formed by the network partners.

The success of the research activities accomplished in the CEEPUS network can be measured through:

- Number of published joint papers authored by researchers from different partner institutions (without joint doctoral students);
- Number of partners involved in the joint doctoral program;
- Number of countries involved in the joint doctoral program;
- Number of doctoral students enrolled in the joint doctoral program;
- Number of joint doctoral theses defended;
- Number of published joint papers with doctoral students and co-supervisors;
- Number of new bilateral projects between network partners;
- Number of applications for European projects involving two or more network partners;
- Number of funded European projects involving two or more network partners;
- Number of awards and recognitions.

Table 1.2 presents the numbers of these measures for the CEEPUS network BG-1103.

Consortiums from the network applied for two projects in response to calls to National Science Fund in Bulgaria, three Calls for an Erasmus+ Strategic partnership, one Call for Erasmus+ Capacity Building in Higher Education (CBHE), and one call for ERA-NET CHANSE and two COST calls. The network was successful with one research project within National Science Fund in Bulgaria, where three network partners are involved, and one Erasmus+ CBHE with a Consortium involving five partners from the network countries.

The awards and recognitions received in the CEEPUS network BG-1103 are:

Innovations in a CEEPUS Academic Network 19

Table 1.2 Measures of the research activities in the CEEPUS network BG-1103

Research activity measure	Numbers in the CEEPUS network BG-1103
Number of published joint papers authored by researchers from different partner institutions (without joint doctoral students)	18
Number of partners involved in the joint doctoral program	7
Number of countries involved in the joint doctoral program	5
Number of doctoral students enrolled in the joint doctoral program	12
Number of joint doctoral theses defended	1
Number of published joint papers with doctoral students and co-supervisors	23
Number of new bilateral projects between network partners (Erasmus+, Erasmus+ Credit mobility)	17
Number of applications for National and European projects involving two or more network partners	8
Number of funded National and European projects involving two or more network partners	2

1 Three awards for Best paper awards to joint papers at the conferences ICEST'2018 and IWSSIP'2022. One of the awards was given by Machine Learning and Knowledge Extraction (MAKE) Journal (https://www.mdpi.com/journal/make)
2 The paper Marinova (2019) presenting the achievements and contributions of the CEEPUS network BG-1103 was finalist in the EUNIS (European University Information Systems organization) Doerup e-learning award 2019 at the EUNIS'2019 Congress in Norwegian University of Science and Technology (NTNU), Trondheim, Norway (website of the EUNIS Doerup Award).

Limitations of the Network Development

CEEPUS program is in its third period, starting from 2011 with the agreement signed by the member states (Agreement, 2010). The previous periods were CEEPUS I (1998–2005) and CEEPUS II (2005–2010). The validity of CEEPUS III was planned till the year 2025. The future of the program is discussed and the CEEPUS officers in member states are in a search of the necessary improvements in CEEPUS in the next CEEPUS IV period. The results in the chapter support the advantages of the extension of the CEEPUS program and its potential for research and innovation. CEEPUS could be opened to additional neighbor countries and extend the support to organizational and management costs.

The approach, management tool, and good practices described in the chapter can help to increase the effectiveness of the networks in the current and new program period.

Additionally, some mathematical methods based on decision-making will be implemented to optimize the distribution of events and grants in the network.

Conclusion

The event-based approach adopted in the CEEPUS network BG-1103, the coordinator's tour, and the innovations implemented as the joint doctoral program, the e-management platform IMA-NET and the intensified business partnership have permitted the network to increase its effectiveness in terms of fulfillment of mobilities awarded, have helped it to pass through the COVID 19 period maintaining its dynamics and have created an environment for the research study of doctoral students and successful national and European project applications. The research achievements obtained in the network are already visible in international publications and show citations in Scopus, WoS, Google Scholar, etc., one joint thesis was already successfully defended in the network. The environment created encourages joint research and more efforts are needed for application and success in bigger research projects such as Horizon. The innovations presented in the chapter, especially the IMA-NET platform can be useful for other academic and research networks for increasing the effectiveness of resources invested in them. Besides science and education, the CEEPUS network BG-1103 is also contributing to establishing a spirit of cooperation and development in a specific region with a complicated history and relations. An effort is made to achieve compatibility in doctoral research administrative rules and regulations in the CEEPUS region, to define close or unified criteria for thesis defense. Further efforts will be invested to increase the overall research level, achievements, and involvement in big European and international research projects and to motivate talented young students to select research careers in the CEEPUS countries.

The CEEPUS networks are a good starting point for the new Erasmus+ initiative called European Universities.

Further some efforts are needed to convince the states to engage the successful and effective CEEPUS networks for solving problems and tasks in society as digital transformation, green transformation, security, and social inclusion, development of skills allowing students and young people to succeed on the job market, but also to develop new businesses.

Acknowledgment

The results presented in the chapter are partly supported by the CEEPUS network BG-1103.

References

Agreement concerning the Central European Exchange Programme for University Studies ("CEEPUS III"), Budva, Montenegro, https://www.ceepus.info/content/downloads Accessed 25.03.2010

Heffernan, T. (2020). Academic networks and career trajectory: There's no career in academia without networks. *Higher Education Research and Development*, *40*(1), DOI: 10.1080/07294360.2020.1799948

Holicza, P. (2020). Regional mobility in Europe: The importance of CEEPUS based on Hungarian evidence. In A. Curaj, L. Deca, & R. Pricopie (Eds). *European higher education area: Challenges for a new decade* (pp. 81–89). Cham: Springer. 10.1007/978-3-030-56316-5_6

Johnston, D. (2020). The trouble with Erasmus is not just the cost. *The Spectator*. https://www.spectator.co.uk/article/the-trouble-with-erasmus-is-not-just-the-cost/ Accessed 28.12.2020.

Jonsta, Z., Hernas, A., & Čizek, L. (2004). Contribution of the CEEPUS project on a development the co-operation between the VŠB – Technical University and Universities in Middle European Region. *International conference on engineering education and research "progress through partnership"* (pp. 1567–1571). Ostrava: VŠB-TUO.

Klaus, S. (2019). The uptake of European programmes in the Ceepus Cooperation Area. Wien: Centre for Social Innovation. 10.13140/RG.2.2.11363.30243

Kostelidou, K. & Babiloni, F. (2010). Why bother with a COST action? The benefits of networking in science. *Nonlinear Biomedical Physics, 4 Suppl 1*(Suppl. 1), S12. doi: 10.1186/1753-4631-4-S1-S12. PMID: 20522262; PMCID: PMC2880798

Marinova G. (2019). Impact of University networking on Students' mobility and Motivation. *EUNIS Congress'2019*, 5-7 June 2019, Trondheim, Norway, 2019 <https://az659834.vo.msecnd.net/eventsairwesteuprod/production-ntnu-public/61b925b38daa4ddf9f3527e45c22642a> Accessed 19.01.2023, Finalist in Doerup E-learning Award 2019

Marinova, G., & Tola, K. (2020). IMA-NET: Innovative e-Management Platform for Academic Network. *Proceedings of papers ICEST'2020*, Nis, Serbia, September 2020, pp.69-72, IEEE Catalog Number: CFP20UWE-PRT https://www.scopus.com/record/display.uri?eid=2-s2.0-85096696117&origin=resultslist&sort=plf-f Accessed 19.01.2023

Scheck, H., Zupan, I., & Schuch, K. (2015). *Evaluation CEEPUS III - Evaluation of CEEPUS' Teacher Mobility. Frequent Travellers under the Microscope*, doi: 10.22163/FTEVAL.2015.6 https://repository.fteval.at/id/eprint/13/7/Evaluation%20CEEPUS%20III%20-%20Evaluation%20of%20CEEPUS%E2%80%99%20teacher%20mobility.%20Frequent%20travellers%20under%20the%20microscope.pdf Accessed 06.03.2023

Schuch, K. (2019). *The uptake of European programmes in the CEEPUS cooperation area*, June 2019, https://www.researchgate.net/publication/334226604_THE_UPTAKE_OF_EUROPEAN _PROGRAMMES_IN_THE_CEEPUS_COOPERATION_AREA Accessed 06.03.2023 DOI: 10.13140/RG.2.2.11363.30243

Sorantin, E. (2020). CEEPUS: Active methods in setting up a new regional academic exchange program. *Open Education Studies*, *2*(1), December 2020, 280–284, DOI: 10.1515/edu-2020-0132, License: CC BY 4.0

Tola, K., Marinova, G., & Hajrizi, E. (2021). Probation of IMA-NET platform in the framework of flexible CEEPUS course at the summer academia in UBT. *UBT International Conference*, *3*(2021), 1–12. https://knowledgecenter.ubt-uni.net/conference/2021UBTIC/scs/3 Accessed 19.01.2023

Tola K., & Marinova, G. (2022). Review on e-management approach, methods, and implementation platforms. *57th International Scientific Conference on Information, Communication and Energy Systems and Technologies (ICEST)*, *2022*, 1–4. doi: 10.1109/ICEST55168.2022.9828604. https://www.scopus.com/record/display.uri?eid=2-s2.0-85136090143&origin=resultslist&sort=plf-f Accessed 19.01.2023

Recommended websites

Website of the CEEPUS network BG-1103. (2023). http://ceepusmodcad.ubt-uni.net/ Accessed 19.01.2023

Website of the CEEPUS program. (2023). www.ceepus.info Accessed 19.01.2023

Website of the IMA-NET platform. (2023). https://ima-net.ubt-uni.net/ Accessed 19.01.2023

Website of the EUNIS Doerup Award. (2023). https://www.eunis.org/awards/dorup-award/ Accessed 03.04.2023

2 The Effect of Ethical Leadership and Leadership Effectiveness on Employees' Turnover Intention in High Education Institutions

A Case Study of Ibagué University

Cesar Augusto Díaz Moya and Paula Lorena Rodríguez Ferro

Introduction

Leadership can take a remarkable role in order to fulfill companies' need of competing and remaining; besides it may lead to yield better results when it constitutes a fully developed organizational aspect, in addition to becoming a dynamic element that characterizes the sense of being for current organizations. Leadership can also stand as a valuable asset resulting in a competitive advantage, as it is a unique and non-transferable factor.

As a COVID-19 pandemic consequence, leaders have to face demanding challenges nowadays. A significant number of organizations were widely affected in their commercial operations which resulted in cash flow shortages, labor instability, job positions destruction, reassignment of functions, and massive dismissals. This crisis reality is no different for higher education institutions, universities' problems like discouraging growth trends intensified during pandemic times, as a consequence some institutions were forced to redesign their organizational structures and optimize their budgets, policies as well as their leadership skills.

According to this context, the purpose of this chapter is to address the leadership effect on human resources behavior in a higher education institution case analysis Ibagué University. This case analysis seeks to validate the theory that, an ethical as well as effective leadership approach is more likely to create a productive, ethical, and trusting work environment, leading to employees' commitment, turnover reduction, favoring the organizational objectives achievement, and university durability over time.

Ibagué University Background

Ibagué University is a private, non-profit institution of higher education, it was established on August 27, 1980, as the University Corporation of Ibagué,

DOI: 10.4324/9781003376583-3

Coruniversitaria; it was recognized in 2003 as a university by the Ministry of National Education of Colombia, as described in institutional document called "Informe de Autoevaluación con fines de Acreditación Institucional" (2018).

The institution was founded by a group of 22 businesspersons and civic leaders from the department of Tolima, altogether with the support of the Corporation for Human Development of Ibagué and the Association for the Development of Tolima. Its founders sought to offer alternative higher education programs, clearly differentiated from the traditional careers provided in the region by that time, founders also procured to contribute to the human, cultural, economic, political, and social development of the territory. The university started by offering programs such as Financial Administration, Industrial Engineering, Public Accounting, and Marketing, nowadays the educational offer includes 17 bachelors, 12 specializations, and four master's degrees.

Social labor was one of the main institution's interests early on its establishment, therefore, at the beginning of the 1990s, high school service was offered to people with limited access, as these people could not get enrolled in education programs available in the city by that time due to their workload. Also in this 90s decade, the University's internationalist vow was evidenced through the first cooperation agreements subscription with Louvain and Ghent universities in Belgium, resulting in the design and offer of joined specializations and master degree programs.

During last five years, university missional tasks such as teaching, researching, social projection, and internationalization have guided the institutional path of growth; in addition, the academic-administrative managerial functions have also evolved transversally, as these matters turn out to be key and necessary aspects for the effective and efficient functioning of the University as a whole.

All these previous facts have marked the evolution and growth of the institution and constituted as foundations for the self-assessment process venture for accreditation purposes (Universidad de Ibagué, 2018). This self-assessment initiative led the institution to achieve the High Quality Accreditation seal awarded since 2019 by the National Accreditation Council (MEN, 2019). Since then, every University daily activity has been planned, directed, and executed aiming the alignment and contribution with this high-quality distinction, also this quality seal has led the institution to a constant search for excellence and a continuous improvement in both academic work and administrative processes.

Ibagué University Organizational Structure

Throughout its 42 years of operation, the Ibagué University has adopted organic matrix structures, which have been mainly focused on the Rector's

Office in charge of strategic planning, administrative management, and extension; and the Vice-Rectory Office in charge of academic, curricular, and scientific research management. Normative and action frameworks are concentrated and intermingled in these two functional areas involving the academic and administrative institutional approaches, this organizational structure setting implies the two functional offices' perspectives interaction on the leadership of every project and initiative.

Currently, the institution's organizational structure is undergoing a transition, which is stated in the Institutional Development Project for the year 2025 (Universidad de Ibagué, 2021). This change is aligned with the latest institutional venture called "The Necessary University" consisting of a new meaning proposal for the "University" concept itself. This new organic structure, conformed by 485 staff (Universidad de Ibagué, 2022), seeks to formally implement all necessary operational changes and adjustments derived from COVID-19 affections, those needed changes stand for implementing new practices in the teaching-learning methods, as well as in administrative and academic management processes.

As already mentioned, the structural changes also seek to fight back pandemic negative effects, mainly the personnel dismissal, the job positions destruction, and the functions reassignment; all these are resulting disruptions from the decrease in the student population, therefore the fall in operating income that affected the institutional normal operation prevailing.

This new structure makes it possible to overview the new institution's operative scheme and enables a clear understanding on staff assignment to a specific dependency or functional area, it also permits to recognize levels of command and authority, and identify the leadership line and style promoted and performed by the employees who work in each functional unit. In order to give an example, the following figure represents the structure of a faculty and its operative model (Figure 2.1).

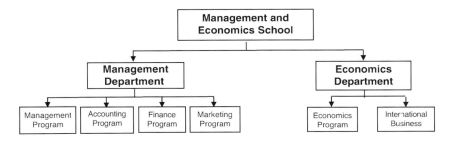

Figure 2.1 Management and economics school structure.

Source: Orozco and Reyes (2021). La Universidad Necesaria. Una propuesta de resignificación. Extract from a Ibagué University document.

Some of the main characteristic resulting of the new organizational structure is the faculties changing for training schools, also researching groups have become in researching institutes and thinking tanks. All these changes have led the institution to adopt a transformational leadership model prevailing in the search for interdisciplinarity, as well as the constant interaction of various knowledge actors and the regional problems approach from a transdisciplinary way.

For the Management and Economics School case, top management leadership has led to the academic programs redesign and creating new offerings. In addition, research projects and extension activities are now aimed to solve business, economic and social problems focusing on organic, multisystemic and transformational approaches, as well as the initiatives are now designed with practical application for the regional business and entrepreneurs. In this way, the university's departments directors and academic program leaders promote transformational and motivational leadership, encouraging the exchange of knowledge whereas giving a new meaning for concepts like "teaching" and "researching", leaders also seek changes in teaching traditional ways used by teacher teams so they develop authentic learning outcomes aligned with the business, commercial and social sector needs.

All this entire new paradigm in institutional organizational model and leadership style has direct effects on function manuals, communication systems, and monitoring and control mechanisms at all hierarchical levels along the line of command. This can also cause uncertainty, nonconformity, work overload, and discouraging in administrative and academic staff who are directly involved in the initiatives of such an ambitious project; therefore, it is necessary to measure, motivate and guarantee ethical, effective, efficient, and aligned behavioral practices with proposed goals resulting from the reconceptualization exercise of the post-pandemic university needed.

In accordance with this changing and challenging context, it constitutes a pertinent initiative to develop a case study to measure the relationship between the ethical and effective leadership executed by Ibagué University first- and second-line managers, with the perception of the collaborators and subordinates, coupled with the employees' commitment level and turnover intention.

Literature Review

Companies have various concerns associated with market issues, financial sustainability, productive capacities, strategic alliances, and innovation, among others, but companies also leave aside human talent matters, which can become the most important organizational aspect, as it has internal implications with repercussions towards the environment. It is important to analyze how people who are in management positions use command and authority to guide, inspire, and retain their employees, looking for the development and achievement of success not only individually, but also for the entire organization.

Leadership constitutes the basis for running a company and the people who make it up, the concept itself can be understood as the "phenomenon that allows increasing competitiveness, promoting productivity and guaranteeing the sustainability of organizations" (Contreras, 2008, p. 64); all these last three aspects stand out as widely desirable goals; but leadership execution has challenges to achieve desired goals, mainly due to individuals complexity, and the interaction and teamwork associated dynamics (Ahumada, 2004).

Despite the multiple definitions, conceptions, and implications associated with leadership, Burns (1978) shares appreciations that are not only widely applied to companies in the productive sectors; but it presents an affinity with educational institutions. Burns' main thesis is socially based on the relationship between leader and followers, this interaction has two perspectives; "behavior" understood from the leader's characteristics and actions, and followers "needs and desires" in particular or specific moments of the organization or community.

Burns also conceives transactional and transformational leadership as two major categories of leadership. Transactional category is possibly the most used due to its practicality in achieving goals, in this style, the leader exerts on his followers, intentionality for activities, objectives, or tasks accomplishment, in exchange for job and employee satisfaction, thus resulting in a linkage between the involved participants.

For transformational leadership, Burns remarks the need of a crisis situation to work as a starting point. This crisis scenario represents a prevailing need to make a change which embraces all the members of an institution or a company. This definition is also validated by Weber (1978, 1979), who emphasizes this type of leadership emerges in difficult and unstable contexts. Transformational leadership is based on the leader executing actions for empowering his team and generating a synergy that involves other groups or actors, thus everyone appropriates and exercises leadership, leaving aside the conventional structure of leader-follower, passing to a figure of moral agent and leader.

Linked to these conceptions, the new moral agent role understood as the evolution of the leader within the transformational framework, leads to an ethical leadership concept review, presenting it as "the demonstration of normatively adequate conduct through personal actions and interpersonal relationships, and the promotion of such behavior among followers through two-way communication, reinforcement, and decision making" (Brown et al., 2005, p. 120).

This is how, according to Paz et al. (2016), leader behavior is structured through his social behavior, which is based on his action willingness against good or evil, meaning, acting responsibly and complementary in a transparent way and with an ethical sense. However, the reality associated with this type of behavior is complex, as each individual can understand what is good and what is bad in a different way, since each person is unique and autonomous, with physical and mental capabilities that allow them to carry out harmful or beneficial actions and decisions according to their opinion (Horta & Rodríguez, 2006).

Due to these situations, ethical leadership becomes a relevant matter in organizations, alluding to the actions that are executed from and to individuals, under the principles of trust, credibility, and coherence, in order to develop suitable, correct activities that place the company as a responsible entity before society (Guaiquirima & Seijo, 2010); (Ferrer et al., 2010); (Eisenbeiss, 2012) and (Quijada et al., 2017) and for employees "a sense of belonging, providing ethical commitments among its members to achieve shared goals, naturally creating competitive advantages" (Paz et al., 2016).

As a complement, Ciulla raises the following question: What is good leadership? (2014, p. 16), possibly a question with various valid answers, depending on the organization or perspective in which it is analyzed; however, this author reflects on the term "good", what is a good thing? It is indicated that under the ethical meaning, the good is something morally accepted while from the technical meaning the good is the effective.

Cuilla's approach introduces the effective leadership concept, an always-evolving concept, which changes at the same pace as the business environment. This occurs as effectiveness is linked to the expected outcome resulting from leadership execution in the organization. Given this situation, according to Maxwell (1998), leaders must motivate their employees to get involved in the actions leading the organizations to the objectives fulfillment. This requires empowerment, responsibility, and gratification for those who really participate and adopt this working style in their daily practices.

However, the effectiveness achievement brings with it challenges for the organization, explained by Mc. Farland et al. (1996) when determining the importance of sharing information and especially power with the hierarchical levels, which requires leadership roles assignment that leads to objectives achievement, enhancing staff capabilities; only by doing this is how effective leadership is built, framed according to Zaleznik (2004) and Bacon (2008) in a managerial order ethics, which allows its employees to be linked with their own daily actions planning processes, avoiding a very common phenomenon in the business environment as power centralization.

This ethical leadership and effective leadership linkage leads to the proposal for the first hypothesis: H1: Ethical leadership is positively and significantly related to leadership effectiveness in High Education Institutions.

Employee well-being together with the work commitment is another important aspect to be considered, as long as the effectiveness, when reflected in the improvement of productivity, can affect individuals due to situations such as work overload, the reassignment of functions derived from positions destruction, poorly oriented guidelines, loss of focus towards the objectives achievement, among others. Therefore, effective leadership must be imparted towards human relations in the first instance, followed by the achievement of tasks and thus the positive result will be both in job satisfaction and organization productivity (Boumans & Landeweerd, 1993).

Gyensare et al. (2019) validated this previously mentioned relationship, considering that effective leadership is understood as the ability to create positive perceptions by a leader and drive the subordinates' intention to procure organizational objectives fulfillment. This can result and generate a close relationship with labor commitment, reflected in work practices and cooperative behaviors benefiting the entire organization. From this approach emerges the following hypothesis: H2: Leadership effectiveness is positively and significantly related to employee's work engagement in High Education Institutions.

From the ethical leadership perspective, for Hansen (et al., 2013) commitment to work should be understood as a social exchange between the leader and the employees. As a result of this, there will be a greater staff's effort and dedication in the work environment when they consider they are being treated ethically, prioritizing, according to Den Hartog and Belschak, values such as honesty, justice, a sense of responsibility, and care for others (2012). From these assessments arises hypothesis H3: Ethical leadership is positively and significantly related to employee's work engagement in High Education Institutions.

It should be sought that employees feel and develop a commitment sense to the company, it constitutes a desirable scenario, in which employees get involved in their functions, in their company's vision fulfillment, enjoy their work, and feel fulfilled (Schaufeli & Bakker, 2004); therefore, according to Bratton (2007), managers task is to establish a lasting relationship, lasting over time to generate a culture of retention and thus company can take advantage and promote the human resources.

Companies are constantly in search of sustainable competitive advantages and thereby ensure their permanence in the market. For Albrecht et al. (2015) a "committed employee" is the individual who seeks his permanence throughout his productive life in a single company, this committed employee is the basis for the construction and consolidation of a competitive advantage. Thus, organizational knowledge is increased, experience and expertise are used to the maximum, training, and inductions costs are avoided, and labor absenteeism is reduced (Swathi, 2014); therefore, the hypothesis resulting from these considerations is H4: Work engagement is negatively and significantly related to employee turnover intention in High Education Institutions.

Research Methodology

For this researching project, authors replied to the methodological model developed by professors Georgios Theriou, Dimitrios Chatzoudes, and Cesar Díaz which was used in their academic article entitled "The Effect of Ethical Leadership and Leadership Effectiveness on Employee's Turnover Intention in SMEs: The Mediating Role of Work Engagement". The following figure represents the model built by the mentioned researchers and adopted by this document's authors as a guide for the development of the case study of the Ibagué University (Figure 2.2).

These project researching characteristics constitute an empirical, explanatory, deductive, and quantitative study, based on the collection of primary information. Data was obtained through a structured survey-type instrument applied to academic and administrative areas staff from Ibagué University.

In order to examine the cause-and-effect relationship and hypothesis testing for the adopted research model, 131 staff members were asked, all of them belonging to the different university hierarchical levels, as a consistent characteristic all of the respondents report their performance to a direct boss and act as subordinates.

For controlling and avoiding biases or omissions in the respondents' answers, data collection process from the demographic perspective, only

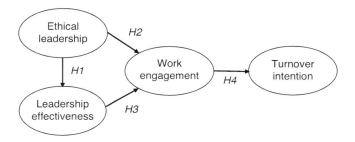

Figure 2.2 Adopted research model.
Source: Theriou et al., 2020.

The Effect of Ethical Leadership and Leadership Effectiveness 31

included variables such as gender, level of education, working area or dependency, and working time in the organization.

Measures in Factor Analysis

The following scheme compiles the measurement scales used for each of the analysis factors and contained in the structured questionnaire used for primary data gathering (Table 2.1).

Applied questionnaire was made up of four sections, each with their respective questions; section one, on Ethical Leadership, was structured with ten questions; section two, on Effective Leadership, contained four

Table 2.1 Measures in factor analysis

Factors to be analyzed	Authors' adapted from	Scale context	Number of items
Ethical Leadership	Brown et al., 2005	Focused on analyzing bosses' ethical conduct by using Ethical Leadership Scale (ELS) ranging from 1 (strongly disagree) to 5 (strongly agree)	10
Leadership Effectiveness	Avolio and Bass, 2004	Focused on analyzing bosses' work effectiveness by using Leader Effectiveness (Multifactor Leadership Questionnaire) scale ranging from (1 strongly disagree to 5 strongly agree	4
Work Engagement	Schaufeli and Bakker, 2004	Focused on analyzing workers' attitude about their job by using Work Engagement was measured using the shortened version of the Work Engagement Scale (WES) consisting of 0 (never) 1 (almost never) 2 (rarely) 3 (sometimes) 4 (often) 5 (very often) 6 (always)	9
Turnover Intention	Meyer et al., 1993	Focused on analyzing workers' intention to leave their job (1 strongly disagree to 5 strongly agree)	3

Source: Theriou et al. (2020).

questions; section three, on Commitment to Work, had nine questions; and section four, on Intention to Resign, had three questions.

For questionnaire creation, authors made an extended literature review. Questionnaire was preserved and applied in its original Spanish version; however, taking into account the current working conditions of the institution resulting from COVID-19 pandemic; demographic data was not taken, this is to generate confidence about anonymity and avoid bias in the responses.

Data Collection

The questionnaire was applied in person, at the facilities of the Ibagué University, addressing the employees related to substantive functions of the institution, staff from the following dependencies were asked: Teaching (deanships, departments, academic programs, and curricular management area); Research (group leaders and researchers); Extension (peace and region program, business training center, permanent education center, "Ibagué Cómo Vamos" office); Internationalization and Administrative offices (Institutional Marketing, University Well-being, Library, Psychological Counseling, and Nursing).

Data collection was carried out in August 2022 for a four-week period, research yields a total of 131 valid questionnaires for data processing.

Validity and Reliability

The researching factors were submitted to a validity test for evaluating their unidimensionality and reliability. Unidimensionality examination used Explanatory Factor Analysis tool (Fabrigar & Wegener, 2011) including following measures: The statistical test of "Kaiser-Mayer-Olkin" (KMO), Bartlett's test of Sphericity, the criterion of "eigenvalue" and the factor loadings; for analysis of Reliability the statistical measure "Cronbach Alpha" was used.

Tests concluded the scales used for the measurement of the factors are valid and reliable, as expressed in the Table 2.2. Amos Software, version 26.0 (Arbuckle, 2019) was used for testing purposes.

Data Triangulation

Triangulation of data analysis was used in order to complement the case study methodology, thus obtained results from questionnaires were contrasted with another data collecting method aimed at factors study and hypothesis validation.

As this case study was applied to an educational institution, Vallejo and De Franco (2009) recommend, for this type of organization, to use a

Table 2.2 Mean scores, validity, and reliability of research model

Factors	KMO	Bartlett	Bartlett_p	The criterion of "eigenvalue"	TVE	The factor loadings	Cronbach Alpha
Ethical leadership	0.863	630,69	2,66E-104	4,864	48.6%	0.581/0.66/0.718/0.662/ 0.783/0.886/0.766/0.663/ 0.517/0.667	0.902
Leadership effectiveness	0.777	204,23	2,39E-41	2,417	60.4%	0.781/0.737/0.825/0.764	0.859
Work Engagement	0.863	941,83	2,45E-174	5,553	61.7%	0.928/0.892/0.864/0.795/ 0.853/0.809/0.683/ 0.648/0.5	0.935
Turnover intention	0.755	242,66	2,53E-52	2,366	78.9%	0.906/0.846/0.911	0.917

Source: The authors.

triangulation allowing the use of different data-collecting methods. This triangulation acts as a filter for the results obtained and provides a greater accuracy, avoiding human intervention misinterpretations and subjectivity as they constitute the main source of information.

Researching Technique

Used contrasting method was based on qualitative research techniques, through the application of in-depth individual interviews (Sandoval, 2002) conducted to university staff in middle and top managerial positions working in different functional, academic, and administrative areas.

This technique, understood by Stake (2005) as a professional interview to be applied in a case study, allows the interviewer to obtain information from a respondent, on a topic, process, or specific experience. Through this technique Selltiz (1980) recognizes that the interviewer is able to extract what the interviewee considers as important and significant data; therefore, it will make possible research data contrast with the first applied method obtained results.

Samples and Qualitative Research Measurement Tool

Applied interviews are based on a structured questionnaire, made up of five open questions associated with the factors of Ethical Leadership, Effective Leadership, Work Commitment, and Rotation Intention, keeping their relationship with the previously stated hypotheses.

The interviewer, as a guide, interacts with bosses to obtain the required information from his role as leader and subordinates' counselor. In this exercise, nine individual and private interviews were conducted with nine area chiefs, representative from all of the university substantive functions.

Secondary Data Collection

Institutional documentary containing regulatory, strategic, and operational information was collected and analyzed, in order to consolidate the triangulation process. All these documents stand out as evidence and describe university intentions and practices associated with the leadership exercise and also characterize university current situation as well as employees' attitude. All this documental analysis complements the triangulation required for the study method as it constitutes the third axis of data analysis. Analyzed Institutional Documents include:

- Good Governance Code – "Código de Buen Gobierno";
- IDP Institutional Development Plan 2022–2025 "PDI 2022–2025";
- "The Needed University" – "La Universidad Necesaria";

The Effect of Ethical Leadership and Leadership Effectiveness   35

- "Rector's Letter" Communication "Carta de Rectoría";
- Megaprojects Infographics.

Results

Demographic Aspects

The first aspect to consider was to inquire exclusively officially contracted employees; therefore, 131 questionnaires and nine valid interviews were obtained and analyzed. Regarding the gender variable, the female staff with (54.2%) predominated over the male with (42.7%), and 3.1% preferred not to say so.

The education level shows the bachelor's degree level with (49.6%) followed by post-graduate degree level with (39.7%). Other results show Technical School and Secondary – High School with 6.9% and 3.8% respectively.

Another aspect to consider was employees' labor allocation within three institutional substantive functions, it shows teaching with (37.4%), researching with (19.1%), and extension with (14.5%). Also main supporting areas such as academic administration with (11.5%), the financial and administrative area with (8.4%) and others with (9.2%).

Finally, the years of employment contractual relationship to the University was considered; here the most representative was from 11 to 15 years with (29,8%), followed by six to ten years with (26.7%). The longest employment contractual relationship for more than 20 years with (14.5%) and from 15 to 20 years with (15.3%). Those with the least participation in the study are people with a recent employment relationship ranging from one to five years with (13.7%).

Mean Scores

Information gathered through 131 questionnaires, as well as the qualitative data from nine interviews with offices' leaders, and current institutional documents extracts, were analyzed for data triangulation and hypothesis verification related with the case analysis variables.

Observations for the four variables are based on a Likert-type scale ranging from 1 to 5 or 1 to 7. Ethical leadership (4.31) as well as leadership effectiveness (4.43) results are located in the average score above 4.0 value (Likert of five points, with 5 being "totally agree"); work engagement (6.10) had a mean score above 6.0 (7-point Likert, with 7 being a frequency of "always"); and turnover intention (2.01) variable scored below 3.0 (5-point Likert, being 1 the "totally disagree with job changing intention").

Results indicate that questionnaire surveyed employees consider their leaders to be ethical and effective, which influences positively the subordinates' daily functions and tasks performance. It establishes ethical precepts in

36 *Cesar Augusto Díaz Moya and Paula Lorena Rodríguez Ferro*

subordinates, leading them to work commitment, therefore to obtain satisfactory results in their offices/departments as in the entire organization.

Hypotheses Testing

Hypotheses group testing was performed by applying a Structural Equation Modeling (SEM), specifically the modified structural model which was adjusted according to provided data. It showed a variance of the main dependent factor "work engagement" in 49.1% and 31.5% of the dependent factor "turnover intention".

For work engagement factor analysis, a new route was built, based on modification indices of IBM AMOS 26, which allows visualizing a structural model with improved fit and explanatory (predictive) power, as shown in Table 4.3. It evidenced a new emerging dependent variable from the model, called "Work Pride" with a variance of 52.7%, this constitutes then as a new relevant dependent factor for the Ibagué University case study.

All the extracted adjustment values are at acceptable levels and validate the hypotheses (H1, H2, H3, and H4), additionally, they support the emergence of the new proposed causal relationship which is presented as follows: from leadership effectiveness to work pride and from work pride to work engagement (Table 2.3).

Based on these facts, the initial model that was taken for the case study presents a new structure which is displayed in Figure 2.3. For the construction of this new model, the necessary sensitizations were made and the trajectory coefficients were considered. (r) and adjusted R2 scores. This

Table 2.3 SEM results

Model fit summary		Squared multiple correlations (R2)	
Variable	*Measure*		*Estimate*
Sig. (p)	0.977	Leadership effectiveness	0.474/47.4%
GFI	0.902	Work engagement	0.491/49.1%
CFI	1.000	Work pride	0.527/52.7%
RMSEA	0.000	Turnover intention	0.315/31.5%

		Standardized Regression Weights			
		Path	*r*	*p*	*Result*
H1	Ethical leadership	→ Leadership effectiveness	0.689	<0.001	Supported
H3	Ethical leadership	→ Work engagement	0.182	<0.001	Supported
H4	Work engagement	→ Turnover intention	−0.233	0.008	Supported
NP1	Ethical leadership	→ Turnover intention	−0.345	<0.001	**New path**
NP2 (H2)	Leadership effectiveness	→ Work pride	0.942	<0.001	**New path**
NP3 (H2)	Work pride	→ Work engagement	0.701	<0.001	**New path**

Source: The authors.

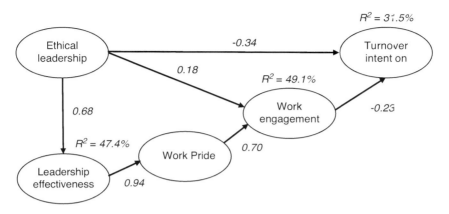

Figure 2.3 New model in Ibagué University case study.
Source: The authors.

allows validation of the four hypotheses (H1, H2, H3, and H4) combined for the case of the University of Ibagué; a relevant factor not considered is the initial approaches. R Core Team Software (2022) was used for data processing.

For leadership effectiveness, the new model shows a significant effect on work pride (r = 0.94 new path), followed by a no less relevant impact of this emerging factor on work engagement (r = 0.70 new path); on the other hand, the expected and validated relationship of the initial model for ethical leadership towards leadership effectiveness is maintained (r = 0.68). The results also indicate a smaller, but existing impact between ethical leadership and work engagement (r = 0.18).

Regarding the indirect effects with considerable importance, there is ethical leadership on work pride (r = 0.64), as on work engagement (r = 0.45), this through the positive relationship that is maintained with leadership effectiveness and a significant direct involvement in the turnover intention factor (r = −0.34 new path). From the leadership effectiveness factor, the relevance is on work engagement (r = 0.66) and this has subsequently a moderate direct effect on turnover intention (r = −0.23). These findings show processed constructs present strong and moderate relationships, as mentioned in the proposed conceptual model.

Discussions

The main objective of this research was to explore ethical leadership and leadership effectiveness effects on employees' turnover intention in higher education institutions, case of Ibagué University. In addition, this case study sought to validate the previously proposed model in a prior research conducted in SME's, but this time in a higher education institution.

Originally formulated hypotheses were tested by performing an SEM. Results demonstrated credible evidence that ethical leadership is positively and significantly related to leadership effectiveness in higher education institutions as proposed by H1. For H2, which states that leadership effectiveness is positively and significantly related to the employees' work commitment in higher education institutions, the model demonstrates that, in effect, "leadership effectiveness" generates employee "work engagement". New resulting model additionally highlights the importance of workers' pride feeling when doing their job, this is reflected in the previous emergence of a pride feeling variable called "work pride", this variable together with the execution of "leadership effectiveness" generates "work engagement" and turns out in the reduction of "turnover intention".

Results also validated hypotheses H3 and H4, demonstrating that "work engagement" mediates the effects of "ethical leadership" and "leadership effectiveness" on "turnover intention".

Practical Implications

The case study findings may have important implications for universities, mainly because rectors and directors are drivers for organizations' success, directors also stand out as a role model for their subordinates. Results demonstrate that an ethical and effective leadership approach is likely to create a productive, goal oriented, and trusting work climate conducive to the work engagement turnover intention reduction and workers' pride enhancing.

Higher education institutions should consider creating policies which include good governance practices and stimulates employees' ethical conduct, additionally universities may provide training to subordinates, develop functional and continuous communication means such as periodic informative reports on institutional projects advancement and managerial challenges, also provide discussion environments for employees to align performance appraisal with ethical conducts and cause reflection on managerial and direction acting.

Universities principals and directors should strive for establishing an ethical climate by appreciating and enhancing ethical decision-making. They can be more effective in their institutions and hence obtain a strong competitive advantage which contributes to human resources promotion and a remarkable belonging sense.

Contributions

The new arising model from this case study could be applied in future studies in other higher education institutions. By this way, future case analysis may validate the causal relationships from formulated hypotheses, as well as the emergence of the new variable "Work Pride" which is a significant contribution to the analysis of the effects of ethical leadership and leadership effectiveness on employee turnover intention.

These case results are useful as a managerial tool or model to be reapplied for those higher educational institutions with similar size, coverage, availability of resources, and current post-pandemic challenges. Case study validates ethical leadership is positively related to more efficient ways of human resources management, companies' goals achievement, organizational value creation, and organizational culture setting up.

Therefore, ethical leadership models complement labor commitment practices and reinforce compensation systems while developing pride and workplace belonging sense. This induces employees to a greater sense of transparency and fairness, increasing trust, improving communication, and clarifying staff career plan expectations.

The resulting model examined additional contextual variables in order to find out if ethics and leadership affect turnover intention through job commitment or other factor, indeed "work pride" emerged as a relevant element. Other factors such as motivation, trust, and the workplace can be explored in other future analyses.

Finally, some of the structural changes and actions taken by Ibagué University and previously described evidenced COVID-19 pandemic consequences in high education institutions. Those changes and actions may work as guidance for other universities to face affections in their labor stability such as job position destruction, reassignment of functions, and massive dismissals.

Limitations

Some employees' reluctance to provide information stands out as the main case analysis limitation; this behavior was derived from the uncertainty resulting from the organizational structural changes implemented in the post-pandemic period. Members of the staff felt intimidated by being asked about concepts like their turnover intention, their bosses' behavior, and their own work commitment level; respondents also doubted regarding their answers' anonymity degree.

Another limitation for the project was having only one institution as the subject of inquiry; in the future, the case can be repeated as a comparison

40   *Cesar Augusto Díaz Moya and Paula Lorena Rodríguez Ferro*

between more universities. Also, this study can be continued in a subsequent stage, by analyzing the new relationships proposed within the resulting model involving "work pride" factor. Future research may also test proposed relationships with larger universities thus differences in results may arise.

References

Ahumada, L. (2004). *Liderazgo y Equipos de Trabajo, una Nueva Forma de Entender la Dinámica Organizacional.* Ciencias Sociales Online, Vol. III, N° 1. Universidad de Viña del Mar, Chile.

Albrecht, S., Bakker, A., Gruman, J., Macey, W., & Saks, A. (2015). Employee engagement, human resource management practices and competitive advantage. *Journal of Organisational Effectiveness, 2*(1), 7–35.

Arbuckle, J. (2019). *Amos (Version 26.0) [Computer Program].* Chicago: IBM SPSS.

Avolio, B., & Bass, B. (2004). *Multifactor leadership questionnaire. Manual and sampler set.* Redwood City, CA: Mind Garden.

Bacon, T. (2008). Balanced leaders. Balance affects effectiveness. *Leadership Excellence, 11,* 11.

Boumans, N., & Landeweerd, J. (1993). Leadership in the nursing unit: relationships with nurse's well-being. *Journal of Advanced Nursing, 18,* 767–775.

Bratton, J. (2007). Strategic human resource management. In J. Bratton and J. Gold (Eds), *Human resource management,* 37–71.

Brown, M., Treviño, L., & Harrison, D. (2005). Ethical leadership: A social learning perspective for construct development and testing. *Organizational Behavior and Human Decision Processes, 97,* 117–134. DOI: 10.1016/j.obhdp. 2005.03.002.

Burns, J. (1978). *Leadership.* New York: Harper & Row.

Contreras, F. (2008). Leadership: Prospects for development and research. *Colombia International Journal of Psychological Research, 1*(2), 64–72. ISSN 2011-7922.

Ciulla, J. (2014). *Ethics, the heart of leadership.* 3ª ed. Santa Barbara, California: Praeger.

Den Hartog, D., & Belschak, F. (2012). Work engagement and Machiavellianism in the ethical leadership process. *Journal of Business Ethics, 107,* 3547.

Eisenbeiss, S. (2012). Re-thinking ethical leadership: An interdisciplinary integrative approach. *The Leadership Quarterly, 23*(5), 791–808.

Fabrigar, L., & Wegener, D. (2011). *Exploratory factor analysis.* Oxford University Press, UK.

Ferrer, J., Colmenares, F., & Clemenza, C. (2010). Un líder ético para el cambio: plataforma de gestión estratégica en Instituciones Universitarias. *Revista de Ciencias Sociales (Ve), XVI*(4), 642–653.

Guaiquirima, C., & Seijo, C. (2010). *Liderazgo ético: Un constructo ambiguo en la administración pública.* En C. Seijo (Comp.), *La gerencia en la sociedad. Un camino para la construcción de organizaciones futuras con rostro humano* (pp. 57–73). Editorial Astro Data.

Gyensare, M., Arthur, R., Twumasi, E., & Agyapong, J. (2019). Leader effectiveness: the missing link in the relationship between employee voice and engagement. *Cogent Business & Management*, 6(1), 1634910.

Hansen, S., Alge, B., Brown, M., Jackson, C., & Dunford, B. (2013). Ethical leadership: assessing the value of a multifoci social exchange perspective. *Journal of Business Ethics*, 115(3), 435–449.

Horta, E., & Rodríguez, V. (2006). *Ética General*. Ecoe Ediciones. Sexta edición. Bogotá, Colombia.

Maxwell, J. (1998). *The 21 irrefutable laws of leadership*. Nashville, TN, USA: Thomas Nelson.

Mc. Farland, L., Senn, L., & Childress, J. (1996). *Liderazgo para el siglo XXI* (E. Hoyos & L.H. Ramírez, Trads.). Bogotá, Colombia: McGraw Hill.

Meyer, J., Allen, N., & Smith, C. (1993). Commitment to organizations and occupations: extension and test of a three-component conceptualization. *Journal of Applied Psychology*, 73, 538–551. DOI: 10.1037/0021-9010.78.4.538.

Ministerio de Educación Nacional. (2019). *Resolución No. 010440 del 3 de octubre de 2019*.

Orozco, L., & Reyes, A. (2021). *La Universidad Necesaria. Una propuesta de resignificación de la Universidad de Ibagué*.

Paz, A., Núñez, M., García, J., & Salom, J. (2016). Rol del liderazgo ético en organizaciones académicas. *Opción*, 32(12), 148–168.

Quijada, G., Pulgar, C., Prieto, R., & Rincón, Y. (2017). Inteligencia ética: Un enfoque teórico hacia el liderazgo. En R. Prieto & A.M. Cazallo (Comps.), *Desarrollo organizacional y gestión humana en contextos globalizados* (pp. 269–310). Ediciones Universidad Simón Bolívar.

R Core Team (2022). *R: A language and environment for statistical computing*. Vienna, Austria: R Foundation for Statistical Computing.

Sandoval, C. (2002). *Investigación cualitativa*. Bogotá, Colombia.: ARFO Editores e Impresores.

Schaufeli, W., & Bakker, A. (2004). Job demands, job resources and their relationship with burnout and engagement: A multi-sample study. *Journal of Organizational Behavior*, 25, 293–315.

Selltiz, C., Wrightsman, L.S. & Cook, S.T. (1980). *Métodos de investigación en las relaciones sociales*. (pp. 151- 15). Rialp, Madrid.

Stake, R.E. (2005). *Case studies. Handbook of qualitative research* (pp. 236–247). London: Sage.

Swathi, B. (2014). A comprehensive review on human resource management practices. *International Journal of Business and Management*, 2(5), 183–187.

Theriou, G., Chatzoudes, D., & Diaz, C. (2020). The effect of ethical leadership and leadership effectiveness on employee's turnover intention in SMEs: The mediating role of work engagement. *European Research Studies Journal*, XXIII(4), 2020 947–963.

Universidad de Ibagué. (2018). *Informe de autoevaluación con fines de acreditación institucional "Construimos sobre lo construido"*. 17–20.

Universidad de Ibagué. (2021). *Proyecto de Desarrollo Institucional "Hacia la Universidad necesaria 2022-2025"*.

Universidad de Ibagué. (2022). *Estadísticas planta de personal - Sem 2022B*. Oficia de Gestión Humana.

Vallejo, R. & De Franco, F. (2009). La triangulación como procedimiento de análisis para investigaciones educativas. *REDHECS. Revista electrónica de Humanidades, Educación y Comunicación Social, 4*(Núm. 7 Pág), 117–133.

Weber, M. (1978). *Economy and society [Economía y sociedad]*. Londres: University of California Press.

Weber, M. (1979). *La ética protestante y el espíritu del capitalismo*. México: Premiá.

Zaleznik, A. (2004). Directivos y líderes ¿Son diferentes? *Harvard Business Review, 82*(1), 64–71.

3 Digital Transformation in Education

A Case Study of Teacher Information Network (TIN) in Turkey

Emrah Tosun, Hüseyin Can Barutcu, Suat Şahin, Zümrüt Ecevit Sati, and Sevinç Gülseçen

Introduction

The Main Elements of Digital Transformation

Undeniably, digitalization in business environments, production lines, products/services, and processes, as well as in-service training and professional and personal development, plays a significant role in competition and effective management. The ever-expanding digital transformation literature appears as an indicator of this (see Figure 3.1). Moreover, especially in the last decade, many academic works have been published within digital transformation studies, and digital transformation has found significant responses in professional life.

Digital transformation, which almost all organizations must adapt to, has been conceptually defined differently in different studies. In general, digital transformation is a continuous process where digital talents redefine business processes, business models, and corporate relationships (Borštnar & Pucihar, 2021). Gökalp and Martinez (2021) describe digital transformation as disruptive technological acquisitions that bring together new business and operational models in all business fields. Teichert (2019) expresses the concept of digital transformation in a more general sense as the organization's processes to adapt to digital changes to meet the digital expectations of customers, partners, and employees. Morakanyane et al. (2017) compared many definitions in the literature and defined digital transformation as a set of evolutionary technological processes that increase digital capacity and add value to customer experience, business models, and operational processes.

On the other hand, Mahraz et al. (2019) highlight three characteristic digital transformation features to develop a better understanding of them. The first characteristic feature is "irreversibility"; it emphasizes that digital transformation is a concept/subject that has constantly expanded and progressed since the beginning. The second characteristic feature is that it is

DOI: 10.4324/9781003376583-4

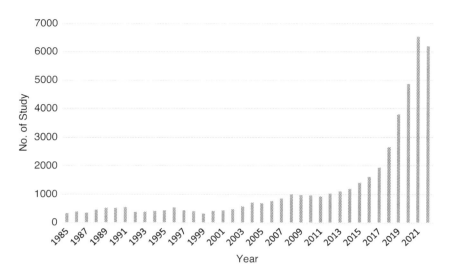

Figure 3.1 Scopus database – digital transformation studies by year.

seen as "inevitability"; it refers to being accepted sooner or later and embraced by institutions. Finally, the last feature is the state of "uncertainty" created by its irreversibility and inevitability; it refers to the future state of digital transformation, which undergoes constant change and transformation and is unpredictable.

Although the characteristics mentioned above emphasize the difficulty of digital transformation, the concept of digital transformation constitutes the framework of a systematic approach. This systematic approach includes important strategic and technological components. Since the emergence of digital transformation, these components have changed with today's technologies. Today, the strategic issues and applications of digital transformation are used in many areas, from finance to production, from education to public administration, and they are constantly improving. Verina and Titko (2019) examined the strategic and technological components that form the basis of transformation under three headings (see Table 3.1); a) The driving forces in digital transformation, b) The main elements of digital transformation, and c) The results of digital transformation. The driving forces consist of elements that can motivate the initiation of digital transformation and its dissemination within the organization (for example, increasing competitiveness, reducing costs, etc.). Management, technology, and human resources appear as the main elements in achieving digital transformation goals. These main elements constitute a broad spectrum ranging from data ownership to cyber

Table 3.1 Main elements of digital transformation

Technologies	Management	People
• Data • Big data • Cloud • Mobile devices • Social media • Software • Analytics • Embedded devices • Artificial intelligence • The Internet of Things • Cybersecurity • App marketplaces	• Business models • Operating models • Operational processes • Strategies • Business activities • Organizational structure • Organizational culture • Coordination mechanism • Products • New services	• Customers • Employees/workforce/people • Managers • Executives • Talents • Owners • Suppliers • Partners • Stakeholders • Competencies

Source: Verina & Tikko (2019).

security, from business models to organizational culture, and all stakeholders of the institution with all its inclusiveness. Based on these main elements, the efficient need-oriented use and management of the available technological sources and the provision of stakeholder support in this focus play an important role in achieving the targeted results in digital transformation.

In today's world, where digital transformation goals are approached step by step, it is seen that constantly developing information and communication technologies, together with Industry 4.0 and globalization, affect and transform all areas. Digital transformation has application areas and potential in almost every field, especially in education, health, agriculture, art, media, management, industry, and the economy (Yıldız, 2021). One of the most striking of these areas is the education sector. In other words, technological development and change affect the teaching process by changing the method and speed of accessing information (Yinanç et al., 2020). As a natural result of digitalization in daily life, the expectation of digital transformation is inevitable in the field of education, where many people are involved (Taşkıran, 2017).

Digital Transformation in Education

Twenty-first-century skills have been examined by different institutions and organizations under various titles, from using information and communication technologies to social life skills, from thinking-problem-solving skills to learning skills (OECD, 2005). Instead of protecting traditions and values, civic awareness, and mass production, high-level skills such as producing information and transferring it to different fields, using digital technologies actively, problem-solving, producing, processing, and using data are demanded from the new generations in the 21st century (Uçak & Erdem, 2020).

The use of technology for teaching purposes has become inevitable to respond to the teaching needs of the changing generation and improve their teaching environment. From this perspective, it is seen that digital transformation is a necessity rather than a preference, and it should be applied in fields that will add quality to our lives such as education, health, public administration, and industry (Karoğlu et al., 2020). Technological tools used in the field of education are increasingly diversified. In recent years, digital content such as video projectors, smart boards, mobile devices, e-books, downloadable music, uninterrupted audio and video networks, and online social networks are technological developments that affect the lives of the majority. Since the use of technology in the field of education makes the education process more effective and motivating, it has become more and more widely used in educational institutions (Temizyürek & Ünlü, 2015). These rapid changes and transformations affect education as a structure and learning environment. In the digital transformation process, for an effective learning environment, managers must create a vision that can produce and manage it. It is also possible for school stakeholders to participate in this transformation process by allowing them access to space and time by supporting technologically appropriate content and infrastructure. It is thought that education administrators and program experts should be ready for this transformation and have the qualifications to manage (Balyer & Öz, 2018).

Considering the developments in the field of education, opportunities, and applications are integrated into the digital world. Moreover, education, which is a subject that significantly affects the development of society, needs to provide digital transformation before other fields. In education, many applications can be expressed as digital transformation (Parlak, 2017). Thanks to these applications, obstacles in education can be identified, and the education process can be improved. As a result, it is possible to raise more qualified students with a better learning environment (Horzum & Demircioğlu Diren, 2022).

Lean activities, such as upgrading the hardware or software put into practice to improve education and training processes, may need to be revised for digital transformation in education and training. Yinanç et al. (2020) state that to successfully realize digital transformation in education and training, some basic principles that overlap with the essential components of the digital transformation process should be considered.

- It should not be forgotten that the technology, devices, and applications to be used in the digital transformation of education and training are tools, and the transformation will not occur only by including these tools in the education and training processes.

- Transformation should be considered a cultural change. Therefore, along with the technology used, detailed studies should be carried out on educational content, software, and the quality of educators. In addition, qualified training should be given to trainers, who are critical for realizing this cultural change, in a way that will enable them to use innovative technologies.
- Digital transformation in education and training should be planned as a long-term process.
- Professional/academic experts should manage the transformation process by the project management approach.

There are different practices in various countries for the vocational training of teachers. In Germany, Japan, and France, participation in in-service training seminars (training that teachers receive while working) is compulsory for teachers by law. In Denmark, in-service teacher training is compulsory only on the first employment entry. When starting a job in England, the condition of attending professional development courses is accepted by signing a contract. In-service training is a prerequisite for recertification in the USA and Switzerland. Although it is not compulsory in Australia, the only way to be promoted is to receive in-service training (Serin & Korkmaz, 2014). Participating in in-service training in our country is optional or compulsory, depending on the purpose and characteristics of the training activity. For example, it is compulsory to attend the in-service training program given at the first entry of employment, as well as the seminars given at the beginning and end of the year (Yazıcı & Gündüz, 2011).

Digital Transformation in Education in Turkey

In the digital transformation process in education in Turkey, questions like "How should educational institutions approach this change?" and "how should the necessary adaptation be ensured?" are increasingly important. The existence of digital transformation in education is accepted. It is seen that various initiatives such as the Movement for Increasing Opportunities and Improving Technology (FATİH – Fırsatları Arttırma ve Teknolojiyi İyileştirme Hareketi) at the K12 (It is a term used in place of 12-year preschool, primary, and secondary education) level, Education Information Network (EBA – Eğitim Bilişim Ağı) applications, and Digital Transformation Project at various universities (Şener & Gündüzalp, 2018). Furthermore, within the scope of out-of-school education, "Deneyap Technology Workshops", "Design-Skill Workshops", and "81 Cyber Heroes in 81 Cities" projects that support digital transformation in education and are carried out with public support are implemented. In addition, the "Teknofest" event has been organized every year since 2018 by the Ministry of Technology and Industry of Turkey and the Foundation of Turkey Technology Team (Teknofest, 2022) the world's largest technology festival, with the participation of many public and private sector institutions, draws attention. At the same time, the initiatives made at primary, secondary, high school, and university levels in Turkey during the pandemic process announced as of March 2020 have an important place in the scope of digital transformation in education.

On the other hand, Human-Education Infrastructure Development and Qualified Workforce Training policies, which have an important place in the Digital Turkey Roadmap of the Ministry of Industry and Technology, have an essential place in education and digitization initiatives in Turkey (T.C. Sanayi ve Teknoloji Bakanlığı, 2018). In the transformation from the traditional system to a digital one, the MEB Information System (MEBBİS) and e-school systems were established to solve these problems. While resource management can be done with MEBBİS, parent-teacher communication can be provided with the e-school system (Karoğlu et al., 2020).

Apart from many activities for students, activities suitable for digital transformation are carried out for teachers and educators affiliated with the ministry. The most important of these activities is the Teacher Information Network (TIN) platform, which has been implemented to increase their digital skills and professional capabilities and benefit from in-service training. In January 2022, the TIN platform was established where teachers could receive remote in-service training (ÖBA, 2022).

The platform provides with

- Central and local in-service training plans;
- In-service training organized synchronously and asynchronously through distance education;
- Virtual library;
- Professional development societies;
- Teacher-administrator mobility programs;
- The school-based professional development program;
- Promotion of good practices by teachers.

An exact number of 175,309 teachers preferentially attended the training seminars. Ten different training options were offered, from climate change to waste management, from event-based course design to first aid training. While 142,425 teachers received at least one training, 444,850 training was completed during the two-week semester break (MEB, 2022a). In the TIN, teachers can see the training they can receive and apply for the training they want through this platform. In addition, the teachers working in the

Ministry of Education have divided into three career steps a teacher, a specialist teacher, and a head teacher after the candidacy period. The career ladder training specified in The Teaching Profession Law that came into force in 2022 was offered for the first time in 2022 through the TIN platform. From this training, 603,864 were made, and 533,359 of these applications were made in specialist teaching and 70,505 in head teacher (MEB, 2022b). Teachers must continue their personal and professional development and transfer the knowledge they have acquired to their students by following technology development. For this reason, activities to improve the qualifications of teachers in developed and developing countries are considered very important in terms of teachers' personal and professional development and ensuring the continuity of education.

Method and Case Study

This chapter used semi-structured interview questions within the in-depth interview technique, one of the qualitative research methods. Qualitative research uses the most preferred methods of collecting qualitative data such as observation, interview, and document analysis. It can be defined as research in which the process is followed impartially in order to reveal the perceptions and events in a realistic and holistically in their natural environment (Yıldırım & Şimşek, 2021).

The in-depth interview technique is a data collection method that includes all dimensions of the research subject. It enables comprehensive answers to be obtained by mainly asking open-ended questions and allowing information to be collected through one-to-one and face-to-face interviews (Tekin & Tekin, 2012). Within the scope of the research, an in-depth interview technique was applied with teachers and administrators from all levels (preschool, primary school, secondary school, and high school) at the K12 level.

Data Collection and Analysis

A form consisting of 13 items containing TIN evaluation interview questions developed by the researchers was used to collect the data. The content modules of digital education platforms and the literature were examined in preparing the interview questions. Categories, indicators, and items derived from the "Teacher Opinion Survey on the Content of Mathematics Courses in the Education Information Network" by Arslan (2016), the "Evaluation Questionnaire for Opinions of Science Teachers of EBA" conducted by Ceylan & Gündoğdu (2017), and "Development of the Digital Education Platform Evaluation Scale" by Özerbaş & Yazıcı (2021) were used.

50 *Emrah Tosun et al.*

Table 3.2 Demographics of participants

Specs		*f (frequency)*	%
Gender	Female	6	50
	Male	6	50
Age	26–30 years old	1	8.33
	31–35 years old	2	16.67
	36–40 years old	3	25
	41–45 years old	3	25
	46–50+	3	25
Level of Edu.	Bachelor's	5	41.66
	Master's Degree	5	41.66
	Ph.D.	2	16.67
Seniority/Experience	5–10 years	2	16.67
	10–14 years	3	25
	15–19 years	3	25
	20 and above	4	33.33
Type of School	Preschool	3	25
	Elementary School	3	25
	Secondary School	3	25
	High School	3	25
Freq. of TIN Use	A few times a week	2	16.67
	A few times a month	5	41.66
	Only in case of necessity	5	41.66

These categories are Scope and Content, Technical and Design Features, Teacher Competencies, and Motivation. The data obtained from the participants were analyzed and presented by creating themes and codes under categories.

Participants

Teachers working in MEB in Turkey constitute the participants of the research. In-depth interviews were conducted with three volunteers from all levels, a total of 12 participants. Some demographic characteristics of the participants are shown in Table 3.2.

Scope and Content of the TIN

In this section, the teachers were asked the following questions: "Can you list the training you have received from TIN so far?", "Do you find the content offered in the TIN sufficient? What do you think about how the contents should be of the TIN?", "What do you think about the strengths and weaknesses of TIN?" and "What aspects of the TIN need improvement?" The themes, codes, and frequencies created from the answers received are shown in Table 3.3.

Digital Transformation in Education 51

Table 3.3 Codes obtained from the dimension of scope and content

Theme	Code	*f*
Most liked training	Training for developing digital skills	5
	Training on psychology, protection of women's and children's rights	5
	Specialized teacher training	3
	Environment and energy-themed training	3
Adequacy of the contents	I find it partly sufficient	7
	I don't find sufficient	3
	I find it sufficient	2
Strong aspects	Being easily accessible	8
	Having enough content to appeal to everyone	7
	Saving time and costs	4
	Giving training by experts	2
Weak aspects	Poor presentation and monotonous methods of expression	4
	Lack of interactive, insufficiency of follow-up and evaluation system	4
	Lack of diversity in training	4
	Failure for training to continue in modules	2
Features that need improvement	Training needs to be made interactive	5
	More and various training should be added	4
	Topics should be handled in a lively and entertaining way.	2

The most liked and preferred training by teachers in the TIN are determined as training that develops digital skills (robotics, Web 2.0 tools, Excel, etc.) (n = 5) and training for the protection of psychology, women's, and children's rights (n = 5). While some of the participants stated that they liked the specialized teacher training (n = 3), some of them stated that they found the environment and energy-themed training (n = 3) valuable and productive. Apart from these, painting analysis training (n = 1), guidance training (n = 1), SRC training (n = 1), personal development training (n = 1), and storytelling training (n = 1) are the training liked by the participants.

Most participants stated that they found the TIN partially sufficient in terms of the content presented (n = 7). While some of the teachers said that they found the content sufficient (n = 2), some of them stated that it was not sufficient (n = 3). The most considerable criticism brought by the participants towards the content presented on the TIN is that the narrations in the videos are too traditional, boring, and longer than necessary (n = 4). In addition, some participants stated that they saw the lack of interaction in the videos as a vital deficiency (n = 2). The lack of sufficient training content for some branches (n = 2), the lack of application aspects of the training for applied fields (n = 2), and the lack of orientation to training (n = 1) are the criticisms brought to the TIN platform in terms of content.

Most participants described the strength of the TIN as being easily accessible (n = 8). In addition, a significant portion of the participants stated that having enough content to appeal to everyone is a strength (n = 7). Some teachers found the TIN strong because it saves time and costs (n = 4), and some stated that the training is given by academicians who are experts in their fields (n = 2).

According to the opinions reported for the weaknesses of the TIN, a significant part of the participants (n = 4) stated that they found the system weak due to poor presentation and uniform expression methods. In addition, most participants stated that the lack of interactiveness of the training, the inability to monitor the extent to which the trainees participated in the training, and the lack of an evaluation system are the weaknesses of the TIN (n = 4). While some participants defined the lack of different content as a weakness (n = 4), some described training that does not continue in modules as the weak side of the system (n = 2). Furthermore, technical problems (n = 1), lack of application in training (n = 1), not being able to access the content after the training expires (n = 1), long training periods (n = 1), not meeting teachers' material needs such as computers and internet (n = 1) and the high level of completion rate (n = 1) for the success criterion were stated as the weaknesses of the TIN by the teachers.

K7: "I think the contents are not very sufficient. Access to resources related to the subject covered in the videos can be provided. After training, a referral to another related training can be made".

K8: "Contents are given in a boring way. I think the topics in the videos should be handled in a more lively, exciting, and interesting way".

K9: "The strengths of the TIN I find are that it is easily accessible and offers every teacher the opportunity to improve themselves. In this respect, it provides equality of opportunity among teachers. I see the lack of mutual communication in training as its weakness."

K2: "Maybe watching time of the training can increase a little more. You can continue from where you left off. A few different activities can be done on feedback after watching the video."

K12: "The interface could be more useful. Videos can be interactive".

K3: "The aspects that need improvement; I can't get it again because the training I wanted has expired".

K10 (Participant 10): "I am currently taking personal development seminars, psychology, general culture, use of digital tools courses, and robotic coding and web 2.0 training through the TIN."

K12: "Web 2.0 Tools Training and Specialist Teacher Training are the training I received on the TIN."

A significant portion of the interviewees stated that the training should be carried out interactively so that the trainees would also be effective, and the reorganization of the evaluation system by following the video-watching times as the aspects of the TIN that should be improved (n = 5). In addition, the participants stated that more and various training should be added to the TIN platform (n = 4). Some of the participants stated that teaching methods should be arranged in a way to make the training lively and entertaining (n = 2). Moreover, participants stated that some aspects of the TIN need to be improved; extending the training video time (n = 1), organizing the videos to continue from where learners left off (n = 1), reopening the expired training (n = 1), strengthening the infrastructure (n = 1), improving the interface (n = 1), recruiting young trainers (n = 1), developing the library application (n = 1), adding training in the form of short presentations like public service announcements (n=1).

Technical and Design Features

In this section, the teachers were asked the following questions: "Do you encounter technical problems in the TIN?", "What do you do for a solution when you have a technical problem?", "How do you evaluate the TIN in terms of interface design and visual content design?". The themes, codes, and frequencies created from the responses received are shown in Table 3.4.

Table 3.4 Codes obtained from the dimension of technical and design features

Thema	Code	f
Methods Followed for Solving Technical Problems	Consulting with an IT specialist	6
	Searching for the solution online	5
	With their own means	4
	Contacting the help desk	2
	waiting for it to fix itself	2
Interface Design	The interface is simple, clear, and effective	7
	Interface needs improvement	3
	The interface is poor and useless	2
Visual Content Design	Not lively, fun, and functional enough	9
	Contents are monotonous	4
	Lively and interesting	2

54   *Emrah Tosun et al.*

Teachers stated that one of the most common technical problems they encounter on the TIN platform is accessing problems in the system. They stated that another critical problem is that some videos are viewed as unwatched by the system even though they have been watched. For specified technical problems, most teachers stated that they tried to find a solution by asking an IT specialist (n = 6) or by searching the internet (n = 5). Some teachers stated that they sought solutions to problems with their own efforts (n = 4). It has been observed that the number of teachers (n = 2) who expect the problem to be solved by itself (n = 2) or who seek a solution by applying to the help desk (n = 2) is less than those who apply other methods.

Most of the participants stated that they liked the interface design of TIN because of its simple, clear, understandable, and effective features (n = 7). Some of the participants stated that they partially liked the interface and that it should be improved (n = 3), while others stated that they did not like it because it was inadequate and unusable (n = 2). Some participants stated that the orientation to the training was incomplete, and they could not reach the content they were looking for (n = 2). Some of the participants stated that the training should be divided into branches and presented in advance with weekly-monthly plans (n = 2). Some participants also stated that it would be appropriate to organize the training in stages and arrange the system in a way that allows asking questions immediately (n = 2).

Most teachers who participated in the interview stated that the visual content design was insufficient because it was not lively, entertaining, and functional (n = 9). A significant part of the participants stated that the video lessons were not memorable and were taught with the traditional lecture method (n = 4). The number of teachers who stated that they consider visual content design to be lively and interesting is lower than the opposite opinion (n = 2). Some of the teachers' opinions that created these codes are given below:

K7: "Sometimes, the videos watched are seen as if they were not watched by the system. To solve this problem, I rewind videos. B-Sometimes, there is a problem accessing the site."

K8: "Sometimes there is a problem in accessing the site. To solve this problem, I deal with myself first. If I can't find a solution, I look for the solution to the problem on the internet. Finally, I ask for help from the IT teacher at the school".

K9: "It's positive that it has a simple and plain interface, but I can't find where the content I'm looking for is. Details about the training are missing".

K3: "*The interface is quite directive; I think it is useful. It has a simple use. The menus are in the right place*".

K4: "*I find the homepage beautiful. The first pages of some tutorials are very good, but the inside pages are not as good.*"

K7: "*The visual content design is not very sufficient; it can be improved. More beautiful and interesting visuals can be used in the content*".

K3: "*I find visual content designs attractive in general. The visual design keeps us in education. Among the training contents, I find the contents attractive in some training, but not in all*".

Teachers' Competencies

In this section, the participants were asked the following questions; "What do you think about the TIN whether it increases your skills in using digital technologies?" and "Do you consider yourself competent to use digital educational content such as EBA, the TIN, Interactive Board … ? Why?". The themes, codes, and frequencies created from the answers received are shown in Table 3.5.

Nine of the participants stated that they improved their ability to use digital technologies with some training on the TIN (n = 9). Two of the participants stated that their skills in using digital technologies were developed before the TIN platform (n = 2). In addition, two of the participants stated that with digital content training on the TIN, those who have very limited ability to use digital technologies could develop these skills very well (n = 2). Nine of the participants consider themselves sufficient to use digital educational content (n = 9). They expressed that there are interactive whiteboards in schools, and in-service training has been taken to use these interactive whiteboards, thanks to the Fatih Project.

Table 3.5 Codes obtained from the dimension of teacher competencies

Theme	Code	f
Teacher Competencies	the TIN contributes	9
	I consider myself sufficient	9
	Developed with previous experience and training	3
	the TIN can also improve the one who does not know	2
	I see partly enough	2
	It should be used more often	2

56 *Emrah Tosun et al.*

Two participants who participated in the study stated that they considered themselves half-sufficient in using digital educational content (n = 2). In addition, two of the participants stated that the TIN platform should be used more frequently in order to reach a sufficient level while using digital education content (n = 2). Some of the teachers' opinions that created these codes are given below:

K1: "It contributes to increasing my digital skills".

K5: "I have solved the digital problems I have faced for years, so I consider myself sufficient".

K5: "Since I do not use the TIN platform very often, I think it does not contribute to my ability to use digital technologies. I have improved myself on this subject with the training I have received before".

K11: "Even someone who does not know this subject can improve their skills in using digital technologies with the training on the TIN".

K6: "I consider myself half-sufficient in this regard".

K2: "I think that more improvement can be achieved when the TIN platform is used more frequently in order to use digital educational content effectively".

Motivation

In this section, "Why do you prefer to use the TIN?", "Do you use the TIN for purposes other than compulsory use?", "What would you like to say if you compare the TIN platform offered within the scope of digital transformation in education with previous traditional in-service training?" questions were posed. The themes, codes, and frequencies created from the answers received are shown in Table 3.6.

K4: "I receive more than one TIN every month".

K6: "I use the library on the TIN".

K11: "the TIN provides quality, accurate and scientific information in the digital environment".

K7: "Face-to-face training is more beneficial for practical training. For other training, the TIN is a very useful platform."

Digital Transformation in Education   57

Table 3.6 Codes obtained from the dimension of motivation

Thema	Code	f
Motivation	Personal and professional development	8
	Benefits	9
	More than one training per month	4
	Request to use the library	2
	The traditional method in applied training	2
	Mandatory use	2
	Keeping up with the digitalizing world	1
	professional structure	1
	Offering equal opportunity	1
	Social development	1
	Learning by doing and experiencing	1

K2: "I have difficulty in finding educational content that suits their wishes. That's why I only use it when necessary."

K11: "We have to resort to digital environments in the digitalizing world. Therefore, teachers need to improve themselves in order to keep up with society".

K9: "The positive side is that it provides equal opportunities for all teachers. It is easily accessible by all teachers in the country. For example, even a distant teacher can benefit from the training given by a famous person on a subject".

K10: "In terms of social communication (gathering the participants, exchanging ideas, etc.), traditional face-to-face education is more advantageous than distance education".

K5: "Learning by doing and experiencing provides more permanent learning".

K10: "For my personal development, I check the TIN every 2–3 days to see if the appropriate course has been added for me".

K3: "in contrast to traditional education, It is much more beneficial in terms of time, space, and cost".

Nine participants stated that they use the TIN for personal and professional development (n = 9). Nine participants found the TIN training more beneficial than the traditional in-service training (n = 9). These participants find the TIN more beneficial than traditional education in terms of time, space, and cost. Four of the participants stated that they received more than one training per month on the TIN (n = 4). In addition, two participants stated that they always use this platform to use its library (n = 2). Two of the participants stated that it would be more effective if the theoretical parts of the courses planned to be given to the teachers were done through the TIN platform and the application parts with traditional face-to-face methods (n = 2). Two participants, on the other hand, stated that they use the TIN only in compulsory situations (n = 2). One of the participants stated that it has become mandatory to use digital tools in the digitalizing world and that teachers need to improve themselves to keep up with this world (n = 1). One participant also stated that they use the TIN platform because it has a professional structure, and the training includes accurate and reliable information (n = 1). At the same time, one of the participants sees the platform as it offers equal opportunities for all teachers (n = 1) to participate in in-service training (access from anywhere). One of the participants said that traditional education improves teachers socially, while the TIN platform is weak in the interaction of teachers with each other (n = 1). One of the participants stated that the training by doing and experiencing is more permanent, so traditional face-to-face in-service training is more beneficial (n = 1).

Conclusion

In similar studies in the literature, it has been stated that e-learning mediates the in-service learning process and that accessibility is high because the training provides advantages in terms of time and space (Hofmeister & Pilz, 2020; Siemens et al., 2015). The strengths of the TIN platform can be expressed as follows:

• It is easily accessible;
• There are lots of training that can appeal to every teacher;
• It is economical in terms of time and finance;
• Experts give the training.

In this vein, similar results were obtained from the literature (Hofmeister & Pilz, 2020).

The weak aspects of the platform; It was concluded that the teaching method and the evaluation system should be developed, the diversity in the pieces of training needed to be improved, and some pieces of training do not continue as a series. In the study in which the blog-based in-service training system of teachers was evaluated (Ciampa & Gallagher, 2015), the shortcomings of the blog platform; time limits; technical problems; He stated that there is a lack of closeness and simultaneous interaction and that the system should be improved with these aspects. In this study, making the pieces of training available on the TIN platform interactive, more and more diverse training, and explaining the subject in a more lively and entertaining way are the features of this platform that need to be developed. The study is similar to the literature (Ciampa & Gallagher, 2015). Some of the pieces of training available on the TIN platform are highly appreciated; these pieces of training are given in the findings section. While some of the pieces of training were found sufficient, some were partially sufficient, and some needed to be developed.

In Lehiste's (2015) study evaluating the teacher in-service training program developed within the framework of Technological Pedagogical Content Knowledge (TPACK), it has been concluded that most of the teachers consider themselves technologically competent, find the platform technically useful, can solve technical problems with their means, and also increase their technological competence thanks to the in-service platform. Considering the technical and design features of the TIN platform in this study, as a result of the data received from the participants: When faced with a technical end, it was concluded that a solution was reached by consulting people who are experts in this field, by searching the internet, by applying to the help desk or by their means. While some teachers found the interface design simple and understandable, some teachers stated that it should be improved, while others stated that it was useless. In these respects, this study is mainly compatible with the literature (Lehiste, 2015). It has been concluded that the visual content design is not lively, entertaining, and functional enough.

According to Damşa et al. (2021) stated that teachers' digital competencies are a prerequisite for online learning and that the e-learning system contributes to teachers' digital competencies. Tang et al. (2022) stated in their study that teachers' digital competencies are important to improve their professional skills and provide students with a better teaching experience. They proposed an online system to measure teachers' digital competencies. Considering the characteristics of teacher competencies in this study, as a result of the information received from the participants, it was concluded that the TIN platform contributed to the ability to use digital technologies and that the teachers considered themselves competent in using digital technologies. In this respect, the study is compatible with the literature (Damşa et al., 2021; Tang et al., 2022).

Considering the motivation dimension of the TIN platform, as a result of the information received from the participants: It is stated that the teachers use the TIN platform for personal and professional development, they find this platform useful, and some teachers receive more than one training every month, the library in the platform is useful, it provides equal opportunities and opportunities, and it is necessary to adapt to the digitalized world. The result is obtained. Hou et al. (2009) examined an online environment for teachers in which problem-solving strategies are used, experimental observations are noted, and discussion activities for knowledge sharing are included. According to the research results, it was stated that face-to-face environments should support online environments used in the training of teachers in terms of increasing interaction and motivation. In a study on online in-service training of teachers in Greece, it is stated that most secondary school teachers prefer in-service teacher training programs based on traditional (face-to-face) and online learning methods (Chatzipanagiotou & Katsarou, 2015). Some teachers who participated in this study stated that traditional in-service training should be done in practical training and that the TIN platform is very useful in other cases. The findings are similar to the literature in this aspect. Again, in some studies similar to this study, it is stated that online in-service training for teachers is vital and necessary in terms of improving teachers' professional skills and competencies (Ernest et al., 2013; Jung, 2005; Robinson & Latchem, 2003).

In a study conducted by Lin et al. (2011) in Thailand, a web-based platform for teacher education called TEACH was developed and tested. The study's findings showed that online education supports teacher education, and the participants found the web-based platform useful. It was concluded that some of the teachers participating in this study only use the TIN platform when there is compulsory education, and they support face-to-face education in in-service training. Therefore, the study is compatible with the literature (Lin et al., 2011) in terms of finding the platform valuable and supportive of face-to-face education.

References

Arslan, Z. (2016). *Eğitim bilişim ağı'ndaki Matematik dersi içeriğine ilişkin öğretmen görüşleri: Trabzon ili örneği [Teachers' views on the content of the Mathematics course in the Education Information Network: The case of Trabzon province] | AVESİS*. https://avesis.gazi.edu.tr/yonetilen-tez/f0620c8b-1243-4e13-9931-4b503844396b/egitim-bilisim-agindaki-matematik-dersi-icerigine-iliskin-ogretmen-gorusleri-trabzon-ili-ornegi Accessed 27.02.2023

Balyer, A., & Öz, Ö. (2018). Academicians' views on digital transformation in education. *International Online Journal of Education and Teaching (Iojet)*, 5(4), 809–830.

Borštnar, M., & Pucihar, A. (2021). Multi-attribute assessment of digital maturity of SMEs. *Electronics*, 10(8), 885. 10.3390/electronics10080885

Ceylan, V.K., & Gündoğdu, K. (2017). Öğretmenlerin e-içerik geliştirme becerileri: Bir hizmet içi eğitim deneyimi. [E-Content Development Skills Of Teachers: An In-Service Training Experience]. *Journal of Education and Humanities*, 8(15), 48–74.

Chatzipanagiotou, P., & Katsarou, E. (2015). The effective use of distance learning model in in-service teacher education in Greece. In L. Gomez Chova, A. Lopez Martinez, & I. CandelTorres (Eds.), *EDULEARN15: 7th International Conference on Education and New Learning Technologies* (pp. 4193–4206).

Ciampa, K., & Gallagher, T.L. (2015). Blogging to enhance in-service teachers' professional learning and development during collaborative inquiry. *Educational Technology Research and Development, 63*(6), Article 6. 10.1007/s11423-015-9404-7

Damşa, C., Langford, M., Uehara, D., & Scherer, R. (2021). Teachers' agency and online education in times of crisis. *Computers in Human Behavior, 121,* 106793. 10.1016/j.chb.2021.106793

Ernest, P., Guitert Catasús, M., Hampel, R., Heiser, S., Hopkins, J., Murphy, L., & Stickler, U. (2013). Online teacher development: Collaborating in a virtual learning environment. *Computer Assisted Language Learning, 26*(4), Article 4. 10.1080/09588221.2012.667814

Gökalp, E., & Martinez, V. (2021). Digital transformation capability maturity model enabling the assessment of industrial manufacturers. *Computers in Industry, 132,* 103522. 10.1016/j.compind.2021.103522

Hofmeister, C., & Pilz, M. (2020). Using e-learning to deliver in-service teacher training in the vocational education sector: Perception and acceptance in Poland, Italy, and Germany. *Education Sciences, 10*(7), 182. 10.3390/educsci10070182

Hou, H.T., Sung, Y.-T., & Chang, K.-E. (2009). Exploring the behavioral patterns of an online knowledge-sharing discussion activity among teachers with problem-solving strategy. *Teaching and Teacher Education, 25*(1), 101–108.

Horzum, M.B., & Demircioğlu Diren, D. (2022). Dijital Dönüşüm Çağında Eğitim [Education in the Digital Age], Efe A. M. İ. Editor Dijital etkileşimler: Sektörel Yaklaşımlar [Digital Interactions: Sectoral Approaches] 1, Akademi Yayınları.

Jung, I. (2005). ICT-Pedagogy integration in teacher training: Application cases worldwide. *Educational Technology & Society, 8*(2), 94–101.

Karoğlu, A.K., Bal, K., & Çimşir, E. (2020). Toplum 5.0 Sürecinde Türkiye'de Eğitimde Dijital Dönüşüm. [Digital Transformation of Education in Turkey in Society 5.0]. *Üniversite Araştırmaları Dergisi, 3*(3), 147–158.

Lehiste, P. (2015). The impact of a professional development program on in-service teachers' TPACK: A study from Estonia. *Problems of Education in the 21st Century, 66*(1), 18–28.

Lin, T.C., Hsu, Y.S., & Cheng, Y.J. (2011). Emerging innovative teacher education from situated cognition in a web-based environment. *Turkish Online Journal of Educational Technology-TOJET, 10*(2), 100–112.

Mahraz, M.-I., Benabbou, L., & Berrado, A. (2019). A Systematic literature review of Digital Transformation. *Proceedings of the International Conference on Industrial Engineering and Operations Management,* 917–931.

MEB. (2022a, February 11). *Yariyil Tatilinde 142 Bin Öğretmen, Öba'dan Eğitim Aldı.* http://bursa.meb.gov.tr/www/yariyil-tatilinde-142-bin-ogretmen-obadan-egitim-aldi/icerik/3874 Accessed 27.02.2023

MEB. (2022a, June 19). *Öğretmenlik Kariyer Basamakları Eğitimine 603 Bin 864 Başvuru Yapıldı.* https://www.meb.gov.tr/ogretmenlik-kariyer-basamaklari-egitimine-603-bin-864-basvuru-yapildi/haber/26729/tr Accessed 8.03.2023

Morakanyane, R., Grace, A., & O'Reilly, P. (2017). Conceptualizing digital transformation in business organizations: A systematic review of literature. *Digital Transformation – From Connecting Things to Transforming Our Lives*, 427–443. 10.18690/978-961-286-043-1.30 Accessed 27.02.2023

OECD. (2005, May 27). *The Definition snd Selection of Key Competencies.* https://www.oecd.org/pisa/definition-selection-key-competencies-summary.pdf Accessed 27.02.2023

ÖBA. (2022). *Öba | Öğretmen Bilişim Ağı [The Teacher Information Network]*, 2022. https://www.oba.gov.tr/ Accessed 27.02.2023

Özerbaş, M.A., & Yazici, E.B. (2021). Dijital Eğitim Platformu Değerlendirme Ölçeği'nin (DEPDÖ) Geliştirilmesi Çalışması. [Development of the Digital Education Platform Evaluation Scale (DEPDÖ)]. *Manas Sosyal Araştırmalar Dergisi, 10*(2), 901–917. 10.33206/mjss.890538

Parlak, B. (2017). Dijital çağda eğitim: Olanaklar ve uygulamalar üzerine bir analiz. [Education in Digital Age:An Analysis on Opportunities and Applications]. *Süleyman Demirel Üniversitesi İktisadi ve İdari Bilimler Fakültesi Dergisi, 22*(Kayfor 15 Özel Sayısı), 1741–1759.

Robinson, B., & Latchem, C. (2003). *Teacher education through open and distance learning.* Boca Raton: Routledge Falmer.

Serin, M.K., & Korkmaz, İ. (2014). Sınıf Öğretmenlerinin Hizmet İçi Eğitim İhtiyaçlarının Analizi. *[Analysis of Classroom Teachers' In Service Training NeedsAhi Evran Üniversitesi Kırşehir Eğitim Fakültesi Dergisi, 15*(1), 155–169.

Siemens, G., Gasevic, D., & Dawson, S. (2015). Preparing for the digital university. *A review of the history and current state of distance, blended, and online learning.* In Athabasca AB Canada: Athabasca University Press.

Şener, G., & Gündüzalp, S. (2018). Akademisyenlerin üniversitelerde dijital dönüşüm ile ilgili görüşleri. *[Views of Academicians on digital transformation at universities], 1*(1), 177–182.

Tang, L., Gu, J., & Xu, J. (2022). Constructing a digital competence evaluation framework for in-service teachers' online teaching. *Sustainability, 14*(9), 5268. 10.3390/su14095268

Taşkıran, A. (2017). Dijital çağda yükseköğretim. [Higher Education in the Digital Age]. *Açıköğretim Uygulamaları ve Araştırmaları Dergisi, 3*(1), 96–109.

T.C. Sanayi ve Teknoloji Bakanlığı (2018). *Türkiye Cumhuriyeti Cumhurbaşkanlığı Dijital Dönüşüm Ofisi—Proje Açıklaması.* Dijital Dönüşüm Ofisi. https://cbddo.gov.tr/projeler/dijital-turkiye-v1.0/ Accessed 27.02.2023

Teichert, R. (2019). Digital transformation maturity: A systematic review of literature. *Acta Universitatis Agriculturae et Silviculturae Mendelianae Brunensis, 67*(6), 1673–1687. 10.11118/actaun201967061673

Tekin, H.H., & Tekin, H. (2012). Nitel araştirma yönteminin bir veri toplama tekniği olarak derinlemesine görüşme. [In-depth interview as a data collection technique of qualitative research method]. *İstanbul Üniversitesi Sosyoloji Dergisi, 3*(13), 101–116.

Teknofest. (2022). Teknofest Aerospace and Technology Festival. https://www.teknofest.org/en/corporate/organizations/ Accessed 4.12.2022

Temizyürek, D.D.F., & Ünlü, O.N. (2015). Dil Öğretiminde Teknolojinin Materyal Olarak Kullanımına Bir Örnek: "Flipped Classroom". [The Use of Technology in Language Teaching Material as an Example: "Flipped Classroom"]. *Bartın University Journal of Faculty of Education, 4*(1), 64–72.

Uçak, S., & Erdem, H.H. (2020). Eğitimde Yeni Bir Yön Arayışı Bağlamında "21. Yüzyıl Becerileri ve Eğitim Felsefesi". [On The Skills Of 21st Century And Philosophy Of Education In Terms Of Searching A New Aspect In Education]. *Uşak Üniversitesi Eğitim Araştırmaları Dergisi, 6*(1), 76–93. 10.29065/usakead.690205

Verina, N., & Titko, J. (2019, May). Digital transformation: conceptual framework. *In Proc. of the Int. Scientific Conference "Contemporary Issues in Business, Management and Economics Engineering'2019", Vilnius, Lithuania,* 719–727. 10.3846/cibmee.2019.073

Yazıcı, Ö., & Gündüz, Y. (2011). Gelişmiş Bazı Ülkeler İle Türkiye'deki Öğretmenlerin Hizmet İçi Eğitimlerinin Karşılaştırılması. [A Comparison Of Inservice Training Of Teachers In Some Developed Countries And Turkey]. *Kuramsal Eğitimbilim, 4*(2), 1–15.

Yıldırım, A., & Şimşek, H. (2021). *Sosyal Bilimlerde Nitel Araştırma Yöntemleri* (12nd ed.). *[Qualitative research methods in the social sciences].* Ancara: Seçkin Yayıncılık.

Yıldız, E.P. (2021). *Bilgi ve İletişim Teknolojileri ile Eğitimde Dijital Dönüşüm ve Ötesi* (1st Ed.) *[Digital Transformation with Information an Communication Technologies and its beyond].* Ancara: Gece Kitaplığı Yayınevi.

Yinanç, A., Zallıhoğlu, A.E., Ünal, A., Yalçınsoy, A., Aşçı, B., Akkoyun, B., Aksoy, C., Doğan Cansaran, D., Bayarçelik, E.B., Gökalp, E., Özkan Pir, E., Yılmaz, F., Taşel, F., Bumin Doyduk, H., Gökırmak, H., Akben, İ., Gökoğlan, K., Mızrak, K.C., Karadağ, M., Süllü, Z. (2020). *Dijital Yönetim* (1st Ed.). *[Digital Management].* Ancara: Nobel Akademik Yayıncılık.

4 Ambient, Guerilla, and Event Marketing in Education of Marketers, and Development of Creative Abilities

A Case Study

Katarína Fichnová, Łukasz P. Wojciechowski, and Edita Štrbová

Introduction and Aims of the Chapter

The aim of the chapter is to confirm, identify, and exemplify the results of targeted stimulation of creative abilities through a proprietary approach (based on a holistic model) in a specific area of higher education in the field of creative forms of marketing communication.

In the professional discourse in the field of creativity research, there is a fairly good agreement that originality and relevance are considered the basic attributes of creativity (e.g., Runco & Garrett, 2012; Pichot et al., 2022 and others). Both factors become particularly important in the context of media communication or advertising. Marketers are currently looking for more effective forms and shapes of communication, by which they would attract the attention of recipients, who are already over-saturated with advertising and media content. In this highly competitive and congested environment, creative advertising, unlike ordinary advertising, can attract attention (Reinartz & Saffert, 2013, Till, 2005), improve attitudes toward advertising (Ang et al., 2007), and be more effective (Choudhary, 2021).

Some types of advertising already incorporate the principles of creativity in their essence – these undoubtedly include ambient, guerrilla, and event marketing communication (for more details, see the subsections below). For such advertising to be created, it requires competent marketers with a high degree of creativity, who have a university education. Creativity is considered one of the key competencies for the 21st century – it enables flexible responses and provides the ability to effectively solve challenges that are part of an often complex and rapidly changing world (Ritter & Mostert, 2017), it helps in solving demands during crisis situations or adaptation (Solodukhova, 2009). It is essential for success in the workplace, and finally, it increases the meaning of life (Kaufman, 2018). Lucas

DOI: 10.4324/9781003376583-5

and Venckuté (2020) see creativity as a transversal skill that is necessary but beneficial to improve throughout life.

Theoretical Background

Creativity and Its Development

Considering the above, universities should pay due attention to the development of creativity. At the same time, it can be proven that creativity supports the employability of university students (Bernabéu Brotóns & De la Peña, 2021), provides a competitive advantage to the individual and the institution (Acar et al., 2019), and is part of effective organizations (Haselhuhn et al., 2022). Despite the undoubted advantages of creativity, it is not a standard part of educational curricula and even in some cases, it is possible to believe that the school not only does not develop creativity, but even the preferred activities in schools inhibit it. There is a recorded decrease in creativity tests in children after starting compulsory school attendance (Torrance, 1968; Rosenblatt & Winner, 1988), although this may be related to the transition to a new education system, a change in supported types of thinking toward convergence. Torrance (1968) also attributed the decline to a conformist acceptance of authority. This is also supported by research that shows a decrease in creativity during university studies. For example, Sola et al. (2017) found out that senior engineering students were significantly less creative than first-year students. Similarly, the results of the research by the authors Cheung et al. (2003) in a group of university students from various fields point to a trend of decreasing creativity with the years of study. However, there are studies that indicate that creativity does not have to decrease with age (Lorenzen-Huber, 1991) and even in adulthood and old age, it can help to achieve developmental tasks and find the meaning of life (ibidem).

At the same time, creativity is an ability that can be developed (e.g., Torrance, 1968; Sierpina & Cole, 2004, and many others). Developability is even considered one of the basic axioms of creativity (Zelina, 1996). All the mentioned facts underline the need to pay increased attention to the development of creative abilities in education, however, Gao et al. (2019) state that there is a general lack of courses in this type.

Specifically targeted courses (e.g., Glover, 1980; Gao et al., 2019; Gu et al., 2022 and others) and activation methods are known (Stanek & Soltysik-Piorunkiewicz, 2011). Ritter and Mostert (2017) prove that creativity can be developed even with programs that are domain-specific and very short (1.5 hours). The effectiveness of the programs is not only immediate, but the effect is recordable also after a longer period of time (Glover, 1980; Fichnová & Vinterová, 2002 and others).

A quantitative meta-analysis of 70 previous studies of creativity development programs by Scott et al. (2004) revealed that various training characteristics (course design, content, procedures used, creativity development methods) ultimately differ in their effects on increasing the creativity of course participants. Similarly, approaches and levels of action can be very diverse. Zelina (1997) and Szobiová (2014) describe in detail the specific level of implementation through the methods of *facilitation, cultivation, interaction,* to *conditioning methods,* and *complex creation of creative personality.* In the context of confluence theories of creativity, such as the Bio-psycho-social approach of Dacey and Lennon (2000), it is also necessary that broader contexts are considered.

Based on the above, some of the authors of this chapter initiated special courses in the marketing communication study program; (and related programs) at Constantine the Philosopher University in Nitra, but also at University of Creative Communication in Prague. Experience has shown that when designing a program for the development of creativity, it is necessary to consider its multidimensionality and complexity. For the above reasons, a holistic approach appears to be the most appropriate for us. Based on this approach, we prepared and verified the proprietary *Holistic-Oriented Approach to Stimulating Creative Competences* (for the purposes of practice, acronymed/labeled GOTCHA = Gaining on the creativity: Holistic Approach). We illustrate its framework model in the working diagram (Figure 4.1, see Fichnová et al., in press) which will be continuously supplemented based on wider research beyond the scope of this publication. We present more detailed information about the course in the empirical part.

Ambient and Guerilla Marketing Communication

Ambient and guerilla marketing uses non-traditional media, such as large areas of buildings, public space, and so-called street furniture, which can be used by a student (a team of students) in an improvisational way and also in the premises of the school and its surroundings. During the preparation of the project, the fact that the chosen position should be clearly connected and related to the message of the communication is emphasized, so that the use of an unconventional place is not for its own sake. Their potential lies in the interaction with the environment and context in which the message appears, as well as in the environment of students who may know it intimately (Wilczek & Fertak, 2004). This form extends to the most diverse communication tools that it uses, while secondarily, it most often benefits from the dissemination support of other popular media (Azhari & Kamen, 1984), e.g., using the reference of other recipients or influencers (see, e.g., Mikuláš & Světlík, 2016).

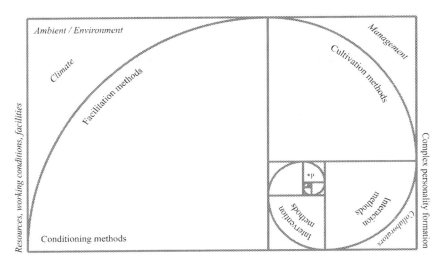

Figure 4.1 Holistic model of creativity development.

Legend: *P = Personality

Source: Authored processing created using the golden ratio scheme, 2022.

At the same time, when presenting this topic, it is necessary to emphasize to the audience the fact that guerilla and ambient marketing can be met with misunderstanding and controversy. There are cases where the implementation of such a communication is to some extent illegal, at the edge of legality (Flyvbjerge, 2006).

During the implementation, when teaching the topic of ambient marketing communication, we must emphasize that novelty, attractiveness, and deviation from the usual standards should be the common denominators of the activities, and the project should carry the value of ingenuity, which is offered, supported, and appreciated to the students during the course.

Event Marketing and Marketing Communication

The increased degree of oversaturation and fragmentation of current markets causes a decrease in the efficiency of using traditional marketing communication tools and a significant shift in consumer behavior. In addition to the adequate quality of the goods and services provided, the consumer also expects added value in the form of original and unrepeatable experiences in which he does not act as a passive recipient of the experience. On the contrary, they are interested in active participation in its creation and dialogue

(Štrbová, 2022; Sistenich, 1999). This results in the fact that consumer behavior is led to increased orientation and active participation in recreational and leisure activities. This is also connected to the preference for entertainment and the application of consumers in new subcultures (Cova & Cova, 2002; Moravčíková, 2022).

Event marketing can be considered a tool with a multi-sensual effect as it mainly benefits from direct personal face-to-face communication and, among other things, it is oriented towards experiences (Weinberg & Nickel, 1998), interactivity (Zanger & Sistenich, 1996), self-education (Nufer, 2002), and dramaturgy (Sistenich, 1999). This determines the use of the topic of event marketing as one of the forms that is attractive to students, who can fulfill themselves more clearly in group projects, each in a different area that is close to them. Therefore, student teams have the potential to create projects that implement elements of experience, internship, innovation, dramatization, originality, surprise, etc., which are actually events as well as ambient marketing.

Case Study

Research Problem and Hypotheses

This chapter addresses the following research question (RQ): Is there a significant difference between performance in creativity before and after the implementation of a specific program/proprietary course aimed at the development of creativity intended for the field of marketing communication?

Based on the stated research problem and the above-specified theoretical starting points, we postulated the following hypotheses:

H1 We assume that the GOTCHA program compiled by us will significantly increase the creative abilities of the participants after a weekly application in the components of:

H1.1 fluency
H1.2 flexibility
H1.3 originality
H1.4 overall score

H2 We assume and identify significant differences in the creativity retest score between the control group and the experimental group (with the implementation of the GOTCHA program) in favor of the experimental group, in the total score and the components of:

H2.1 fluency
H2.2 flexibility
H2.3 originality

At the same time, the focus will be placed on the description and categorization of some specific findings of differences in the quality level of the outputs of individual student works realized.

Methodological Framework and Methods

The basic methodological framework of the current study was the case study research approach, which is a selection from more broadly conceived research. For the purposes of this chapter, the most significant data from the case study are presented. From the point of view of the object of investigation (Gary, 2011), the presented case study is, the so-called evaluation study (in the intentions of the types according to Yin (2003)), in which the program focused on the development of skills in the creation of marketing communication campaigns, but also soft skills, especially the creative abilities of the course participants, were evaluated. In terms of design, this study covered a single case with a holistic approach (Yin, 2003) and theory testing (Gary, 2011). Based on the division of case types according to Creswell (2017), the so-called single instrumental case study is applied. Hence, the researcher focuses on a problem or issue and then selects a limited case for illustration (Creswell, 2017), while the case study is a tool for working with theory (Kořan, 2008). This is a case bounded by time: the duration of the specific event of the 11th International Week at the EU in Katowice in the spring of 2022, during which highly specialized and thematically specifically focused courses were implemented. In our case, these were two classes within the IntWeek learning process and one within the standard course schedule at the same university (groups as sources of information according to Hancock & Algozzine, 2006). A theory that defines creativity as a trainable ability (Sternberg, 2010; Bulut et al., 2022 and others) was tested.

In the intentions of Flyvbjerge's typology of cases, this was the so-called critical case selected by the so-called purposeful sampling (Patton, 1990) by "criterion" and "opportunistic" strategy. The presented study uses a triangulation research approach: an experimental research plan complemented by a qualitative approach focused on the contents of solutions implemented by students.

The classic standardized Torrance test of creative thinking (TTCT, Torrance, 1971; Jurčová, 1984) subtest "Circles" was chosen to identify the creativity of the participants. The task of the respondents is to create the most original pictures possible from sketched unfinished shapes (circles) within the time limit and label them with the most creative name possible. The test offers the possibility of identifying several components of creativity. Therefore, the following factors were chosen for the purpose of this study: fluency (number of solutions), flexibility (diversity), and originality. For the

70   *Katarína Fichnová et al.*

purposes of scoring the originality, a frequency analysis of the ideas in the studied set was carried out. The total number of participants' ideas in a total of 73 protocols was 1005. Solutions that appeared in less than 1% of protocols received 3 points for originality, similarly, $1\% \le x \le 3\%$ received 2 points, $3\% < x \le 5\%$ received 1 point, above 5% received 0 points. Where "x" represents the % of logs that contain a particular solution. As part of a more broadly conceived research project, other procedures aimed at identifying the creativity of student products – individual or group ones – were also used; due to the lack of space, outputs from TTCT are only dealt with in this chapter. The data were subjected to statistical confrontation. The data were tested for normality (K-S test statistic), and the results were corrected with the Šidák correction.

Research Sample

The case study was carried out on a total of 39 participants of university courses at the University of Economics in Katowice (communication and journalism, business, economics, and related fields). Thirteen of the participants were in the experimental group and 26 were in the control group. The number of participants identifying as women was 24, as men 14, and one participant chose the other option. The average age of the respondents was 21.02 years (sd = 3.28, K-S test (D) = .19118. p = .10099). The experimental and control groups did not differ statistically in terms of age or in terms of the entry score of the observed variables. A total of 95.12% of the participants stated that they had completed secondary education with a secondary school-leaving certificate. The sample was part of a more broadly conceived research. The method of selecting participants, which respected their allocation to groups according to their interest in the courses, as well as the multidisciplinary composition of the group, could have an impact on the data obtained.

"Ambient Marketing Creative Skills Development" Course and the Holistically Oriented Approach to Stimulating Creative Competences

Based on the synthesis of previous approaches, our own model of creativity development was presented. Based on this model, individual procedures, methods, techniques, and activities were specified into our own program for the development of creative abilities for a specific area of marketing communication in the thematic circle of creative marketing communication – guerrilla, ambient, and event marketing (GOTCHA). The program is focused on the personality of a creative individual, including the development of knowledge in the relevant domain with the integration of the development of creative thinking. The time allocation of the course was

24 teaching hours in blocks during the week. Due to spatial reasons, its detailed description cannot be given here; the reader is asked to refer to our more broadly conceived work (in press). Briefly presenting some of its elements at this point, the researchers started from several premises: (1) creativity is a trainable ability (see above); (2) it develops in a context with all its known sources (Dacey & Lennon, 2000); (3) approaches should include all levels of intervention (see Figure 4.1), including the environment (e.g., the psychological climate); (4) student's activity is an essential part.

When designing specific tasks, the researchers also worked with Gehlbach's taxonomy (Gehlbach, 1991; Zelina, 1993). The researchers used: (a) original methods – verbally and figuratively divergent tasks, group and individual ones; (b) original content and presentation of case studies within guerrilla, ambient, and event marketing communication; (c) active-learning procedures based on Person-Centered Education (Rogers, 1983), since this approach consists, for example, of the project education. Specifically in our course, students prepared their own proposals of strategies. Instead of a directive evaluation by the teacher, the students were encouraged to make self-evaluations, etc.; (d) climate monitoring (Ekvall, 1999); (e) work with physical environments either in the classroom or outside; (f) specific methods of supporting creative production (applied imagination, SCAMPER (Osborn, 2009)), and others.

Analysis and Interpretation of Results

The collected data were scored according to the standards with the addition of frequency analysis of specific student ideas. Qualitative analysis of the pre-tests showed a higher incidence of irrelevant solutions. Non-incorporation of specified objects into the final designs or the shape did not form an important part (see Figure 4.2a). A total of 54.05% of the pre-test protocols contained this type of answer. We recorded 54.55% of inadequate solutions in the experimental group and 53.85% in the control group. The groups did not differ in the aspects stated at the beginning of the study. The ability that enables subjects from the perceptual field to identify relevant elements and compose them in new and unusual contexts based on shape, is part of the set of skills that are expected of workers in creative industries, especially workers in communication advertising agencies who mainly prepare campaigns, as mentioned at the beginning of this chapter. Therefore, it should be developed in a standard higher education program. After the implementation of our GOTCHA program in the experimental group, the number of such protocols dropped to 16.57%. In the control group, 50.00% of them were recorded in the re-test.

From a qualitative point of view, originality is traditionally considered the most essential element of creativity (Shamay-Tsoory et al., 2011, and

72 *Katarína Fichnová et al.*

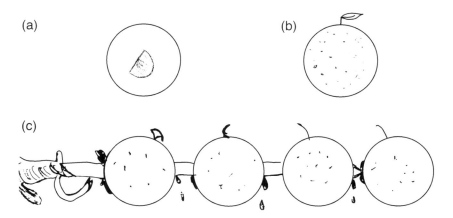

Figure 4.2 Examples of TTCT solutions in both groups of subjects: irrelevant (a), relevant low creativity (b), and relevant high creativity (c).

Legend: a. Slice of orange. b. An orange. c. Sword piercing fruit.

Source: Authored processing using TTCT (Torrance, 1971), and protocols of research participants, 2022.

others). Since Torrance's (1971) manual contains norms for the American population, we used the modification of Jurčová (1984) containing norms for the Slovak population for the sake of this study. Hence, in the first phase of the study, a detailed qualitative and quantitative analysis of all the answers of male and female subjects had to be carried out with the aim of identifying the usual as well as non-standard original answers. The number of original solutions (unusual, non-frequently used ones) in both groups at the beginning of the study was comparable in terms of average scores (Table 4.1), which was confirmed by statistical comparison (Table 4.2). Examples of non-original and original solutions are presented in Figures 4.2b and 4.2c. Original solutions often exceeded established frameworks, combined several topics, and objects, or brought unusual views and perspectives. In the case of original solutions, there were quite often well-formulated solution names, while in the case of the less original ones, the name either did not appear at all or was trivial and did not enrich or make the picture special. These abilities are again very important in the implementation of marketing-communication campaigns in which a slogan, claim, or other text component is part of the solution.

In addition to qualitative analysis, the obtained data were subjected to a more thorough statistical comparison using standard procedures of the experimental research plan. Both groups were compared before the implementation of activities in the experimental group within GOTCHA

Ambient, Guerilla, and Event Marketing 73

Table 4.1 Scores of the pretest and retest of the investigated groups in dimensions of creativity and the standard deviation

		Fluency		*Flexibility*		*Originality*		**Total**	
		AM	*sd*	*AM*	*sd*	*AM*	*sd*	*AM*	*sd*
pretest	Experimental group	11.45	*4.13*	7.82	*4.14*	5.82	*4.83*	25.09	*10.53*
	Control group	9.46	*6.91*	4.88	*4.25*	5.92	*6.29*	20.27	*16.56*
retest	Experimental group	20.67	*6.08*	12.25	*3.02*	16.33	*7.80*	49.25	*13.99*
	Control group	16.00	*6.78*	7.67	*3.04*	9.93	*5.46*	31.50	*15.50*

Source: Own.

Table 4.2 Results of statistic confrontation of dimension of creativity between the control group and the experimental group, ante, and post

	Sign. t-test			
	Fluency	*Flexibility*	*Originality*	**Total**
Pretest control group and experimental group	*0.3807 n.s./Šn.s.*	*0.0612 n.s./Šn.s.*	*0.9609 n.s./Šn.s.*	*0.3802 n.s./Šn.s.*
Retest control group and experimental group	*0.0362 */Šn.s.*	**0.00015 ***** **Šidák corr sig.**	*0.0053**//Šn.s.*	**0.0018 **** **Šidák corr sig**
Pretest-retest experimental group	**0.0010 **** **Šidák corr sig.**	0.0257 **/Šn.s.*	**0.0017**** **Šidák corr sig.**	**0.0005 **** **Šidák corr sig.**
Pretest-retest control group	0.8326 *n.s./Šn.s.*	0.0109 **/Šn.s.*	0.0499 **/Šn.s.*	0.0419 **/Šn.s.*

Source: Own.
Legend: n.s. = not significant result; * = significant/ $p \leq 0.05$; ** = highly significant/ $0.01 \leq p \leq 0.05$; *** = very highly significant/ $0.001 \leq p \leq 0.01$, */Šn.s. = *after Šidák correction - insignificant result; Šidák corr sig.* = *after Šidák correction – significant result, Šidák correction* = 0.00321

program. The average score in the pre-test of both groups regarding the significance of the differences between the compared averages in all monitored factors of creativity, i.e., fluency, flexibility, originality, and total score, can be considered equivalent without significant differences. This fact is documented in Table 4.2, while all the obtained data are corrected by means of the Šidák correction, considering the larger number of comparisons made.

After the implementation of a weekly targeted stimulation of creativity in the experimental group which was incorporated into educational activities focused thematically on creative types of marketing communication, a re-test measurement was implemented. The effects of the GOTCHA program were monitored at two levels: a) by changes in the level of creativity expressed in the experimental group and b) by comparing the level of creativity of the experimental and control groups in the re-test.

74 *Katarína Fichnová et al.*

Performance increases in all monitored indicators of creativity were enormous in the experimental group and visible even at the level of a simple comparison of average scores. After the Šidák correction, a significant difference was confirmed in the fluency factor and the originality factor as well as the overall creativity score (Table 4.2), which means that hypotheses H1.1, H1.3, and H1.4 can be considered as confirmed. Flexibility after correction showed only an insignificant increase, so H1.2 can be considered as rejected. The program put together by the authors of this chapter had positive and demonstrable effects on two of the three monitored factors of creativity, and these in principle also influenced the overall result of the identified level of creativity. A similar analysis in the control group, also taking into account the correction, confirmed that creativity does not increase significantly without targeted stimulation, although before the correction, it was particularly flexibility that was close to it (Table 4.2). No significant increases were found in all indicators of creativity.

The comparison of the experimental and control groups in the re-test (Table 4.2) showed significant differences in performance before correction for all indicators; after correction, this result can be confirmed in the overall creativity and in the flexibility factor (the average score of the experimental group increased by 5.67 points (from 7.82 to 12.25)). For the control group, the increase was by 4.88 points, so hypotheses H2.2 and H2.4 can be considered as confirmed. On the other hand, the findings disprove hypotheses H2.1 and H2.3.

Based on the above, the GOTCHA program, created specifically for marketing communication departments, can help accelerate the growth and development of creative abilities in its various components, but especially in flexibility. However, inter-individual differences between the participants of the course are quite likely considering the relatively high values of the standard deviations. In the experimental group, the deviations were particularly high in the re-test in the originality factor, which increased from the initial value of AM = 5.82 to 16.33 points with sd = 7.80. So, it is likely that increases could have been significantly differentiated within the group and the group was quite heterogeneous. In such cases, an analysis of the so-called extreme groups is usually implemented as there is evidence in the literature that higher increases were recorded in respondents with lower initial scores and vice versa (Meinel et al., 2019). However, this type of analysis is beyond the scope of this chapter, and it will be addressed in another study.

Limits and Discussion

The presented findings point to impulses for the possibilities of targeted stimulation of creativity of future experts in marketing communication and related fields. Despite the above, it is necessary to perceive the data with a certain academic caution, especially regarding the limits of the presented research within the case study. In principle, the findings within any case study are always linked to the specific conditions described in the case study (compare, e.g. Yin, 2003; Daymon & Holloway, 2010, and others). The above relates mainly to the selection of participants for the presented study by means of the so-called self-selection as a type of the research sample set selection from the population (see e.g. Hendl, 2016). Further, students chose and signed up for courses according to their preferences. It can be therefore assumed that mainly those who are expected to have a procreative orientation, reacted more sensitively to stimuli in activity tests during the course. They also tended to choose a course having the word "creativity" in the description of activities. These students most likely expected an increase in their own creativity in accordance with the goals of the course, and they could also have been influenced by the name of the implemented method, which could have induced placebo effect or Hawthorne effect (Mayo, 1945). Use of the identical forms for the test and re-test could be seen as another limitation of the presented study. Another factor influencing the results is the fact that the students and teachers implemented the program in a language other than their mother tongue. Thus, the performance of the participants in the test did not have to correspond to the real level of their creative abilities, but rather to the extent of their vocabulary, even if the scores were significantly influenced by figurative, i.e., non-linguistic productions. In tasks requiring creativity, students were asked to create appropriate and original names, which requires certain language skills. Vocabulary in bilingual performances is more related to convergent thinking, even if handling language and solving tasks already stimulates a divergent area (modern methods of education through mobile apps, see, e.g., Hurajová, 2019). DeSouza Fleith et al. (2002) found that the effects of the divergent thinking program were not related to the placement of students in monolingual or bilingual classes, which would suggest that this factor may not have biased the results identified, although it should be considered. Therefore, the validity of the methods as well as the smaller scope of the research sample can be limiting.

Apart from the mentioned limits, the findings correspond to earlier studies that confirmed the positive effects of targeted stimulation of creativity. In the presented study, the most significant effects were manifested in area of the flexibility of thinking (identified by means of the comparison of the experimental and control groups), although even the changes in the comparison of the group's performance before and after the implementation cannot be considered negligible. These, in turn, highlighted shifts in area of originality and fluency. Similar results were shown by the research dealing with the semester course of creativity, implemented by Vally et al. (2019).

76 *Katarína Fichnová et al.*

The data confirmed the effectiveness of targeted stimulation of creativity, just as in the case of the study presented, for the areas of flexibility, originality, and elaboration, although the authors also expected impacts on neuro-executive functioning. The research was carried out in a group of university students studying mainly humanities (in total 40.5%, of which 14.5% were business students). Their course was one of the longest, lasting 13 weeks. As it is clear from the above comparison, similar effects can be achieved in a shorter time and at a higher intensity. This corresponds to the conclusions of the meta-analysis by Ma (2006) that the training effect is independent of the duration of the training and consistent across different instruments for measuring creativity. However, the literature also documents quite different findings. From all of them, let us mention the research of Perry and Karpová (2017), who after the implementation of the course found a significant increase in the average scores of the group, but at the individual level, a decrease in creativity was demonstrated in several participants. The subsequent analysis revealed that behind the decline it is possible to identify a low belief in one's own abilities and/or a reluctance to take risks. In the research sample of this study, all participants benefited from the program even at the individual level in the overall creativity score. The differences were only in the degree of increase in this score (from 1 point to an increase of up to 23 points), the average increase in the experimental group was 10.52 points. On the contrary, in the control group, although individual increases in scores were also recorded, in 18.52% of participants a decrease in scores from −1 to −9 points was identified. Therefore, it is possible to assume that the program created by the authors of this study also has a preventive effect against a spontaneous drop in the creativity score due to various causes (impacts of external adverse factors, loss of motivation, and others).

Conclusion

The presented case study aimed at verifying the effectiveness of the creativity development model GOTCHA for the gradual training of future experts in the field of marketing, marketing communication, business, and related fields, including the application of the program in a specific course at the 11th International Week (IntWeek) in Katowice, demonstrated positive effects on the level of creativity of the participants. Undoubtedly, the international dimension of the form of the implemented courses plays a role in the outputs – experts from all over the world brought inspiration not only to the students but also developed a professional dialogue among themselves. Intercultural stimuli as well as diverse perspectives are generally important catalysts of creativity (Simonton, 1997; Leung et al., 2008). The above-mentioned facts can be perceived as one of the explanations why in some of the monitored factors of creativity, at the level of averages, certain progress in the control class (in the case of comparing pre-test and re-test scores) was also noted. However, when comparing the control and experimental groups in the re-test, i.e., after creativity stimulation in the experimental class, the data show a significant superiority of the performance of the experimental group in the following areas:

- Fluency – the number of ideas increased significantly in the experimental group compared to the pre-test. The program significantly supports the ability to produce a high volume of ideas.
- Flexibility – in the experimental group, a significant increase in scores in the re-test compared to the control group was noted. The program also contributes to the flexibility of thinking and develops the ability to produce diverse ideas.
- Originality – in the experimental group at the end of the implementation of the program, the participants significantly improved in the pre-test in producing new ideas (the score increased by 11.23 points on average, in the control group by 4.01). The program had an impact on the ability to bring new and unusual ideas.

The results were also reflected in the overall score, in which the experimental group also dominates in the re-test. Likewise, on a qualitative level, progress in the subjects of the experimental group was noted. Thus, the findings are quite encouraging, although generalizations have their limitations, considering the identified numerical limits presented in the relevant section of this chapter.

With some academic caution, it can be stated that the research results presented in this case study provide a reference for the design of innovative educational courses aimed at developing the creative abilities of course participants at universities. The findings of this case study can be incorporated into the theory of the study field and implied for the needs of practice in the field of communication and social sciences, marketing communication, marketing, organizational management, education, and related fields.

The data are part of a more broadly conceived research project and will be the subject of further analyses which will help refine the content of the proprietary program and gain insight into other related contexts of creativity performance and variables. In the near future, the authors plan to identify whether the climate perceived by the course participants during the implementation of group projects has an effect on their creative performance and to clarify the impact on real performance in the creativity of projects.

78 *Katarína Fichnová et al.*

Acknowledgment

The text is a partial outcome of the scientific project supported by KEGA No. 018UCM-4/2021 "Art in mass media – ambient media" and VEGA No. 1/0650/22 "Mass-media communiqués in digital and printed form and their comprehension by various target groups".

References

Acar, O.A., Tarakci, M., & Van Knippenberg, D. (2019). Creativity and innovation under constraints. *Journal of Management, 45*(1), 96–121.

Ang, S.H., Lee, Y.H., & Leong, S.M. (2007). The ad creativity cube. *Journal of the Academy of Marketing Science, 35*(2), 220–232. 10.1007/s11747-007-0042-4

Azhari, A.G. & Kamen, J.F. (1984). Study shows billboards are more effective than recall, attitude-change scores indicate. *Marketing News, 18*(24), 11.

Bernabéu Brotóns, E. & De la Peña, C. (2021). Creatividad en educación superior. [Creativity in higher education]. *Profesorado, Revista De Currículum Y Formación Del Profesorado, 25*(3), 313–330. 10.30827/profesorado.v25i3.9546

Bulut, D., Samur, Y., & Cömert, Z. (2022). The effect of educational game design process on students' creativity. *Smart Learning Environments, 9*(8), 1–15. 10.11 86/s40561-022-00188-9

Cheung, C.K., Rudowicz, E., Yue, X., & Kwan, A.S. (2003). Creativity of university students. *The Journal of Creative Behavior, 37*(1), 42–63.

Choudhary, H. (2021). Creativity in advertising. *Asian Journal of Management, 12*(2), 144–146. doi: 10.52711/2321-5763.2021.00021N

Cova, B. & Cova, V. (2002). Tribal marketing: The tribalisation of society and its impact on the conduct of marketing. *European Journal of Marketing, 36*(5–6). http://visionarymarketing.com/_repository/wanadoo/cova-tribe-2001.pdf

Creswell, J.W. & Creswell, J.D. (2017). *Research design: Qualitative, quantitative, and mixed methods approaches* (4th ed.). SAGE publications.

Dacey, J.S. & Lennon, K.H. (2000). *Kreativita* [Creativity]. Bratislava: Grada.

Daymon, Ch. & Holloway, I. (2010). *Qualitative research methods in public relations and marketing communications* (2nd ed.). London: Imprint Routledge. 10.4324/9780203846544

DeSouza Fleith, D., Renzulli, J.S., & Westberg, K.L. (2002). Effects of a creativity training program on divergent thinking abilities and self-concept in monolingual and bilingual classrooms. *Creativity Research Journal, 14*(3–4), 373–386. doi: 10.1207/S15326934CRJ1434_8

Ekvall, G. (1999). Creative climate. In M. Runco & S. Pritzker (Eds.). *Encyclopedia of creativity. Vol. 1 Ae–h* (1st ed., pp. 403–412). Cambridge, Massachusetts: Academic Press.

Fichnová, K. & Vinterová, K. (2002). Efekty stimulačného programu. [Effects of the stimulation program]. *Technológia vzdelávania, 10*(5), 10–14.

Fichnová, K., Wojciechowski, Ł., & Štrbová, E. (in press). *Creative abilities and guerilla, ambient and event marketing.*

Flyvbjerge, B. (2006). Five misunderstandings about case-study research. *Qualitative Inquiry, 12*(2), 219–245. 10.1177/1077800405284363

Gao, X.-R., Tan, Y., & Li, S.-Y. (2019). Research on the construction of creativity training course in universities in the age of innovation and entrepreneurship. *DEStech Transactions on Social Science, Education and Human Science.* 10.12783/dtssehs/eiem2018/26910

Gary, T. (2011). A typology for the case study in social science following a review of definition, discourse, and structure. *Qualitative Inquiry, 17*(6), 511–521. 10.1177/1077800411409884

Gehlbach, R.D. (1991). Play, Piaget, and creativity. *The Journal of Creative Behavior, 25*(2), 137–144.

Glover, J.G. (1980). A creativity-training workshop: short-term, long-term, and transfer effects. *The Journal of Genetic Psychology, 136*(1), 3–16. 10.1080/00221325.1980.10534091

Gu, X., Ritter, S.M., Delfmann, L.R., & Dijksterhuis, A. (2022). Stimulating creativity. *The Journal of Creative Behavior, 56*(3), 312–327. 10.1002/jocb.531

Hancock, D.R. & Algozzine, B. (2006). *Doing case study research.* Teachers College Press.

Haselhuhn, M.P., Wong, E.M., & Ormiston, M.O. (2022). Investors respond negatively to executives' discussion of creativity. *Organizational Behavior and Human Decision Processes, 171*(July), 1–12. 10.1016/j.obhdp.2022.104155

Hendl, J. (2016). *Kvalitativní výzkum. Základní metody a aplikace.* [Qualitative research. Basic methods and applications]. https://www.databazeknih.cz/knihy/kvalitativni-vyzkum-zakladni-metody-a-aplikace-139067 Accessed 09.03.2022

Hurajová, A. (2019). Learning a language as part of life – how to learn a foreign language in the digital age. In Z. Bučková, L. Rusňáková & M. Solík (Eds.). *Megatrends and media* (pp. 186–191). Trava: FMK UCM.

Jurčová, M. (1984). *Torranceho figurálny test tvorivého myslenia* [Torrance figural test of creative thinking]. Bratislava: Psychodiagnostické a didaktické testy.

Kaufman, J.C. (2018). Finding meaning with creativity in the past, present, and future. *Perspectives on Psychological Science, 13*(6), 734–749. 10.1177/174569161 8771981

Kořan, M. (2008). Jednopřípadová studie [Single-case study]. In P. Drulák et al. (Eds.). *Jak zkoumat politiku.* [How to research politics] (pp. 29–60). Praha: Portál.

Leung, A.K.Y., Maddux, W.W., Galinsky, A.D., & Chiu, C.-Y. (2008). Multicultural experience enhances creativity. *American Psychologist, 63*(3), 169–181. 10.1037/0003-066X.63.3.169

Lorenzen-Huber, L. (1991). Self-perceived creativity in the later years: case studies of older Nebraskans. *Educational Gerontology: An International Quarterly, 17*(4), 379–390.

Lucas, B. & Venckuté, M. (2020). *Creativity – a transversal skill for lifelong learning.* JRC Technical Report. Publications Office of the European Union. 10.2760/557196 Accessed 27.02.2023

Ma, H-H. (2006). A synthetic analysis of the effectiveness of single components and packages in creativity training programs. *Creativity Research Journal, 18*(4), 435–446. 10.1207/s15326934crj1804_3

Mayo, E. (1945). *The social problems of an industrial civilization* (4th ed.). Boston: Graduate School of Business Administration: Harvard University. 10.1177/0002 71624624500154

Meinel, M., Wagner, T.F., Baccarella, C.V., & Voigt, K. (2019). Exploring the effects of creativity training on creative performance and creative self-efficacy. *Journal of Creative Behavior*, *53*(4), 546–558. 10.1002/jocb.234

Mikuláš, P. & Světlík, J. (2016). Execution of advertising and celebrity endorsement. *Communication Today*, *1*(7), 93–103.

Moravčíková, E. (2022). The contexts of hyper consumerist culture and social media platforms. *Media Literacy and Academic Research*, *5*(1), 141–160.

Nufer, G. (2002). *Wirkungen von event-marketing*. [Effects of Event Marketing]. Wiesbaden: Deutscher Universitäts-Verlag.

Osborn, A.F. (2009). *Unlocking your creative power*. Buffalo, New York: Creative Education Foundation, Inc.

Patton, M.Q. (1990). *Qualitative evaluation and research methods* (2nd ed.). Thousand Oaks, California: Sage Publications.

Perry, A. & Karpova, E. (2017). Efficacy of teaching creative thinking skills. *Thinking Skills and Creativity Journal*, *24*(June), 118–126. 10.1016/j.tsc.2017.02.017

Pichot, N., Bonetto, E., Pavani, J.B., Arciszewski, T., Bonnardel, N., & Weisberg, R.W. (2022). The construct validity of creativity: empirical arguments in favor of novelty as the basis for creativity. *Creativity Research Journal*, *34*(1), 2–13. 10.1080/10400419.2021.1997176

Reinartz, W. & Saffert, P. (2013). Creativity in advertising. *Harvard Business Review*, *91*(3), 106–112.

Ritter, S.M. & Mostert, N. (2017). Enhancement of creative thinking skills using a cognitive-based creativity training. *Journal of Cognitive Enhancement*, *1*(3), 243–253. 10.1007/s41465-016-0002-3

Rogers, C.R. (1983). *Freedom to learn for the 80's*. Columbus: Charles E. Merrill Publishing Company.

Rosenblatt, E. & Winner, E. (1988). The art of children's drawing. *Journal of Aesthetic Education*, *22*(1), 3–15. 10.2307/3332960

Runco, M.A. & Garrett, J.J. (2012). The standard definition of creativity. *Creativity Research Journal*, *24*(1), 92–96. 10.1080/10400419.2012.650092

Scott, G., Leritz, L.E., & Mumford, M.D. (2004). The effectiveness of creativity training. *Creativity Research Journal*, *16*(4), 361–388. 10.1080/10400410409534549

Shamay-Tsoory, S.G., Adler, N., Aharon-Peretz, J., Perry, D., & Mayseless, N. (2011). The origins of originality. *Neuropsychologia*, *49*(2), 178–185. 10.1016/j.neuropsychologia.2010.11.020.

Sierpina, M. & Cole, T.R. (2004). Stimulating creativity in all elders. *Care Management Journals*, *5*(3), 175–182. 10.1891/cmaj.2004.5.3.175

Simonton, D.K. (1997). Foreign influence and national achievement. *Journal of Personality and Social Psychology*, *72*(1), 86–94. 10.1037/0022-3514.72.1.86

Sistenich, F. (1999). *Eventmarketing*.[Event marketing]. Wiesbaden: Deutscher Universitäts-Verlag.

Sola, E., Hoekstra, R., Fiore, S., & McCauley, P. (2017). An investigation of the state of creativity and critical thinking in engineering undergraduates. *Creative Education*, *8*(9), 1495–1522. 10.4236/ce.2017.89105

Solodukhova, O.G. (2009). Стратегії творчості як засоби активної адаптації особистості [Strategies of creativity as active adaptations of personality]. *Science and Education*, *12*(6), 133–136.

Stanek, S. & Sołtysik-Piorunkiewicz, A. (2011). Building creative decision support systems for project management. *Studia Ekonomiczne*, *88*, 133–142.

Sternberg, R.J. (2010). Teaching for creativity. In R.A. Beghetto & J.C. Kaufman (Eds.), *Nurturing creativity in the classroom* (pp. 394–414). Cambridge University Press. 10.1017/CBO9780511781629.020

Štrbová, E. (2022). *Art & Event marketing kultúrnych inštitúcií* [Art & Event marketing of cultural institutions]. Bratislava: EAMMM.

Szobiová, E. (2014). *Creativity – unravelling the Mistery*. Amsterdam: Wolters Kluwer.

Till, B.D. & Baack, D.W. (2005). Recall and persuasion: Does creative advertising matter? *Journal of Advertising*, *34*(3), 47–57. http://www.jstor.org/stable/4189308

Torrance, E.P. (1968). A longitudinal examination of the fourth-grade slump in creativity. *Gifted Child Quarterly*, 12(4), 195–199. 10.1177/001698626801200401

Torrance, E.P. (1971). Are the Torrance tests of creative thinking biased against or in favor of "disadvantaged" groups? *Gifted Child Quarterly*, *15*(2), 75–80. 10.1177/001698627101500201

Vally, Z., Salloum, L., AlQedra, D., Shazly, S., Albloshi, M., Alsheraifi, S., & Alkaabi, A. (2019). Examining the effects of creativity training on creative production, creative self-efficacy, and neuro-executive functioning. *Thinking Skills and Creativity*, *31*(March), 70–79. 10.1016/j.tsc.2018.11.003

Weinberg, P. & Nickel, O. (1998). *Grundlagen für die erlebnisvermittlungen von marketing-events. Eventmarketing* [Fundamentals of experiential marketing events. Event Marketing]. Wiesbaden: Deutscher Universitätsverlag.

Wilczek, P. & Fertak, B. (2004). Ambient media, media tradycyjne – konkurencja czy współpraca? [Ambient media, traditional media - competition or cooperation?]. *Brief*, 58, 7–12.

Yin, R.K. (2003). *Case study research: design and methods*. Los Angeles: Sage Publications Inc.

Zanger, C. & Sistenich, F. (1996). Eventmarketing [Event marketing]. *Marketing – Zeitschrift für Forschung und Praxis*, *18*(4), 233–242.

Zelina, M. (1993). *Humanizácia školstva* [Humanization of education]. Bratislava: Psychodiagnostika.

Zelina, M. (1996). *Stratégie a metódy rozvoja osobnosti* [Strategies and the methods of personality development]. Bratislava: IRIS.

Zelina, M. (1997). *Ako sa stať tvorivým* [How to become creative]. Bratislava: Fontana Kiadó.

Part 2

Digital Transformation and Perspective Development at Business Organizations

5 Testing and Certification of New Product Development in the Electronics Industry
Case Studies

Dariusz Meiser and Maciej Nowak

Introduction

In this study, we consider New Product Development (NPD) projects in the electronics industry. Such a project can be described as a process aimed at designing, implementing, and launching a new product on the market. The problems faced by companies implementing NPD projects are widely analyzed in the literature.

In one of the earliest works, Myers and Marquis (1969) defined a manufacturing design as a complex operation that begins with the development of a new concept or idea, continues through the development of a solution, and ends with the actual application of a new product of economic and social value. It should be emphasized that the necessary condition for a project to be called a manufacturing project is the implementation, production launch, and market launch of the product or service.

A model of industrial innovation, proposed by Rothwell (1974), combines in one integrated process the identification of market or social needs and new technologies that can meet those needs. Bessant and Francis (1997) described how a company can formulate and implement good patterns of behavior, the accompanying processes and structures necessary to make NPD good practices work for them. Shrivastava et al. (2012) optimized NPD activities against risk factors to minimize time and costs. Based on this, they propose a systematic risk management framework to deal with risk factors, degree of risk, and production problems. Four dimensions of uncertainty and their direct and indirect effects on the performance of NPD projects were investigated by Sicotte and Bourgault (2008). These include technical and project uncertainty, market uncertainty, fuzziness, and complexity.

Keizer et al. (2005) emphasized that empirical research shows that the success rate of large-scale NPD projects is still unsatisfactorily low. They focused on risk factors occurring in a fairly early stage of a project. A very extensive description of NPD-related issues was presented by Kahn (2013).

DOI: 10.4324/9781003376583-7

The main goal of his study was to provide insights into how to make better decisions while traveling through the difficult landscape typical of NPD. Cooper (1983) analyzed what steps an Industrial New Product Manager should take to improve the performance of a new product. He proposed a seven-step model aimed at taking the product from the idea stage to launching the product on the market. In one of his next papers, he tried to bridge the gap between research and practice by advising on the practical application of the results obtained (Cooper, 1988). His conclusions were formulated as a guide for the systematic development of new products, providing practical help to those involved in the NPD process.

Research Plan and Methodology

The case studies described in this chapter are based on the methodology described by Yin (2014). His method includes six stages: plan, design, preparation, data collection, analysis, and sharing of results. Both the case studies and chapter structure follow these stages.

This chapter presents case studies of Polish companies from the electronic device industry that have experienced problems with launching new electronic devices on the market – i.e., completing manufacturing projects.

In the case studies presented, the main source of problems is the need to carry out legally required tests, as well as formal approvals. These activities strongly influence the implementation and risk of a manufacturing project and are usually ignored by various methods, tools, and practices of project management. Their nature is closely related to the specifics of the industry in which the analyzed projects are implemented, i.e., the electronic devices industry, the conditions of the design work, as well as the performed tests. The case study has been chosen as the main research method because it is an empirical study that explores a phenomenon occurring today in a real context. According to Yin (2014), the use of this method is recommended especially when the boundary between the phenomenon itself and its context is not entirely clear. It is equally important that the realization of the case study allows us to explain the causes, conditions, and origin of the phenomena taking place in the analyzed organization. An additional justification for choosing the case study method is that it is impossible to fully understand any phenomenon by analyzing it without taking into account its environment.

The main purpose of the research reported in this chapter was to answer the following research questions:

- Why often, despite the completion of a manufacturing project in the electronic devices industry, the designed device cannot be launched to the market?

- What are the common problems related to the testing of electronic devices before their market launch?
- What issues specific to manufacturing projects in the electronics industry are not described by the most commonly used project management methods?

As part of the research work, a multiple case study was conducted, including nine cases concerning manufacturing projects in the electronics industry. Due to the limited volume of this chapter, only two of them are described in detail. Beyond that, a cross-sectional synthesis of all completed case studies is presented.

Design

As it is pointed out earlier, one of the most important methodological issues is the context of the phenomena studied. This chapter is about the electronic devices industry. Thus, it is necessary to start by defining the main terms used in this study.

First of all, it should be emphasized that the electronic devices industry is not the same as the Information and Communication Technology (ICT) sector, most often described in similar analyses. First, the electronic devices industry does not cover the service segment, which is a significant part of the ICT sector. Second, the scope of the electronic devices industry production area is much wider than that of ICT.

Due to the subject of case studies presented, one of the key terms is an electronic device, which is applied for generating, transmitting, and measuring electric current and electromagnetic fields. The correct operation of this device depends on the electric power supply or the presence of electromagnetic fields. The device may generate electromagnetic disturbances or its operation may be affected by such disturbances.

Such a device is intended for sale on the market to a private (B2C) or institutional (B2B) user, regardless of whether it is an end customer or a broker (e.g., importer, retailer, or distributor). The second part of the definition is extremely important, as the electronic devices that are designed only for experimental or individual users are not subject to EU directives, especially in terms of the approval system, testing, and certification.

Another important term is NPD project. In the case of the electronics industry, a product is understood as an electronic device consisting of integrated and cooperating components such as electronics (hardware), mechanics (housing and chassis), and software (mainly embedded software: firmware). The term "chassis" means an internal element of the device mechanics – the main board on which electrical, electronic, and other components are mounted, constituting the parts of the device.

It should be noted that the necessary condition for introducing such a product to the market is to carry out analysis and tests, including tests in laboratories, certifications, and approvals. These issues are highlighted in many publications on the testing and marketing of electronic devices. Mandrusov et al. (1999) pointed out that no manufacturer of electronic devices can sell a product that does not meet the electromagnetic compatibility (EMC) requirements of a particular country. Yuwono et al. (2022) also emphasized that "an electronic product must meet functional requirements and EMC compliance requirements prior to be commercialized" (p. 23).

At this point, the concept of EMC needs to be clarified. Keller (2023) defined it as follows: "EMC is the ability of equipment or a system to function satisfactorily in its electromagnetic environment without introducing intolerable electromagnetic disturbances to anything in that environment" (p. 1). Montrose (1996) also highlighted the need for a product to be compliant with applicable legislation, notwithstanding the requirement for the product to function properly. Williams (2017) rightly pointed out that "every company that manufactures or imports electrical or electronic products should have in place measures that will enable its products to comply with the Directive. This means that an awareness of EMC must penetrate every part of the enterprise" (p. xiv). Mao and Du (2022) emphasized that "the electromagnetic (EM) risk is difficult to find since the EM weaknesses would be hidden in the system design and no evident symptom can be observed in the normal" (p. 764).

At the same time, as Eroglu and Goodrich (1998) pointed out that no two manufacturers, markets, or products are the same – each of them is unique in its own way. Therefore, it is necessary to develop one's compliance assessment process. Such a process should be as simple as possible, be effectively implemented, and be subject to adaptation as conditions change. Designing a modern electronic device that meets EMC requirements is not easy without iterative tests and design changes (Burneske, 1999). Knowledge of applicable standards and test methods, theories of electromagnetic phenomena, and techniques to mitigate electromagnetic disturbances is a prerequisite for success.

In the European Union environment, to meet these requirements it is necessary to implement the resolutions of the EU Directive EMC 2014/30/EU (Directive 2014/30/EU of the European Parliament and the Council of February 26, 2014, on the harmonization of the laws relating to compatibility). Each EU Directive provides a list of harmonized standards that apply either to a given environment or to a group of products.

As can be seen, the legal and technical situation is defined hierarchically and in great detail. In general, in most projects, it is known what specific standards the designed electronic device must meet. It is also known what

Testing and Certification of New Product Development 89

tests are necessary to be performed. Nevertheless, there are two types of uncertainty associated with this stage of the project:

- Despite consulting with experts, the project leaders are not always able to fully, accurately, and correctly assess all aspects of these tests and certification, e.g., selecting the severity levels in the case of a series of EMC tests, precisely assigning the device being tested to a specific group or class specified in the regulations, precisely defining the target electromagnetic environment in the normative sense.
- During the design it is difficult to take into account all issues which are necessary for a positive result of all tests and certifications that the final device must pass – even those predefined 100% correctly.

Despite the more and more technologically and functionally advanced Computer Aided Design (CAD) software, which offers among others EMC modeling, actual results can be obtained only by carrying out tests on a physical model – a prototype of a designed device.

Both issues are associated with project risk if any of the required standards are not taken into account or if the results of the tests are negative. Generally, this issue is described in the literature on EMC research. However, there are relatively few papers in this field – surveys and case studies. Some of them are briefly discussed later.

Research conducted by the Polish Institute of Telecommunications showed that Polish companies producing electronic equipment have the greatest problems with EMC, and more specifically with excessive emission, i.e., ensuring that the device does not emit electromagnetic disturbances above the limits allowed by the standards (Bogucki et al., 2007). Importantly, according to the same studies, it is estimated that the costs of the elements necessary to ensure EMC constitute approximately 10% of the costs of all elements used in the device.

Case studies on this topic can be found in the literature. A very extensive review of 890 examples of EMC problems, covering the years 1992–2020 was presented by Armstrong (2020). Some of the reported cases come from official research reports, some are the result of research or personal Armstrong experiences. While some of the cases described in his study did not have serious consequences, some involved significant losses of time and resources and even bankruptcy for companies involved in the projects. Worse still, some events have caused (or could easily cause) human injury and death. As Armstrong (2018) wrote in the introduction: "My experience is that these stories only represent the very tip of a large iceberg, with unguessable costs for manufacturers and society as a whole" (p. 1). He emphasized the growing role of EMC, paying attention to the increasing degree of complexity of modern electronic devices, which means that problems with ensuring EMC would become more frequent, generating more and more costs and noticeably affecting user safety.

Therefore, technical issues related to carrying out analyses and tests, including tests in external laboratories and certification or approval and, in particular, issues of compliance with EU Directives, especially EMC, are a distinct risk factor, typical for manufacturing projects in the electronics industry.

In the case studies presented in this chapter, the examples analyzed are manufacturing projects implemented by Polish companies from the electronic device industry that have experienced problems with the market launch of new electronic devices. The framework of the research was determined, on the one hand, by the industry of a given company (electronic devices industry), the nature of the project being implemented (manufacturing project), the type of product of the manufacturing project made (electronic device), and on the other hand, whether there were any problems related to testing of electronic devices before their market launch.

Preparation

One of the stages of preparation for the research was a review of possible case studies and the final selection of some of them to be performed. Such a selection was possible from among dozens of cases to which the researchers had access. As mentioned earlier, the research area concerned manufacturing projects in the electronics industry. Therefore, the following projects were not taken into account: typical IT projects (no EMC tests), electronic devices from the special services, and military industries (placing such devices on the market is governed by specific regulations, and the design and tests are kept secret).

As part of the preparations for the research, a pilot case study was carried out. The authors took part in the preparation, supervision, and performance of EMC tests in a laboratory. As in the first attempt, the EMC test result was negative, the device prototype was modified. Such iterations were performed twice and the results of the third series of EMC tests in the laboratory were positive. During this pilot study, the methodological and practical aspects of the case studies were developed and refined.

In preparation for the research, a single case study protocol was also developed. This protocol was also used to carry out a multiple case study involving nine cases concerning manufacturing projects in the electronics industry.

An important issue related to the implementation of case studies is to ensure the protection of research participants. As far as the research discussed in this chapter is concerned, it was quite a delicate and sensitive

Testing and Certification of New Product Development 91

issue, especially in two aspects. On the one hand, manufacturing projects in the electronic devices industry include new devices, usually with high market potential, which are tested in strict confidence long before their official market launch. The problems with obtaining positive test results and access to the intellectual property devices of the company are therefore confidential and may not be disseminated to the public. Often, the laboratories carrying out tests for external clients have to ensure the confidentiality of their work. On the other hand, possible problems with performing and passing device tests may harm the image of the company or its specific employee. Therefore, all information presented in this chapter has been anonymized and the details of the devices have been described in a way that minimizes the likelihood of associating them with specific products or companies.

Data Collection

The next step in the case study analysis is data collection. In terms of data collection, it is important to identify, select, and collect data from several sources. This type of procedure, i.e., data triangulation, is an important element in strengthening the construct validity of the case study (Yin, 2014). The selection of data sources mainly depends on the possibilities available to researchers to reach these data. In the described studies, it was helpful that one of the authors was for about three years an employee of the EMC laboratory, and later – as the project manager – had access to such laboratories and their staff, participating in research conducted there. Therefore, he was able to conduct interviews, direct observations, and participant observations and had access to documents, archival files, and physical artifacts (tested devices). It should be emphasized that in terms of data collection, the case studies are based on all six data sources described in the Yin methodology (Yin, 2014). The two case studies are described later. They concern electronic devices (outcomes of manufacturing projects of two Polish companies from the electronics industry). In both cases, the companies encountered problems with completing these tests with a positive result and, consequently, were unable to launch these devices onto the market.

These cases were selected to diversify as much as possible the context, including the size of the company, the type of tested devices, the problems encountered during tests, and the experience and knowledge of the company ordering the tests.

Case Study 1: Video Game

One of the authors took part in the tests as an expert cooperating with the EMC laboratory. The data were collected using participant and direct observation. During the research, the authors also had access to documents providing a test program, a functional description of the tested device, and full construction documentation of the device. Another source of data was archival files, i.e., the program and test results of similar devices tested in the laboratory, and the documentation of previous versions of devices manufactured by the company ordering the tests. The authors also used physical artifacts – two prototypes of video games provided by the client. The data for this case study were collected over a two-and-a-half-month period during subsequent customer visits to the EMC laboratory.

The analyzed problem took place in one of the Polish EMC Laboratories. One of its clients was a company producing video game machines. The company independently designed electronic devices and manufactured them using components purchased from reputable global producers.

It is worth noting that when purchased components are applied to the electronic device, there is a great temptation not to carry out EMC tests of the entire device, but to be content with the fact that all these components have positive EMC test results and meet all the required standards. Such thinking – often caused by ignorance – is unfortunately wrong. Not only is this a case in the field of EMC, but "a complex system does not simply function as a collection of subsystems" (Shenhar & Dvir, 2007, p. 38). The fact that individual elements and components of the device meet all the required EMC standards does not automatically mean that their assembly in the form of a finished device will also meet these standards. Each time it is necessary to verify this empirically through analyses, simulations, and preferably by performing a complete cycle of required tests.

Preparing a test program for a newly designed device requires defining its intended use in a specific so-called "EMC environment". It is the responsibility of the designer or manufacturer of the device. In the analyzed situation, the equipment under test was designed for use in residential, commercial, and light industrial environments, which means that the EMC requirements were not too high. After the test program was designed and its scope approved, testing began.

During one of the EMC tests, the excess emissivity of the radiated and conducted route was observed. Due to the quite geometrically extensive topology of the device, conducting a thorough analysis and finding the cause of the excessive emission was quite a complex and time-consuming task. The tested device had large dimensions (approx. $150 \times 60 \times 50$ cm) and weight (approx. 60 kg). The electrical and electronic components were placed in various, often spaced apart places inside the enclosure, and the electrical and signal wiring was long and complicated. In such a situation, the analysis and remedial measures required a long time and additional visits to the laboratory. The remedial actions consisted of the replacement of the central unit (computer) with a different model, modification of the cabling, including length adjustments and topology changes, replacement of the power supply, and addition of network filters. After three iterations of the modifications described earlier, the new version of the video game machine successfully passed the complete EMC test cycle.

It's worth mentioning that the client properly defined the environment, in which the tested device was to operate, taking into account the applicable regulations. The device documentation provided by the client was sufficient, including functional description, design documentation, and test program. The test program (specific test standards, levels of electromagnetic immunity, emission limits, operation or non-operation criteria) was developed with the help of the EMC laboratory staff.

The problems identified during testing had negative consequences for the entire project including exceeding the project schedule and going over the budget. The delay was related to the need to make modifications and corrections to the design and technology documentation, as well as physical modifications to the prototype, and the necessity to make three additional visits to the laboratory.

The consequences for the entire project were as follows:

- Extending the project duration by 2.5 months – from the planned 14 months to 16.5 months, i.e., by approx. 20%.
- Increasing the project budget by approx. 10% due to the additional costs resulting from design modifications, hardware changes, and three additional visits to the EMC Laboratory.

Case Study 2: Technological Device: Wire Breaking Strength Tester

Like in the previous case, one of the authors personally participated in this research, but this time as the head of the EMC laboratory. Again, the primary sources of the collected data were participant observation and direct observation. Due to his role, the co-author had access to the full documentation provided by the client, which included a functional description of the device and the full documentation on mechanics, electronics, and software. He also participated in the formulation of the test program, which was aided by the archival records provided by the client including the program and test results as well as the documentation on previous versions of the devices. Access to physical artifacts in the form of prototypes of two devices, provided by the client for testing, completed available data sources. Data for this case study were collected over a two-month period during subsequent customer visits to the research laboratory.

The problem emerged at the EMC Laboratory, which provides commercial EMC testing services for third-party customers. This time, the client was a company producing technological and measuring instruments, testers, and other unusual technological and production devices. A specific feature of this company's activity was that it did not have any typical, mass-produced devices of this type in its portfolio. Each time, the devices were designed and manufactured according to the strictly defined requirements of an external customer. The production was usually unitary, although in the past it happened that the customer ordered, for example, several dozen of identical pieces of a particular tester or device so that it could be installed at all stands of their production lines. According to popular opinion, devices manufactured individually or on the so-called "own needs" – under applicable regulations – do not have to be EMC tested. However, a deeper analysis of the applicable regulations leads to the conclusion that such a situation can only take place when the manufacturer and user of the unique device are the same company. Then, the "for own use" clause is legally fulfilled. Therefore, in this situation, the tests were necessary, especially since it was one of the requirements specified in the customer's order, who wanted to make sure that the devices would be electromagnetically compatible with their other devices and installations.

In the described case, EMC tests were performed on a specialized technological device for testing the breaking strength of cables. The client (the future end user of this tester) ordered 20 pieces of such devices. Such a tester was to be used to test the breaking strength of cables in bundles produced, among others, for the automotive industry. Cables used in various devices and installations are usually terminated with plugs, sockets, or connectors. Occasionally, significant kinetic forces (e.g., sudden accelerations or strong vibrations) act on such bundles and cables, which in extreme conditions may cause the cable to break or pull the cable out of the socket, plug, or connector. Therefore, the performance of wire break tests is part of the quality control cycle performed in the cable and harness manufacturing industry. After the customer developed the test program and agreed on the scope of the tests to be carried out, EMC tests were started.

During one of the EMC tests, the problem was the immunity of the tested device to electrostatic discharge ESD (one of the EMC tests required by the applicable standards). In particular, contact discharges directed at the touch display (part of the device) were problematic. The structure of the tester consisted mostly of ready-made mechanical elements and parts: motors, actuators, and gears, as well as the electrical and electronic ones: industrial controller, power supply, display with a touch screen, strain gauge force sensors, and wiring. All components used in the tester construction were certified and tested, also in terms of EMC, but it turned out that assembling electromagnetically compatible components into a finished device did not automatically ensure its EMC as a whole.

In the described case, it turned out that the touch display had all the necessary CE certificates and declarations and, as a separate part, it also successfully passed the ESD immunity tests. Such a test of the separate display – at the customer's request – was repeated with a positive result in the EMC laboratory. However, the same tests of the complete device (tester) gave negative results. After a deeper analysis, it turned out that the problem was the topology of the entire tester, especially the geometry of the cabling used, including the signal and power cables. The remedial actions taken by the tester designers included changes in the geometric layout of the cabling, modification of the physical arrangement of individual components, addition of special electrostatic discharge connections, and mechanical changes to the chassis and housing related to the modifications made. After another three visits to the EMC laboratory – it was necessary to repeat the entire test program due to the significant scope of the design changes – the new version of the tester successfully passed the complete EMC test cycle. As a result, the production of testers ordered by the customer could be launched.

The problems identified during the EMC tests had budgetary consequences for the entire project, especially regarding the project time overruns and – to a slightly lesser extent – project costs. The additional time was related to the necessity to visit the EMC Laboratory three times more to perform tests after modifications, and the necessity to perform adjustments and corrections in construction documentation and physical alterations of the prototype.

The consequences for the budget of the entire project were as follows:

- The project was delayed by two months – from the planned six to eight months, i.e., by approx. 33%.
- The project budget was increased by approx. 12% due to the additional costs resulting from hardware changes of mechanics and cabling and three additional visits to the EMC Laboratory.

Data Analysis

Data analysis described in this section consists of three parts: an analysis for each of the two described case studies separately, and an analysis summarizing both case studies combined. According to Yin (2014), data analysis consists of checking, classifying, compiling, testing, and other methods of processing evidence to obtain results on an empirical basis. The analytical strategy used in the case studies consisted mainly of referring to the theoretical assumptions that had been made before the research began. These assumptions, made for the case study project, were reflected in the research questions formulated earlier.

The main technique employed to analyze the data was pattern matching. It consists in comparing patterns emerging from the collected evidence with

96 *Dariusz Meiser and Maciej Nowak*

patterns predicted before starting the data collection. Such predicted patterns are described in the section "Design".

Case Study 1: Video Game

The project of the video game machine was neither complex nor in any way innovative or technologically advanced. The concept of such video game machines is a twilight solution and technologically rather outdated. Nevertheless, such devices still find their buyers in niche markets.

Analyzing the data collected in this case study, the following characteristic phrases and events can be observed: an electronic device, manufacturing project, EMC tests, exceeding the permissible limits, especially emission, complex and time-consuming search for the cause of exceeding standards, the need to iterate (project – corrections – re-tests), design modifications, project delay, project budget overruns, and additional cost. After a deeper analysis (including semantics), the data were aggregated into the following codes:

- Scope of the project and industry: manufacturing project from the electronic equipment industry, EMC.
- Negative test results: excessive emission, exceeding the permissible levels.
- Iteration of design activities: the need to perform several cycles of design – corrections – re-testing.
- Project budget overruns: project delay – time-consuming diagnosis, corrections, and re-tests, cost overruns – related to the project delay, the need to make modifications, and the costs of additional visits to the laboratory.

The main cause of the problems was ignoring EMC issues during the design phase and trusting in the heuristic described earlier: failing to take into account the fact that assembling the device from electromagnetically compatible components does not automatically make the entire device EMC compatible. Another reason was the insufficient knowledge and experience of the device's developers in designing with EMC requirements. An additional factor contributing to the negative test result was the lack of even preliminary (pre-compliance) EMC tests of the prototype at an early stage of design works.

The main sources of this information were interviews with device designers, participant observation, direct observation, documentation, and physical artifacts. In contrast, archival documentation (in the form of technical documentation of previous devices manufactured by the company) was used to a lesser extent.

It is worth emphasizing that the described situation involves the need to return to the earlier phases of the manufacturing project, i.e., to perform

Testing and Certification of New Product Development 97

several iterations: research – design modification – implementation of planned corrections – testing, etc. Standard linear project management models, most often used in companies, generally do not accommodate such situations. In the discussed case, the company designing and manufacturing the device had a "bureaucratic and accounting" problem of going back to one of the previous design phases. This was because both the design phase and the prototyping phase had already been closed and pre-accounted for. Therefore, it was not formally possible to return to these design phases and assign the necessary costs related to modifications and the cost of additional tests to them. It pertained to the linear model of project management adopted in this company.

Case Study 2: Technological Device: Wire Breaking Strength Tester

The design of the tester was neither complex nor in any way innovative or technologically advanced. Its only distinction was that it was not a standard mass-produced device intended for mass use. However, it was a typical product of the company and was built with components typically used in such devices.

The data collected during the case study were aggregated and coded. Analyzing these data, the following distinctive events and phrases could be observed: manufacturing project, electronic device, EMC tests, failure to meet the requirements specified by standards, time-consuming search for identified non-conformities, the need to introduce structural corrections and implementation of several iterations of the process (design – modifications – repetition of tests), exceeding the time and budget of the project. These patterns were then aggregated into the following codes:

- Scope of the project and industry: manufacturing project from the electronic equipment industry, EMC.
- Negative test results: failure to meet the required levels according to the standards.
- Iteration of design activities: the need to perform several cycles of design – corrections – re-testing.
- Project budget overruns: project delay – time-consuming analysis of the reasons for the negative test results, the need to make structural changes and re-tests, cost overruns – related to the project delay, the need to make modifications, and the costs of additional visits to the laboratory.

The main reason for the problems was the insufficient analysis and consideration of EMC issues at the construction stage and an overly optimistic assumption that the use of EMC-compliant components will automatically result in the finished product also being electromagnetically compatible. In this case, as in the previous one, no preliminary EMC ("pre-compliance") testing of the prototype was carried out during the early stage of the project.

The analysis of the causes was conducted using the following data sources: participant observation and direct observation, interviews (with device designers), archival documentation (construction documentation of similar products designed and manufactured by the company), and physical artifacts (two prototypes of the devices under test).

As in the previous case, also for this company, the return to the initial phases of the project was associated with certain inconveniences. This time it was related to the "closed" and "fixed" budget of the project, as the device was to be produced in a small number of copies according to specific customer requirements. Thus, it was not possible either to sell this device to another customer or sell more units of it. According to additional interviews with company representatives, it used one of the linear project management models for manufacturing projects.

Data Analysis Summary

All the data collected during the implementation of the nine case studies were analyzed with the following as a starting point:

- Reference to theoretical assumptions.
- Matching patterns and referring to formulated research questions.

Our research has confirmed that problems can occur during EMC testing of newly developed electronic devices. It should be emphasized that these conclusions apply to all nine case studies, not just the two discussed in this chapter.

At this point, it is worth recalling Mao and Du's (2022) conclusion that "the electromagnetic (EM) risk is difficult to find since the EM weaknesses would be hidden in the system design and no evident symptom can be observed in the normal" (p. 764). Also, Yuwono et al. (2022) pointed to the fact that "complex electronic products with smaller sizes and denser components will be a challenge for compliance with EMC standards" (p. 23).

The analysis of observed patterns examined whether their occurrence could be found in all the cases analyzed. This part of the research was carried out iteratively, and the results of each case study were examined both independently, as well as in the relation to the results obtained for other cases. In each case, the patterns discussed in detail in the two case studies described in this chapter were confirmed, and they were aggregated in the form of codes: project scope and industry, negative test results, iteration of project activities, and project budget overruns. It is also worth adding that the repetition of these patterns was also found in the other case studies we conducted, which are not discussed here. The other seven case studies included the following devices: industrial power supply, plug-in power supplies, professional GSM concentrator for industrial applications, cash register, high-end audiophile tube amplifier, production line safety system, and industrial measuring device.

Given the evidence collected and analyzed, as well as the patterns identified, the following answers to the previously formulated research questions can be provided.

Question 1: Why often, despite the completion of a manufacturing project in the electronic devices industry, the designed device cannot be launched to the market?

Answer: A necessary condition for introducing an electronic device to the market is to carry out – with a positive result – analysis and tests, including tests in laboratories and obtaining certification or approval. This is confirmed by both the previously cited publications (Montrose, 1996; Mandrusov et al., 1999; Williams, 2017; Yuwono et al., 2022), as well as the results of a multiple case study presented here. At the same time, it is important to emphasize the growing awareness of designers and manufacturers of electronic devices – in all the described cases, representatives of manufacturing companies had general knowledge (at varying levels, however) that testing is necessary before launching a device on the market.

Question 2: What are the common problems related to the testing of electronic devices before their market launch?

Answer: The most common problem is the lack of positive test results, certification, and approval in the area of EMC, especially during the first attempt. Other difficulties include too little knowledge about and experience with EMC and dependencies related to these tests, as well as the overoptimistic assumption that the use of components that meet EMC requirements automatically results in the finished product being electromagnetically compatible. Another major problem – in fact, the most important from a business perspective – is the time and budget overruns of manufacturing projects. Moreover, the project management methods used by the analyzed companies do not take into account the need to iterate several cycles: design – corrections – re-testing. These conclusions are confirmed by both the previously cited publications (Eroglu & Goodrich, 1998; Burneske, 1999; Armstrong, 2018), as well as the results of the multiple case study.

Question 3: What issues specific to manufacturing projects in the electronics industry are not described by the most commonly used project management methods?

Answer: The most important issues that are ignored by the most commonly used project management methods include: insufficient emphasis on the importance of the need to conduct testing, approval, and certification and a frequent situation when the first approach to testing yields a negative result and it is necessary to repeat several cycles: design – corrections – re-testing.

These conclusions are confirmed by both the previously cited publications and the results of a multiple case study.

Findings

The final step in Yin's case study method is the findings' presentation. Apart from the conclusions presented earlier, one more point is worth noting. The information collected during the research, the analysis carried out and the conclusions drawn indicate that it is necessary to provide information feedback, in the form of gathering the knowledge acquired during the tests in the laboratory, and then to return with this knowledge to the earlier stages of the project. Such knowledge, accumulated iteratively, should also provide important information input for assumptions in subsequent projects implemented in a company. It is worth pointing out that the significance and scope of changes made in the project may be different each time, and therefore the depth of the return to the earlier stages of the project may also vary. For example, in case study 1, it was not necessary to make any changes to the functional and technical assumptions of the device. The modifications covered only one (of three) ranges of the device's design: electronics (the other two were mechanics and software). In turn, in case study 2, the modifications covered all these components of the electronic device design.

The results of the case studies lead to the general conclusion that, in addition to other key aspects of managing a manufacturing project in the electronics industry, it is extremely important to consider issues related to testing, certification, and approval.

Conclusions

The results presented here indicate that it is necessary to develop an adaptive method of project risk management, appropriate to the conditions in which manufacturing projects are implemented in the electronics equipment industry. The leading assumption of this method is that the project risk management process should be an integral part of the project management process itself because the implementation of each project is inherently associated with the risks involved. Therefore, these two management

Testing and Certification of New Product Development 101

processes cannot be carried out side by side or independently of each other. In doing so, risk management must also take into account changing conditions during the project implementation. Therefore, it cannot be implemented in a static and linear manner, but constantly adapt to the changes that occur. Adaptation in project risk management can be understood as a continuous adjustment to the changing conditions in which the project is implemented when any changes occur that may affect its risk. Contrary to passive management, the adaptive approach emphasizes continuous monitoring of the environment and search for possible changes, as well as ongoing updating of risks, development, and modification of preventive and contingency plans.

In the process of project risk management, a clear distinction should be made between reducing the likelihood of a given risk, and reducing its impact when that risk actually does occur. Reactive risk management comes down to the second aspect only – minimizing the undesirable effects of risk. In contrast, proactive management focuses on both threads: reducing the possibility that the risk will occur, and reducing the impact of the risk when it actually materializes (Smith & Merritt, 2002).

The adaptive risk management process should consist of two loops: a risk management loop and an incident management loop. The main purpose of the risk management loop is to reduce the likelihood of a given risk occurring. In the incident management loop, on the other hand, the main objective is to minimize the impact of an incident on the project when a given risk has turned into an incident. The risk management loop is iterative and continuous. If any of the risks becomes active and turns into an event (an incident), then there is a smooth transition to the second loop – incident management. Proposing this type of approach to manufacturing project management in the electronics equipment industry will be the subject of our future work.

References

Armstrong, K. (2018). _New EMI Stories_. Cherry Clough Consultants Ltd.
Armstrong, K. (2020). _EMI Stories. A Collection of 890 Real-Life Short Stories about the Dangers of Electromagnetic Interference (EMI)_. Cherry Clough Consultants Ltd.
Bessant, J., & Francis, D. (1997). Implementing the new product development process. _Technovation, 17_(4), 189–197. doi:10.1016/S0166-4972(97)84690-1
Bogucki, J., Chudziński, A., & Połujan, J. (2007). Emisja elektromagnetyczna urządzeń w praktyce. _Telekomunikacja i techniki informacyjne, 1–2_, 85–95 (in Polish).
Burneske, G.W. (1999). Exorcise the demon: Managing EMC in product development. In _1999 IEEE International Symposium on Electromagnetic Compatability. Symposium Record (Cat. No. 99CH36261)_ (Vol. 1, 257–262).

Cooper, R.G. (1983). A process model for industrial new product development. *IEEE Transactions on Engineering Management* (1), 2–11. doi:10.1109/TEM.1983.6448637

Cooper, R.G. (1988). The new product process: A decision guide for managers. *Journal of Marketing Management*, *3*(3), 238–255. doi:10.1080/0267257X.1988.9964044

Eroglu, K., & Goodrich, D. (1998). Regulatory compliance, a manufacturer's perspective. In *1998 IEEE International Symposium on Electromagnetic Compatibility. Symposium Record (Cat. No. 98CH36253)* (Vol. 1, 250–252).

Kahn, K.B. (2013). *The PDMA Handbook of New Product Development*. Wiley.

Keizer, J.A., Vos, J.P., & Halman J.I. (2005). Risks in new product development: Devising a reference tool. *R&D Management*, *35*(3), 297–309. doi:10.1111/j.1467-9310.2005.00391.z

Keller, R.B. (2023). *Design for Electromagnetic Compatibility – in a Nutshell Theory and Practice*. Springer Nature.

Mandrusov, V., Jackman, T., Roaque, T., & Friesen, D. (1999). EMC development process for information technology equipment. In *1999 IEEE International Symposium on Electromagnetic Compatibility. Symposium Record (Cat. No. 99CH36261)* (Vol. 1, pp. 121–126). IEEE.

Mao, C., & Du, C. (2022). Overview and progress of risk assessment for EMC. In *2022 Asia-Pacific International Symposium on Electromagnetic Compatibility (APEMC)*, 764–766.

Montrose, M.I. (1996). *Printed Circuit Board Design Techniques for EMC Compliance*. IEEE Press.

Myers, S., & Marquis, D.G. (1969). *Successful Industrial Innovations: A Study of Factors Underlying Innovation in Selected Firms* (Vol. 69, No. 17). National Science Foundation.

Rothwell, R. (1974). Factors for success in industrial innovation. *Journal of General Management*, *2*(2), 57–65. doi:10.1177/030630707400200210

Shenhar, A.J., & Dvir, D. (2007). *Reinventing Project Management: The Diamond Approach to Successful Growth and Innovation*. Harvard Business Review Press.

Shrivastava, R., Singh, S., & Dubey, G.C. (2012). Optimization of different objective function in risk management system to launch new version of product. *International Journal of Theoretical and Applied Sciences*, *4*(1), 41–47.

Sicotte, H., & Bourgault M. (2008). Dimensions of uncertainty and their moderating effect on new product development project performance. *R&D Management*, *38*(5), 468–479. doi:10.1111/j.1467-9310.2008.00531.x

Smith, P.G., & Merritt, G.M. (2002). *Proactive Risk Management*. Productivity Press.

Williams, T. (2017). *EMC for Product Designer*. Elsevier.

Yin, R.K. (2014). *Case Study Research. Design and Methods*. Sage Publications.

Yuwono, T., Baharuddin, M.H., Misran, N., Ismail, M., & Mansor, M.F. (2022). A review of measurement of electromagnetic emission in electronic product: Techniques and challenges. *Communications in Science and Technology*, *7*(1), 23–37.

6 Role of Information System Support in Project Management

Case of Companies Competing at Publicly Funded Calls for Projects

Jerneja Šavrič and Blaž Rodič

Introduction

In this chapter, we examine the project management practices and the role of information systems (IS) in the function of project management on the case of companies competing at national and EU funded calls/tenders for project proposals in Slovenia against the background of STS (Science, Technology & Society), a field of social science dedicated to the research on the interplay between technology and society.

Public calls or tenders for R&D (Research and Development) project proposals represent an important source of co-financing for development of new products and services, particularly for small and micro enterprises with limited own R&D budget. Unfortunately, many SMEs find participation in national and EU funded calls for project proposals challenging due to a lack of competent personnel capable of developing and managing a complex development project according to EU or national rules. Consequently, some companies don't participate in calls that require comprehensive project proposals (e.g., with a detailed financial plan), or the quality and thus success rate of their proposals is poor. As the complexity of expected project proposals roughly correlates to the amount of financing, companies with lacking project development capacity cannot obtain significant development and research funding, which has negative consequences for the development of these companies and their added value.

Official reasons for failure of proposals or projects may include low quality of applications, i.e., poor content (state of the art of the project, project planning, capabilities of project partners), not meeting formal requirements of call, and inadequate project management. Some of these issues can be avoided or mitigated with the use of good project management methodology and associated IT support – the use of appropriate software for development and management of projects.

Since specialized project development and management software aims to facilitate the planning and implementation of projects, providing the employees

DOI: 10.4324/9781003376583-8

104 *Jerneja Šavrič and Blaž Rodič*

with such IT support and associated training (in use of software as well as project management methodology) represents an opportunity for companies to escalate their participation in public tenders and improve the quality of their project proposals. We therefore wanted to explore what kind of software is used in successful companies and how it is integrated in the project development and management process.

In the second part of this chapter, we present the theoretical backgrounds of IS research, research on the interaction of IT and society, i.e., the field of STS, and introduce the term "project" and models of project management. In the third part of this chapter, we present the methodology used in our research case. Fourth part of this chapter contains the results of our research. In the conclusion of this chapter, we look at how the most successful Slovenian companies perform their project planning and management in the role of public tender applicant. Through their practices, we have identified the characteristics of IT solutions and other factors that affect the performance of companies in public R&D tenders.

Theoretical Background

When researching IS from a sociological point of view we rely on theories of STS. STS is a field of social science dedicated to the research on the interplay between technology (e.g., information technology support) and society (e.g., the organization of project work). Information and communication technologies (ICT) are key technologies of the information society and, as is typical of general-purpose technologies, they are present in all modern societies. According to STS theories, we can study ICT as a key influencing factor in the development of the information society, or we can study the influence of society on the emergence, development, and dissemination of new ICT.

The STS

Whether technology shapes the society (in our case, we examine companies as an important part of society) and whether the society influences the development of technology are the key questions in the STS field. The subject of our research was companies that partly finance their research and development from EU funds. To implement their processes, companies use technology, which affects the way of work, structure, and processes in the company, while the development of companies' technology is on the other hand influenced by the company itself, i.e., the users.

If we limit ourselves to ICT, we can present the main STS issues in this way: after a company chooses and implements a certain software solution, it adapts its organization to the new technology in certain aspects, for example, it distributes work differently among employees, introduces additional processes, or eliminates some processes. This represents the impact of technology on society (a company). Regardless of whether the technology is purchased, its development outsourced, or it's developed in-house, the choice of technology is influenced by the company's needs. A company typically chooses the technology that corresponds to the existing work process as much as possible or offers such advantages, that the company is willing to adapt its processes to the new technology. Technological change is obviously a never-ending development process and doesn't bring a kind of final equilibrium to the socio-technical system. Instead, technological development is always open-ended, as its result without a known absolutely optimal solution.

Companies may find themselves in the following technological development dilemma: choose a technology that is highly adapted to their current needs and processes, bringing limited improvements, but requiring little organizational change; or a technology that allows them to greatly improve their business, but only if they also significantly adapt (reengineer) their processes, train and motivate the employees. In any case, we can assume that the successful use of technology depends on the alignment of the company's needs with the chosen technology and its ability to adapt to new technology. In this dilemma, we can therefore identify mutual influence of technology and society and thus an interesting research problem for the field of STS.

STS originates in period before second world war, however, the most notable early achievement in this field, according to Harvard Kennedy School (2016), is Thomas Kuhn's paper, *The Structure of Scientific Revolutions* (Kuhn, 2012). Today, STS is an interdisciplinary field that encompasses several scientific disciplines: history, philosophy, sociology, political science, economics, management and innovation, psychology, semantics, cultural studies, and anthropology with one research goal – to investigate the role of science and technology in society (Rip, 1994). However, since scientists have generally studied this question from the point of view of their own field, the interdisciplinary approach to STS is still lacking (Cozzens, 2001, pp. 51–64). Two modern approaches derived from STS are Constructive Technology Assessment and Critical Theory of Technology, which avoid leaning toward either extreme and represent the first attempts to connect the two currents within STS research. The complex interaction between people and technology organizations and the society's complex infrastructures and human behavior is also recognized by the socio-technical systems approach, also known as the socio-technical systems design (STSD) paradigm, which considers technology from a broader perspective, conveyed by the original meaning of the word technology (Greek techne "craft, art" + logos "opinion, discourse").

IS Research

We can consider all parts of the organization, both physical and abstract, which contribute to the formation and dissemination of information to be a part of an IS. When studying an IS with the goal of its improvement, it is necessary to establish a systematic way of measuring the relevant properties of the system to allow comparison with other IS, either existing or planned.

Laudon and Laudon (2022) have defined an IS as a set of interdependent components (hardware, communication equipment, software, people) that collect, process, store, and distribute data and thereby support the key and decision-making processes in the organization. Cordella and Iannacci (2011) have defined IS as a set of interconnected parts that collect or acquire, process, store and transmit information to support decision-making, coordination, and control of activities in the organization and enable analysis and visualization of data and system operation. In the study of IS, and not limited to STS, IS are perceived as socio-technical systems that comprise both technical and social variables. Therefore, the planning, development, and introduction of IS have far-reaching consequences that go beyond the technological aspect and the elements of the IS itself.

Most IS researchers consider them from one of three perspectives: technical, cognitive, and behavioral (Cordella & Iannacci, 2011). The characteristic of the technical approach is in the development and study of mathematical models of IS, physical properties and limitations of IS, and this approach uses data modeling as the main tool for analyzing IS. The technical approach originates in management sciences, operations research, and computer science. The cognitive approach is based on socio-psychological theories and studies how decision-makers perceive and use information and uses decision modeling as the main tool. The behavioral approach is based on behavioristic economics and examines problems that arise in the context of the development and long-term maintenance of IS. It uses the transaction cost model as the main tool for IS analysis.

Quality of IS

The IS's properties, degree of their correspondence with the needs of the organization, and the IS implementation process affect IS effectiveness and the productivity of IS users and the organization itself. According to Abugabah et al. (2009), organizations must use adequately rigorous approaches to properly assess the impact of an existing or planned IS on their operations. In this way, they can achieve positive effects of IS on the efficiency and effectiveness of the organization. A key part of evaluating the impact of IS on an organization is studying the impact of IS on the performance and productivity of the end users of the system. Early approaches in this area focused on identifying factors that facilitate the use of IS and formalizing these factors into models for analyzing the ease of use of systems.

Despite the quantity of research on the subject of the connection between IS and the performance of organizations, demonstrating the impact of a specific IS on the results of the organization's operations has proven to be very difficult (Alpar & Kim, 1990; Rai & Welker, 2002). The connection between IS and business results is multidimensional and includes many aspects, such as the user's workplace, the set of tasks, the matching of the IS process model with the organization's processes. At the same time, it is difficult to isolate the impact of other factors on the organization's business due to the long process of introducing a new IS. We can summarize that the impact of the IS on the organization and the quality of the same IS are not entirely identical concepts.

There are several current frameworks for IS evaluation which allow the studying the impact of IS on both the organization and the individual user. The most frequently and widely used are the Technology Acceptance Model (TAM), the Task-Technology Fit (TTF) model, and the DeLone & McLean (D&M) model. TAM and TTF overlap to a large extent, and when integrated, they represent a coherent and robust model for assessing the impact of technology on an organization. D&M and TAM are related, as TAM investigates the possible effects of ease of use and perceived usefulness of the system on the user's performance, while D&M specifies the quality and final characteristics of the system and/or the method of its implementation to achieve the maximum level of usability, which ultimately also affects the user's performance and ease of use (Abugabah et al., 2009). What defines a good IS depends on the choice of stakeholders, the aspects evaluated and the purpose of the system. To paraphrase Ashby (1991), there is no such thing as an "absolutely good" IS. IS planners must be familiar with the goal of system development, and their customers must be able to determine whether the goal has been achieved. Using a set of criteria to check the achievement of the goal, it is possible to compile a list of questions that need to be checked before, during and after the planning phase. In this way, we could check whether the new system works as planned and how well it performs its tasks compared to, for instance, previous systems.

Project Management

To understand the role of IS in project management, we need to be familiar with fundamentals of project management. Different experts and institutions interpret the term "project" differently. Wysocki defines it as a sequence of unique, complex, and interconnected activities with a single goal, which must be completed in a certain time, within the set financial plan and in accordance with specifications (requirements) (Wysocki, 2019). The Project Management Institute in its PMBOK®Guide, which is recognized as the standard of project management in the USA, defines a project as "a temporary endeavor with a beginning and an end and it must be used to create a unique product, service or result" (Project Management Institute, Inc., 2021). PRINCE2 "Projects in a Controlled Environment", originally developed by a UK government ICT support agency, is a method for structured project management, which defines project as "a temporary organization that is created for the purpose of delivering one or more business products according to an agreed Business Case" (AXELOS Ltd, 2023). The definition of project found in the ISO standard ISO 21502:2020 "Project, programme and portfolio management—Guidance on project management" is "temporary endeavour to achieve one or more defined objectives" (International Organization for Standardization, 2020). While these definitions of project differ, they all refer to the goal-directed and time-limited nature of a project.

Based on his many years of experience, Wysocki (2019) developed the theory that the project management life cycle (PMLC) model is a sequence of five activities (research, planning, initiation, monitoring and control, completion). It defines several PMLC models based on the type of project we manage: traditional, agile, extreme with an unknown path to a known goal, or extreme with a known goal but an unknown path. With these approaches, we can create the following models of project management:

1 Traditional project management (TPM) approach: using a linear or primary model.
2 Agile project management (APM) approach: using an iterative model.
3 Extreme project management model (xPM or MPx): using one of two different PMLC.
4 Hybrid project management model or adaptive project framework (APF): a hybrid that takes the best from TPM and xPM.

The third model (extreme) is developed using one of two approaches, which Wysocki (2019) labeled xPM and MPx. They differ in that former has both an undefined goal (or final product) and the process to achieve the goal. In the latter approach, at least the goal (or final product) is known, but we do not know how achieve it. Which model to use therefore depends on criteria that include the characterization of the goal and the process.

Methods and Techniques Included in This Case Study

Research Aims

Our research aimed to identify the factors related to project development and management IT support that influence the success of companies at national and EU public calls for R&D project proposals, using a sample of Slovenian SMEs as well as medium and large companies according to EU classification.

Our fundamental research question was: "What is the nature of IT support in companies successful at national and EU project tenders?" This research question was then divided into specific research questions:

1 How is project development and management work organized in companies successful at national and EU project tenders?
2 How and what kind of specialized project development and management software do these companies use?
3 How do these companies train employees in use of the software?
4 What is the attitude of employees toward the use of this specialized software in companies successful at national and EU project tenders?

Research Methodology

This study research was conducted on a sample of privately owned companies, registered in Slovenia, which successfully participated in one or several national or EU funded calls for research and development project proposals. In order to focus on projects that require significant development and planning effort, we have limited our research to calls for projects with a mandatory detailed financial plan. Our investigation of 31 past calls for project proposals has revealed 1,254 successful project proposals (i.e., selected for financing), which have been submitted by 704 different companies. This data was obtained from intermediary bodies, i.e., national ministries, agencies and EU program contact points. Data included public calls in EU's Framework programs (FP6, FP7, Horizon 2020) and national R&D calls co-funded by the EU.

As our goal was to discover new knowledge, i.e., how successful companies organize their project development and management and support it with IT, we have decided to use qualitative methodology (semi-structured interviews) to obtain and analyze data from key employees in a sample of companies. Coordination and execution of interviews is time consuming; therefore, we needed to keep the sample size manageable. As we were interested in the data from successful companies, the companies in the sample were selected according to their success at public calls. To compare only companies with similar human and financial resources and avoid the domination of large companies in the sample, we have divided the research population into three groups: small and micro; medium; and large companies according to the EU criteria (European Commission, 2020).

The method for sample selection was a novel multicriteria model for classification of companies according to their success at public calls, which is presented in Šavrič and Rodič (2020). The model uses the following criteria to measure relative success at public calls: total funds acquired (in EUR), total number of successful project proposals, the proportion of public funds in company, and total number of employees. Four best rated companies from each size category were selected as the sample for qualitative research.

In second part of our research, we have applied qualitative methods such as semi-structured interviews (Edwards & Holland, 2013), qualitative content analysis of interviews, and formation of a well-grounded theory (Chametzky, 2016) and a paradigmatic model (Fischbein, 2005) with the goal of identifying the role and impact of IT support and other factors that influence the success of companies in public tenders for co-financing of R&D projects. According to the presented theoretical background, in order to assess the impact of IT on the performance of companies, it is necessary to examine the quality of the IS, its efficiency, the user experience, the motivation of the users and their IS competence.

The process of qualitative content analysis, which we carried out in the empirical part of the doctoral thesis, is roughly divided into six steps: (1) editing of the material, (2) determination of coding units, (3) open coding, (4) selection and definition of relevant concepts and categories, (5) respective coding, and (6) creation of the final theoretical formulation. The main goal of the qualitative content analysis was the creation of concepts, hypotheses, and explanations, i.e., a grounded theoretical formulation, which can be read as a narrative about the use of specialized project management software and its impact on the performance of both large- and medium-sized as well as small and micro companies when applying on national and community tenders.

Results

Through the interviews, we have discovered that companies use at least two IS (in combination) for project development and management: ISARR project management and reporting software package, mandated by the administrative body responsible for cohesion policy in the Republic of Slovenia, and an internal IS, which varies from company to company. Companies are autonomous in choosing its internal project management IS, and if developed in-house, the IS tends to be treated as their trade secret, with companies reluctant to reveal much information about it. Due to this

Role of Information System Support in Project Management   111

heterogeneity and restricted access to information, we could not directly and formally assess the quality of their project development and management IS; however, we were able to assess the adequacy of the systems in use based on the opinions of the interviewees.

We have formed the grounded theory by "selectively coding" (Glaser & Strauss, 1967) the categories formed in the process of qualitative content analysis in such a way that we connected them to each other and displayed the relationships between them within a schema or paradigmatic model. The paradigmatic model has demonstrated that the influence of IT support for project development and management on success of companies at national and EU public calls for R&D project proposals can be conditioned by (1) the degree of structuring of work organization, (2) the competence of employees in terms of exploiting the possibilities offered by specialized software (3) the attitude of employees toward the use of specialized software and, last but not least, the mode of software usage itself. Here we find that the way that companies train their employees to use specialized software indirectly affects the attitude of employees toward the software and its effective use when participating in national and community tenders.

In the following subsection, we summarize the responses of interviewees.

Work Organization in Project Development and Planning

Collected empirical data indicate that there are differences between companies regarding the way work is organized when applying in calls for projects. First, we can perceive the difference in the degree of structuring of the employees' work when applying for projects, starting with the decision of whether to submit a project proposal. In both large- and medium-sized companies that participated in our research, we notice that they have a very transparent work organization when applying for projects.

Even among the interviewees from small or micro companies, we detected a certain degree of structure in the organization of work when applying in calls for projects. Just like large- and medium-sized companies, small and micro companies also try to clearly divide the work of team members participating in the project application into administrative and professional, but in this context, a smaller distinction between the duties of employees can be observed.

The interviewees from large- or medium-sized companies said that the entire process of project preparation is the domain of the project office or team members who participate in the preparation of the project application. In small and micro enterprises, however, it seems that the decision-makers (owners, directors, or heads of departments) are involved in all phases or in the entire process of preparing the tender application, both in making the decision to submit a proposal and also in the process of filling out the tender forms/documentation and taking care of complete and submitted final form of application within the expected time limit.

The third difference in the way work is organized in project preparation is related to seeking help from external experts. None of the interviewees from large- or medium-sized companies mentioned that they would rely on the help of external experts when preparing project documentation. Small and micro companies, on the other hand, are faced with staff shortages in complex project applications and therefore look for solutions in the activation of external experts.

The testimonies of the interviewees also demonstrated the difference regarding the "idea funnel" a.k.a. innovation funnel (Chesbrough, 2003, p. 37), a mechanism that facilitates the screening and prioritizing the stream of ideas for new development projects/innovations. Within the idea funnel, ideas are first screened for viability, then prioritized according to company strategy and relevant financing mechanism deadlines. The metaphor of a funnel suggests a high number of innovative ideas "floating" around at the top (where there is unlimited brainstorming), with their number reduced according to their "weight" (priority) as they flow down the funnel toward implementation. The idea funnel also works as an innovation idea repository, i.e., a database that offers an overview of all recorded innovation ideas, their feasibility, stage of implementation, involved staff, thus facilitating the management and analysis of the organizations innovation process. The efficiency of the idea funnel depends on the effectiveness of the screening process – too many ideas may slow down the innovation process.

All interviewees in large- or medium-sized companies say that they have an annual plan for the development of products and technologies. This plan, prepared by development departments in large/medium-sized companies, is based on the most promising ideas collected and ranked with the method of "idea funnel".

Most similarities between companies regarding work organization were identified in the phases of project proposal development. The process is mostly divided into six or fewer phases: (1) continuous monitoring and identification of calls for projects or tenders; (2) suggesting participation to decision-makers; (3) evaluation of the correspondence between call/tender objectives and company development strategy and identification of suitable project ideas in the "idea funnel"; (4) confirmation of the suitability of the proposed project idea; (5) designation of the project manager and creation of a group (team members) that will be responsible for the preparation of the project proposal and (6) review and evaluation of the quality of the project proposal before the submission to the

Role of Information System Support in Project Management   113

calls for projects or tender. All companies implement the first phase - monitoring and identification of potential tenders. All companies also conduct a formal decision process whether to submit a proposal. The main difference between the companies is in terms of who makes the decision to submit a proposal or not.

Usage and Types of Project Development and Management Software

We can divide the use of specialized project development and management software into two areas: specialized software for (administrative) project management and specialized software for financial management and reporting. All companies regardless of their size mostly use Microsoft Office tools (i.e., Excel and Word) for the financial management of both project proposals and ongoing projects. Most of the interviewees use Excel to create a transparent tabular project planning structure.

In addition to Excel, interviewees in large companies use specialized software: SAP (a type of ERP system) and/or PRIMAVERA (an Oracle Project Portfolio Management package) when preparing a project proposal and managing projects. Interviewees in medium-sized companies also use specialized software: Perftech.Largo, Infor LN or another ERP system which includes project management functionality.

The key difference between small and micro companies, and larger companies is the use of specialized project development and management software. Small and micro companies use only Microsoft Excel (a general-purpose tool) for financial planning and management, which has severe shortcomings (compared to specialized solutions) regarding support for collaboration, data management and data security.

Another key difference between small or micro enterprises and large enterprises is the methodology used. Most of the interviewees from small or micro companies do not even mention that they use a project management methodology. Meanwhile most of interviewees employed in large companies manage projects according to the PRINCE2 project management methodology, and they consider the methodology more important than the use of specialized software. The interviewees in large companies also state that the number and size of projects affect the need for purchase or development of specialized software.

Some of the interviewees stated that the call for project or tender conditions (which influence project development and management) vary a lot. Companies of these interviewees have developed their own software solutions that support and simplify certain processes in project development and management instead of seeking specialized project development and management software on the market.

Training of Employees

The interviewees in large- and medium-sized companies are familiarized with the software they use to prepare project proposals systematically, during initial job training. Meanwhile, the employees in small or micro companies stated that the competence of the use of software is already required upon employment and a high degree of self-initiative is expected from employees regarding independent learning of any software used for project management.

Attitude Toward Software

Most of the interviewees believe that their attitude and the attitude of other employees in the company toward the use of software is positive. The interviewees describe the software as indispensable in preparing project proposals.

Conclusion

We have conducted research on a sample of Slovenian companies, successful in EU funded public calls for projects / tenders for co-financing of research and development. We have investigated how companies in the role of applicant carry out project development and management, and through their practices and the use of sociological theories, identified the properties of IT support and other factors that influence the performance of companies in calls for projects.

The results of qualitative research contained in the paradigmatic model (Rodic & Šavrič, 2016) show that the impact of information support on the project organization of work in companies in successful participation in national and community calls can depend on the following:

- The degree of structure in work organization.
- The competencies of employees in the use of specialized project development and management software.
- Employee attitude toward specialized project development and management software.
- The role of the specialized software in companies' project development and management process.

We have also found that all interviewed companies, regardless of their size, use distinct software for administrative project management and financial project management; size and number of projects influences the company need for specialized software; companies prefer electronic (i.e., web based) call applications and project reporting; all interviewed employees are motivated to use project management software.

Companies indirectly influence the attitude of employees toward the software and its effective use through their software training methods. Organization of work in the project proposal development process also depends on the size of the company, with large- and medium-sized companies having a greater transparency and more structured work, and mostly implement the "idea funnel". Regardless of the size of the company, they implement a complete separation of work on the administrative and R&D aspects of a project proposal, and their process of project development follows a sequence of pre-defined phases. The detailed description of the developed grounded theory is available in Šavrič (2016) and will be the subject of further publications.

Authors hope to have contribution to sociological research on interplay of IT and society and have a potential impact in the design and management of public calls for project proposals and contribute to the development of methodology for identifying key factors of company performance in public tenders.

Recommendations

Strategic and project planning must necessarily be closely connected when planning the development of companies, especially if they want to finance their product development from EU funds and thus compete with other companies for the funds. In each of the projects they must in some way clearly demonstrate that the project "matches" the EU strategy (as referred to in the call for projects), which can only be convincingly achieved by developing the company strategy and managing the "idea funnel" of projects with a good working knowledge of the EU development programs. In our research, we found that the most successful large companies with a clear development strategy operate in this way when drawing funds from EU funded calls for projects.

The theoretical aspect of STS states that society affects technology and technology also affects society. If society (i.e., a company as a part of society in the context of this research) does not sufficiently influence the technology (its usability, adaptability to work characteristics, and user suitability), the technology will not be adopted by the users, as it will have more negative than positive effects on the society (increased time to perform a task, duplicated work, inadequate functions, and accessibility of information), which will be manifested in inferior work output. In contrast, an IS, prepared and evaluated with the participation of users and, if necessary, corrected, perhaps even upgraded, will be well received by users, their user experience will be positive, and the positive effect will also be shown in work results.

In the future, it would be interesting to expand the quantitative aspect of the research by conducting a wider survey, based on the results of the interviews. It would also be interesting to study the formal reasons for failure of rejected project proposals; however, as these projects are not funded with public money, these data are not publicly available, and we assume that companies themselves would be reluctant to share their rejection letters. A quantitative survey would provide insight into the relevance of quantitative research results in a wider sample of companies and allow us to examine project development and management process and assess the impact of work methodology and use of IT in both "successful" and "less successful" companies.

References

Abugabah, A., Sanzogni, L., & Poropat, A. (2009). The impact of information systems on user performance: A critical review and theoretical model. *International Conference on Computer Science and Engineering (ICCSE 2009)*. Griffith University, Nathan, Australia: WASET.

Alpar, A., & Kim, M. (1990). A microeconomic approach to the measurement of information technology value. *Journal of Management and Information Systems, 7*, 55–69.

Ashby, W. (1991). *Principles of the Self-organizing Systems: Facts of Systems Science*. New York: Plenum Press.

AXELOS Ltd. (2023). *PRINCE2® Project Management Certifications*. Retrieved 16 6, 2023, from Axelos, https://www.axelos.com/certifications/propath/prince2-project-management

Chametzky, B. (2016). Coding in classic grounded theory: I've done an interview; now what?'. *Sociology Mind, 4*(6), 163–172. doi:10.4236/sm.2016.64014.

Chesbrough, H. (2003). *Open Innovation: The New Imperative for Creating and Profiting from Technology*. Cambridge, MA: Harvard Business School Press.

Cordella, A., & Iannacci, F. (2011). *Information Systems and Organisations*. University of London.

Cozzens, S. (2001). Making disciplines dissapear in STS. In S. Cutcliffe & C. Mitcham (Eds.), *Visions of STS: Counterpoints in Science, Technology and Society Studies* (pp. 51–64). Albany: State University of New York Press.

Edwards, R., & Holland, J. (2013). *What Is Qualitative Interviewing?* London: Bloomsbury.

European Commission. (2020). *SME Definition - User Guide 2020*. Retrieved 3 12, 2023, from https://ec.europa.eu/growth/smes/business-friendly-environment/sme-definition_en

Fischbein, E. (2005). Paradigmatic models. In *Intuition in Science and Mathematics* (Vol. 5, pp. 143–153, doi:10.1007/0-306-47237-6_13). Kluwer Academic Publishers.

Glaser, B., & Strauss, A. (1967). *The Discovery of Grounded Theory: Strategies for Qualitative Research.* Mill Valley, CA: Sociology Press.

Harvard Kennedy School. (2016, 09 06). *Harvard University, Harvard Kennedy School.* Retrieved 3 12, 2023, from Program on Science, Technology & Society, http://sts.hks.harvard.edu/about/whatissts.html

International Organization for Standardization. (2020). *Project, Programme and Portfolio Management—Guidance on Project Management.* Retrieved 3 10, 2023, from https://www.iso.org/standard/74947.html

Kuhn, T.S. (2012). *The Structure of Scientific Revolutions, 1962 (50th Anniversary Edition: 2012).* Chicago: University of Chicago Press.

Laudon, J., & Laudon, K. (2022). *Management Information Systems: Managing the Digital Firm* (17th Edition). Prentice Hall.

Project Management Institute, Inc. (2021). *A Guide to the Project Management Body of Knowledge (PMBOK Guide)* (7th Edition). Newtown Square, PA: Project Management Institute, Inc.

Rai, S.L., & Welker, R.B. (2002). Assessing the validity of IS success models: An empirical test and theoretical analysis. *Information Systems Research, 13*(1), 50–69.

Rip, A. (1994). Science and technology studies and constructive technology assessment. *European Association for the Study of Science and Technology EASST Review, 13*(3), 11–16.

Rodic, B., & Šavrič, J. (2016). Success factors in public calls for project proposals. *39th International Conference on Organizational Science Development: Organizations at Innovation and Digital Transformation Roundabout* (pp. 675–686, doi:10.18690/978-961-286-388-3.53). Maribor: University of Maribor Press.

Šavrič, J., & Rodič, B. (2020). Success factors in public calls for project proposals. In P. Šprajc (Ed.), *39th International Conference on Organizational Science Development Organizations at Innovation and Digital Transformation Roundabout: Conference Proceedings* (pp. 675–685, doi:10.18690/978-961-286-388-3.53). Maribor: Maribor University Press.

Wysocki, K.R. (2019). *Effective Project Management: Traditional, Agile, Extreme, Hybrid.* Indianapolis, IN: John Wiley & Sons, Inc.

7 Comparison of Multi-Criteria Decision Methodologies
Case of Water Management Investment Project

Marjan Brelih and Blaž Rodič

Introduction

Water utility management companies are facing several challenges: aging utility networks, growth of population and populated areas, and rising environmental standards, and thus require a methodological, decision analysis-based approach to modernization and growth of water supply networks. Reliability of supplying consumers with drinking water refers to the capability of a water supply system to provide a steady supply of safe drinking water to its final consumers in the long term. The management of water supply systems has been the subject of several research projects as presented in Cohen (2003), Alegre et al. (2013), Gunnarsdottir et al. (2015), Marie et al. (2013), and Menaia et al. (2015). To ensure that water supply systems fulfill their goals, it is necessary to optimize the operation of existing water supply networks (Cherchi et al., 2015). This process can take several years, even decades (Creaco et al., 2014). A large number of experts from interdisciplinary fields, such as project management, information and communication technologies, finance, hydraulic modeling, and management of water supply systems, collaborate in this process, thus a formal decision-making methodology and a IT-based decision support system are necessary to ensure decision quality and consistency.

The water management investment project case selected for the Multi-Criteria Decision Methodology (MCDM) comparison and development comes from our research and development work with a 70-year-old multi-utility service company (subsequently referred to as "operator"), which manages numerous projects in the field of water management for various customers (water utility companies). With 4,000 employees, it is one of the largest companies of this type in South Europe. Due to the complexity of the decision problem, the operator has requested our assistance in building a decision model to evaluate the possibilities for participation in projects with potential customers.

DOI: 10.4324/9781003376583-9

Research Aims

The main goal of this project was to use design science and MCDM methodologies to develop a hybrid decision-making model combining two diverse MCDMs and implementing the decision rules and criteria based on the operator's expert knowledge and expectations. To this end, we have compared several existing MCDMs in terms of differences in decision model results, model complexity, and model transparency.

Our main research question that we have sought to answer was: what are the potential benefits of combining qualitative and quantitative MCDM methodologies in a single water management investment decision model?

Theoretical Background – Multi-Criteria Decision Methodology

Our approach to project selection is based on Multi-Criteria Decision Methodology (MCDM). An overview of MCDM and development of this methodology is available in Fishburn (1967), Keeney and Raiffa (1976), Keeney and Fishburn (1974), Keeney (1982), Chankong and Haimes (1983), Fülöp (2005), Bohanec et al. (1995), and Kolios et al. (2016). The main characteristic of MCDM methods is that the decision problem is broken down into sub-problems, down to the level of individual option characteristics, which are easier to define or measure than a large complex problem. The decision problem is then structured as a hierarchical set of criteria, which can be presented as a tree, with end nodes ("leaves") representing the elementary (measurable) characteristics of the options, joined into aggregated criteria, with the final node ("root") of the tree structure representing the aggregated score of an option, used to rank all options. Formal description of such a model involves one or several utility functions used to calculate utility of each option according to the decision-makers' preferences (Krause et al., 2015).

Use of MCDM is a proven approach in project planning (Bohanec et al., 1995; Nowak & Nowak, 2013), with solid theoretical basis (Fishburn, 1967; Keeney & Fishburn, 1974; Keeney & Raiffa, 1976; Chankong & Haimes, 1983), and a large choice of tested methodologies (Keeney, 1982; Kolios et al., 2016).

According to Zavadskas et al. (2016), formal decision-making methods can be used to help improve the overall sustainability of industries and organizations. While history of MCDM can be traced to Benjamin Franklin, who allegedly had a simple paper system for deciding important issues, modern MCDMs started to emerge with the development of Operations Research and Management Science. Recently, there has been a significant development of new decision methodologies combining diverse MCDM techniques, i.e., hybrid MCDM (HMCDM) methods.

Zavadskas et al. (2016) presented an overview of hybrid approaches as improvements for decision-making related to sustainability issues using on a sample of 2,450 HMCDM related scientific publications the Web of Science Core Collection published from 1999 to 2015. The authors state that while several new approaches for HMCDMs have been developed and published in recent years, there is a lack of a critical review of these methods. An interesting observation is that water management ranks lowest in research volume in the overview of 32 research areas that utilize HMCDMs, which illustrates the importance of research presented in this chapter.

According to Zavadskas et al. (2016), several shortcomings of singular MCDMs can be solved by combining two or more methods into a hybrid method and developing a set of recommendations for decision-makers. Mardani (2015) and Zavadskas et al. (2016) state that for complex decision problems the selection of an appropriate method involves compromises and trade-offs. No method can be considered as the "best" either for a general or for a particular problem. Furthermore, different MCDMs can yield different rankings of decision variants. Zavadskas et al. (2016) proposed the modeling of a problem using several methods and integrating results. However, the integration of results poses an additional decision problem.

Previous Research – MCDM in Water Management Projects

Miscalculated decision-making in asset acquisition and project execution can have long-lasting economic consequences for the operator as well as for the manager of the water supply system (Cherchi et al., 2015). A strong link exists between water supply and energy consumption (Olsson, 2015). Understanding this relationship can ensure profound energy savings through thorough technical and managerial planning. This awareness creates and increases management efficiency, which ensures that consumers receive high-quality service while minimizing energy and water consumption (Basupi & Kapelan, 2013; Hoque, 2014). In an urban environment, efficiency in the water sector is closely related to managing the efficiency of the public (subsequently referred to as "consumer") drinking water supply, as well as efficient water use at the consumer level (Fan et al., 2014). The management processes of drinking water supply are mostly inefficient, as a large quantity of drinking water is lost in the distribution network even before it reaches the final consumer (Barry, 2007).

We have decided to use MCDM methodologies verified in the field of water management and other environmental fields as presented in Hoque (2014), Fan et al. (2014), Menaia et al. (2015), Olsson (2015), EU reference document (2015), Barry (2007), Kabak and Ruan (2011), Lipušček et al. (2010),

Velasquez and Hester (2013), Karni et al. (1990), and Zanakis et al. (1998). To gain the benefits of both qualitative and quantitative methodologies, we have decided to develop a new hybrid methodology combining both approaches.

The Multi-Attribute Utility Theory (MAUT) methodology was selected to model the quantitative aspects of the decision, while the Decision Expert (DEX) methodology was selected to model the qualitative aspects of the decision (Keeney, 1977). An overview of MAUT is available in Dyer (2005), while DEX is documented in Bohanec (2014) and Bohanec et al. (2013b).

MAUT is a structured quantitative decision-making methodology designed to handle the trade-offs among multiple objectives, developed in the 1960s. MAUT is based on expected utility theory (Von Winterfeldt & Edwards, 1986; French, 1988), i.e., it uses a systematic approach for quantifying the decision-makers' preferences by rescaling the values of criteria using a given scale (e.g., price in EUR, weight in kg) onto a $[0\ldots1]$ scale with 0 representing the worst utility and 1 the best. Due to its quantitative nature and thus precision, MAUT enables us to differentiate between similar options. However, it is not always possible to define exact numerical values for criteria of real-life projects Zanakis et al. (1998).

DEX methodology has been originally developed in 1979 as an expert system shell and continues to undergo improvements (Bohanec et al., 2013b). In the last 30 years, a broad range of complex decision models have been applied to diverse areas, such as industry, agronomy, health sciences, finance, and ecology (Bohanec et al., 1995; Bohanec et al., 2000; Kontić et al., 2006; Bohanec et al., 2007; Bohanec et al., 2008; Žnidaršič et al., 2008; Rozman et al., 2009; Lipušček et al., 2010; Bohanec et al., 2013a; Bohanec et al., 2013b; De Feo & De Gisi, 2014). DEX methodology combines elements of expert systems and MCDM. The main recognizable characteristic of the DEX methodology is its ability to use qualitative instead of numerical variables. Values are expressed in classes rather than numbers, for instance, "low", "appropriate", and "excellent". Therefore, the DEX methodology is more suitable for decision support in less struc-tured problems or where criteria cannot be measured on a numerical scale. In addition, for assessing projects, the DEX methodology uses simple if-then rules, which the decision-makers may find easier to express their knowledge with and to understand than mathematical models. Descriptive grades entail approaches different from numeric values, where we may use mathematical utility functions to calculate values of aggregated criteria. Utility functions in the DEX methodology are determined by sets of criteria and are thus non-linear and discrete. The advantage of defining functions with simple if-then rules lies in the freedom in expressing utility functions. Complex utility functions may be easier to express with a set of simple rules than with relatively limited numerical functions as in the case the MAUT methodology.

Methods and Techniques Included in This Case Study

The research methods used within the presented case study include design science as the research framework, and MCDM as the main artefact development methodology. Design science has been an important strategy in decision support systems (DSS) research since the field's inception in the early 1970s, as evidenced by the overview of 1,466 DSS design-science research papers presented by Arnott and Pervan (2012, 2014). Our approach to investment project selection modeling is based on MCDM (Kabak & Ruan, 2011). We used known and tested methodologies, quantitative (i.e., MAUT methodology) and qualitative (i.e., the DEX methodology), in the decision-making model.

Design Science Research

Design science research is a process of creating new knowledge through design of novel and innovative artefacts and analysis of their performance with reflection to enable improvement and understand the behavior of aspects of Information Systems (IS) (Vaishnavi & Kuechler, 2015). According to Hevner et al. (2004), design science research in IS addresses the so-called "wicked" problem, characterized by unstable requirements and constraints, complex interaction between subcomponents, inherent flexibility to change design processes, dependence on human cognitive and social abilities. Considering all these characteristics, we concluded that the problem of water management investment decision modeling matches the description given.

Hevner (2007) introduces the three design science research cycles in a design research project: the relevance cycle, the rigor cycle, and the design cycle. The research process model as presented in Vaishnavi and Kuechler (2015) consists of awareness of the problem, suggestion, development, evaluation, and conclusion. These steps and cycles, together with the design science research checklist (Hevner & Chatterjee, 2010), were used as a guideline to develop the artefact.

A design science research project begins and ends with the relevance cycle: first the application domain and problems and opportunities are identified, and the requirements and testing criteria are developed. The relevance cycle in our project was done with continuous communication with the operator's experts, through which we were able to identify and represent the opportunities and problems in the actual application environment and test the project results as presented in the project evaluation subsection.

The aim of our design science research project was to develop a technology-based solution, i.e., a new and innovative decision support

Comparison of Multi-Criteria Decision Methodologies   123

system, to a relevant problem of water management investment project selection. This has provided the application context and the required inputs for our development: user requirements and the evaluation or acceptance criteria for the developed solution.

Selection of MCDM Methodologies

In this part of the project, we have examined previous related MCDM, HMCDM, and water management project related research, existing decision support methods and tools used by the operator (client), as well as their experiences and expertise that define the state of the art in the application domain of the research. This has provided the grounding theories and methods along with domain experience and expertise from the foundation's knowledge base into the research, which corresponds with the rigor cycle in the design science research methodology. The rigor cycle provides past knowledge to the research project to ensure its innovation. It is contingent on the researchers to thoroughly research and reference the knowledge base to ensure that the designs produced are research contributions and not routine designs based upon the application of well-known processes (Hevner et al., 2004).

Neither the quantitative nor the qualitative methodologies meet all the necessary requirements for solving the operator's decision problem. We have considered combining quantitative and qualitative values in one decision-making model, with the intention to assess even small differences between projects, which we consider decisively influence the final assessment. When using purely qualitative methodology it often happens that two or more projects receive the same final utility score, making the ranking and final selection difficult. Thus, we aimed to use weights for the quantitative criteria and if-then rules for the qualitative ones in the same decision-making model. The small quantitative differences between projects, which are otherwise in the same qualitative class (i.e., having same utility score), make it possible to rank the projects or select one for implementation. Since the combination of quantitative and qualitative MCDM methods in a single model has not been previously used to solve the presented water management investment decision modeling problem, our contribution can be seen as a significant improvement to the decision-making methodology.

Due to its quantitative nature, MAUT enables precise evaluation of options, while allowing the use of different (linear, non-linear) utility functions, making one of the more popular MCDM methods (Velasquez & Hester, 2013). However, decision problems can involve both quantitative and qualitative assessments. When dealing with qualitative criteria, where the emphasis is on subjective assessment, or which may be difficult to express numerically, it is difficult to define strict formal features. A similar situation arises in cases where qualitative information is easier to understand. We could define numeric values to qualitative assessments, e.g., 0, 1, and 2 for unacceptable, acceptable, and excellent, respectively. In many cases, it may be difficult or perhaps impossible to imagine the differences between the various transformations. In such instances, the usage of a qualitative methodology like the DEX methodology is preferred. If we want experts from different fields to understand the process of modeling knowledge, we should allow them to use natural language instead of converting values. Consequently, it becomes easier for them to interpret the final grade. A good understanding of grades plays a key or crucial role in the decision-making process.

Through the years, the DEX methodology has been proven to be simpler to understand (Bohanec et al., 2013), but less precise than MAUT methodology. The operator's experts conveyed that while MAUT provides a higher resolution, its results are less understandable, especially when we include the numerical values of the qualitative criteria in the model.

MCDM Model Development

In this part of the project, we have developed the software artefact with integrated novel HMCDM. Development was done in close cooperation with the operator (client) experts providing constant feedback in the development loop, which relates to the design cycle in the design science research methodology. The essence of design cycle lies in generating design alternatives and evaluating the alternatives against requirements until a satisfactory design is achieved. The internal design cycle is the heart of any design science research project, and it iterates more rapidly between the construction of an artifact, its evaluation, and subsequent feedback to refine the design further (Hevner, 2007).

To allow the use of most appropriate modeling method for each criterion, we have combined both qualitative (DEX) and quantitative (MAUT) methods in the developed decision model. We have implemented the IT artefact containing the decision model and the user interface in Visual C#.NET programming language. The quality of our research designs has been tested through inclusion of operator (client) experts in the development loop and the evaluation of the developed artefact using a real-life decision problem involving several options in a water management investment project.

We have initially designed an unstructured criteria list to evaluate projects by incorporating expert knowledge during a brainstorming session with the operator's experts (Keeney, 2012). From this list, we eliminated double entries, overlapping criteria, or criteria that did not significantly affect the final decision. Together with the operator's experts, we divided these criteria into

Investment project evaluation

Customer assessment	Investment criteria	Data analysis
Risk assessment	Performance criteria	Adequacy and quality of GIS data
Customer size class	Financial criteria	Adequacy and quality of process data
	Strategic importance	

Figure 7.1 Overview of the top-level criteria in the proposed hierarchical multi-criteria decision-making model.

three main groups (Figure 7.1), that is, "customer assessment", "investment criteria", and "data analysis", which include the suitability of geographical information system (GIS) data and process data of the water supply system. To evaluate the "customer assessment" criterion, we need the following information: size of the customer's organization, the number and availability of employees to work on the project, the educational level of the employees, credit ratings of the organization, its ownership structure, and assessment of business risk in a long-term collaboration with the customer. The "investment criteria" criterion is evaluated from the perspective of profitability, the amount of bank guarantee, funding sources, project deadline, contractual obligations, and type of contract. We also assess the strategic importance of the project from the viewpoint of the operator.

As mentioned, the tree of criteria is composed of quantitative and qualitative criteria. We assigned all criteria short, unique, and easy-to-understand names. To facilitate the operator's understanding, we added a brief description for each criterion. As we used different types of criteria, that is, quantitative and qualitative, we represented them in the tree of criteria with the following symbols: $\boxed{1}$ for quantitative criteria and $\boxed{a}$ for qualitative criteria.

In Figure 7.2, the tree of criteria provides the descriptions and value domains. Quantitative criteria are described as units of measurement and their value domains (upper and lower value limits). The value domains of qualitative criteria are described as an ordered set of preference values, starting with the least desirable value (appearing in **bold**) and ending with the most desirable value (depicted in ***bold italics***) (Bohanec, 2014).

Utility Function

After defining the tree of criteria and its value domains, we have defined the utility functions. The presented decision-making model contains the

Criteria tree	Description	Original value domain
Evaluation	Final evaluation	Unacc., Acc., Good, *Excel.*
Customer	Customer assessment	Unacc., Acc., Good, *Excel.*
Risk	Risk business assessment	High, Med., *Low*
Shareholder	Shareholders structure	Private, Mixed, *Public*
Payment habits	Customer ability to pay	Defaulting, Irregular, *Regular*
Risk assessment	The assessment of the risk	High, Med., *Low*
Size class	Customer size class	Unacc., Acc., Good, *Excel.*
Enterprise size	Company size category	Micro, Small, Med., *Large*
Employees	Assessment of properly trained employees	Unacc., Acc., Good, *Excel.*
Number	Number of assigned employees	Small, Med. *Large*
		$0 - 25$ [people]
Structure	Educational structure of employees	Unacc., Good. *Excel.*
Availability	Working hours per week	None, Small, Med. *Large*
		$0 - 40$ [hour]
Investment	Investment assessment	Unacc., Acc., Good, *Excel.*
Performance	Performance assessment	Unacc., Good, *Excel.*
Contract model	Type of contract model	Purchase, Installation, *Optimisation*
Contractor	Contractor structure	Subcontr., Mixed, *Own*
Deadline	Project deadline	Short, Middle, *Good*
		$0 - 60$ [months]
Finance	Financial construction assessment	Unacc., Acc., Good, *Excel.*
Funding	Available funding sources	Credit, Fee, *Cohesion*
Bank guarantee	Size of bank guarantee	High, Med., *Low*
		$1000 - 0$ [monetary unit]
Profitability	Expected profitability	Unacc., Acc., Good, *Excel.*
Effectiveness	Effectiveness points criteria	Low, Med., *High*
		$0 - 100$ [points]
Excellence	Excellence points criteria	Low, Med., *High*
		$0 - 100$ [points]
Strat.importance	Strategic importance evaluation	Low, Med., *High*
Internal	Strategic importance for the operator	Low, Med., *High*
Buyer	Buyer type	Existing, New cust., *New market*
Collaboration	Collaboration type	Purchase only, Short-term, *Long-term*
New research	Developing new services	None, Partial, *New study*
External	Strategic importance for the purchaser	Low, Med., *High*
Spare capacity	Available water after losses and consumption	High, Med., *Low*
		$50 - 0$ [%]
User growth trend	The growth rate of the water customers	No, Small, *Large*
Data	Adequacy of data	$0 - 100$ [points]
GIS	Adequacy and quality of GIS	$0 - 100$ [points]
Process data	Adequacy and quality of process data	$0 - 100$ [points]
Operation data	Adequacy and quality of operation data	$0 - 100$ [points]
Sales data	Adequacy and quality of sales data	$0 - 100$ [points]
Customer profiles	Adequacy and quality of customer profiles	$0 - 100$ [points]

Legend: Unacc. - Unacceptable, Acc. - Acceptable, Excel. - Excellence, Med. - Medium,
New cust. - New customer, Subcontr. - Subcontractor

Quantitative criteria   Values of quantitative criteria are converted into qualitative classes
Qualitative criteria

Figure 7.2 The tree of criteria with definitions and value domains.

quantitative as well as the qualitative criteria, and therefore, the functions were defined for conversion from one type of criterion to another type.

Regarding the quantitative criteria: as all criteria are not equally important, and their relative importance is expressed in weights. To calculate the value of the aggregated criterion "Data", we used Eq. (7.1) for the weighted sum:

$$Data_{P_i} = GIS_{P_i} * W(GIS) + Process\ data_{P_i} * W(Process\ data) \qquad (7.1)$$

where P_i presents project i and $W(X)$ presents the weight of criterion X.

Regarding the qualitative criteria, the DEX methodology uses simple if-then rules as its fundamental decision mechanism (Bohanec et al., 2013a). For each combination of the value domains of the subordinate criteria, we chose an appropriate value domain of the superior criterion. For example, consider the aggregate criterion "Risk". It was divided into three subcategories: "Shareholders", "Payment habits", and "Risk assessment". Each one of them has a three-point scale:

Shareholders$_{V.D.}$ = {Private, Mixed, Public}
Payment habits$_{V.D.}$ = {Defaulting, Irregular, Regular}
Risk assessment$_{V.D.}$ = {High, Med., Low}

Below is an example for easier understanding of a single rule:

IF Shareholders Is Public
AND Payment habits Is Regular
AND Risk assessment Is Med.
THEN Risk Is Low

There are 27 rules or combinations. They are defined as the following Cartesian product [Eq. (7.2)]:

$$Shareholders_{V.D.} \times Payment\ habits_{V.D.} \times Risk\ assessment_{V.D.} \qquad (7.2)$$

Regarding the conversion of values from quantitative to qualitative, we first provide the justification for converting a quantitative scale into a qualitative one, namely, a better and easier understanding of the utility functions. Experts can use one type of utility function to express the relationship between sub-criteria, even though the same function could also be written mathematically. Consider the following example: if the value lies between 30 and 50, then this criterion has a weight of 100%. Operator's experts found it easier to read and understand simple rules than mathematical expressions that may include complex programing logic. In the latter case, experts lose the focus necessary for understanding decision problems.

Project Evaluation

In this part of the project, we have tested the developed artefact which integrated the novel HMCDM. Testing was done using a real-life example

128   *Marjan Brelih and Blaž Rodič*

investment project, which relates to the final part of the relevance cycle in the design science research methodology. As elaborated by Hevner (2007),

> ... the relevance cycle initiates design science research with an application context that not only provides the requirements for the research (e.g., the opportunity/problem to be addressed) as inputs but also defines acceptance criteria for the ultimate evaluation of the research results.

The key question of the relevance cycle therefore is: "Does the design artifact improve the environment and how can this improvement be measured?" As output from the design science research must be returned into the environment for study and evaluation in the application domain, the user feedback provided an important input in the process of artefact and HMCDM methodology refinement.

The artefact has been tested on a decision problem which included four projects as decision options. The projects were named P1, P2, P3, and P4. We assessed them according to the basic criteria (Table 7.1). We marked the least and the most desirable value domains for the qualitative and

Table 7.1 Basic criteria values for options P1, P2, P3, and P4

Criterion	*P1*	*P2*	*P3*	*P4*
Shareholders	**Public**	**Public**	**Public**	**Public**
Payment habits	**Regular**	**Regular**	**Regular**	**Regular**
Risk assessment	Med.	Med.	**Low**	Med.
Enterprise size	Med.	Med.	**Large**	Med.
Number	3 →**Large**	1 → **Small**	8 → **Large**	3 → **Large**
Structure	Good	**Excel.**	**Excel.**	**Excel.**
Availability	5 → Small	9 → Med.	24 →**Large**	8 → Med.
Contract model	Installation	**Optimization**	Installation	**Optimization**
Contractor	Mixed	Mixed	**Subcontr.**	**Own**
Deadline	5 → **Short**	59 →**Good**	24 → **Good**	6 → **Short**
Fundings	**Cohesion**	Fee	**Credit**	Fee
Bank guarantee	675 → **High**	803 → **High**	471 → Med.	99 → **Low**
Effectiveness	60	54	66	78
Excellence	35	25	37	38
Buyer	New cust.	**New market**	**New market**	New cust.
Collaboration	Short term	**Long term**	**Long term**	Short-term
New research	Partial	**New study**	None	**New study**
Spare capacity	25 → Med.	8 →**Low**	33 → **High**	25 → Med.
User growth trend	**No**	**Large**	**Large**	Small
GIS	75	80	65	95
Operation data	94	95	85	97
Sales data	91	88	75	93
Customer profiles	80	80	70	90

Comparison of Multi-Criteria Decision Methodologies 129

Table 7.2 Simple if-then rules for the criterion "external"

Rule	Spare capacity	User growth trend	External
1	**High**	**No**	**Low**
2	**High**	Small	**Low**
3	**High**	*Large*	Med.
4	Med.	**No**	**Low**
5	Med.	Small	Med.
6	Med.	*Large*	Med.
7	*Low*	No	Med.
8	*Low*	Small	*High*
9	*Low*	*Large*	*High*

quantitative values in **bold** and ***bold italics***, respectively, depending on the defined value domain for each individual criterion.

Criteria have been aggregated using simple if-then rules, as shown in Table 7.2. For example, the first rule states that if the "spare capacity" criterion is assessed as **High** and the "user growth trend" is assessed as **No**, then "external" equals **Low**.

Using aggregation utility functions, the decision-making model can calculate values of superior (aggregated) criteria. The result is the final evaluation score for each project. The advantages of the presented decision-making model include the use of both quantitative and qualitative types of criteria and the preservation of original values; therefore, in addition to a qualitative estimation, we gain a quantitative value. Because we preserved all the input data, we can now distinguish between projects in the same class.

For every qualitative aggregation function, the result consists of a qualitative value and a numeric value that describes that project more precisely. Value domains of qualitative criteria are an ordered set of preference values (also referred to as qualitative classes), while the numeric value ([0..1]) defines the position of the project within a qualitative class. Using this principle, all aggregated criteria are assigned both a qualitative value and a numeric value. However, a linear or non-linear (part-wise) conversion function needs to be defined for each of the quantitative criteria. Since such criteria have both quantitative and qualitative value domains, their qualitative values are shown in brackets following a quantitative value that was calculated prior to using a conversion function. Table 7.3 showing the complete project evaluation includes two such criteria: "profitability" and "data".

Figure 7.3 presents the graphical view of project evaluation by the final score (evaluation) and its direct sub-criteria, with quantitative and qualitative values, respectively, represented via points and intervals (horizontal

130 Marjan Brelih and Blaž Rodič

Table 7.3 Evaluations of projects for aggregated criteria

Criteria	P1	P2	P3	P4
Evaluation	*Excel.* [0.37, 0.45]	*Excel.* [0.72, 0.80]	*Excel.* [0.56, 0.64]	*Excel.* [0.79, 0.86]
Customer	*Excel.* [0.44, 0.70]	*Excel.* [0.46, 0.73]	*Excel.* [0.70, 0.98]	*Excel.* [0.47, 0.73]
Risk	*Low* [0.35, 0.90]	*Low* [0.35, 0.90]	*Low* [0.46, 1.00]	*Low* [0.35, 0.90]
Size class	Good [0.51, 0.69]	Good [0.63, 0.80]	*Excel.* [0.66, 0.88]	Good [0.65, 0.82]
Employees	Good [0.18, 0.37]	Good [0.40, 0.60]	*Excel.* [0.42, 0.74]	Good [0.45, 0.65]
Investment	Acc. [0.33, 0.54]	*Excel.* [0.36, 0.58]	Good [0.43, 0.64]	*Excel.* [0.39, 0.58]
Performance	*Unacc.* [0.47, 0.85]	*Excel.* [0.43, 0.82]	Good [0.26, 0.63]	Good [0.50, 0.87]
Finance	Good [0.24, 0.65]	Good [0.18, 0.59]	Good [0.57, 0.98]	*Excel.* [0.43, 0.83]
Profitability	47.50 [Good]	39.50 [Good]	51.50 [*Excel.*]	58.00 [*Excel.*]
Strat. importance	*Low* [0.48, 0.71]	*High* [0.58, 0.86]	Med. [0.53, 0.76]	Med. [0.48, 0.71]
Internal	Med. [0.30, 0.86]	*High* [0.48, 1.00]	*High* [0.13, 0.66]	*High* [0.13, 0.65]
External	*Low* [0.45, 0.73]	*High* [0.38, 0.68]	Med. [0.31, 0.58]	Med. [0.18, 0.45]
Data	78.25 [Good]	81.98 [*Excel.*]	67.92 [Good]	94.72 [*Excel.*]
Process data	89.15	88.63	77.70	93.80

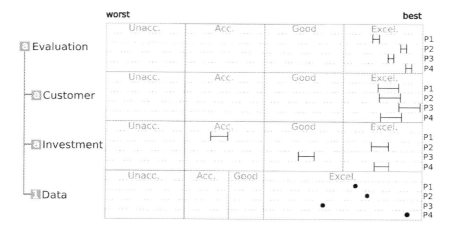

Figure 7.3 Graphical representation of projects ranked by selected criteria.

bars), extending from the minimal to the maximal value within a qualitative class. Similar visualizations can be used to explain any aggregate criterion in the model. This type of presentation helped us to easily explain the final evaluation to the decision-makers. The experts found this ability of the model to explain assessments as the most important advantage of the novel (HMCDM) decision-making methodology.

Conclusion

We have developed a novel hybrid decision-making (HMCDM) methodology and used it to develop an artefact (software), a decision support system intended to be used for the selection of water management investment projects. The main part of the artefact is a decision model within which we have implemented several utility. We have created a tree of criteria after consulting and brainstorming with the operator's experts. For each criterion, we defined value domains, and we created appropriate utility functions for aggregated criteria. Choice of value function per criterion depended on what the operator's expert group found to be the most applicable. The artefact was then tested on a real-life example decision problem and used to evaluate four options, i.e., four potential projects (P1–P4). The transparency of the model structure and its easily understandable utility functions allow the decision-maker to comprehend the result of evaluation immediately. The operator provided us with data describing each project in terms of the basic criteria listed in the tree structure. The final evaluation results were presented to the operator's expert team.

We were able to answer our main research question: What are the potential benefits of combining qualitative and quantitative MCDM methodologies in a single water management investment decision model?

Therefore, the advantage of the presented decision-making model over purely quantitative models is its ability to include qualitative criteria where required. Despite the absence of exact numerical values, the proposed model allows the evaluation of all options and the aggregation of qualitative and quantitative criteria into a single value, used to rank the options. Quantitative methodologies tend to be preferred over qualitative methodologies as quantitative criteria assessments are not transformed into classes, and we can distinguish between projects within the same class. Combining the quantitative and the qualitative criteria in the same decision-making model maintains the criteria-level differences between the projects within the decision tree all the way to the root criterion (overall project utility value). The ability to conduct quantitative and qualitative assessments for an individual criterion represents a novel and valuable functionality for the participants in decision-making process.

The artefact containing the novel decision-making model combining qualitative and quantitative MCDM methodologies offers new possibilities, as it allows the operator's experts to gain a better understanding of the decision problem and assess projects according to individual project criteria. The results of the analyses allowed the decision-makers to analytically perceive the differences between the projects, and consequently, to make more informed decisions. We tested our decision-making model on a real-world problem with actual projects, namely, the selection of the most suitable investment water supply systems project. Using the proposed decision-making model, we can conduct the quantitative and qualitative assessments of all potential projects. Limitations of our research stem from the specifics of the water management investment processes, which are mostly dependent on the size of the operator's water supply network. Therefore, the developed approach and (adapted) artefact can be reliably expected to be valuable to water utility operators of similar size.

Recommendations

The presented methods represent an innovative approach to business decision modeling in the field of water utility management, with potential for improvement of decision quality and transparency and consequently business management as well as environmental management, thus supporting sustainable water management development policies. The potential for future development includes the integration of further MCDM methods, and custom value functions, which would improve the method and artefact flexibility and potential for use in other decision domains. Additionally, the documentation of the decision-making process could be enhanced to facilitate the monitoring of decision quality and comparison with non-MCDM supported project decisions.

References

Alegre, H., Coelho, S.T., Covas, D.C., Almeida, M.D., & Cardoso, A. (2013). A utility-tailored methodology for integrated asset management of urban water infrastructure. *Water Science and Technology, 13*(6), 1444–1451. doi:10.2166/ws.2013.108

Arnott, D., & Pervan, G. (2012). Design science in decision support systems research: An assessment using the Hevner, March, Park, and Ram Guidelines. *Journal of the Association for Information Systems, 13*(11), 923–949. doi:10.17705/1jais.00315

Arnott, D., & Pervan, G. (2014). A critical analysis of decision support systems research revisited: The rise of design science. *Journal of Information Technology, 29*(4), 269–293. doi:10.1057/jit.2014.16

Comparison of Multi-Criteria Decision Methodologies   133

Barry, J.A. (2007). *Watergy: Energy and water efficiency in municipal water supply and wastewater treatment.* Retrieved from http://www.gwp.org/globalassets/global/toolbox/references/watergy.-water-efficiency-in-municipal-water-supply-and-wastewater-treatment-the-alliance-to-save-energy-2007.pdf

Basupi, I., & Kapelan, Z. (2013). Flexible water distribution system design under future demand uncertainty. *Journal of Water Resources Planning and Management, 141*(4), 1–14. doi:10.1061/(ASCE)WR.1943-5452.0000416

Bohanec, M. (2014). *DEXi: Program for multi-attribute decision making, user's manual, version 4.01. IJS Report DP-9989.* Ljubljana, Slovenia: Jožef Stefan Institute. Retrieved from http://kt.ijs.si/MarkoBohanec/pub/DEXiManual401.pdf

Bohanec, M., Aprile, G., Costante, M., Foti, M., & Trdin, N. (2013a). Decision support model for the assessment of bank reputational risk. *Proceedings of the 16th International Conference Information Society IS, Ljubljana, Slovenia, October 7–11*, 11–14.

Bohanec, M., Cortet, J., Griffiths, B., Žnidaršič, M., Debeljak, M., Caul, S., ..., Krogh, P.H. (2007). A qualitative multi-attribute model for assessing the impact of cropping systems on soil quality. *Pedobiologia, 51*(3), 239–250. doi:10.1016/j.pedobi.2007.03.006

Bohanec, M., Messean, A., Scatasta, S., Angevin, F., Griffiths, B., Henning Krogh, P., ...Džeroski, S. (2008). A qualitative multi-attribute model for economic and ecological assessment of genetically modified crops. *Ecological Modelling, 251*(1-3), 247–261. doi:10.1016/j.ecolmodel.2008.02.016

Bohanec, M., Rajkovič, V., Bratko, I., Zupan, B., & Znidarsič, M. (2013b). DEX methodology: Three decades of qualitative multi-attribute modelling. *Informatica, 37*, 49–54.

Bohanec, M., Rajkovič, V., Semolič, B., & Pogačnik, A. (1995). Knowledge-based portfolio analysis for project evaluation. *Information and Management, 28*(5), 293–302. doi:10.1016/0378-7206(94)00048-N

Bohanec, M., Zupan, B., & Rajkovič, V. (2000). Applications of qualitative multi-attribute decision models in health care. *International Journal of Medical Informatics, 2000*(58-59), 191–205. doi:10.1016/S1386-5056(00)00087-3

Chankong, V., & Haimes, Y. (1983). *Multiobjective Decision Making: Theory and Methodology.* Amsterdam: North-Holland.

Cherchi, C., Badruzzaman, M., Oppenheimer, J., Bros, C.M., & Jacangelo, J.G. (2015). Energy and water quality management systems for water utility's operations: A review. *Journal of Environmental Management, 153*, 108–120. doi:10.1016/j.jenvman.2015.01.051

Cohen, J. (2003). Human population: The next half century. *Science, 302*(5648), 1172–1175. doi:10.1126/science.1088665

Creaco, E., Franchini, M., & Walski, T.M. (2014). Accounting for phasing of construction within the design of water distribution networks. *Journal of Water Resources Planning and Management, 140*(5), 598–606. doi:10.1061/(ASCE)WR.1943-5452.0000358

De Feo, G., & De Gisi, S. (2014). Using MCDA and GIS for hazardous waste landfill siting considering land. *Waste Manage, 34*(11), 2225–2238. doi:10.1016/j.wasman.2014.05.028

134 Marjan Brelih and Blaž Rodič

Dyer, J.S. (2005). *Maut-Multiattribute Utility Theory*. New York: Springer. doi: 10.1007/0-387-23081-5_7

European Union. (2015). *EU reference document – Good practices on leakage management WFD CIS WG PoM*. Luxembourg: Office for Official Publications of the European Communities. Retrieved from https://circabc.europa.eu/sd/a/1ddfba34-e1ce-4888-b031-6c559cb28e47/Good%20Practices%20on%20Leakage%20Management%20-%20Main%20Report_Final.pdf.

Fan, L., Wang, F., Liu, G., Yang, X., & Qin, W. (2014). Public perception of water consumption and its effects on water conservation behavior. *Water, 6*(6), 1771–1784. doi:10.3390/w6061771

Fishburn, P. (1967). Conjoint measurement in utility theory with incomplete product sets. *Journal of Mathematical Psychology, 4*(1), 104–119. doi:10.1016/0022

French, S. (1988). *Reading in Decision Analysis*. London: Chapman and Hall.

Fülöp, J. (2005). *Introduction to decision making methods*. Retrieved from http://academic.evergreen.edu/projects/bdei/documents/decisionmakingmethods.pdf

Gunnarsdottir, M.J., Gardarsson, S.M., & Bartram, J. (2015). Developing a national framework for safe drinking water: Case study from Iceland. *International Journal of Hygiene and Environmental Health, 218*(2), 196–202. doi:10.1016/j.ijheh.2014.10.003

Hevner, A.R. (2007). A three cycle view of design science research. *Scandinavian Journal of Information Systems, 19*(2), 87–92. Retrieved from http://aisel.aisnet.org/sjis/vol19/iss2/4

Hevner, A., & Chatterjee, S. (2010). *Design Science Research in Information Systems*. New York: Springer. doi:10.1007/978-1-4419-5653-8_2

Hevner, A., March, S., Park, J., & Ram, S. (2004). Design science research in information systems. *MIS Quarterly, 28*(1), 75–105.

Hoque, S.F. (2014). *Water Conservation in Urban Households: The Role of Policies, Prices and Technology*. London: IWA Publishing.

Kabak, O., & Ruan, D. (2011). A comparison study of fuzzy MADM methods in nuclear safeguards evaluation. *Journal of Global Optimization, 51*(2), 209–226. doi:10.1007/s10898-010-9601-1

Karni, R., Sanchez, P., & Rao Tummala, V.M. (1990). A comparative study of multiattribute decision making methodologies. *Theory and Decision, 29*(3), 203–222. doi:10.1007/BF00126802

Keeney, R. (1977). The art of assessing multiattribute utility functions. *Organizational Behavior and Human Performance, 19*(2), 267–310. doi:10.1016/0030-5073(77)90065-4

Keeney, R.L. (1982). Decision analysis: An overview. *Operations Research, 30*(5), 803–838. Retrieved from http://links.jstor.org/sici?sici=0030-364X%28198209%2F10%2930%3A5%3C803%3ADAAO%3E2.0.CO%3B2-Y

Keeney, R. (2012). Value-focused brainstorming. *Decision Analysis, 9*(4), 303–313. doi:10.1287/deca.1120.0251

Keeney, R., & Fishburn, P. (1974). Seven independence concepts and continuous multiattribute utility functions. *Journal of Mathematical Psychology, 11*(3), 294–327. doi:10.1016/0022-2496(74)90024-8

Comparison of Multi-Criteria Decision Methodologies 135

Keeney, R., & Raiffa, H. (1976). *Decisions with Multiple Objectives*. New York: John Wiley & Sons.

Kolios, A., Mytilinou, V., Lozano-Minguez, E., & Salonitis, K. (2016). A comparative study of multiple-criteria decision-making methods under stochastic inputs. *Energies*, *9*(7), 566 (21). doi:10.3390/en9070566

Kontić, B., Bohanec, M., & Urbančič, T. (2006). An experiment in participative environmental decision making. *Environmentalist*, *26*(1), 5–15. doi:10.1007/s10669-006-5353-3

Krause, M., Cabrera, J.E., Cubillo, F., Diaz, C., & Ducci, J. (2015). *Aquarating: An International Standard for Assessing Water and Wastewater Services*. London: IWA publishing.

Lipušček, I., Bohanec, M., Oblak, L., & Zadnik Strin, L. (2010). A multi-criteria decision-making model for classifying wood products with respect to their impact on environment. *International Journal of Life Cycle Assessment*, *15*(4), 359–367. doi:10.1007/s11367-010-0157-6

Mardani, A., Jusoh, A., Nor, K.M., Khalifah, Z., Zakwan, N., & Valipour, A. (2015). Multiple criteria decision-making techniques and their applications – a review of the literature from 2000 to 2014. *Economic Research-Ekonomska Istraživanja*, *28*(1), 516–571. doi:10.1080/1331677X.2015.1075139

Marie, K.J., Cano, J., Insua, D.R., & Arroyo, O. (2013). Multiobjective decision support for the Kwanza River management. *International Journal of Information Technology & Decision Making*, *12*(5), 999–1020. doi:10.1142/S0219622013400063

Menaia, J., Joao Rosa, M., Mesquita, E., Pocas, A., & Bruaset, S. (2015). Guidelines for improved operation of drinking water plants and maintenance of water supply and sanitation networks. In A.E. Hulsmann (Ed.), *Climate Change, Water Supply and Sanitation: Risk Assessment, Management, Mitigation and Reduction*. London: IWA Publishing.

Nowak, M., & Nowak, B. (2013). An application of the multiple criteria decision tree in project planning. *Procedia Technology*, *2013*(9), 826–835. doi:10.1016/j.protcy.2013.12.092

Olsson, G. (2015). *Water and Energy: Threats and Opportunities* (2nd ed.). London: IWA Publishing.

Rozman, Č., Potočnik, M., Pažek, K., Borec, A., Majkovič, D., & Bohanec, M. (2009). A multi-criteria assessment of tourist farm service quality. *Tourism Manage*, *30*(5), 629–637. doi:10.1016/j.tourman.2008.11.008

Vaishnavi, V.K., & Kuechler, B. (2015). *Design science research in information systems overview of design science research*. Retrieved July 28, 2017, from http://desrist.org/desrist/content/design-science-research-in-information-systems.pdf

Vaishnavi, V.K., & Kuechler, W. (2015). *Design Science Research Methods and Patterns: Innovating Information and Communication Technology* (2nd ed.). Boca Raton: CRC Press.

Velasquez, M., & Hester, P.T. (2013). An analysis of multi-criteria decision making methods. *International Journal of Operational Research*, *10*(2), 56–66. doi:10.1.1.402.1308

Von Winterfeldt, D., & Edwards, W. (1986). *Decision Analysis and Behavioural Research*. Cambridge: Cambridge University Press.

Zanakis, S.H., Solomon, A., Wishart, N., & Dublish, S. (1998). Multi-attribute decision making: A simulation comparison of select methods. *European Journal of Operational Research, 107*(3), 507–529. doi:10.1016/S0377-2217

Zavadskas, E.K., Govindan, K., Antucheviciene, J., & Turkis, Z. (2016). Hybrid multiple criteria decision-making methods: A review of applications for sustainability issues. *Economic Research-Ekonomska Istraživanja, 29*(1), 857–887. doi:10.1080/1331677X.2016.1237302.

Žnidaršič, M., Bohanec, M., & Zupan, B. (2008). Modelling impacts of cropping systems: Demands and solutions for DEX methodology. *European Journal of Operational Research, 189*(3), 594–608. doi:10.1016/j.ejor.2006.09.093

8 Augmented Reality in Medical Training of Patient Referrals

A Nursing Case Study of Children's Hospital in Taiwan

Shu Ru Uen and Yuh Wen Chen

Introduction

Nursing is critical to support the success of the medical operation, which is an act that requires complex skills and intensive experience, and its success is accompanied by patient morbidity and mortality. With the advancements in information technologies (ITs), performing spatial alignment and information integration is crucial to transform the traditional process digitally. Wüller et al. (2019) tried to overview the current research regarding AR in nursing to identify possible research gaps (Wüller et al., 2019). They suggested the use of augmented reality (AR) in nursing may have positive implications and should focus on performing long-term evaluations and considering the long-term consequences of AR. Curran et al. (2022) used affordable extended reality (XR) technologies to an outstanding level of fidelity, providing compelling experiences for medical education. Their applications have the potential to create immersive learning experiences that are engaging and lead to learning outcomes that appear to be equivalent to, or in some areas, potentially more effective than, traditional methods for teaching and learning in medicine. Moran et al. (2018) suggested educators should play a crucial role in how advanced technology transforms medical education in tradition. Increasingly integral to medicine, technology endeavors to streamline a clinician's work and to offer credible, easily accessible information are necessary to enhance trainee growth and empower innovative hospital leaders. Winkler-Schwartz et al. (2019) confirmed that although emphasized points in reporting were different between medical and computer science journals, both discussion quality and study design are important in the related research in adding values to virtual reality (VR) of surgical education by artificial intelligence. Winkler-Schwartz et al. (2019) confirmed that although emphasized points in reporting were different between medical and computer science journals, discussion quality and study design are both essential in the related research when adding values to VR of

DOI: 10.4324/9781003376583-10

surgical education by artificial intelligence. The use of VR or AR has become an implicit trend in medical training nowadays.

A patient referral is a dynamic process in which medical personnel at one level of the health system has insufficient resources; for example, drugs, equipment, and skills to manage a clinical condition and seek the assistance of a better or differently resourced facility at the same or higher level (Levin, 2000). An effective referral is crucial to maintaining the high survival rate of patients in an emergency (Chen et al., 2009). Bashar et al. (2019) validated the value of the e-referral system for it improving communication, increased access to care, seamless exchange of information, improved knowledge management, and decreased waiting times. Straus et al. (2011) also supported the effectiveness of e-referral system. According to the complicated and dynamic characteristics of clinical referral operation, Nuti et al. (2020) summarized that referral networks might represent the most effective accountability level for chronic disease management since they encompass the multiple care settings experienced by patients. Nuti et al. (2020) suggested an integrated approach to evaluation and performance management that considers the naturally occurring links between professionals from different backgrounds to enable more efficient, integrated care and quality improvements. From the advanced view of the point above, integrating the e-referral system and clinical experiences from medical professionals everywhere for patients should be very valuable. Zhu et al. (2014) proposed the review framework to discuss the role of AR in corresponding literature: AR is still viewed as a novelty or prototype in the study. They thought more exploration of this AR in medical applications should be necessary.

This study innovatively collects the clinical responses from nurses of National Taiwan University Children's Hospital (NTUCH) to survey the acceptance of the new operational model in order to test the possibility of using AR in the patient referrals. We use a modified technology acceptance model (TAM) to calibrate questionnaire responses (Mugo et al., 2017). The second section briefly introduces the technological background. The third section presents the methodology and how the questionnaire items come. The fourth section provides the calibrated results and discussions. Finally, in the fifth section, we summarize the conclusions and recommendations.

Technological Background

In this section, we review the clinical experiences of patient referral for children, theory basis of TAM, and training applications of VR and AR in medicine.

Patient Referral for Children

The patient referral is an official, complicated, and dynamic request from one health professional to another health professional or health service, asking them to diagnose or treat the transported patient for a particular condition by integrating various medical resources such as the dimension of families, doctors and nurses in hospitals, and emergency medical technicians (Levin, 2000; Chen et al., 2009). Considering the vital characteristic of children, pediatric critical care transport becomes a low-volume, high-cost, high-complexity specialty (Ratcliffe, 1998). According to the WHO guidelines (https://www.emro.who.int/child-adolescent-health/imci/referral.html), in the pre-referral stage, the health provider should be professionally trained to administer any pre-referral, urgent treatment as needed, to reduce the delay in initiating treatment at the referral site caused by the long time that the referral process may take. In the stage of emergency triage, the medical professionals provide immediate emergency treatment where needed, prioritize severe cases over other waiting patients, and distinguish emergency and priority cases from those who do not need urgent care. No matter whether in the pre-referral or emergency triage stage, skilled professionals are always needed during the process, and public support is necessary (Hoghughi, 1998). We summarize the steps as follows:

Matching the patients to the appropriate hospital

In the first step, we should triage factors such as age, physical factors, environment, vital signs, disease or trauma characteristics, and hospital capacity to improve the survival rate of patients. In addition, providers need to consider the attention, memory, perception, cognitive level, and patient temperament when evaluating and selecting appropriate patients for the appropriate hospital, as well as the patient's vision, hearing, medical history, and current vital limitations of patients.

Scheduling the Patient Referral

The patient referral can be scheduled by the facility scheduling department, the therapist via telephone interaction or a web-based scheduling application with synchronized capabilities. We should confirm the scheduled referrals in advance by both parties: the sender and the receiver to maintain consistency and ensure adequate preparation. If the referral is confirmed and available, two parties appoint prior to the referral to minimize the no-show rate. Referrals should be conducted once the additional/involved support staff is available. Additional consideration should be given to the schedules, for example, some burned children may need special equipment for burn rehabilitation, and the nursing staff should be present to assist with burn-related medical and rehabilitation interventions. The serious trauma patients could have the similar considerations.

Launching the Patient Referral

Critically, the referral patient in the children hospital has a changing range of illnesses and pathophysiology from early infancy to adolescence, which is far different from that of critically sick adults (Ratcliffe, 1998). Therefore, all the vital signs of children patients should be continuously monitored until they arrive at the reception professional safely. Instructions and monitoring data should be constantly provided on accessing the referral platform. Furthermore, real-time interaction online or by telephone provides patients with real-time feedback on how to maximize their survival successfully.

The referral team for children's patients in NTUCH was built in 1989, the team composes of the following staff, medical director, referral/transport coordinator, and the operational team, which is summarized in Figure 8.1. The clinical situation of patient referral at NTUCH is simply illustrated in Figure 8.2. Administrative functions interact based on the various functional members include the medical director group, referral/transport coordinator, and operational team. Team managers are supervisors and nursing leaders. They organize regular meetings to ensure quality management and improvements concerning each clinical case of success or failure. The abilities for the referral team to launch smoothly consist of the following: (a) medical knowledge of unique disease or

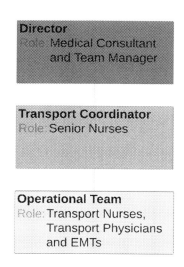

Figure 8.1 The organization of NTUCH referral team.

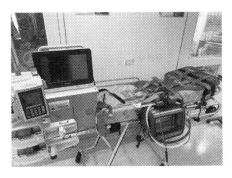 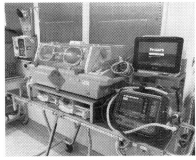

Figure 8.2 The clinical situation for patient referral of NTUCH.

trauma, (b) professional assessment, (c) technical skills, and (d) cross-functional communication.

The number of accepted patient referrals to NTUCH is increasing to 130 visits yearly in 2022, which is still climbing.

VR/AR Applications in Medical Training

Bruno et al. (2022) validated that VR and AR offer great potential to improve critical care medicine for patients, relatives, and healthcare providers. They summarized three involved parties that will perceive the values of VR and AR: patients, relatives, and healthcare providers. They regarded VR is valuable for distracting patients during critical care therapy or invasive procedures: treatment VR to enhance the rehabilitation of patients during critical care therapy; information VR to inform the patient during and after the intensive care treatment about critical care therapy. As for the perspective of relatives, VR educated the family or relatives during and after the intensive care treatment about critical care therapy, and establish virtual ward rounds for better communication. Furthermore, the healthcare provider may use VR to establish virtual ward rounds and AR to help during virtual ward rounds – VR is also helpful to help relax stress for them; however, AR enhances the operation effectiveness for them.

We search the latest Scopus by utilizing PyScopus, a Python wrapper of Elsevier Scopus API, for fast filtering of the documents we desire in the scientific database. The keywords AR, VR, medicine, and education are combined to focus the key papers. We select some key papers after filtering here to support the idea of this study. Bradley (2006) viewed clinical simulation in medicine as a technique that enables the learning and training of individuals and teams through the re-creation of the actual clinical situation. It is a spectrum of educational activities involving technological and computerized facilities and critical human interactions: one-on-one within or between teams. It is essential not to disintegrate simulation into a dichotomy between low and high fidelity but to regard it as a continuum with roles to fulfill at all levels of seniority within and between professional groups. Munzer et al. (2019) validated that AR has utility and feasibility in clinical care delivery in patient care settings, operating rooms, and inpatient settings, and the education and training of emergency care providers; therefore, a role in telehealth is suggested. Albrecht et al. (2013) built an AR app for fast trauma triage of wounds in legal medicine. The participants in this study were interviewed regarding their emotions while using the app. Users consistently confirmed that using the app was stimulating and fascinated them, and they also favor its interactivity. Park et al. (2007) provided the VR simulators to help prepare residents for live clinical experience. They concluded that, although the VR simulator's performance metrics showed limited concurrent validity and a need for further refinement, residents trained on a colonoscopy simulator performed significantly better in the clinical setting than controls, demonstrating skill transfer to live patients. Heinrichs et al. (2008) showed that trainees under VR simulation to be adequately realistic to "suspend disbelief", and they quickly learn to use Internet voice communication and user interface to navigate to and work with their online critical care team. The findings demonstrate that this virtual emergency department (ED) environments fulfill their promise of providing repeated practice opportunities in dispersed locations with uncommon, life-threatening trauma cases in a safe, reproducible, flexible setting. Klemenc-Ketis et al. (2021) expected to evaluate the effectiveness of AR in teaching medicine based on a clinical case of anaphylactic shock at the primary care level. With this study, they will be able to assess their long-term impact. Carenzo et al. (2015) thought the Google Glass is a promising AR device for telemedicine applications to increase operators' performance, helping them to make better choices on the field in time. In addition, AR technology finally represented an excellent option to take professional education to a higher level. Duarte et al. (2020) supported the AR/VR simulator reproduces real-life conditions without time limitations, patient discomfort, and student shame. It is consistently associated with significant effects on the results of knowledge, skills, and behaviors. The visual aids of AR/VR are a highly effective teaching method, and studies now show an increase in memory retention compared to more traditional teaching methods (Bui et al., 2021). Gerup et al. (2020) reviewed reports of AR and mixed reality (MR)-based applications for healthcare education beyond surgery. Studies based on display technologies across various specialties and subjects state an increased number of established applications moving the research base away from feasibility studies on prototypes. Future studies are essential and emerging required for researchers, educators, and developers to build an evidence base defining suitable research designs and instructional objectives achievable by AR- and MR-based applications.

Some observations are briefly summarized as follows by our deep survey of Scopus:

1 When comparing the number of publications between VR applications and AR applications, the role of VR contributes to 495 related papers and high citations more than 200 times; however, the amount of AR only has 57 articles and low citations about 100 times. This imbalance may arise from the high cost of AR devices to limit the exposure of corresponding applications.

2 The ideas from the top cited articles between the VR and AR area are not significantly different, most of them are devoted to the field of surgery, healthcare, and medical training/education. More interestingly, the AR application could be embedded in a physical model/organ with 3D printing to provide the highlights during training (Huang et al., 2018; Wake et al., 2020).

3 We use the medical and professional noun "Referral" to find related articles in Scopus and only see one paper by Datta et al. (2012). The authors discussed and confirmed the value of simulation in five situations: undergraduate teaching, postgraduate training, continuing medical education, disaster management, and military trauma management. We know the patient referrals of this study is a particular case of military trauma management; therefore, using AR devices to learn about some experiences in this rarely studied topic is worthy of exploration.

The TAM

The TAM can analyze behaviors and determinants influencing individuals' adoption of new technologies; the model is shown in Figure 8.3. The TAM was introduced by Davis (1985, 1989) and extended by Davis et al. (1989), and was designed to address the behavior of computer users as they embrace new information systems. It is the most widely used theoretical model for studying the acceptance of new technologies. It is also an effective tool for predicting and explaining individuals' intentions toward new technologies and information use in healthcare (Holden & Karsh, 2010).

The TAM explains individuals' acceptance of new technologies and techniques, analyzes the differences between different groups, and explains consumer behavior. The TAM was originally designed to investigate the acceptance of computer information technology. Suppose we want to analyze the factors that influence individuals' acceptance of new technologies. In that case, the TAM using the Theory of Rational Behavior (TRB)

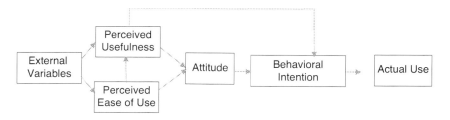

Figure 8.3 Framework of TAM.
Source: Davis et al. (1989).

is a basis for understanding the external factors influencing individuals' behavioral attitudes, internal beliefs and motivations, and intention to use new technologies. It also helps researchers understand why new technologies are not accepted and make appropriate corrections and improvements. The rational behavior theory and the TAM believe that individual beliefs influence behavioral attitudes, and attitudes affect individuals' intentions to adopt. The sensible behavior theory and the TAM is that the pragmatic behavior theory emphasizes that behavioral attitudes and subjective norms jointly influence behavioral intentions. Individuals adopt specific behaviors out of intentions; the TAM believes that behavioral attitudes are more influential than subjective norms.

TAM has been frequently utilized in the information systems literature to explore the determinants of technology acceptance as a robust model to analyze the determinants of subject acceptance. Various educational studies related VR/AR have demonstrated the explanatory power of TAM in acceptance and adoption studies (Jang et al., 2021; Lai et al., 2009; Yavuz et al., 2021). Perceived usefulness (PU) and perceived ease of use (PEOU) are the two main components of TAM. The degree to which a person feels that utilizing a system would enhance their job performance is referred to as PU (Aggelidis & Chatzoglou, 2009). PEOU is a person's belief that implementing a specific strategy would not increase performance (Su et al., 2012). TAM proposes linking the above central and other constructs, namely "behavioral intention to use technology" (BI). BI is the extent to which a person has to make a conscious plan to perform or not to perform some specified future behavior (Briz-Ponce & García-Peñalvo, 2015).

The theory of reasoned action (TRA), proposed by Fishbein and Ajzen (1975), has been used to model the TRA. The idea of reasoned action (TRA) has been widely used in the past few decades to explore the validation of individual behavior. TRA suggests that an individual's behavioral beliefs and assessments directly affect an individual's attitude toward behavior. This attitude and subjective norms affect an individual's BIs, which are the determinants that directly affect an individual's behavior. Davis (1985) proposed the TAM based on TRA to explore the relationship between external factors on users' beliefs, attitudes, and intentions. The TAM continues the core concept of the rational behavior theory, which suggests that beliefs influence attitudes, which further influence BIs, which affect actual use.

We can find some/limited literature using TAM for medical training/education by adopting AR/VR. Basoglu et al. (2018) suggested developers of AR should pay attention to healthcare-specific requirements for improved utilization and more extensive adoption of AR in healthcare settings. Alawadhi et al. (2022) validated that PEOU and PU significantly influenced the medical students' inclination to use AR/VR technology. Adenuga et al. (2019) emphasized the widespread adoption of AR in clinical perspectives, most especially toward enhancing medical practice and education in developing countries: Sub-Saharan African countries. This paper also examined some of these influencing factors in TAM and proposed a modified model to be validated in future studies. Özdemir-Güngör et al. (2020) used TAM as an imperative and empirical study to analyze user perceptions, attitudes, and intentions. For this purpose, five external factors are extracted from the literature and field study to improve TAM: integration with information systems, external effects, hands-free features, technological compatibility, and documentation. Klinker et al. (2020) thought the features of hand-free and real-time audio from AR devices support healthcare professionals dealing with wound treatment better by TAM analysis. Gorman et al. (2022) identified that there is potential acceptability for AR in stroke rehabilitation. The needs identified by the participants may inform development of current and future technology.

Research Framework and Hypotheses

According to the previous literature review, we confirm the scope of the past literature on the AR use of patient referrals needs to be broadened and expanded. The following research framework is similar to that of Huang et al. (2023): they modified the TAM by embedding the flow theory (Csikszentmihalyi, 1975); however, we modify the TAM by including two external variables: social media addiction (SMA; Baumgartner & Steenkamp, 1996; Amadu et al., 2018) and perceived enjoyment (PE; Huang et al., 2023). We review the literature and theoretical basis for the research framework as follows by some related references:

1 Wang et al. (2016) define PU as "the user's perception that the use of an AR device is advantageous for maintenance instructions". Meanwhile, in

the TAM model, PU and PEOU are considered the most influential factors in adopting new technologies like AR. PU is a predictor of new technology acceptance in studies across multiple domains; similarly, PU is one of the pretest predictors of intention to use a wearable device. We hypothesized that PU actually affects BI. The perceived efficacy will impact consumers' PU of healthy wearable technologies after using AR devices: hamlets or glasses in the patient referrals. Therefore, the first hypothesis of this study is as follows:

H1: Individuals' perceived usefulness affects nurses' attitude to wear the AR device.

2 PEOU as one of the main components in the TAM model, Davis (1985, 1989) proposed that an individual's motivation toward technology would be influenced by PU and PEOU, which TAM researchers as facilitators of technology use and adoption have extensively studied. These studies found that researchers generally agree that PEOU positively impacts individuals' BIs to use new technologies directly and indirectly. This finding was consistent with previous studies and recognized in the context of augmented or VR in training professionals (Basoglu et al., 2018). As a result, in the context of wearable health devices, PEOU refers to how the product design is simple to use and how the end user anticipates the AR device to be simple to understand and utilize. Therefore, this study proposes the second hypothesis:

H2: Individuals' perceived ease of use affects nurses' attitude to wear the AR device.

3 Lee et al. (2019) proposed the perception of enjoyment and social tie (SMA) may influence the intention to use virtual devices. They empirically analyzed how introducing social network characteristics as a diffusion strategy for VR devices affects the end users' intentions. This survey was conducted with 350 people from South Korea, and TAM was used to analyze the acceptability of VR. User adoption behaviors were analyzed rigorously, adding PE, social interactions, and strength of the social ties to the basic TAM. Research indicates that social interactions and the strength of social ties increase PE, and PE has a more significant effect on the intention to use than PU, which is the main element of TAM. These results have theoretical implications for consumer adoption behavior and empirical implications for adopting VR devices. In addition, Amadu et al. (2018) also suggested significant mediation effects exist on the relationship between social media usage dimensions and attitude to collaborative learning. Therefore, we follow the research of Lee et al. (2019) and Amadu et al. (2018) to propose the following two hypotheses:

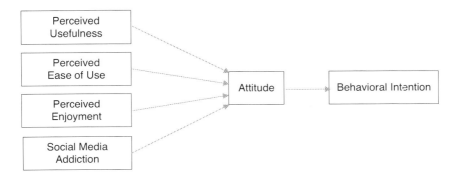

Figure 8.4 Research framework.

H3: Individuals' perceived enjoyment affects nurses' attitude to wear the AR device.

H4: Individuals' social media addiction affects nurses' attitude to wear the AR device.

Finally, we again tested the effect of attitude on behavior intention and proposed the fifth hypothesis.

H5: Individuals' attitude affects nurses' intention to wear the AR device.

We organize the data and explore them according to the literature above; the initial structure of this study modified from Figure 8.3 is shown in Figure 8.4. In addition, the items of questionnaire for testing the hypotheses are summarized in Table 8.1.

Case Study Results and Discussions

We present the case study, calibration results, and discussions in this section.

Case Study

This study selects Microsoft HoloLens (https://www.microsoft.com/en-us/hololens/hardware) and Realwear HMT-1 (https://www.realwear.com/) to launch the AR experiment in the beginning. However, the nurse team decided to use the HMT-1 in the operation of patient referrals because of its characteristics of voice communication rather than hand gesture communication from HoloLens. The Realwear HMT-1 is an AR device with a small digital screen located to the side of one of the user's eyes and attached to the helmet (Figure 8.5, left and middle). The distance and the angle to the eye are adjusted, so the user sees the screen in focus. The small screen displayed slides or videos (Figure 8.5, right). The mass of the HMT-1 is 0.37 kg, and the group of the HMT-1 and helmet combined with

148 *Shu Ru Uen and Yuh Wen Chen*

Table 8.1 Questionnaire design

Dimension	Item	Reference
Perceived usefulness (PU)	1 I believe that using AR will increase productivity (x1). 2 I think using AR will increase operational efficiency (x2). 3 AR in the patient referrals is useful (x3). 4 AR will improve the quality of operation (x4). 5 Using AR is effective for my job (x5).	Davis (1989) Cho and Fiorito (2009) Wang et al. (2016)
Perceived ease of use (PEOU)	1 Using AR is accessible to me (x6). 2 It is easy to achieve the goal of patient referrals by AR (x7). 3 AR is clear and easy to understand (x8). 4 The interactions within the team become more vivid through AR (x9). 5 It just takes a little while to be skilled personnel with this AR device (x10).	Davis (1989) Gefen and Straub (2000) Basoglu et al. (2018)
Perceived enjoyment (PE)	1 I enjoy using AR in patient referrals (x11). 2 I find fun when using AR in my job (x12). 3 It is exciting to use AR in patient referrals (x13). 4 Using AR is an enjoyable experience (x14).	Lee et al. (2019) Huang et al. (2023)
Social media addiction (SMA)	1 I keep noticing the latest status of my social community is up to date (x15). 2 I often read the pop-out news from my social community (x16). 3 It is wasting time to communicate with the social gathering online (x17). 4 I often watch the latest promotion and shop the commodities online (x18).	Baumgartner and Steenkamp (1996) Lee et al. (2019) Amadu et al. (2018)
Attitude (A)	1 It is lovely to use the AR device (y1). 2 I am favorable toward using AR (y2).	Davis (1989)

(Continued)

Table 8.1 (Continued)

Dimension	Item	Reference
	3 I am satisfied after using AR (y3).	
	4 I like to use AR in my job (y4).	
	5 I am happy to use the AR device (y5).	
Behavioral intention (BI)	1 I am very willing to use the AR device shortly (z1).	Davis (1989) Basoglu et al. (2018)
	2 I want to use this AR to improve the quality of patient referrals (z2).	
	3 I will within the coming months (z3).	
	4 Using AR in patient referrals is essential to my job (z4).	

Figure 8.5 AR system of patient referrals in children hospital by HMT-1 and Webex.

attachment hardware is 0.76 kg. The nurse team chose the HMT-1 with less weight because the safety helmet is redundant in the hospital environment. The experimental protocol is built online on the Webex (https://www.webex.com/) meeting system (Figure 8.5, left). Any nurse of a children's hospital joining the patient referral team can use HMT-1 and Webex to communicate with each other in real time to set the appropriate sending and accepting circumstances for transferred patients so as to maximize their survival chance.

The study surveys the opinion of nurses in the patient referral team to investigate how they evaluate the AR effectiveness of TAM. Every nurse's intensive and laborious load restrains the time and the number for completing the questionnaire in Table 8.1. The survey period started on August 1, 2022 and ended on October 31, 2022. The number of responses is only

150 *Shu Ru Uen and Yuh Wen Chen*

29 returned by the paper sheet. We summarize a questionnaire of 27 items in Table 8.1. The primary purpose of reliability is to analyze the consistency and stability of the responses in the questionnaire. Among many methods to examine the reliability, Cronbach's alpha is now a prevalent method to examine reliability indicators. In this study, we use Cronbach's alpha to analyze the reliability of the questionnaire, which is used to measure the consistency of the scale. Cronbach's α value must be at least greater than 0.7 to indicate high reliability and in the acceptable range. If Cronbach's α value is between 0.35 and 0.7, it means medium reliability, and the questionnaire is generally acceptable (Rauschnabel & Ro, 2016). In general, it is recommended that Cronbach's alpha value be more significant than 0.7 to be considered a good questionnaire. The overall Cronbach's alpha value of this questionnaire was checked and reached 0.8973, which implies the questionnaire response in Table 8.1 is excellent and appropriate for further analysis.

In terms of validity, the study used the Kaiser-Meyer-Olkin (KMO) measure of sampling adequacy proposed by Kaiser (1974) and the Bartlett sphericity test offered by Bartlett (1951) to determine the suitability of the questionnaire for analysis. KMO > 0.9 is excellent, KMO > 0.7 is suitable, KMO > 0.6 is ordinary, and KMO < 0.5 is unusable. This study tests each response variance for every question as unequal according to ANOVA (p-value tends to be 0). Moreover, our KMO is 0.6016 in this study, which means the validity is ordinarily acceptable. Our limited respondents say Kaiser's KMO value is low in this study.

Calibration Results

This study optimizes the structural equation model in Python with the open-source Semopy package (https://semopy.com/). We compare the results of the calibration by the coefficient of influence (label) and statistical significance (p-value) during calibration, check the explanatory power of the measurement variables (items are denoted by x, y, and z in Table 8.1), and examine whether the hypothesis of the framework in Figure 8.4 holds. When we try to include all items (variables) into the model, the calibrated results could be more satisfying initially, resulting from no statistically significant path in the initial model.

Our intuition leads us to reduce the scale of this model is necessary because we only collect 29 available responses. Therefore, we use the following principles to check all the possible models by various calibrations. The priority is to keep the relationship from Attitude (A) to BI by gradually reducing the dimension of PU, PEOU, PE, and SMA. Suppose the relationship from Attitude (A) to Behavioral Intention (BI) still fails to validate or keep. In that case, we only keep the Attitude (A) and continue

Augmented Reality in Medical Training of Patient Referrals 151

Table 8.2 Path analysis

Hypothesis	Path	Coefficient	p-value
H1	PU->A	Unclear/uncalibrated	Not available, because PU is not included in model
H2	PEOU->A	0.604	0.00
H3	PE->A	Unclear/uncalibrated	Not available, because PE is not included in model
H4	SMA->A	−0.435	0.03
H5	A->BI	−1.438	0.02

to gradually reduce the dimension of PU, PEOU, PE, and SMA. Following this logic to test all the possible models, finally, we find one satisfying model below according to the limited data after trying more than 20 calibrations. This model is compromised with considerable dimensions and the relationship from A to BI. And the path, influence coefficients, and *p*-values are organized in Table 8.2. The final model didn't include the PU and PE because they performed poorly during more than 20 calibrations tests. In such a case, PU and PE won't render a coefficient (relationship) to A; thus, no *p*-values will be available in Table 8.2 for these paths (Figure 8.6).

Discussions

According to the limited data and the calibrated results on hand, we have a 95% confidence level to say PEOU has a positive impact on A, SMA has a negative impact on A, and the surveyed nurses' attitude has a negative impact on the behavioral intention of using AR. Although the calibrated results are not very satisfying, we discuss our findings by reviewing some literature with similar responses as follows:

1 Although two AR devices, Microsoft HoloLens and Realwear HMT-1, are prepared for the nurses, they arbitrarily decided to use Realwear HMT-1 for patient referral finally. This decision could result from some reasons: (a) the nurses need to constantly work by hand to help the children patients in clinical circumstances, and the real-time/fast response to the outside (outside the AR device) is primary and critical. Microsoft HoloLens has large eyeglass lenses covering the face. This property somewhat isolates the user's subjective perception from the environment outside, (b) the nurses are in charge of the initial setting of AR before use; the scene of Microsoft HoloLens needs to approve the entry by the virtual keyboard in the air; this is not convenient for the professionals want to

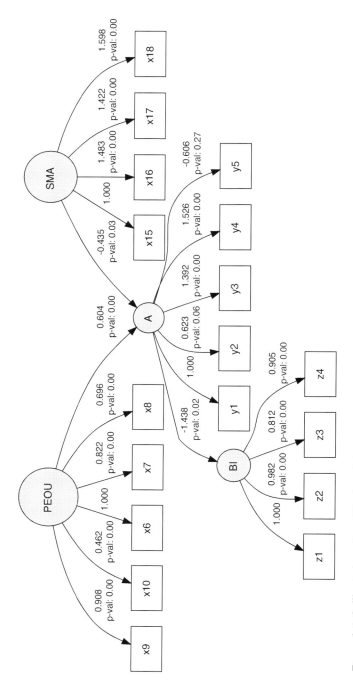

Figure 8.6 Calibrated results of final model.

Augmented Reality in Medical Training of Patient Referrals 153

"hand free". Interestingly, the decision to choose AR also matches the relationship between PEOU to Attitude (A) in Figure 8.5.

2 Individuals' PEOU affects nurses' attitude to wear the AR device.

In addition to the discussion (1) above, the support of H1 matches our previous expectations. We can also find literature to validate this point. The AR study of Wang et al. (2016) supported the PEOU from the responses of training aviation students. Whether aviation students or nurses in this study are skilled professionals, straight and simple use of AR is the top emphasized issue for these people. Huang et al. (2016) built a prototype 3D VR learning system and used it to survey 167 university students toward learning via VR applications. They also supported that immersion and imagination features of VR-mediated course contents have a positive impact on PEOU. Sagnier et al. (2020) suggested that the intention to use VR is positively influenced by PEOU and negatively influenced by cybersickness. We also find the nurse with cybersickness gave our questionnaire a low score. However, we didn't collect enough samples of cybersickness to test their finding. Lee et al. (2003) also exerted PEOU as an influence on attitudes of distance training/learning online.

3 Individuals' SMA affects nurses' attitude to wear the AR device.

SMA impacts attitude, but our calibrated parameter is negative. Rauschnabel and Ro (2016) thought these end users of AR are likely to use social media platforms to discuss the AR devices such as smart glasses. Examples include Microsoft's official discussion forum (http://forums. windowscentral.com/microsoft-hololens/) or other user-generated forums. In addition, the study of Uymaz and Uymaz (2022) also confirmed that social influence/media had a positive and significant influence on using AR. Interestingly, although we validated the relationship between SMA and attitude, our finding is somewhat opposite to the studied results above. We think this may have three possible explanations; first, the patient referral team viewed the AR device as a working tool, and using it only in the medical operation, and the operation process is just a job without so much fun. Therefore, they don't have the opportunity to share anything after a tough day and intensive work. Second, the sharing culture of AR may have hospital competency and patient privacy; thus, it is less prevalent in such a circumstance than in other general social communities. Third, our studied AR object is communicated by speaking voice rather than typing text; the user experience is quite different when they use Line, Instagram, or Facebook in leisure.

4 Individuals' attitude affects nurses' intention to wear the AR device.

The support of H5 goes beyond our previous expectations partially. We previously expected a positive impact from attitude on behavioral intention. Basoglu et al. (2018) found attitude may be the primary determinant of intention within the attitude/intention research domain, and a high correlation between these two factors we always expected in the literature. However, their calibrated results demonstrate that attitude may not always be the only antecedent to intention. In other words, that attitude alone could not explain the variation in intention appropriately. The nurses in the patient referral team may have other concerns in addition to attitude: this should be explored further. For example, they may care the privacy issues during the referral. While AR technology has the potential to improve or replace some conventional medical training methods, the systematic review of Tang et al. (2020) also demonstrated inconsistency in focus, quality, driver, and conclusion of the published studies. Therefore, we need to collect more data to validate the point based on evidence.

Conclusions and Recommendations

AR technology in medical education/training for patient referrals may still be in its early stages and needs more evidence-based support for its current implementation. Future research should adopt long-term and large-scale cohort study designs in keeping with the proposed model to evaluate the efficacy of AR applications.

This study coincided with the late stage of the COVID-19 epidemic in Taiwan, which means congested patient traffic in hospitals. We add a manageable and acceptable load for nurses by simplifying the questionnaire design to complete this study. The limited response time from nurses and the approval by Institutional Review Board (IRB) hampers the study's progress beyond our expected delay, and the return of respondents still needs to be improved further. Using the TAM for validating the AR revealed that although all SEM-oriented measurement variables (items) met the statistical reliability requirements, the model for calibrating results still has much room to improve, extend and validate. The study indicates that end users have a strong interest in and the ability to use AR only when they perceive its ease of use (or show the practitioner value to them). In other words, the PEOU of AR is a strong predictor of medical professionals' attitudes. The "hand free" characteristic is seldom discussed in the previous academic paper for medical personnel adopting AR; there could be more hidden considerations for the practitioners in the front line of emergency medicine. The other hypothesizes beyond our previous imagination and needs more data to finalize.

Rigorous and standardized validation of commercially viable applications will contribute more value to be readily integrated into the medical operation. Furthermore, the research framework of TAM here could be too simple to ignore some managerial implications. More improvements for this study are needed shortly.

References

Adenuga, K.I., Adenuga, R.O., Ziraba, A., & Mbuh, P.E. (2019). Healthcare augmentation: Social adoption of augmented reality glasses in medicine. In *Proceedings of the 2019 8th International Conference on Software and Information Engineering* (pp. 71–74).

Aggelidis, V.P., & Chatzoglou, P.D. (2009). Using a modified technology acceptance model in hospitals. *International Journal of Medical Informatics, 78*(2), 115–126.

Alawadhi, M., Alhumaid, K., Almarzooqi, S., Aljasmi, S., Aburayya, A., Salloum, S.A., & Almesmari, W. (2022). Factors affecting medical students' acceptance of the metaverse system in medical training in the United Arab Emirates. *South Eastern European Journal of Public Health, 5*, 1–14.

Albrecht, U.V., Noll, C., & von Jan, U. (2013). Explore and experience: Mobile augmented reality for medical training. *MEDINFO, 2013*, 382–386.

Amadu, L., Muhammad, S.S., Mohammed, A.S., Owusu, G., & Lukman, S. (2018). Using technology acceptance model to measure the use of social media for collaborative learning in Ghana. *JOTSE, 8*(4), 321–336.

Bartlett, M.S. (1951). The effect of standardization on a $\chi 2$ approximation in factor analysis. *Biometrika, 38*(3/4), 337–344.

Bashar, M.A., Bhattacharya, S., Tripathi, S., Sharma, N., & Singh, A. (2019). Strengthening primary health care through e-referral system. *Journal of Family Medicine and Primary Care, 8*(4), 1511–1513.

Basoglu, N.A., Goken, M., Dabic, M., Ozdemir Gungor, D., & Daim, T.U. (2018). Exploring adoption of augmented reality smart glasses: Applications in the medical industry. *Frontiers of Engineering Management, 5*(2), 167–181. doi:110.15302/J-FEM-2018056

Baumgartner, H., & Steenkamp, J.B.E. (1996). Exploratory consumer buying behavior: Conceptualization and measurement. *International Journal of Research in Marketing, 13*(2), 121–137.

Bradley, P. (2006). The history of simulation in medical education and possible future directions. *Medical Education, 40*(3), 254–262.

Briz-Ponce, L., & García-Peñalvo, F.J. (2015). An empirical assessment of a technology acceptance model for apps in medical education. *Journal of Medical Systems, 39*(11), 1–5.

Bruno, R.R., Wolff, G., Wernly, B., Masyuk, M., Piayda, K., Leaver, S., ... & Jung, C. (2022). Virtual and augmented reality in critical care medicine: The patient's, clinician's, and researcher's perspective. *Critical Care, 26*(1), 1–13.

Bui, D.T., Barnett, T., Hoang, H.T., & Chinthammit, W. (2021). Tele-mentoring using augmented reality technology in healthcare: A systematic review. *Australasian Journal of Educational Technology, 37*(4), 68–88.

Carenzo, L., Barra, F.L., Ingrassia, P.L., Colombo, D., Costa, A., & Della Corte, F. (2015). Disaster medicine through Google Glass. *European Journal of Emergency Medicine, 22*(3), 222–225.

Chen, Y.W., Wang, G.J., Li, T.H., Yang, T.M., Shiu, T.W., Tasi, M.S., ... & Chen, C.W. (2009). A RFID model of transferring and tracking trauma patients after a large disaster. In *2009 IEEE/INFORMS International Conference on Service Operations, Logistics and Informatics* (pp. 98–101).

Cho, H., & Fiorito, S.S. (2009). Acceptance of online customization for apparel shopping. *International Journal of Retail & Distribution Management*, *37*(5), 389–407.

Csikszentmihalyi, M. (1975). *Beyond Boredom and Anxiety*. Jossey-Bass Publishers.

Curran, V.R., Xu, X., Aydin, M.Y., & Meruvia-Pastor, O. (2022). Use of extended reality in medical education: An integrative review. *Medical Science Educator*, *33*(1), 275–286.

Datta, R., Upadhyay, K.K., & Jaideep, C.N. (2012). Simulation and its role in medical education. *Medical Journal Armed Forces India*, *68*(2), 167–172.

Davis, F.D. (1985). *A Technology Acceptance Model for Empirically Testing New End-User Information Systems: Theory and Results*, Doctoral dissertation. Massachusetts Institute of Technology.

Davis, F.D. (1989). Perceived usefulness, perceived ease of use, and user acceptance of information technology. *MIS Quarterly*, 319–340.

Davis, F.D., Bagozzi, R.P., & Warshaw, P.R. (1989). User acceptance of computer technology: A comparison of two theoretical models. *Management Science*, *35*(8), 982–1003.

Duarte, M.L., Santos, L.R., Júnior, J.G., & Peccin, M.S. (2020). Learning anatomy by virtual reality and augmented reality. A scope review. *Morphologie*, *104*(347), 254–266.

Fishbein, M., & Ajzen, I. (1975). *Belief, Attitude, Intention, and Behavior: An Introduction to Theory and Research*. Reading, MA: Addison-Wesley.

Gefen, D., & Straub, D.W. (2000). The relative importance of perceived ease of use in IS adoption: A study of e-commerce adoption. *Journal of the Association for Information Systems*, *1*(1), 1–28.

Gerup, J., Soerensen, C.B., & Dieckmann, P. (2020). Augmented reality and mixed reality for healthcare education beyond surgery: An integrative review. *International Journal of Medical Education*, *11*, 1–18.

Gorman, C., Gustafsson, L., & Gomura, C. (2022). The perspectives of stroke survivors and health professionals on the use of augmented reality for inpatient stroke rehabilitation: An anticipatory exploration. *Brain Impairment*, *23*(2), 206–215.

Heinrichs, W.L., Youngblood, P., Harter, P.M., & Dev, P. (2008). Simulation for team training and assessment: Case studies of online training with virtual worlds. *World Journal of Surgery*, *32*(2), 161–170.

Hoghughi, M. (1998). The importance of parenting in child health: Doctors as well as the government should do more to support parents. *BMJ*, *316*(7144), 1545.

Holden, R.J., & Karsh, B.T. (2010). The technology acceptance model: Its past and its future in health care. *Journal of Biomedical Informatics*, *43*(1), 159–172.

Huang, H.M., Liaw, S.S., & Lai, C.M. (2016). Exploring learner acceptance of the use of virtual reality in medical education: A case study of desktop and projection-based display systems. *Interactive Learning Environments*, *24*(1), 3–19.

Huang, T.K., Yang, C.H., Hsieh, Y.H., Wang, J.C., & Hung, C.C. (2018). Augmented reality (AR) and virtual reality (VR) applied in dentistry. *The Kaohsiung Journal of Medical Sciences*, *34*(4), 243–248.

Augmented Reality in Medical Training of Patient Referrals 157

Huang, Y.C., Li, L.N., Lee, H.Y., Browning, M.H., & Yu, C.P. (2023). Surfing in virtual reality: An application of extended technology acceptance model with flow theory. *Computers in Human Behavior Reports*, 9, 100252–100261.

Jang, J., Ko, Y., Shin, W.S., & Han, I. (2021). Augmented reality and virtual reality for learning: An examination using an extended technology acceptance model. *IEEE Access*, 9, 6798–6809.

Kaiser, H.F. (1974). An index of factorial simplicity. *Psychometrika*, 39(1), 31–36.

Klemenc-Ketis, Z., Susič, A.P., Gorenjec, N.R., Miroševič, Š., Zafošnik, U., Selič, P., & Tevžič, Š. (2021). Effectiveness of the use of augmented reality in teaching the management of anaphylactic shock at the primary care level: Protocol for a randomized controlled trial. *JMIR Research Protocols*, 10(1), e22460.

Klinker, K., Wiesche, M., & Krcmar, H. (2020). Digital transformation in health care: Augmented reality for hands-free service innovation. *Information Systems Frontiers*, 22(6), 1419–1431.

Lai, C.M., Huang, H.M., Liaw, S.S., & Huang, W.W. (2009). A study of user's acceptance in three-dimensional virtual reality applied in medical education. *Bulletin of Educational Psychology*, 40(3), 341–362.

Lee, J., Kim, J., & Choi, J.Y. (2019). The adoption of virtual reality devices: The technology acceptance model integrating enjoyment, social interaction, and strength of the social ties. *Telematics and Informatics*, 39, 37–48.

Lee, J.S., Cho, H., Gay, G., Davidson, B., & Ingraffea, A. (2003). Technology acceptance and social networking in distance learning. *Journal of Educational Technology & Society*, 6(2), 50–61.

Levin, A. (2000). Consequences of late referral on patient outcomes. *Nephrology Dialysis Transplantation*, 15(suppl_3), 8–13.

Moran, J., Briscoe, G., & Peglow, S. (2018). Current technology in advancing medical education: Perspectives for learning and providing care. *Academic Psychiatry*, 42(6), 796–799.

Mugo, D.G., Njagi, K., Chemwei, B., & Motanya, J.O. (2017). The technology acceptance model (TAM) and its application to the utilization of mobile learning technologies. *British Journal of Mathematics & Computer Science*, 20(4), 1–8.

Munzer, B.W., Khan, M.M., Shipman, B., & Mahajan, P. (2019). Augmented reality in emergency medicine: A scoping review. *Journal of Medical Internet Research*, 21(4), e12368.

Nuti, S., Ferré, F., Seghieri, C., Foresi, E., & Stukel, T.A. (2020). Managing the performance of general practitioners and specialists referral networks: A system for evaluating the heart failure pathway. *Health Policy* 124(1), 44–51.

Özdemir-Güngör, D., Göken, M., Basoglu, N., Shaygan, A., Dabić, M., & Daim, T.U. (2020). *An Acceptance Model for the Adoption of Smart Glasses Technology by Healthcare Professionals*. Cham: Palgrave Macmillan.

Park, J., MacRae, H., Musselman, L.J., Rossos, P., Hamstra, S.J., Wolman, S., & Reznick, R.K. (2007). Randomized controlled trial of virtual reality simulator training: Transfer to live patients. *The American Journal of Surgery*, 194(2), 205–211.

Ratcliffe, J. (1998). Provision of intensive care for children. *BMJ*, 316(7144), 1547–1548.

Rauschnabel, P.A., & Ro, Y.K. (2016). Augmented reality smart glasses: An investigation of technology acceptance drivers. *International Journal of Technology Marketing, 11*(2), 123–148.

Sagnier, C., Loup-Escande, E., Lourdeaux, D., Thouvenin, I., & Valléry, G. (2020). User acceptance of virtual reality: An extended technology acceptance model. *International Journal of Human–Computer Interaction, 36*(11), 993–1007.

Straus, S.G., Chen, A.H., Yee Jr, H., Kushel, M.B., & Bell, D.S. (2011). Implementation of an electronic referral system for outpatient specialty care. In *AMIA Annual Symposium Proceedings* (pp. 1337–1346).

Su, S.P., Tsai, C.H., & Chen, Y.K. (2012). Applying the technology acceptance model to explore intention to use telecare system in Taiwan. In *2012 13th ACIS International Conference on Software Engineering, Artificial Intelligence, Networking and Parallel/Distributed Computing* (pp. 353–356).

Tang, K.S., Cheng, D.L., Mi, E., & Greenberg, P.B. (2020). Augmented reality in medical education: A systematic review. *Canadian Medical Education Journal, 11*(1), e81.

Uymaz, P., & Uymaz, A.O. (2022). Assessing acceptance of augmented reality in nursing education. *PloS One, 17*(2), e0263937.

Wake, N., Nussbaum, J.E., Elias, M.I., Nikas, C.V., & Bjurlin, M.A. (2020). 3D printing, augmented reality, and virtual reality for the assessment and management of kidney and prostate cancer: A systematic review. *Urology, 143*, 20–32.

Wang, Y., Anne, A., & Ropp, T. (2016). Applying the technology acceptance model to understand aviation students' perceptions toward augmented reality maintenance training instruction. *International Journal of Aviation, Aeronautics, and Aerospace, 3*(4), 3–15.

Winkler-Schwartz, A., Bissonnette, V., Mirchi, N., Ponnudurai, N., Yilmaz, R., Ledwos, N., … & Del Maestro, R.F. (2019). Artificial intelligence in medical education: Best practices using machine learning to assess surgical expertise in virtual reality simulation. *Journal of Surgical Education, 76*(6), 1681–1690.

Wüller, H., Behrens, J., Garthaus, M., Marquard, S., & Remmers, H. (2019). A scoping review of augmented reality in nursing. *BMC Nursing, 18*(1), 1–11.

Yavuz, M., Çorbacıoğlu, E., Başoğlu, A.N., Daim, T.U., & Shaygan, A. (2021). Augmented reality technology adoption: Case of a mobile application in Turkey. *Technology in Society, 66*, 101598.

Zhu, E., Hadadgar, A., Masiello, I., & Zary, N. (2014). Augmented reality in healthcare education: An integrative review. *PeerJ, 2*, e469.

9 The Use of Blockchain Technology in the Sports Sector

The Case of AC Milan Football (Soccer) Team

Kacper Zagała and Mario Nicoliello

Introduction

The coronavirus pandemic (COVID-19) has hit all sectors of the global economy, including sports, which is particularly affected by the crisis in a way that has never been seen before. It is therefore not surprising that since March 2020, there have been numerous contributions from international business and economic literature dedicated to the effect of COVID on the sports sector. The first line of study (Alon et al., 2020; Kraus et al., 2020; Liguori & Winkler, 2020; Nicola et al., 2020) inserted sport into the sectors affected by COVID, the second field of research (Ferreira et al., 2020; Parnell et al., 2020) instead focused on the effects of the virus on different sports, analyzing the consequences in terms of event organization. The third field of study was instead dedicated to the effects of COVID on the management of sports clubs, with particular attention to the consequences of entrepreneurship (McSweeney, 2018; Ratten, 2020; Hammerschmidt et al., 2021). Finally, the fourth strand concerned the legislative aspects of sport and the necessary regulatory adjustments caused by COVID (Garcia-Garcia et al., 2020). Following the third field of research, this case study aims to analyze how football clubs have responded to the managerial challenges imposed by the pandemic by leveraging much more technology to create new revenue streams.

Technology is developing fast, and the sports sector is trying to adapt to the newest solutions in the market. In the third decade of the 21st century, one of the leading technology paths is blockchain, which has been used in many sectors, including sports. In particular, the aim of this case study is to find an answer on how one of the biggest football clubs in the world – AC Milan – is using the newest blockchain technology to increase revenues, improve engagement with their fanbase, and increase the number of supporters who become customers. This case study was placed in the context of technology usage in the sports sector, from the past to the newest innovations, such as Non-Fungible Tokens (NFTs) and Fan Tokens.

DOI: 10.4324/9781003376583-11

The Use of Technology in the Sport Sector

Broadcasting, Wearables, and Video Assistance

The usage of technology in sports is common. Given the technological advances that are taking place in every sector, it should come as no surprise that sports are also becoming more advanced in this regard. Initially, new developments were applied in two areas: sports statistics and broadcasting the game. While in the beginning, all this was handled by trained people supported by technology, in the 21st century, very often, all statistical analyses are carried out using algorithms, artificial intelligence, and advanced systems. In the case of sports broadcasting, people still play the most significant role, but technology has developed significantly too. Live commentary and analysis, replays from many different cameras, or the ability to personalize the experience are just a few examples from a large group of innovations (Goebert et al., 2022). In the context of sports broadcasting, streaming services are also worth mentioning. They are gaining an increasing share of the sports market and give viewers a different opportunity and a different perspective on experiencing sports emotions (Qian, 2021; Lee Ludvigsen & Petersen-Wagner, 2022).

Another example of the technology used in sports is the set of devices that people wear. This refers to all wearables, specially designed items that contain the appropriate technological tools to monitor players, for example, football players wearing special vests under their shirts or wristbands and watches that are worn by professional athletes and amateurs to allow them to record their parameters (Burland et al., 2020; Girginov et al., 2020). Innovation in sports can be seen best in disciplines where players and teams must constantly increase speed of actions. An example of this is auto racing, such as Formula 1, where even the slightest change or innovation can determine the victory in the race or even in the whole season or prevent the drivers from serious injuries (Dhanvanth et al., 2022).

In the context of technology in sports, mention should also be made of the increasingly sophisticated systems designed to assist in the conduct of competitions or individual matches. In some sports (i.e., basketball, tennis, or volleyball), video verification (often called challenge) has been introduced earlier than in other sports. The main goal of this technology is to help better judge a given match situation. Football has also begun to use similar technological solutions. The first example is the Goal-Line Technology (GLT) system, which tells the referee whether the ball has crossed the end line of the pitch in goal and whether a goal should be awarded. Responsible for assessing the situation is a set of cameras, which are placed above the pitch and aimed at the goal. Their task is to record the position of the ball (Winand & Fergusson, 2016). An additional system that was introduced in 2016 is Video Assistant Referee (VAR). The function of this system is that

The Use of Blockchain Technology in the Sports Sector 161

certain pitch situations can be reviewed by a referee who is off the pitch and has replays from multiple cameras at his disposal. The VAR referee assists the head referee in making the best decision and can suggest him to see a given situation on a screen next to the pitch (Carlos et al., 2019; Spitz et al., 2020). Although already used in many top leagues and championship events, this technology still generates some controversy and mixed feelings (Chen & Davidson, 2021). Some of the reasons are the mistakes made by referees, different regulations in different countries, or the lack of VAR in some games (Zglinski, 2020; Scanlon et al., 2022).

Technology can be used to improve performance, monitor fitness, or analyze and broadcast the game. The next step was to improve the business side of sports by using new solutions. Clubs and athletes began to be active on social media and consciously build their brands on these sites to reach new audiences and keep existing fans interested all the time (Anagnostopoulos et al., 2018; Doyle et al., 2020). Another example of increasing fan engagement and increasing revenues are well-run online stores, where fans can purchase club gadgets or apparel.

Blockchain

The solutions described earlier, and their widespread use in sports suggested that the latest technology would also be of interest to the sports sector. This technology is blockchain. Blockchain is a growing list of records, which are called blocks. They are linked together using cryptography. Each block contains a timestamp, i.e., information about when the event associated with the block occurred, transaction data, and encrypted information about the previous block, from which the unidirectionality of the chain results. Each subsequent block is linked to all previous blocks. An important feature of blockchain is also that it is immutable. It is not possible to alter the data in a block without altering the data in the other blocks. Blockchains are usually managed by P2P (peer-to-peer) networks, in which all nodes with the same privileges decide to add or verify new blockchain transactions based on the rules of communication protocols. The advantages for which blockchains are used are transparency, anonymity, independence, security, and efficiency (Lee, 2019; Rajasekaran et al., 2022).

After the first implementations in IT-related industries, more fields have begun to see that using some blockchain solutions can be possible and beneficial. One example is the financial industry, where blockchain technology is helping with currency transactions, conducting many types of contracts or the usage of cryptocurrencies (Ciaian et al., 2016; Farning & Centers, 2016). Another example is the health sector, where blockchain is useful in storing various types of confidential information, such as patients' health status (Agbo et al., 2019). Blockchain is also used by governments and other institutions for many public services (Datta, 2021). Since so many different sectors are taking advantage of the technology and the opportunities offered by blockchain, the sports industry has also begun to implement it.

With the development of information technology, the amount of data that needs to be processed and protected is increasing. One of the advantages of using blockchain is the security (Chen et al., 2019). The data can involve a diverse set of topics, for example, private information about a particular athlete (Yu, 2021). Another way to protect the data is to use the so-called Smart Contracts, which allow bypassing various types of intermediaries in each transaction, thus making it possible to carry out the transaction faster and additionally secure it using cryptography (Singh et al., 2020; Khan et al., 2021). Smart Contracts may be used on different occasions, such as negotiating contracts with athletes or a new deal with a business partner or sponsor. Another example of potential blockchain use in sports is ticket sales, same as in tourism (Kwok & Koh, 2018). Because of the use of cryptography, the entire operation is more secure. Beyond that, each ticket uniqueness, due to the blockchain technology, allows for more efficient management of seats, as well as the elimination of fraudulent practices when reselling tickets on the black market. Each ticket is unique, and its authenticity can be verified automatically (Naman et al., 2021). Some sports clubs have also considered using cryptocurrencies as a means of payment for tickets to their matches (Naraine, 2019). This shows that there is no shortage of ways to use blockchain in sports.

The motivations behind the use of blockchain technology are the desire to innovate, improve technological systems, or increase security in different areas. However, sports clubs and organizations also have business purposes. In addition to their sports activities, they are most often also profit- and growth-oriented businesses, and they are constantly looking for new opportunities to make money and grow.

The Use of Non-Fungible Tokens (NFTs) and Fan Tokens

Television and Internet broadcasts, ticket sales, sponsorship deals, or the sale of club gadgets and merchandise are sources of income of sport organizations (Cox, 2012; Mondello & Fortunato, 2022). In all these ways, fans and their involvement are not insignificant, as they are the ones who consume content and purchase club items. In some sports or leagues, there is a noticeable downward trend in participation in sporting events. In reality less and less people are coming to sport events. This was certainly influenced by the COVID-19 pandemic, through which many games were suspended, played without an audience, or postponed, but there might be other reasons

The Use of Blockchain Technology in the Sports Sector 163

too (Majumdar & Naha, 2020). Sports organizations have therefore begun to think about how to increase fan engagement, which will also lead to better financial results. Also here, blockchain technology, especially NFT (Non-Fungible Token) and Fan Token, was considered as a solution.

NFT is a blockchain-based digital data unit. Its important advantages are uniqueness and indivisibility. This means that it is not possible to represent a particular data string with two different tokens, and it is not possible to divide one token into smaller parts. In the case of NFTs, it is also important to remember that if they represent an object, it does not mean that the holder of the token also holds the copyrights to that object. Most often, the tokens themselves are separate from the copyrights, and an additional legal agreement is required in this regard (Nadini et al., 2021). NFTs are most often used in digital art, and this industry has contributed significantly to the popularity of tokens. The most expensive artworks have been sold for millions of dollars (Ante, 2022). NFTs are also used in games to represent various unique goods in a game, as well as in the music or film industry. However, many NFTs were linked to some online objects, and their value depended on how much someone was willing to pay, and it did not necessarily represent any use value. Different case was with Fan Tokens, the possession of which was also linked to the ability to engage in different activities and participate in events. The sports industry tried to use Fan Tokens to increase fan engagement by offering something in return.

After successful implementation in many sectors, sports has also joined in the use of NFTs. Once popular cards and other collectibles began to appear in virtual form as NFTs. Fans could buy unique tokens that were associated with their favorite player or favorite team. For example, fans of the American basketball league NBA, in addition to collectible cards, can buy the best moments from the NBA's history. The program is called NBA Top Shot, and it has its own website with information about new collectible items and its own marketplace where people can buy items from other fans (Zaucha & Agur, 2022). The items can be purchased in dollars but also in cryptocurrencies. A similar formula is considered by the authorities of UFC fights, the NFL football league, or the Spanish La Liga football league. In football, virtual collectible cards are popular too, and new companies are emerging to offer fans further opportunities to collect their favorite players or moments associated with them. In addition to NFTs, the previously mentioned Fan Tokens have also been developed, which are different from NFTs. Most often, they are fungible, and having more of them comes with more benefits. They can be compared to shares, the number of which corresponds to greater power in a company. While in the case of NFTs, there is a speculative aspect, in the case of Fan Tokens, they represent use value. By holding the tokens, fans can take part in various kinds of votes and polls on, for example, the club's new motto, the inscriptions on the shirts or captain's armband, and the songs played before matches or after a goal is scored (Demir et al., 2022). One of the first teams to take advantage of the new technology was the Italian club Juventus Turin, and many others followed. One of the most popular platforms for buying tokens and the benefits associated with them, Socios already has more than 150 partners from different sports (football, basketball, field hockey or, even gaming). It is being used by major football clubs such as FC Barcelona, Manchester City, PSG, and AC Milan to increase the loyalty of their fans by offering them active participation in building the club, thereby gaining a new source of revenue. This case study describes how Italy's Serie A champion from the 2021/2022 season, AC Milan, is using new blockchain technology to achieve its goals.

Methods

Following the case study method (Yin, 2017), the work focused on the case of AC Milan. The choice of the club was made in successive steps. First of all, wanting to find a link between COVID-19 and the balance sheets of football clubs, the analysis focused on the Italian Serie A, the European league that was most affected by COVID-19 among the five main ones of the old continent (Deloitte, 2022). Within Serie A, after analyzing the budgets of the last three years, the focus was dedicated to Milan, the winning team of the last championship in the 2021/22 season.

To collect the data, the authors proceeded with a detailed analysis of the balance sheet numbers of the AC Milan club, then a detailed investigation of the communications made by the club was carried out, analyzing all the press releases published in the year 2022 and published on the website www. acmilan.com. Within these press releases (1,232 news published on the website from January 1, 2022, to October 15, 2022), those relating to the commercial area (36 news) were chosen. The analysis of the selected press releases allowed to reconstruct the events related to the use of blockchain and NFTs. The authors also requested an interview with the chief revenue officer (CRO) of AC Milan, as the analysis is aimed at understanding how the use of technology can impact revenues, but the company has not granted permission, therefore in the analysis, there are only the public statements made by the CRO during the launch of the specific campaigns.

The Case Study

A Brief History of AC Milan

AC Milan is an Italian Football Team based in Milan. Associazione Calcio, commonly referred to as AC Milan or simply Milan, is a professional football club in Milan, Italy, founded in 1899. "We will be a team of

The Use of Blockchain Technology in the Sports Sector   165

devils. Our colors will be red like fire and black to invoke fear in our opponents!" These were the words that Herbert Kilpin used as he founded AC Milan on December 16, 1899. Just a year and a half later, the Rossoneri became the champions of Italy for the first time after beating Genoa 3-0 at Ponte Carrega on May 5, 1901. The first celebration took place at AC Milan's first headquarters, the Fiaschetteria Toscana on Via Berchet in Milan, in 1899. The club has spent its entire history, with the exception of the 1980–81 and 1982–83 seasons, in the top league of Italian football, known as Serie A, since 1929–30. AC Milan's 18 FIFA and UEFA trophies are the fourth highest out of any club (joint with Boca Juniors) and the most out of any Italian club. Milan has won a joint record of three Intercontinental Cups and one FIFA Club World Cup, seven European Cup/Champions League titles (Italian record), the UEFA Super Cup a joint record five times, and the Cup Winners' Cup twice. With 19 league titles, Milan is tied as the second most successful club in Serie A with local rivals Inter Milan (also with 19 league titles), behind Juventus (36 league titles). They have also won the Coppa Italia (Italian Cup) five times and the Supercoppa Italiana (Italian Supercup) seven times. Milan's home games are played at San Siro, also known as the Stadio Giuseppe Meazza. The stadium, built by Milan's second chairman Piero Pirelli in 1926 and shared since 1947 with city rivals Internazionale, is the largest in Italian football, with a total capacity of 75,923. They have a long-standing rivalry with Inter, with whom they contest the Derby della Madonnina; it is one of the most followed derbies in football.

The Rossoneri's last trophy came on May 22, 2022, when Stefano Pioli's men won the Scudetto. In September 2022, Red Bird Capital Partner became the new owner, buying the shares from Elliott Management Corporation.

The Use of Blockchain

Using the press release, the authors reconstructed the main steps regarding the projects of AC Milan in the Blockchain Sector.

In April 2022, AC Milan, in collaboration with Fansea, launched its first NFT project, through which the Club sold a 3D, limited edition NFT of a special Rossoneri jersey from South Sudan. Proceeds from the sale favor the Milan Foundation and its charitable initiatives worldwide, including those dedicated to the humanitarian crisis in Ukraine. The NFT in 3D, created by Fansea using modern and eco-sustainable technology, costs €45 and is available in only 75,817 units, a number that corresponds to the capacity of the San Siro stadium. Fans can purchase one or more NFT copies on the website: acmilan.fansea.io. The limited edition NFT represents a special AC Milan shirt from South Sudan, which hit the headlines in December 2021. The shirt, dating back to the 2016/17 season, was discovered during a trip by Danish war photographer Jan Grarup, who was engaged in documenting the devastating effects of the severe floods that have afflicted South Sudan for years. This shirt was then donated to the Club, which decided to exhibit it in the Mondo Milan Museum at Casa Milan, the Rossoneri headquarters in Milan, in a new section dedicated to the educational and social initiatives of the Milan Foundation. The Club and the Milan Foundation have also made a donation to UNICEF, which actively works in the country to guarantee every child their right to a childhood.

On the occasion of the last home match of the season, on May 15, 2022, Milan launched two initiatives related to Fan Tokens. For the last home game of Serie A 2021–2022, the one against Atalanta, Milan decided to let their supporters choose a memorable phrase to print on the pennant as an encouraging slogan for the penultimate step toward the Scudetto. A survey among all the holders of fan tokens decreed which motto to select from the proposals made available to the community. In addition, the signed Milan-Atalanta pennant was purchased by the fastest user in the fan rewards list of the dedicated application. Among the Rossoneri fans, those who had enough experience points (Ssu) to convert tried the company to beat the competition to secure the heirloom.

On Sunday of winning the Scudetto, May 22, 2022, there were two initiatives related to the NFTs. The first one was placed a few minutes after the end of the last match against Sassuolo – an invitation for all the fans to participate in the celebrations on the dedicated app. The additional motivation was the chance to win an official signed shirt. The second surprise came about an hour later – in the fan rewards list (on which prizes are redeemed in exchange for experience points – Ssu), the experience of meeting the players at Casa Milan was made available. Those who were connected at the time of the tweet – and qualify – got their hands on the treasure.

In July 2022, AC Milan and OneFootball announced a new partnership to create exclusive digital collectibles, in the form of video highlights and images, for over 500 million Rossoneri fans worldwide. As part of the new multi-year agreement, OneFootball becomes the new Official NFT Video Highlight Moment Partner and new Premium Partner of AC Milan. The goal of the partnership is to improve further the engagement of the Rossoneri fans in the digital world, allowing them to collect and exchange official digital collectibles and offering a multidimensional experience that can accompany them from real life during a new digital era.

The new digital collectibles allow the Milan fans to collect, own, and exchange exclusive moments from AC Milan matches in Serie A, Coppa Italia, and Supercoppa Italiana: the best actions, saves, and defensive interventions, but also the most spectacular goals. Through OneFootball, fans can purchase a unique moment of a specific AC Milan match, owning it forever in real life. Created on the Flow blockchain, Aera by OneFootball is the largest football media platform in the world, where fans can easily buy their favorite moments, and it is safe through a Dapper wallet. The new partnership with OneFootball is part of AC Milan's broader Web 3.0 strategy, which sees the Club working with industry experts to create unique digital experiences for fans, increasing the degree of participation and closeness to their team.

In July 2022, AC Milan and Sorare announced a new exclusive multi-year partnership. The aim was to engage in the crypto fantasy football game, which is based on collectible digital cards that can be purchased in the form of NFT. In addition, Sorare became the Official NFT Fantasy Football Game Partner and new Premium Partner of AC Milan. With this new agreement, AC Milan officially joins the NFT-based Sorare fantasy football. It allows users to buy, sell, trade, and manage their team of official digital cards, which provide a global and immersive gaming experience. From the 2022/23 season, the more than two million registered users on the Sorare platform will also be able to purchase, exchange, and manage AC Milan trading cards, further strengthening the link between AC Milan fans around the world and the Club in the digital world.

The partnership with Sorare, a leading company in the rapidly evolving sector of NFTs, offers AC Milan a new crucial digital tool for fan engagement, a platform available to fans and users to enhance and share their passion for football. The agreement also involves a new source of revenue created through the licensing of NFTs. The new partnership with Sorare is part of AC Milan's broader Web 3.0 strategy, with the Club working with industry experts to create unique digital experiences for fans, increasing participation and closeness to their favorite team.

In September 2022, AC Milan announced a new partnership with MonkeyLeague, a digital football game for the web3 and built on the Solana blockchain. This cooperation allowed MonkeyLeague to become Rossoneri's new NFT Gaming Partner. MonkeyLeague is a strategy-based soccer game in which all users create and manage their dream team of at least six MonkeyPlayer NFTs (attacker, midfielder, defender, and goal-keeper), compete against real players, and climb the ranks based on their achievements. The game's economy revolves around an internal currency, the MonkeyBucks ($MBS), and internal assets with intrinsic value inside and outside the game. This new strategic partnership between MonkeyLeague and AC Milan allows creating the exclusive NFT assets branded AC Milan, such as game outfits, special tournaments, co-marketing events, and many other initiatives, such as the participation of AC Milan players themselves in the playtest of the game. The partnership involves the close collaboration between MonkeyLeague and the club to launch a new collection of NFT assets related to the game and branded AC Milan, such as new MonkeyPlayers, skins, and stadiums. The first and exclusive part of the collection auctioned from October 2022 on MagicEden allows buyers of some of AC Milan's MonkeyPlayers to receive an original physical shirt signed by the AC Milan team.

With this partnership, AC Milan sponsors some prestigious esports tournaments that bring together the best players in the world of MonkeyLeague, who compete to take home exclusive prizes. At the same time, there are additional prizes, such as VIP tickets for the big matches played at the San Siro stadium, signed AC Milan shirts, and other accessories. The game benefits from the input of AC Milan stars, as some players have participated in a test phase of the game to provide feedback and guidance to ensure that the gameplay is as realistic and engaging as possible.

Discussion

The purpose of this case study is to show how the use of blockchain and NFT can positively impact the football club's revenues. Therefore, it is noteworthy to report the comments of the Rossoneri management following the projects presented. The statements are taken from the press releases issued by the company AC Milan. According to Casper Stylsvig, chief revenue officer of AC Milan:

> It is in the nature of AC Milan to explore innovative ways of interacting with its fanbase of over 500 million fans around the world, spreading the most positive values of sport at the same time. We are therefore proud to have been able to merge both these aspects of our Club into a single project.

After the agreement with OneFootball, the chief revenue officer said: "We are thrilled to launch this project, which will bring us even closer to the more than 500 million Rossoneri fans around the world. Plus, we believe that this territory can improve the experience of our fans".

Meanwhile, after the agreement with Sorare, the management was optimistic about the new project, and Stylsvig said that this is a special moment for the club and the fans:

> A new era is opening for us, together with a young and dynamic brand, at the forefront of the NFT revolution, and that has been able to combine digital collectibles and fantasy sports games. We are an innovative club, and we intend to explore this sector with a well-defined strategy. The goal

is to offer our more than 500 million fans around the world new opportunities to connect with their favorite team.

Finally, following the partnership with MonkeyLeague, the CRO said about a cooperation:

> That will allow us to strengthen our position in the field of digital innovation. We are proud to be the first football club to forge a partnership with MonkeyLeague. Through this collaboration, we will bring this game to our fans around the world by offering them an innovative new way to interact with their favorite team.

The exploration of this business area was necessary because Milan needed to improve the turnover of its commercial sphere. Many financial reports showed that the Milan club in the years from 2017 to 2020 reduced its commercial revenues. In 2021, there was growth, but the numbers were still lower than the ones from 2016. There is, therefore, the objective of increasing commercial revenues, at the base of which is the activity of the fans. The more fans are involved in the club's business, the greater the chances for a club to increase revenue from sponsorship and merchandising. Blockchain and NFTs, therefore, act as business levers in the commercial area, and in this perspective, they constitute a driving force for increasing revenues.

Conclusion

Technology in sports is being used in many different areas, whether to improve security, conduct a fair game, or grow as a company in the sports sector. Sports organizations try to follow the trends and implement innovative solutions to be competitive from both sports and business perspectives. That is why many teams started using blockchain technology with all its benefits. Some of them focused on data security, and others saw the potential to engage with their fanbase on a different level, make them more active, and eventually increase revenue. That is the case of AC Milan, which is one of the most active football clubs in this manner. This case study is a summary of the new solutions implemented and actions taken by the club to connect with their fans and secure another way of income.

This case study aimed to place the AC Milan football team in the context of the technology used in the sports sector and show how they implement blockchain solutions to improve their bond with the existing fans, gain new supporters, and increase revenue. The case study shows that AC Milan benefited from blockchain technology and implemented many different solutions such as NFTs with the greatest moments from the history of the club, Fan Tokens that allow fans to decide on various aspects related to the club, and also the games where fans can interact with the club even more.

This case study of the AC Milan football team can be analyzed from two perspectives. The first one is the sports perspective. The usage of blockchain technology by the club addressed in this study can be viewed as a source of inspiration or as a benchmark for other teams that are either struggling to engage with their fans or just trying to grow as a sports team. The usage of NFTs and Fan Tokens by AC Milan, presented in this case study, can become a model for others to copy the solutions or adjust them to their own needs. The other perspective is the business one. AC Milan is a football club but also a company with important business goals. Technology innovations help them build a stronger connection with their fans, who are also their clients. Having a more engaged fanbase means that the supporters are more eager to invest their money in new projects because they see value in them. For the club, it means that they have another way of income. That is why this case study can be beneficial not only for the sports organizations but also for the ones from other sectors. They may need to adjust some solutions to match their business goals, but the idea of building a loyal group of clients and increasing revenue can be a motive to use blockchain technology. The case study of AC Milan contributes to many fields of science, including sports, technology, and business. It shows how technology can be used in sport organization to help them reach their sports and business goals. However, this case study represents the perspective of the organization. To fully understand the process of new technology implementation, an additional study can be conducted in which the main focus will be on the fans' perspective. Their involvement and their opinions might be beneficial in future research like the development of this result.

References

Agbo, C.C., Mahmoud, Q.H., & Eklund, J.M. (2019). Blockchain technology in healthcare: A systematic review. *Healthcare 2019*, *7*(2), 56. 10.3390/HEALTHCARE7020056

Alon, I., Farrell, M., & Li, S. (2020). Regime type and COVID-19 response. *FIIB Business Review*, *9*(3), 152–160. 10.1177/2319714520928884

Anagnostopoulos, C., Parganas, P., Chadwick, S., & Fenton, A. (2018). Branding in pictures: Using Instagram as a brand management tool in professional team sport organisations. *European Sport Management Quarterly*, *18*(4), 413–438. 10.1080/16184742.2017.1410202

Ante, L. (2022). The non-fungible token (NFT) market and its relationship with bitcoin and ethereum. *FinTech 2022*, *1*(3), 216–224. 10.3390/FINTECH1030017

The Use of Blockchain Technology in the Sports Sector 171

Burland, J.P., Outerleys, J.B., Lattermann, C., & Davis, I.S. (2020). Reliability of wearable sensors to assess impact metrics during sport-specific tasks. *Journal of Sports Sciences, 39*(4), 406–411. 10.1080/02640414.2020.1823131

Carlos, L.P., Ezequiel, R., & Anton, K. (2019). How does video assistant referee (VAR) modify the game in elite soccer? *International Journal of Performance Analysis in Sport, 19*(4), 646–653. 10.1080/24748668.2019.1646521

Chen, J., Lv, Z., & Song, H. (2019). Design of personnel big data management system based on blockchain. *Future Generation Computer Systems, 101*, 1122–1129. 10.1016/J.FUTURE.2019.07.037

Chen, R., & Davidson, N.P. (2021). English Premier League manager perceptions of video assistant referee (VAR) decisions during the 2019–2020 season. *Soccer & Society, 23*(1), 44–55. 10.1080/14660970.2021.1918680

Ciaian, P., Rajcaniova, M., & Kancs, d'A. (2016). The economics of bitcoin price formation. *Applied Economics, 48*(19), 1799–1815. 10.1080/00036846.2015.1109038

Cox, A. (2012). Live broadcasting, gate revenue, and football club performance: Some evidence. *International Journal of the Economics of Business, 19*(1), 75–98. 10.1080/13571516.2012.643668

Datta, A. (2021). Blockchain enabled digital government and public sector services: A survey. *Public Administration and Information Technology, 36*, 175–195. 10.1007/978-3-030-55746-1_8/COVER

Deloitte. (2022). *Annual review of football finance 2022.* https://www2.deloitte.com/uk/en/pages/sports-business-group/articles/annual-review-of-football-finance.html. Accessed February 2, 2023.

Demir, E., Ersan, O., & Popesko, B. (2022). Are fan tokens fan tokens? *Finance Research Letters, 47*. 10.1016/J.FRL.2022.102736

Dhanvanth, S., Rajesh, R., Samyukth, S.S., & Jeyakumar, G. (2022). Machine learning-based analytical and predictive study on Formula 1 and its safety. In A. Tomar, H. Malik, P. Kumar, & A. Iqbal (Eds.), *Proceedings of 3rd International Conference on Machine Learning, Advances in Computing, Renewable Energy and Communication. Lecture Notes in Electrical Engineering* (Vol. 915, pp. 257–266). Singapore: Springer. 10.1007/978-981-19-2828-4_25

Doyle, J.P., Su, Y., & Kunkel, T. (2020). Athlete branding via social media: Examining the factors influencing consumer engagement on Instagram. *European Sport Management Quarterly, 22*(4), 506–526. 10.1080/16184742.2020.1806897

Fanning, K., & Centers, D.P. (2016). Blockchain and its coming impact on financial services. *Journal of Corporate Accounting & Finance, 27*(5), 53–57. 10.1002/JCAF.22179

Ferreira, J.J., Fernandes, C., Ratten, V., & Miragaia, D. (2020). Sports innovation: A bibliometric study. In V. Ratten (Ed.), *Sport Entrepreneurship and Public Policy: Contributions to Management Science* (pp. 153–170). Cham: Springer. 10.1007/978-3-030-29458-8_10

Garcia-Garcia, B., James, M., Koller, D., Lindholm, J., Mavromati, D., Parrish, R., & Rodenberg, R. (2020). The impact of Covid-19 on sports: A mid-way assessment. *The International Sports Law Journal, 20*(3), 115–119. 10.1007/S40318-020-00174-8

Girginov, V., Moore, P., Olsen, N., Godfrey, T., & Cooke, F. (2020). Wearable technology-stimulated social interaction for promoting physical activity: A systematic review. *Cogent Social Sciences, 6*(1). 10.1080/23311886.2020.1742517

Goebert, C., Greenhalgh, G., & Dwyer, B. (2022). A whole new ball game: Fan perceptions of augmented reality enhanced sport broadcasts. *Computers in Human Behavior, 137.* 10.1016/J.CHB.2022.107388

Hammerschmidt, J., Durst, S., Kraus, S., & Puumalainen, K. (2021). Professional football clubs and empirical evidence from the COVID-19 crisis: Time for sport entrepreneurship? *Technological Forecasting and Social Change, 165.* 10.1016/J.TECHFORE.2021.120572

Khan, S.N., Loukil, F., Ghedira-Guegan, C., Benkhelifa, E., & Bani-Hani, A. (2021). Blockchain smart contracts: Applications, challenges, and future trends. *Peer-to-Peer Networking and Applications, 14*(5), 2901–2925. 10.1007/S12083-021-01127-0

Kraus, S., Clauss, T., Breier, M., Gast, J., Zardini, A., & Tiberius, V. (2020). The economics of COVID-19: Initial empirical evidence on how family firms in five European countries cope with the corona crisis. *International Journal of Entrepreneurial Behaviour and Research, 26*(5), 1067–1092. 10.1108/IJEBR-04-2020-0214

Kwok, A.O.J., & Koh, S.G.M. (2018). Is blockchain technology a watershed for tourism development? *Current Issues in Tourism, 22*(20), 2447–2452. 10.1080/13683500.2018.1513460

Lee, W. M. (2019). Understanding blockchain. In *Beginning Ethereum Smart Contracts Programming* (pp. 1–23). Berkeley, CA: Apress. 10.1007/978-1-4842-5086-0_1

Lee Ludvigsen, J.A., & Petersen-Wagner, R. (2022). From television to YouTube: Digitalised sport mega-events in the platform society. *Leisure Studies.* 10.1080/02614367.2022.2125557

Liguori, E., & Winkler, C. (2020). From offline to online: Challenges and opportunities for entrepreneurship education following the COVID-19 pandemic. *Entrepreneurship Education and Pedagogy, 3*(4), 346–351. 10.1177/2515127420916738

Majumdar, B., & Naha, S. (2020). Live sport during the COVID-19 crisis: Fans as creative broadcasters. *Sport in Society, 23*(7), 1091–1099. 10.1080/17430437.2020.1776972

McSweeney, M.J. (2018). Returning the 'social' to social entrepreneurship: Future possibilities of critically exploring sport for development and peace and social entrepreneurship. *International Review for the Sociology of Sport, 55*(1), 3–21. 10.1177/1012690218784295

Mondello, M., & Fortunato, J. (2022). The economics of sport broadcasting. *Sport Broadcasting for Managers*, 55–69. 10.4324/9781003140061-5

Nadini, M., Alessandretti, L., di Giacinto, F., Martino, M., Aiello, L.M., & Baronchelli, A. (2021). Mapping the NFT revolution: Market trends, trade networks, and visual features. *Scientific Reports, 11*(1), 1–11. 10.1038/s41598-021-00053-8

Naman, V., Daliyet, S.P., Lokre, S.S., & Varaprasad Rao, K. (2021). Secure event ticket booking using decentralized system. *Intelligent Systems Reference Library, 203*, 221–242. 10.1007/978-3-030-69395-4_13

Naraine, M.L. (2019). The blockchain phenomenon: Conceptualizing decentralized networks and the value proposition to the sport industry. *International Journal of Sport Communication, 12*(3), 313–335. 10.1123/IJSC.2019-0051

Nicola, M., Alsafi, Z., Sohrabi, C., Kerwan, A., Al-Jabir, A., Iosifidis, C., Agha, M., & Agha, R. (2020). The socio-economic implications of the coronavirus pandemic (COVID-19): A review. *International Journal of Surgery, 78*, 185–193. 10.1016/J.IJSU.2020.04.018

Parnell, D., Widdop, P., Bond, A., & Wilson, R. (2020). COVID-19, networks and sport. *Managing Sport and Leisure, 27*(1–2), 72–78. 10.1080/23750472.2020.1750100

Qian, T.Y. (2021). Watching sports on twitch? A study of factors influencing continuance intentions to watch Thursday Night Football co-streaming. *Sport Management Review, 25*(1), 59–80. 10.1080/14413523.2021.1930700

Rajasekaran, A.S., Azees, M., & Al-Turjman, F. (2022). A comprehensive survey on blockchain technology. *Sustainable Energy Technologies and Assessments, 52*. 10.1016/J.SETA.2022.102039

Ratten, V. (2020). Coronavirus disease (COVID-19) and sport entrepreneurship. *International Journal of Entrepreneurial Behaviour and Research. 26*(6), 1379–1388. 10.1108/IJEBR-06-2020-0387

Scanlon, C., Griggs, G., & McGillick, C. (2022). 'It's not football anymore': Perceptions of the video assistant referee by English Premier League football fans. *Soccer & Society, 23*(8). 10.1080/14660970.2022.2033731

Singh, A., Parizi, R.M., Zhang, Q., Choo, K.K.R., & Dehghantanha, A. (2020). Blockchain smart contracts formalization: Approaches and challenges to address vulnerabilities. *Computers & Security, 88*. 10.1016/J.COSE.2019.101654

Spitz, J., Wagemans, J., Memmert, D., Williams, A.M., & Helsen, W.F. (2020). Video assistant referees (VAR): The impact of technology on decision making in association football referees. *Journal of Sports Sciences, 39*(2), 147–153. 10.1080/02640414.2020.1809163

Winand, M., & Fergusson, C. (2016). More decision-aid technology in sport? An analysis of football supporters' perceptions on goal-line technology. *Soccer & Society, 19*(7), 966–985. 10.1080/14660970.2016.1267629

Yin, R.K. (2017). *Case Study Research and Applications: Design and Methods* (6th ed.). Los Angeles: SAGE Publications, Inc.

Yu, S. (2021). Application of blockchain-based sports health data collection system in the development of sports industry. *Mobile Information Systems, 2021*. 10.1155/2021/4663147

Zaucha, T., & Agur, C. (2022). Newly minted: Non-fungible tokens and the commodification of fandom. *New Media & Society*. 10.1177/14614448221080481

Zglinski, J. (2020). Rules, standards, and the video assistant referee in football. *Sport, Thics and Philosophy, 16*(1), 3–19. 10.1080/17511321.2020.1857823

Part 3

Value Creation at Business Organizations

10 "Pacto pela Industria"

Reindustrialization Opportunities in the Great ABC Region, Brazil

Cristina Fróes de Borja Reis,
Aroaldo Oliveira Santos,
Sheila Ribeiro Marques, and
Amanda Colombo

Introduction

The value chains of Brazilian companies were challenged by the pandemic of COVID-19, with disruptions in the flows of investments, goods, and services. Among the dramatic examples, one can recall the lack of personal protective equipment, respirators, inputs for the production of vaccines and medicines, as well as difficulties in the food, raw materials, and energy chains (Reis, 2021). There were also discontinuities in the supply of semiconductors, affecting several chains dependent on electronics, such as the automotive industry: the most damaged by the pandemic (UNIDO, 2022). They have caused not only commercial problems, but serious social problems, such as unemployment, inflation, food, and energy insecurity. Thus, the problems in global value chains (GVCs) during the pandemic, exacerbating an ongoing crisis related to climate change, new technological paradigm and geopolitical conflicts, negatively affects the realization of the UN Agenda 2030 in the developing world (Reis, 2021; UN, 2022).

Such crisis hits hard the declining industrial regions, such as the Greater ABC Region (ABC). The ABC is located in the metropolitan region of São Paulo and since 1967 has been composed of seven municipalities: Santo André, São Bernardo do Campo, São Caetano do Sul, Diadema, Mauá, Ribeirão Pires, and Rio Grande da Serra. It covers an area of 825 km², with a population of about 2.7 million inhabitants (IBGE estimate for 2021). Having been in the 1950s–1980s the heart of Brazilian manufacturing industry, particularly centered on the automotive, metal-mechanic and petrochemical sectors, with the productive and financial globalization the ABC underwent a productive reconfiguration toward deindustrialization (Reis et al., 2023). Orchestrated by external forces, related to global geopolitics and the governance decisions of large transnational corporations, but aggravated by internal forces, such as the lack of planning, the rising

DOI: 10.4324/9781003376583-13

178 *Cristina Fróes de Borja Reis et al.*

costs of production and commercialization as well as unfavorable macroeconomic regime, deindustrialization has been relentless.

According to a survey by the Observatory of Economics of the Methodist University in April 2020, at the beginning of the pandemic, 4.5% of the EAP lost their jobs, with the unemployment rate – which was already 12.5% – reaching 17% in the Greater ABC region. The ABC pointed to capacity utilization well below the state and national average, in 2021, with an average of 67%, while in the Southeast it was 69% and in Brazil 70%. In July 2022, the three had already reached 71%, which shows that the sector is still very idle. Such that the production level of the national transformation industry has not yet reached the levels of 2010 (Observatorio Economico, 2020, 2022). Loss of income mass, indebtedness and precarious social indicators in the current crisis, by the end of 2022 have not yet been reverted.

In this sense, the tremendous crisis led the various social actors to come together in a joint search for solutions. Around the Greater ABC Economic Development Agency (ADEGABC), an expectation of regional repactuation was formed by industry (Reis, 2022). Such commitment was tremendous and mobilized the so-called quadruple helix: productive sector, public sector, education institutes, and social movements, in search of a bottom-up social agreement such as had not been seen in the region for years. Due to the enormous importance of this case, as a possible example for several other localities facing the same situation, the objective of this article is to describe and analyze the process of construction of the Pact for Industry, led by the Agency for Economic Development of the Greater ABC region. For this purpose, the first section presents a socioeconomic panorama of the ABC region based on Agenda 2030; the second section describes the formation of the ABC Intermunicipal Consortium and the Greater ABC Economic Development Agency; the third section presents the sociological record of the Pact for Industry in the Greater ABC region.

The Great ABC Region: Overview of Socioeconomic Indicators

The seven cities of the ABC region are quite unequal in terms of territory, population, and socioeconomic indicators (see Tables 10.1 and 10.2). On one side is São Bernardo do Campo, with a territory larger than that of the other six municipalities combined, about 850,000 inhabitants and the 16th largest GDP in Brazil. There is also São Caetano do Sul, a smaller city, with 162,000 inhabitants, but the highest GDP per capita (National currency reais – R$85,000 per year). On the other hand, the poorest municipalities, Ribeirão Pires and Rio Grande da Serra, with per capita GDP, respectively, of R$25,000 and R$14,000 per year, less than two minimum wages per month.

In Table 10.2, in turn, the region's disparities become more evident. São Caetano do Sul, out of 5,570 Brazilian municipalities evaluated by the

Table 10. 1 Summary profile of the seven cities in the Greater ABC region

	S. André	S. B. do Campo	S. C. do Sul	Diadema	Mauá	Ribeirão Pires	Rio Grande da Serra
GDP [current R$ billion, 2019]	30.3	51.1	13.7	15.3	16.3	3.1	0.7
Estimated population [2021]	723,889	849,874	162,763	429,550	481,725	125,238	52,009
Territory [km²]	175.78	409.53	15.33	30.73	61.91	99.08	36.34
SM monthly formal jobs [2020]	2.7	3.4	3.1	3.0	2.9	2.5	2.4
Personnel employed [2020]	238,845	283,119	120,965	95,052	72,712	23,885	3,877
% Occupied population [2020]	33.1%	33.5%	74.7%	22.3%	15.2%	19.2%	7.5%
Schooling rate of 6 to 14 year olds [2010]	97.4%	97.6%	97.4%	96.8%	97.4%	97.4%	98.2%
GDP per capita [2019] in R$	42,209.54	60,871.06	85,062.97	36,097.90	34,430.52	25,497.1	14,179.63
Municipal Human Development Index (HDI) [2010]	0.815	0.805	0.862	0.757	0.766	0.784	0.749

Source: Prepared by Reis et al. (2023) based on IBGE Cidades (Brazilian Institute of geography and Statistics, Cities Database) between the years 2010 and 2021.

Table 10.2 SDG achievement indicators in the ABC municipalities

	Sao Caetano do Sul	St. Andre	Sao Bernardo do Campo	Maua	Ribeirao Pires	Diadema	Rio Grande da Serra
Ranking Brazilian Cities (5,570 total)	1	296	423	690	794	1,453	1,838
Point (max 100)	65.6	57.7	56.6	54.9	54.2	50.9	49.5
SDG1							
SDG2							
SDG3							
SDG4							
SDG5							
SDG6							
SDG7							
SDG8							
SDG9							

"Pacto pela Industria" 181

SDG10
SDG11
SDG12
SDG13
SDG14
SDG15
SDG16
SDG17

Source: Prepared by the authors based on Sustainable Development Index for Cities, 2022.
Legend: Black = SDG achieved; Dark grey = there are challenges; Light grey = There are significant challenges; White = there are major challenges.

Institute and the Sustainable Cities Program, based on the methodology developed by the SDSN network (UN Sustainable Development Solution Network), is the best Brazilian city in Agenda 2030, while Diadema and Rio Grande da Serra are in the 1,453rd and 1,838th positions, respectively. Even at the top of the ranking, São Caetano do Sul has eight SDGs (Sustainable Development Goals) classified as the furthest from being achieved (SDGs 1, 2, 3, 4, 5, 10, 15 and 16). All municipalities have seven to ten SDGs in black, coinciding with education (SDG 4), gender equality (SDG 5), reduction of inequalities (SDG 10), and peace and justice institutions (SDG 16). In almost all municipalities, except Rio Grande da Serra, the SDGs of renewable energy (SDG 7), and industry, infrastructure, and innovation (SDG 9) were met (white). SDG 13, on climate change, is in light grey (few challenges remain) in all municipalities as well, and SDG 14 (life on water) was achieved in São Caetano do Sul and Mauá.

The success of SDG 7 is explained by the energy matrix historically based on hydroelectric dams. But as Lampis et al. (2020) state when analyzing the Macrometrópole of São Paulo (MMP) "the concepts of access, equity and energy justice are not yet confirmed". Regarding SDG 9, the region still has high participation of the transformation industry in the region's GDP, comparatively to its state and country. However, deindustrialization has been accelerating, as it can be seen by the sector's loss of participation in total employment in the last decades, in Table 10.3.

This phenomenon was national, but more intense in the ABC. As Reis et al. (2023) point out, the share of manufacturing industry in Brazilian GDP in real terms retracted from 14.5% to 11% between 2003 and 2019 (Morceiro, 2019). The state of São Paulo, which held 43.6% of Brazil's Industrial Transformation Value (ITV) in 2003, fell to 37.5% in 2019 (SEADE, 2019). In the state, the capital São Paulo had a reduction from 14.8% to 9.0% of the VTI between 2003 and 2017, while the municipalities in the Greater ABC region had a drop from 11.4% to 7.2%. Thus, while in 2003, five municipalities of the Greater ABC region were among the 20 cities with the highest manufacturing production in the state of São Paulo, in 2017 there were four: São Bernardo do Campo fell from the fourth to the sixth position (with share in the state VTI falling from 5.0% to 3.0%), Santo André from the 8th to the 13th position (from 2.2% to 1.4%), Mauá from the 11th to the 12th position (with 1.6% stable), Diadema from the 12th to the 18th position (SEADE, 2019).

For Negreiros and Abriko (2020), as to SDG9 in the MMP, local management faces several challenges in face of the dimension and scale of the current problems, which would require articulated and integrated solutions and cooperation of actors and institutions. "It presents as a challenge to governance to equate the differences in characteristics and configuration of the municipalities, metropolitan regions, and urban

Table 10.3 Participation of the sectors of activity in formal jobs in the Greater ABC Paulista Region, 1989–2020

Year	Mineral extraction	Industry	Public utilities	Civil construction	Trade	Services	Public Administration	Agrope-cuary, extraction	Total
1989	0.1%	61.7%	0.1%	2.3%	10.7%	20.5%	4.5%	0.1%	100.0%
1999	0.0%	39.2%	0.6%	2.4%	14.1%	35.9%	7.2%	0.6%	100.0%
2002	0.0%	34.8%	0.5%	2.3%	14.8%	40.6%	6.9%	0.0%	100.0%
2005	0.0%	35.8%	0.6%	2.7%	16.0%	38.2%	6.7%	0.0%	100.0%
2008	0.0%	34.8%	0.6%	4.2%	16.9%	37.7%	5.8%	0.0%	100.0%
2011	0.0%	32.7%	0.6%	0.5%	17.4%	38.2%	6.1%	0.0%	100.0%
2014	0.0%	29.2%	0.6%	0.0%	1.8%	40.8%	6.3%	0.0%	100.0%
2016	0.0%	26.1%	0.6%	4.6%	19.3%	4.3%	6.6%	0.0%	100.0%
2019	0.0%	24.9%	0.5%	4.1%	19.7%	44.9%	5.8%	0.1%	100.0%
2020	0.0%	24.4%	0.5%	4.2%	19.8%	44.7%	6.4%	0.0%	100.0%

Source: Adapted by the authors from Conceição et al. (2018) and Reis et al. (2023) from Annual Social Information Report (RAIS) of the Ministry of Labor and Employment.

184 *Cristina Fróes de Borja Reis et al.*

agglomerations that constitute the MMP" (p. 172), and as we may imply, the ABC. Among these challenges, they highlight:

> improve the business environment; implement and develop sectors and activities intensive in innovation, science and technology; make the environmental issue transversal and internalized by public policies; achieve a balanced offer of environmental sanitation and energy infrastructures; ensure the connectivity of the network of cities and regional units of the MMP, through the supply and integration of transport and logistics infrastructure; develop the potential and opportunities of the territory of the MMP and explore regional complementarities and synergies favorable to development; address the serious liabilities arising from poor urbanization in the MMP; avoid the creation of new urban and environmental liabilities.
>
> (Negreiros & Abriko, 2020, p. 172)

It is exactly in this sense of articulation of the industrial agenda that the Greater ABC Economic Development Agency – in the scope of the Greater ABC municipal consortium – has been acting and, despite the structural and conjunctural difficulties, above all linked to political and economic-financial cycles.

The Greater ABC Economic Development Agency

The crisis in ABC Region caused by productive and financial globalization and the Brazilian neoliberal economic policy in the 1990s led, as explained Bresciani (2011), to the formation in ABC Region of public governance of regional development policies through the Intermunicipal Consortium of Greater ABC. This, in turn, was supported by two other institutions: the Greater ABC Regional Chamber and the Greater ABC Economic Development Agency.

Founded in 1990 for planning, articulation, and definition of actions of regional character, as presented by the Intermunicipal Consortium on its website, in 2010 it became the first multisectoral consortium of public law and autarkic nature in Brazil. On the occasion, the mayors of the seven municipalities formed a General Assembly along the lines of the Public Consortium Contract: a sovereign body that meets once a month to establish the guidelines of the institution's activities. The assembly elects annually the president and the vice-president, and directs deliberations from the Executive Secretariat, assisted by a technical team, assistants, and the work groups. The municipalities commit themselves to financing the consortium from budget revenues.

When adapting to the Law 11.107 of 2005, by which the union only celebrates agreements with public consortiums constituted under the form of public association or that have been converted to this form, the Intermunicipal Consortium has acquired the status of a public organ.

The new legal constitution gave executive power to the autarchy to sign agreements among the administrations and to open bidding processes for works in favor of the seven cities; to receive resources from the federal and state spheres, as well as from international organizations, to give life to regional projects originating from the Consortium's Work Groups. The current model allows the Consortium to open bidding processes for works on behalf of the seven cities; increases the limits of values of the bidding modalities for Public Consortia, due to the consortium of several municipalities; exempts the Consortium from bidding processes to contract with entities of the federation or entities of its direct administration. The new legal structure has tax immunities and procedural advantages.

(Consorcio Intermunicipal, 2022, website)

The creation of the consortium was followed by the Citizenship Forum in 1994 and the Regional Chamber in 1997. The forum remains as an association of movements and environmental, trade union and business organizations of the region, which became a privileged interlocutor of regional articulation according to Rolnik and Somekh (2002). In it emerged the idea of creating the Chamber of Greater ABC, a space for political concert between the seven municipalities, the state government and organized civil society, with a view to overcoming the economic and social crisis experienced by the ABC related to deindustrialization (Bresciani, 2011). The chamber began its work around agreements on water and sanitation, social and economic development, which deflagrated the foundation of the Economic Development Agency in 1998 as an executive arm (Rolnik & Somekh, 2002).

The Agency "acts strategically, through debates, in the proposition and execution of measures to overcome challenges, especially of economic nature, which interfere in the daily lives of entrepreneurs, investors, workers, academics, students, public managers, researchers and residents of the seven cities in the region" (ADEGABC, 2022a). Constituted under a tripartite and mixed entity *status*, the Agency's management includes the seven municipalities of the Greater ABC region (represented by the consortium, with the nomination of five directors), business associations and trade union entities. Subsequently, the universities of the region also began to occupy a seat on the board of the Agency, and the budget allocation obeyed from the beginning the proportion of 49% for the consortium and 51% for all other entities (Bresciani, 2011).

Having been executive secretary of the consortium in 2011/2012, Luis Bresciani considers that the origin of these movements relied on the actions

186   *Cristina Fróes de Borja Reis et al.*

of the Sindicato dos Metalúrgicos do ABC and the studies supported by them. Taking as a reference, the experience of the northern region of Milan, under the coordination of the municipality of *Sesto San Giovanni* in *Agenzia Sviluppo Nord Milano* (ASNM), the corresponding Agency in the Greater ABC region, was materialized from the strong commitment of Mayor Celso Daniel of Santo André, its first director general. As Brazilian professor, engineer, and politician, affiliated to the Workers' Party, he was mayor of Santo André twice: from 1989 to 1993 and from 1997 to 2002, when he was assassinated. Celso Daniel (1951–2002) was in charge of the institutional construction of the Intermunicipal Consortium, the Regional Chamber, and the Development Agency, the three pillars that constitute the regional governance model of the Great ABC throughout the 1990s (Bresciani, 2011).

As analyzes Anau (2019), with initial vigor, the Agency held important initiatives, such as the discussions of the APL (Local Productive Arrangement) Project from 2006, focusing on the metal-mechanic and plastic sectors. Later, in 2010, there was also the creation of APLs in the city of São Bernardo do Campo (in the case of tooling, together with Diadema), in which the Agency, instead of being a leader, was a participant. In 2015, the Agency took over the coordination of most APLs, but the pace of their operation was reduced, as assessed by Anau (2019), due to the weakening of public-private coordination related to political and economic cycles in the region.

> Despite the anticlimax concerning the ADE-GABC and the continuity of business inertia, the Greater ABC region accumulated experience, probably unprecedented at the national level and quite significant even in relation to international standards, with regard to regional articulation, involving the local public power, the private sector and organized civil society. Undoubtedly, this accumulation represents an expressive lever for new advances (…) As far as the effort for economic development is concerned, the focus on innovation, modernization, and diversification was intense, coupling to it some related activities, such as professional qualification and managerial and entrepreneurial training. Seminars, conferences, workshops, lectures, and courses were frequent, although they did not maintain a regular rhythm throughout the time of research observation (2000–2015).
>
> (Anau, 2019, p. 560)

Since the second half of 2021, under the leadership of Aroaldo Oliveira da Silva, member of the board of directors of the ABC Metalworkers' Union, the Greater ABC Development Agency has been sewing the articulation around the industrial agenda. Based on the organization of successive discussion events with various representatives from civil society, it created the Permanent Industry Forum on May 18, 2022. The ABC Industry Forum is permanent and aims to guide the actions of the municipal, state, and federal governments in the region. The Forum also seeks to dedicate itself to the revival of the sector in the seven cities, since the period is a time when Brazil, the state, the region and the municipalities are facing and suffering from the unfolding effects of a health crisis caused by the COVID-19 pandemic. As described in the following section, three meetings of the forum were held in 2022, where it was discussed, based on specific reflections on industrial sectors, financing and socio-environmental impacts of the economic crisis in the region, the preparation of a document to pact the strengthening of industry in the ABC (ADEGABC, 2022b).

Pacto pela Industria do ABC (The Industry Pact of ABC Region)

The event "The Future of Industry in ABC", organized by the Greater ABC Economic Development Agency at the Municipal University of São Caetano do Sul (USCS) on May 18, 2022, was supported by the Intermunicipal Consortium Greater ABC and the Center of Industries of the State of São Paulo (Ciesp). Information about that was presented in report of the ABC Industry Forum, by Agencia de Desenvolvimento do Grande ABC (2022b). The occasion brought together representatives from the State Government, the Legislative Assembly, the National Association of Motor Vehicle Manufacturers (Anfavea), the Brazilian Chemical Industry Association (Abiquim), the National Association of the Industry of Components for Motor Vehicles (Sindipeças), the ABC Metalworkers Union, the ABC Chemists Union, the Petrochemical Pole, in addition to universities, trade associations, municipal secretariats of Economic Development, City Councils, and mayors of the Greater ABC region. The Petrochemical Pole is located in the metropolitan region of São Paulo. The Capuava Refinery (Recap) started operating on December 18, 1954. Currently, it is responsible for the marketing of about 30% of the fuel volume consumed in the Greater São Paulo region. "Due to the ease of obtaining raw materials in the region, its installation in Mauá (Greater São Paulo) attracted other industries, forming the Petrochemical Center of the Greater ABC region" (Petrobras, 2022, website).

The president of the Development Agency, Aroaldo Oliveira da Silva, pointed out at the occasion that the Industry Forum will have members appointed by the seven municipalities, by the universities, by the industry, by the Development Agency, by the ABC Consortium, and by the state government. The solemn opening of the event was attended by the vice-president of the ABC Consortium and mayor of Ribeirão Pires, Clovis Volpi, the mayor of São Caetano do Sul, José Auricchio Júnior, host of the meeting, and the heads of the municipal administrations of Mauá, Marcelo

Oliveira, and Rio Grande da Serra, Claudinho da Geladeira, and the vice-mayor of Diadema, Patty Ferreira.

Governor Rodrigo Garcia of the State of São Paulo was represented at the event by the State Secretary of Economic Development, Zeina Latif, who reaffirmed that state public policies are more efficient when thought in conjunction with local players, such as municipalities, unions, companies, and class entities. Antonio Megale – director of Governmental Affairs at Volkswagen and vice-president of Anfavea (National Association of Vehicle Manufacturers), Ciro Marino – president of Abiquim (Brazilian Association of the Chemical Industry), Rafael Cervone – vice-president of the Federation and Center of Industries of the State of São Paulo (FIESP/ CIESP) spoke. The program included thematic panels on problems faced by the industry in the Great ABC region, opportunities, and the regional agenda. It was remembered that the region stands out for being a knowledge territory, with a local innovation network made up of quality institutions and references in all areas of education. However, there is a lack of data and studies about the region, including with regard to the fulfillment of Agenda 2030.

At the first meeting of the AB Industry Forum, on June 15, 2022, at Santo André, about 60 representatives from the public and private sectors participated, and defined the structuring themes of the industry forum: competitiveness, technology and innovation, management, investment, financing and incentives, professional training, infrastructure, sustainability, regulation. The start was set for the formalization of a Regional Pact. At the second meeting of the ABC Industry Forum, on July 14, 2022, at the headquarters of São Judas Tadeu University in São Bernardo do Campo, with a similar number of participants, the crisis in the region's textile sector was presented by Rhodia Solvay's plant director, Hugo Kitagawa. Next, Gabriel Aidar, the business and technology development superintendent of Desenvolve SP, a state financing bank, presented possibilities for industrial investment in the region. Between 2019 and 2022, R$76.1 million were applied that directly benefited 313 companies and two city halls.

At the third meeting of the ABC Industry Forum, on August 4, 2022, at the headquarters of the Santo André Foundation, the focus was on the scenario of the pharmaceutical and personal care, perfumery and cosmetics industry. Challenges were presented, notably tributary and fiscal, which emerged as demands for the Forum and also solutions, in the sense of opportunities for the region from the presentations of the lawyer from Sindusfarma (Sindicato da Indústria de Produtos Farmacêuticos), Renato Rezende, and Karla Brandão, director of Management, Communication and Marketing from ABIHPEC (Associação Brasileira da Indústria de Higiene Pessoal, Perfumaria e Cosméticos).

In addition to these meetings, the agency has led and/or participated in several events of industrial and service sectors of the seven cities, as well as on general topics such as development and compliance with the 2030 Agenda. On most occasions, the idea of the industry pact and a drafting proposal were presented. In particular, on October 6, 2022, there was a conversation with universities, colleges, and technical schools in the region to discuss the text of the Regional Pact for Industry. The main point highlighted at the meeting was the need to bring universities and companies closer together, so that there can be a joint work, support and collaboration, from High School to College. Moreover, other agendas were also taken to be included in the document, as well as the issues of standardization, certifications, governance, as well as the dialogue between the universities themselves and the companies in the region.

It was established that the pact for industry should be for the great challenges of the ABC region, such as social and sustainability. In other words, it is not about protecting the industry just for itself, but because the industry helps in the other challenges of the region, both social and sustainable, and aligned to the UN Sustainable Development Goals. For the Agency's president, Aroaldo Oliveira da Silva, the Pact's initiative should generate a wave of partnerships and development throughout the region:

> I understand that with the symbolism and potential that our region has, along with the universities, colleges, schools, articulated public power, it is essential that we can synchronize efforts. Organizing the contacts, especially between industry and university, will channel the initiatives and generate a synergy for the entire region.
>
> (AGDEABC, 2022c)

In this sense, throughout the year the text that we reproduce below was consolidated, with the outstanding participation of different representatives of the education sector, who supported the pact's process both from the theoretical and practical point of view.

Regional Pact for Industry of the Greater ABC Region

The signatory entities of the present Regional Pact reaffirm their collective commitment with the strengthening of the industrial activity in the Great ABC region. This commitment should stick to the following guidelines:

i *The increase in competitiveness and quality of the industries, chains, and local productive arrangements, as a means to expand the presence of the Great ABC region in the national and global economy.*
ii *The preservation of industrial activity as a source of job creation and value.*

190 *Cristina Fróes de Borja Reis et al.*

iii *The understanding of education and professional qualification as central elements of productive and technological modernization and human emancipation.*

iv *The recognition of union representation and collective bargaining as elements of social dialogue between workers and companies in the region.*

v *The strengthening of the regional innovation system, guided by a regional plan for science, technology and innovation.*

vi *The structuring of specific support for industrial development in the Greater ABC region, with emphasis on medium and small industries, based on a knowledge repository, with an industrial inventory and consolidated socioeconomic data from the industry observatories and other analysis centers in the region.*

vii *The rationalization of areas for industrial use, through the coordination of municipal master plans by a regional macro-zoning.*

viii *The qualification of regional infrastructures, including standardization, the logistic, energy and connectivity system.*

ix *The improvement of products and industrial processes, with the support of regional technology parks, of the universities present in the Great ABC region, of the FATECs/ETECs network, of Fapesp funding, of the support from the S system, with strategies agreed upon among the players involved.*

x *The search for specific solutions for the viability of low-impact and low-carbon industrial activities, especially in the water source areas, in the Great ABC region.*

xi *Establish governance mechanisms for the coordination, articulation, and synergy of the industrial strategies of the public, private, educational, and labor sectors in favor of the Sustainable Development Goals.*

Conclusion

The ABC Industrial Pact is a unique case study in post-COVID Brazil. It can be an inspiration for several other national and global regions that were once thriving industrial parks but are now undergoing economic, social, and environmental crises caused by the rearrangement of global value chains. When the COVID-19 crisis exacerbated the existing difficulties and made more than urgent the articulation of public and private power to find solutions, with support and participation of the education entities, the regional governance system previously established through the Intermunicipal Consortium, the Regional Chamber, and the Greater ABC Economic Development Agency were essential to make the commitment to industry viable.

This commitment must not boil down to protectionism for specific sectors, but to enabling investments in production and employment that contribute to improve the indicators of Agenda 2030 in the municipalities of Greater ABC. As shown, the agenda is "white" in the case of most SDGs in these municipalities, considering the heterogeneities present. SDG 9, however, presents itself as the one with the best results, evidencing the window of opportunity brought by the existing industry, infrastructure, and innovation system. Regarding the last one, in particular, the ABC region has dozens of educational institutions of all levels, as well as technology labs, which joined forces with the Greater ABC Economic Development Agency to, within one year, in 2022, establish the Industry Forum and the proposed pact, to be signed in early 2023. At this moment, the challenge is to keep governance armored against electoral cycles, preserving the dialogue and will to act of the various actors involved in the pact.

References

ADEGABC. (2022a). *Quem somos*. Agencia de Desenvolvimento Econômico do Grande ABC. https://agenciagrandeabc.com.br/quem-somos/. Accessed December 2, 2022.

ADEGABC. (2022b). *Fórum da Indústria do ABC*. Relatório da Agencia de Desenvolvimento Econômico do Grande ABC. https://agenciagrandeabc.com.br/publicacoes-e-estudos/. Accessed December 2, 2022.

AGDEABC. (2022c). *Agência e Universidades aprofundam debate sobre o Pacto Regional pela indústria do ABC*. Notícia da Agencia de Desenvolvimento Econômico do Grande ABC. https://agenciagrandeabc.com.br/2022/10/06/agencia-e-universidades-aprofundam-debate-sobre-o-pacto-regional-pela-industria-do-abc/. Accessed December 2, 2022.

Anau, R.V. (2019). Impasses e oportunidades para a construção de um Sistema Regional de Inovação no Grande ABC. *Cadernos Metrópole*, *21*, 551–572.

Bresciani, L.P. (2011). Tradição e transição: o caso do Consórcio Intermunicipal Grande ABC. *Cadernos Adenauer*, *12*(4), 161–178.

Conceição, J.J. da, Yamauchi, G., Monea, G.K. de A. (2018) Complexidade tecnológica das exportações do Grande ABC Paulista. *Carta de Conjuntura*, Universidade Municipal de São Caetano do Sul, ed. 2, abr. http://noticias.uscs.edu.br/uscs-lanca-2a-carta-de-conjuntura/. Accessed November 28, 2022.

Consorcio Intermunicipal do Grande ABC. (2022). *O consorcio*. https://www.consorcioabc.sp.gov.br/pagina/81/o-consorcio. Accessed December 20, 2022.

Lampis, A. et al. (2020). ODS 7 – Energia limpa e acessível. In K. Frey et al. (Ed.), *Objetivos do Desenvolvimento Sustentável Desafios para o planejamento e a governança ambiental na Macrometrópole Paulista*. Santo Andre: UFABC Editors.

Morceiro, P.C. (2019). Industrialização e desindustrialização brasileira pela ótica do emprego. *IV* Encontro *nacional de economia industrial e inovação (ENEI)*. Campinas, São Paulo. Sept/2019.

192   *Cristina Fróes de Borja Reis et al.*

Negreiros, I., & Abriko, A. (2020). ODS 9 – Indústria, inovação e infraestrutura. In K. Frey et al. (Ed.), *Objetivos do Desenvolvimento Sustentável Desafios para o planejamento e a governança ambiental na Macrometrópole Paulista*. Santo Andre: UFABC Editors.

Observatorio Economico. (2020). Boletim IndustriABC. Universidade Metodista de Sao Paulo, Ano V - setembro 2020.

Observatorio Economico. (2022). Boletim IndustriABC. Universidade Metodista de Sao Paulo, Ano VII- setembro 2022.

Petrobras. (2022). *Reinaria Capuava*. Informações Gerais. https://petrobras.com.br/pt/nossas-atividades/principais-operacoes/refinarias/refinaria-capuava-recap. htm. Accessed December 20, 2022.

Reis, C.F.B. (2021). The pandemic and the new technologies' boom: New narratives for justifying more power and wealth asymmetries. In G. Rached (Org.), *States and Institutions: International Dialogues and Policies for Tackling the Crisis*. Niteroi: Autografia.

Reis, C.F.B. (2022). Um pacto para fortalecer as cadeias de valor das empresas do ABC Paulista. *Boletim de conjuntura econômica do ABCDMMR*, 2ª edição, CORECON-SP, April 2022.

Reis, C.F.B., Yamauchi, G., & Tourinho, A. de O. (2023). *La pérdida de valor de la industria automotora de ABC Paulista*. Papeles de Europa: Mimeo, 36. 10.5209/pade.84585

Relação Anual de Informações Sociais (RAIS). (2022). *Plataforma de dados da Relação Anual de Informações Sociais do Brasil*. https://bi.mte.gov.br/bgcaged/login.php. Accessed October 10, 2022.

Rolnik, R., & Somekh, N. (2002). Governar as metrópoles: dilemas da recentralização. *Cadernos Metrópole* (08), 105–117.

SEADE. (2019). *Mapa da indústria Paulista 2003-2016*. São Paulo, Fundação Seade 40 anos. https://www.seade.gov.br/produtos/mapa-da-industria-paulista/. Accessed November 28, 2022.

UN. (2022). *Transforming our world: The 2030 Agenda for Sustainable Development*. United Nations. https://sdgs.un.org/2030agenda. Accessed October 3, 2022.

UN Sustainable Development Solution Network. (2022). Índice de Desenvolvimento Sustentavel das Cidades Brasil. *Perfis das sete cidades do ABC Paulista*. https://idsc.cidadessustentaveis.org.br/profiles. Accessed October 31, 2022.

UNIDO. (2022). *International Yearbook of Industrial Statistics*. United Nations Industrial Development Organization.

11 Auditing Human Resource Management Practices

A Case Study in the Egyptian Hospitality Industry

*Hazem Tawfik Halim, Yasser Halim,
Hazem AbdElhady, and Karim Salem*

Introduction

Egypt's hospitality and tourism industry is critical to the country's economic prosperity. Given the severe impact of uncontrollable global and domestic political, environmental, and economic forces in 2022, Egypt has devised a strategy to revitalize the industry. An action plan is already in place to target new markets with massive marketing efforts, in conjunction with a focus on internal factors that drive can encourage local tourism activities. Essentially, the audit function provides assurance to any organization that its objectives are being met. Many businesses have an internal audit function that is in charge of identifying business risks. These risks could include one or more operational, strategic, financial, or compliance risks. The purpose of this study is to determine how Egyptian hotels, both state-owned and privately owned, audit their human resource management (HRM) practices in order to reshape organizational performance, ensure compliance to standards/best practices, mitigate risks, and correlate HRM operational indicators to hospitality financial indicators. The study also includes a full and comprehensive auditing tool for self-assessment.

Background

The Egyptian Hospitality and Tourism Industry

The hospitality and tourism industry is a keystone to Egypt's economic development, with high growth rates and a large contribution to gross domestic product (GDP). Egypt's tourism sector also represents one of the main sources of foreign exchange. In addition, the sector's wide-ranging capacity to absorb labor either directly or in-directly, plays a major role in bringing down the country's unemployment rate.

According to the Central Agency for Public Mobilization and Statistics (2020), Egypt's hospitality and tourism industry accounted for 15% of

DOI: 10.4324/9781003376583-14

GDP prior to the COVID-19 pandemic, generating 2.4 million jobs for the economy. However, the pandemic resulted in a substantial fall in visitor numbers in 2020, with only 3.7 million arrivals and a decrease in hotel and tourism industry employment of 1.9 million jobs. Egypt lost 70% of its tourism revenue in 2020 due to the pandemic.

Another slew of factors evolved to shape and function the sector in general, and its labor market in particular (OECD, 2020). Egypt's economic reform issues between 2013 and 2022, followed by the Russia-Ukraine war in 2022, accelerated the need for an exit and a path out of the crisis.

Given the unfavorable impact of uncontrollable political, environmental, and economic issues in 2022, Egypt has devised a plan to revitalize the industry. A plan of action is already in place (Ministry of Planning and Economic Development, 2021) to target new markets through massive marketing efforts, with an emphasis on internal driving factors that could boost local tourism activities.

Furthermore, Egypt's political leaders have pushed hospitality and tourism properties to take revolutionary steps to reshape the outcome of the labor market in order to improve service standards, manage operational expenses, and increase profit margins. These include improved workforce training, accelerated organizational change, and visionary steps toward corporate governance. Line managers of publicly owned entities were directed to introduce sophisticated technology, realize returns on investments, and reform management practices, while privately owned entities were encouraged and supported to do the same (Egypt's Tourism Reform Program, 2019).

HR departments of all organizations in the hospitality industry are expected to play a strategic and critical role in implementing and sustaining initiatives related to growing profitability and organizational market value. HRM is a functional responsibility of all departmental line managers, not just the HRM department (Heilmann et al., 2020; Mulolli, 2020). The HRM department, on the other hand, ensures that departmental strategic objectives are aligned with organizational objectives and promotes regulatory compliance of employment practices within the property. Effective HRM practices are the roots and stem of profitable business operations (Islami, 2021).

In empirical research, linking the role of HRM practices to enhanced performance would imply the existence of an assessment of HRM practices and an audit for their contribution to growing profits and sustaining departmental objectives' alignment. The HR auditing process is always about diagnosing, analyzing, evaluating, and reviewing present and future HRM lines of action.

Auditing Human Resource Management Practices   195

A Contemporary Perception of HRM

The effectiveness with which organizations select, develop, retain, motivate, compensate, involve, and evaluate employees has always been key determinants of how well those organizations operationally and financially perform. Throughout the past three decades, HRM practices have been linked to profit maximization and market value, helping companies gain a competitive edge (Bratton et al., 2021; Meier et al., 2021; Peccei and Van De Voorde, 2019; Guest, 2017; Wright et al., 2005; Delery and Doty, 1996; Huselid, 1995).

The literature suggests that the future of HR functions has completely evolved to encompass other critical roles. According to KPMG (2019) report, managers who are acting decisively would see HR as a new value driver. They would acquire new skills that are becoming critical to thrive, even survive in the digital era, along with a new employee experience designed to attract and retain the brightest and meet the needs of multigenerational workforce. Accordingly, there need to be some kind of re-alignment of workforce to facilitate collaboration between employees and robotics, automation and artificial intelligence. According to DiClaudio (2019), Chalutz Ben-Gal (2019), and Falletta and Combs (2021), today's HR analytics focuses mostly on what happened and why. For instance, there might be tools for identifying high turnover and diagnosing the reasons. However, HRM is better positioned to be the predictive engine required for the organizational success. In other words, the future of HRM is evolving from descriptive and diagnostic to prescriptive and predictive.

The role of HRM practices has also been extended to the areas of sustainability and green economy. There are many research studies examining the way of incorporating ecological practices into HRM policies. Terms such as "Green HRM" are widely used by academics and practitioners (Hooi et al., 2021; Mukherji & Bhatnagar, 2022; Yan and Hu, 2022; Yong et al., 2022). Moreover, the naming of some tools have changed. For example, employee satisfaction survey has been labeled engagement survey (Mann & Harter, 2016).

The Evolution of HR Auditing Practice

In empirical studies, linking the role of HRM practices to improved performance, digitalization, sustainability, and green economy would imply the existence of some sort of assessment to those practices and an audit for their contribution to increasing profits. The auditing process consists of diagnosing, analyzing, evaluating, and assessing future lines of actions within the framework of HRM. According to Armstrong (2020), it is necessary to evaluate the contribution of the HR function in order to establish how effective it is at both the strategic level and in terms of service delivery and support.

The term "HR contribution" refers to the correlation of HR operational output to organizational financial yield. This is the foundation for determining return on investment (ROI). Phillips et al. (2001, 2016) implicitly linked the intention of auditing and measuring HR practices' functional effectiveness with the objective of determining the monetary value of implementing HR practices.

From 1960 to the beginning of the new millennium, there was a remarkable evolution of the concept of HR auditing and HR functional assessment. HR auditing has evolved from a simple checklist to a comprehensive assessment of interrelated variables, transforming it into a decision-making tool.

There has been a growing interest in quantifying the contribution of HR activities because labor costs are the greatest expenditure in most organizations and have a significant impact on the budget. Moreover, ineffective implementation of HRM practices would lead to undesirable significant financial and operational consequences. Thus, the HRM department must ensure that the functions are managed appropriately and that the different HR programs are subject to a system of accountability (Phillips et al., 2016). Having said that, there have always been attempts to show accountability of HR functions. Figure 11.1 chronologically presents the approaches to HR accountability measurements; not necessarily termed as accountability, yet the core meaning existed in many of the following consecutive measurement trends: management by objectives, HR case studies, HR audit, HR key indicators, HR cost monitoring, HR reputation, competitive HR benchmarking, ROI processes, HR effectiveness indicatorx, human capital measurement, and finally HR profit center indicator

According to Figure 11.1, the term "HR auditing" emerged in the late 1970s. Previously, there have been various attempts to conduct auditing in order to measure the impact of few, sometimes, unrelated HR practices on organizational financial/operational performance. In contrast, few other models were developed after the 1980s to conduct a thorough HR assessment. For example, Delery and Doty (1996) correlated result-oriented appraisals, profit sharing, job descriptions, employment security, training, and participation to financial indicators. However, that would not be considered an all-embracing HR auditing model.

Another similar perspective is underlined in the early writings of Walker (1998) who differentiates between two types of audit based on their context: internal or external. In other words, valuing HRM actions from an internal perspective is based on their ability to provide services at the lowest feasible cost, using operational measurements such as quantity, quality, reliability, cost, and speed.

Auditing Human Resource Management Practices 197

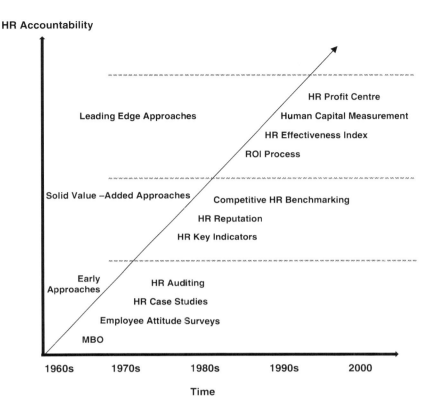

Figure 11.1 The accountability HR measurement trends.
Source: Phillips et al. (2001).

From an external perspective, the ultimate assessment of the effectiveness of HR practices is based on their impact on the company's results. Thus, the measurements encompass outcomes obtained outside of the function. That was partially emphasized in Ulrich's HR effectiveness model (Ulrich, 1996). Ulrich divides HRM into four sections: strategic partner, change agent, administrative expert, and employee champion. For many years, researchers have adopted this model to evaluate the effectiveness of the running HRM practices.

Some of the specifically designed HR audit systems that are utilized globally are based on the proposal of Sacht (2001). He argues that auditing should encompass four main domains: (1) the functional role of HRM–systems, HRM and provision of information; (2) the service role of HRM–customer service and responsiveness; (3) the compliance role of

HRM–legal aspects; and (4) the strategic role of HRM–workforce development and increasing value. Sacht's model is comprehensive, yet lacks the risk management component that needs to be included in the audit exercise. Furthermore, the distribution of "to be audited" HR practices is not correctly classified among the four audit categories. Additionally, practices of diversity management are not covered within the auditing instrument.

Another well-known classification to the approaches of HR audit is based on the difference between three focuses. These are the legal audit of performance conformity, the operative or efficacy-based audit, and the strategic audit (Ollala & Castillo, 2005). It is worth noting that the output of these early studies focuses solely on the efficiency and effectiveness of HR functions.

The term "HR governance" first appeared in the literature in the 2000s. According to Mercer's report (2003), HR governance is the act of leading the HR function and managing investments to optimize performance, fulfil fiduciary and financial responsibilities, mitigate risk, align priorities, and enable executive decision making. This could mean that HR audit is becoming a part of HR governance.

The emphasis shifted away from descriptive and diagnostic-based measures toward prescriptive and predictive-based measures. Shifting to HR governance was essential for organizational structural transformation and the adoption of principles such as ambidexterity (O'Reilly & Tushman, 2004). Within a governance framework, the ambidexterity concept required HR managers to redesign, align, and integrate their practices with the overall organizational strategy.

Since 2012, very few studies have been conducted in the area of auditing HRM practices as a means to a comprehensive and sustainable process that is an integral part of the organization's internal controls, due diligence, and risk management function. Having said that, the auditing process was included as a part of discussing introducing automation via Enterprise Resource Planning Systems (Lewis & Haung, 2019).

In 2016, the International Organization for Standardization published the human governance standards known as ISO 30408:2016 (2016). ISO's criteria help organizations anticipate and manage HRM risks, manage costs, develop an organizational culture, foster communication and collaboration, and optimize performance. According to Kaehler and Grundei (2019), HR governance, in concept, must be a part of corporate governance, but since both concepts are outlined vaguely in the literature, it is still unclear how they might interrelate (Martin & Gollan, 2012; Martin et al., 2016; Zuma, 2018; Anand, 2019; Busrai, 2019).

Despite the different divergence in views regarding the meaning and mechanism of HR auditing, most arguments lead to the conclusion that when utilizing measurement instruments, both inputs (behavior) and outputs (results) need to be included as business performance has a dynamic nature.

It should also be noted that, while HR procedures are seen as launching pads that perpetuate the achievement or failure of organizational objectives, they are sometimes disregarded in the hospitality business. Preliminary investigations in Egypt's hospitality five-star hotels revealed the usage of wide range of financial and operational indicators. However, operational ones appear to be employed separately to reflect the success or failure of a certain division or department; rather than strategically connecting all variables and correlating them to certain practices in a hospitality property. Canning and Hills (2012) supported this notion. They argued that those HR audit systems suffer the deficiencies of an internally oriented activity focusing on best practice and compliance; they are carried out in isolation from the organization in which it operates and finally they employ a problem-avoidance approach, not an improvement-benefits approach. It seems that hospitality properties, particularly in Egypt, have maintained the status quo regarding HR audit.

Another reason that some models of HR measurement has gained general acceptance but not general application could be the existence of non-prescriptive criteria which create a vague picture of how HR models can be used.

Auditing HRM Functions Is a Complicated Process

It is worth noting that HR auditing is a complicated process and its effectiveness is subject to many interrelated variables. Primarily, there is a need to focus on what exactly to audit – functions, final yield, or both? Then, how to audit? In other words, what benchmark or criteria could be used to evaluate HR practices in question? The answer to this particular question is confusing simply because it can be argued that those criteria are not standardized. Best practices implemented in one successful company, would in fact be unsuitable for the local issues of another successful company. This gives rise to the notion of best fit. In doing so, evaluation addresses the gap between expected and perceived HRM practices that would lead to desired outputs at the design, implementation, and experience levels (Wright & Nishii, 2007; Makhecha et al., 2018). There is also a necessity to highlight whether HR practices would be examined in isolation of the overall system of a company or in relation to other processes and operations. The latter makes the argument more intriguing as it raises the following question: Is it more meaningful to assess HR functions within the boundaries of an overall evaluation system such as the European Foundation for Quality Management (EFQM), Malcolm Baldrige National Quality Award (MBNQA) model International Organization for Standardization (ISO), or in isolation of other processes.

The strategy, the nature and scope of business, company structure, its budget, and its decision-making process can all affect the output of the audit. Consequently, the significance or insignificance of the found flaws because of the audit is questionable. Another subsequent dimension is the timing of the audit. In other words, when should audit take place? Timing is critical if aiming for valid results. The audit process must not only highlight existing flaws but encompass the cause and effect as well.

The Theory of the Firm

Whether the hotel property is owned privately or by the state, the balance of power between owners and management companies remains unresolved. Few research studies were conducted in Egypt to examine the role of owners on influencing the decision-making process. Generally, management companies reject interference from owners, while hotel owners use financial and board of directors' power to control decision making. This is fact relate to what has been known as the agency theory or principal agent theory that was developed by Jensen and Meckling (1976). It recognizes that in most firms there is a separation between the owners (the principals) and the agents (the managers). However, the principals may not have complete control over their agents, who may act in ways that are not in accordance with their wishes. This generates what economists call agency costs, which arise from the difference between what might have been earned if the principals had been the managers and the earnings achieved under the stewardship of the actual managers. Within the context of this study, there is a need to examine the extent to which management companies could positively use the influence of the government in state-owned hotels to facilitate compliance related aspects.

A Gap in the Literature

It is worth noting that this study is overcoming an existing gap in the literature pertaining to the hospitality industry particularly in Egypt. This study aims to identify how Egyptian hotels are auditing HRM practices to ensure compliance, mitigate risks, and correlate HR operational indicators to hospitality financial indicators. This study also examines whether Egyptian hotels have proactive tools for assessing HR practices to improve organizational performance.

Methodology

A case study methodology was tailored to suit the qualitative nature of this study. A case study methodology can entail the study of one or more "cases", which could be described as instances, examples, or settings, where the problem or phenomenon could be examined.

Secondary data was collected from relevant textbooks, journals, and online databases. The literature review provided valuable insights regarding the used models of auditing HRM practices.

Primary data was collected using a structured interview form. Two different groupings of hotels were selected as cases under investigation for this study. The first group encompassed three privately owned hotel properties that are managed by three international hotel chains in the three different resort areas of Hurghada (American Chain), Marsa Alam (Belgian Chain), and Sharm El-Shiekh (French Chain). These cities were selected because, according to the Ministry of Tourism report (2021), 65% of tourists coming to Egypt visit South Sinai and the Red Sea, as they represent open areas with water activities. The second group encompassed two state-owned properties that are managed also by American international chains located in Greater Cairo. Greater Cairo was selected because most state-owned hotels are located there. The five chain of hotels are different. Hotel numbers were not the same in the two groups because the purpose was not to compare the two groups of hotels but rather to identify owner-management relationships pertaining to the implementation of related HR activities. It was assumed that the state ownership of hotels would enhance business conformance to functional, service, strategic and risk parameters and would reduce the burden of regulatory compliance to legal and law requirements. It was also critical to examine any differences between the two groups of hotels in the implementation of HR practices as a means of re-shaping organizational performance.

Five-star was the selected hotel category due to its ability to employ sophisticated auditing techniques. Three of the investigated hotels are privately owned, while the two hotels of Greater Cairo are state owned. For reasons of confidentiality, hotel names were hidden. The three hotels of resort cities were named "A", "B", and "C"; while the two state-owned hotels of Greater Cairo were named "D" and "E".

All interview questions were open-ended to collect as much data as possible. The questions covered:

1 The operational or functional role of HR internal systems (HR management and provision of information).
2 The service role of HR (customer service and responsiveness).
3 The compliance role of HR (legal aspects).
4 The strategic role of HR (alignment and integration of objectives and workforce value increasing).

5 The risk management role of HR (mitigation of risk internally or externally).

HR directors and other functional departments' directors were interviewed. The sample size were nine senior managers. Each interview took almost three hours to complete. Most interviews were conducted in two consecutive sessions due to time constraints. Reasons for interviewing functional department directors in addition to the HR directors were the following: (1) those directors are usually responsible for the implementation of the policies and procedures set by the HRM department; (2) there was a need to ensure the credibility of respondents' answers; (3) if there could be a variance in responses, there was a better opportunity to reveal more facts and allow for conducting comparisons; and (4) the used audit instrument required investigating the service role of HR. Accordingly, it was critical to find the gap between what is said to be offered by the HRM department and what is implemented in reality.

The interview form was piloted with an HR director of hotel "D", with changes such as rewriting questions, adding questions relevant to the usage of HR information system (HRIS), and eliminating duplications.

Data were translated, simplified, selected, sorted, and abstracted to obtain meaningful information. Evaluation was conducted against the best practices appeared in the literature taking into consideration the Egyptian context.

It was a necessity to score each practice of HRM within the investigated hotels. As each category of hotel conformed to different standard operating procedures (SOPs), using this approach was thought to be helpful in magnifying the variations between managements' deployment of different approaches. The application of this scoring system was therefore limited to the researchers' discretion. However, using it allowed the researchers to apply a degree of personal consistency. A similar degree of generosity or harshness in assigning a score to a particular HRM practice was extended to the five hotels. Different individuals using the scoring system might come up with higher or lower average scores to HRM practices, but there would still be a reasonably consistent measure. The scoring system of the Malcolm Baldrige National Quality Award (MBNQA criteria, 2020) provided by the National Institute of Standards and Technology – US department of Commerce was used.

Results

In the pages that follow, the results from the five hotels are displayed and discussed. The HRM department's functional, service, compliance, strategic, and risk management roles in reshaping corporate performance were all covered by the audit.

The HR Audit

Through the regional chief HR, hotels managed by American international hospitality management companies execute an HR audit twice a year.

The audit typically lasts two to three days and follows a predetermined audit plan.

The HRM department is aware of the time of the audit in advance. Only the hotel's GM and the director of HR are informed of the audit's findings. On the other hand, in hotels run by European management companies, the HR audit is casually conducted. Hotel "B" highlighted that HR flaws are controlled by the GM and corrective actions are taken to prevent problem recurrences.

The Functional Role of Human Resource Management Department

This part of the audit assessed whether or not there is a systematized process for workforce planning and the determination of the needed manpower. This included information on how different hotels are recruiting and selecting their employees; how do employee on-boarding and off-boarding occur; how is personnel record-keeping system maintained. It also included information on how employee learning and development are managed; how is employee performance managed; the mechanism of handling employee relations and employee rewards; how is HR budgeting developed and processed; what is the role of the HRM department in organizational development activities.

Workforce Planning

American chain hotels use "work study techniques" in determining the right number of employees in every department. Within the boundaries of the yearly business plan, which reveals the expected level of activities and the constraints of the yearly budget, hotels seek to recruit or downsize the number of staff. In hotels (A, D, and E), the process of determining the needed manpower starts in October/November each year. Departmental directors discuss the required personnel numbers on individual basis with the HR director. Then, the HRM department prepares a consolidated manpower plan for the hotel, taking into account turnover rates and staff transfer/promotion. Although interviewees did not corroborate that the job analysis process was carried out every few years, they did confirm the presence of a traditional job description (rather than a result-oriented one) for each job. They have little knowledge of equations such as "Stability

Index" or "Half Life Index", which can be utilized as additional tools to forecast future departmental staffing needs. Interviewees also stated that throughout the year, only the GM approves employee requisitions. The method is nearly identical in hotels "A", "D", and "E", but resort hotels have higher turnover rates than city hotels. However, hotels managed by European management corporations (B and C) do not have established manpower strategies. The pre-planned budget governs all departmental employee requisitions. HR respondents also pointed out the lack of a resourcing strategy. The success of the existing unguided approach to resourcing is determined by the HR directors' level of competence. It was surprising to hear notes like:

> The whole process is based on experience. We have no documentation of a departmental strategy or sub-departmental strategies. The most important thing is to abide by budget limits.
>
> (Hotel "B" HR director)

There is a well-developed HRIS system in Hotels "A", "D", and "E"; yet, it is not used for in-depth analytical purposes. Basic reports are usually the outcome of this system.

Manpower planning has transformed dramatically in recent years and in many different fields. Computer assisted models such as "mathematical programming" and "simulation modeling" (Choudhari & Gajjar, 2018; Willis et al., 2018) have been used to properly calculate the needed numbers of employees keeping attrition rates, staff promotions, staff transfers, productivity standards, performance levels, and staff schedule in the equation. It would seem that the process of workforce planning has to be improved.

Recruitment

There is a recruitment strategy in place in American-managed resort and city hotels alike. With these hotel chains, software programs like "TALEO" or "Hotel Career Path" are frequently used. An internal notice for all open positions is posted on the e-portal for hotels "A", "D", and "E". Employees can apply for promotions or similar positions within the business in any other city or nation. This particular program does placement in accordance with the requirements of chain hotels by compiling prospective successful candidates into a list known as a "Talent List". Having stated that, there is a strict regulation prohibiting using social media, including "LinkedIn", for recruitment in Hotel "A" solely.

These hotels manage to fill their positions through "head hunting" for managerial positions or employment agencies and direct advertisement for rank and file applicants, despite the lack of an employee branding strategy and any analysis of the hotel's advantages and disadvantages as an employer of choice.

Interviewees reported that resort hotels run by European management companies don't have employee branding or recruitment strategies. Rank and file candidates are attracted to the hotels because of the relatively fair perks offered. Additionally, analysis suggested that the high unemployment rate in resorts and the nearby cities would make it simpler to find candidates for this group of workers. Head hunting is a typical practice at higher levels of the hierarchy. The interviewees admitted that they occasionally utilize social media for hiring; yet it's not official; it's more private.

Advertising in newspapers is not a source of candidates for any hotel. It is common knowledge that advertising in local newspapers is expensive and, at times, overpriced; furthermore, in the digital age, newspapers are rarely read. However, if these hotels are in need of qualified individuals, it is imperative that they utilize many recruitment channels. Rarely, an analysis of the capacity of sources of recruitment to generate viable short lists is done.

Selection

According to Black and Esch (2020), people are our most important asset. It is a competitive imperative born of a seismic shift in where firm value and competitive advantage are found. From the turn of the 20th century until the early 1980s, 70%–90% of firm value was tied to tangible assets such as plant, property, and equipment with intangible assets accounting for roughly 65% of the average firm's value (Black, 2019).

Excellent service takes place when a match exists between employees a hotel hire and the customers served. Additionally, when there is compatibility among the many staff members engaged by the hotel, a high degree of service is achieved. Within this context, the recruitment and selection process used to be based on matching people to specific jobs, but now looks for a range of matches, such as interaction with colleagues, and fitting with the current environment of customers, culture, and technology.

In resorts and Greater Cairo, hotels managed by American management companies shared positive characteristics. Hotels "A", "E", and "D" have structured employee selection procedures. In addition, the selection of guest-contact staff is emphasized. The three hotels use advanced selection processes, such as psychometric analysis, aptitude tests, and intelligence tests, for senior management positions. In Hotel "A", tests are administered via the e-portal, but the GM has the last say about the hiring of those candidates. Regarding the recruiting of personnel at lower levels of the organizational structure, the HRM department conducts the preliminary screening and the directors of functional departments make the final hiring decision based only on an interview. The executive chef conducts a practical examination of applicants for technical positions like chef and sous-chef. A director of a functional department in Hotel "A" stated: "In most cases, what is happening in our hotel follows the standard operating procedures (SOPs) of the chain hotel. However, we tweak the Sops to suit our local issues".

The created competence matrices and the hotel value system impart a behavioral element to all administered examinations.

Interviewees of Hotel "A" in particular, however, revealed the existence of only six basic competences for all levels of the hierarchy that are modified slightly each year. That was an uncommon practice in the development of competence matrices. They added that the time to occupy a position is not standardized.

Interviewees denied the presence of a validator who verifies the outcome of psychometric tests. It is widely known that those kind of tests have lower validity rates because they should be administered under perfect settings. In addition, it seems that the directors responsible for the interviewing process are not trained to conduct an interview, notwithstanding the assertions of a few interviewees from Greater Cairo hotels. There are doubts pertaining to the capabilities of all directors/senior managers to find the match between the requirements of the job and the characteristics of the candidate. Another important note is that tweaking the SOPs to suit the local issues could, in fact, make it ineffective.

Hotels "B" and "C" that are run by European management companies in the resorts of Sharm Elsheikh and Marsa Alam employ primitive inefficient and ineffective employee selection approaches. According to the HR director of hotel "B": "Attitude is the most important aspect of any candidate. When the functional department insists on hiring a candidate and I see he is not competent, my word rules".

The director of human resources assumes that the directors of all functional departments are competent interviewers because they exclusively evaluate candidates' technical qualifications. He administers the English language examinations and, through the interview, evaluates the behavioral features of candidates. He asserted that there are no computer-based psychometric, aptitude, or other examinations. The HR director stated: "Do not tell me that all hotels of resorts or even in Greater Cairo apply psychometric tests. They say they have the tests but I have never witnessed their implementation".

It should be emphasized that the recruitment and selection of individuals has changed significantly. According to Black and Esch (2020), firms are currently at the onset of what we refer to as digital recruiting, where artificial intelligence (AI) is used extensively. Computers are now capable of identifying, attracting, screening, assessing, and interviewing candidates at numbers and rates considerably beyond those of humans. Unfortunately, none of the Egyptian hotels investigated in this study have fully embraced the digital age.

On-boarding

In all investigated hotels, the HR directors inform the entire staff about new hires, transfers, and promotions. They are then exposed to a group orientation program during which they obtain hard copies of the employee handbook. The comprehensiveness of the orientation program varies in hotels run by the American management companies. In these hotels, the process of on-boarding is more systematic and encompasses a greater number of critical factors. In every hotel, the HRM department does not conduct follow-up meetings with newly hired employees. In resort hotels, orientation consists primarily of instructions to adhere to the code of conduct, rather than an explanation of the hotel's aims and how departmental deliverables are interrelated.

Off-boarding

All investigated hotels have a termination policy. The turnover rate is calculated for every department. In all hotels, exit interviews are undertaken, but the outcome of the interview is rarely used for analytical purposes. One functional department director in hotel "A" stated: "In critical situations only, managers who proved to be responsible for frequent involuntarily separation of staff members were terminated".

In the majority of investigated hotels, a severance policy exists. Severance package is a bundle of pay and benefits offered to an employee upon being laid off. The negotiation skills of the laid-off employee is a key element of how much he/she would eventually get. Some interviewees alluded obliquely to the preceding piece of information, while others declared their compliance with Egyptian legislation.

Personnel Management

Hotels "B" and "C" in Marsa Alam are still employing manual time-keeping cards to record employees' clocking in and out. Other hotels feature electronic staff record-keeping systems. Respondents from resort hotels said that their personnel are rarely absent.

Employee Training

According to the interviewees of hotels managed by American management companies, there is a consolidated behavioral training plan for all

208 *Hazem Tawfik Halim et al.*

employees. Technical training is conducted by the functional departmental training specialist in all departments or by the deputy director. However, it appears that employee technical training is not planned in these hotels. Directors of departments typically coach employees and provide feedback as they perform their duties. Every employee has a profile of behavioral training.

Training is provided mostly in response to problems identified in yearly employee performance reviews and at the request of functional department directors. "Code of Conducts, Sexual Harassment, Drug Abuse, Effective Communication, and Customer Relationship Management" are some of the featured training subjects.

The analysis of respondent answers revealed that only the junior, supervisory, and middle management levels receive training. Higher managerial levels are exposed to other developmental interventions found on the hotels' software applications such as "SHINE", "ELEVATOR", "GATEWAYS", and others. In spite of the fact that these multinational chains have highly effective core management training programs offered by professional trainers, Egypt's hotels may diverge slightly from these beneficial pathways. Some individuals, especially those on the verge of promotion, are given additional training emphasis. They are permitted to engage in cross-exposure, job enrichment, and work expansion methods.

Employee training needs are not usually determined with reference to behavioral competence matrices and employee proficiency levels. Due to low or high occupancy rates, training sessions may be delayed or canceled. In Hotel "A", the content of all levels of given training programs is identical. Rarely are external training organizations utilized to address topics outlined in the training plan. Thus, it is questionable if the hotel's training manager could adequately cover all training programs' stated learning outcomes. Another interesting finding is that the training budget is accrual in these hotels. This is a good indicator if the training plan is fully implemented. In the hotels of Greater Cairo, external training bodies could be hired to facilitate some training topics.

Staff who seeks higher educational degrees or external training programs are rarely supported by the hotels.

In hotels managed by European management companies, training activities neither adhere to the conventional standards described in the literature nor any established practical norm. Staff training is limited to a bare minimum, with either a high occupancy rate that does not allow for training or a low occupancy rate that results in minimal revenue, therefore restricting staff training. Both Hotels "B" and "C" lacked structured training programs.

Return on investment (ROI) is not measured monetarily in all investigated hotels. Although the training budget is accrual in hotels managed by

American management companies, the business plan provides no financial reason for the increase.

Reaction of the participants toward the efficiency and effectiveness of the delivered training programs is occasionally gathered but not utilized. The acquired learning is not tested except for those senior managers using software development applications in Hotel "A", "D", and "E". Changes in behavior as a result of training are only reflected in the performance evaluation report. The financial results of training are not consistently calculated.

Succession Planning

In hotels managed by American companies, the selection of successors follows a predetermined process. The performance evaluation result is a crucial component of this procedure. Those chosen as successors get extensive training using the hotel chain's online applications.

As noted previously, they are cross-exposed to the tasks of several departments and extensively tested to ensure that they are fully prepared. In hotels administered by European management companies, the procedure is haphazard and lacks a structure. Vacant positions are typically filled through headhunting.

One of the unique statements made by interviewees at Hotel "A" is that "career path" activities are not for everyone. This chance is limited to a select group of people. This raises questions about the thoroughness and impartiality of the whole process.

Employee Retention

The stagnating economic circumstances and high unemployment rate are issues that limit staff retention efforts to a minimum.

Particularly at resort hotels, it is believed that "staff outing", "improved staff meals", and "employee fringe benefits" are the most important retention factors. Work-life balance and planned development activities are not taken into account for all employee categories.

Performance Monitoring

In all hotels, a performance appraisal system rather than a performance management system is utilized. In all hotels, operational and financial factors influence the success of the directorship and management levels, according to respondents. Sets of competences and objectives serve as evaluation criteria. Evaluation outcomes at this level are determined by a mix of quantitative and qualitative measures. On the other hand, personnel at lower levels of the hierarchy are evaluated annually using forms that focus primarily on customer-related competences and other technical aspects. In restaurants, customer feedback might be utilized as a measure of the performance of both the rank-and-file and supervisory employees.

In hotels managed by American companies, the results of the appraisal are used for development purposes. In hotels managed by European firms, it appears that both rank-and-file and management-level performance valuations are undertaken "pour la forme". The output is not effectively utilized by directors/senior managers.

Interviewees highlighted that favoritism could play a part in employee performance. Although there is a wide divergence of views with regard to the effectiveness of the performance monitoring process, it seems logic that hotels are paying close attention to this process as a means of survival in the fierce competition of the marketplace.

It was alarming to learn that Hotel "B" occasionally cancels or skips planned audits for unknown reasons. Only paper audit forms are given to the HR director for completion and return to the parent company. The HR director of Hotel "B" stated: "Sometimes the auditor send the paper forms and do not show up. We do the forms and no problem what so ever".

Employee Relations

Once a year, the level of employee satisfaction in all hotels is acquired through several means. Hotels managed by American companies and one hotel managed by a European company employ web-based anonymous software such as "TIMOS" to gather data; however, Hotel "C" in Marsa Alam solely uses paper form surveys. In Hotels "A", "D", and "E" owned by American companies, the survey results are provided directly to the GMs. It was concluded that a part of the annual objectives established for managers pertain to "Team Member Satisfaction". It has been observed that the degree of satisfaction has not greatly grown throughout the years. The survey results are also distributed to all staff. These kind of surveys are known as "engagement surveys", and systems such as "Gallup" are devoted to collecting, analyzing, and producing output. These hotels do not utilize this software or "Pulse Surveys" as a means for tracking the activities made in response to the survey.

However, one of the functional department directors at Hotel "A" said that there is a committee entitled "Blue Energy" that has been formed.

Its purpose is to analyze, from a practical standpoint, team members' engagement, the community duty of the hotel, and other topics linked to sustainability and green economy.

Not all information is shared with every employee. It was highlighted that only success stories, excellent initiatives, the employment of senior management, and other key hotel events are reported. Aspects pertaining to hotels' strategies, challenges, alterations in market segmentation, and new openings are not communicated to all employees. It is inconceivable that these hotels do not have an integrated communication system, given that the vast majority of businesses seek more efficient means of disseminating information among personnel.

In hotels managed by American Companies, employee recognition programs exist. However, not all directors and managers receive regular training in recognizing and motivating employees. The practice is entirely dependent on their characteristics and abilities.

In all hotels, employees can submit complaints and comments to the HRM department or deposit them in a "Suggestion Box".

These are the sole means through which an employee may communicate their opinions and have a say.

In all hotels, there is a health and safety policy and there is strong emphasis on abiding by health and safety regulations.

Employee Reward Management

In all hotels, reward management practices exist. However, they are labeled as "payroll systems". It was difficult to conclude if there is a reward strategy that helps hotels achieve their objectives or just a practice of compensating staff. Respondents were unable to describe the parameters of their reward strategies. They only indicated that they try to pay employees packages that are similar to the market to maintain their presence within the hotel.

The hotel does not adopt the practice of job evaluation. An informal salary survey is undertaken by hotel HR personnel. Performance-related pay is not implemented as described in the literature. However, annual merit increases and salary increments are determined by annual performance evaluation. It was stated that all employees are aware of their salary's components. They enjoy fringe benefits at all hotels. However, the level of benefits may vary from one hotel to another. The incentive scheme at Hotel "A" is limited to the managerial level. In Hotels "E" and "D", all personnel are covered. Both Hotels "B" and "C" lack incentive schemes. The total reward philosophy is not applied as described in the literature or by best-practice organizations.

It was observed that decisions about salary increments are not routinely disclosed to employees. Nonetheless, it is transmitted informally. The grading system of the salary structure was a topic the interviewees would not discuss.

It appears that reward management is a sensitive and confidential topic, since respondents did not feel comfortable disclosing many information.

Organizational Development

All positions in the hierarchy have an approved job description, as validated by interviewees. The interviewees of hotels "A", "D", and "E", which are managed by American companies, claimed that the SOPs and value systems in place at headquarters guide their daily operations. They noted that the roles of directors and managers are clear. In all hotels, the Egyptian corporate governance codes are not adhered to, and neither a board of directors nor other governing bodies exist.

It appears that the HRM department does not undertake job analysis. Instead, they rely on headquarters-approved forms. This also applies to the hotels' competence matrices and organizational structures. The HRM department does not interfere with the integration, alignment, or monitoring of departmental objectives' accomplishment. Regarding the presence of productivity-boosting programs at the hotels under review, no conclusive result was obtained.

Since there have been no macro or micro interventions in the previous few years, the situation in hotels run by European management companies has worsened significantly. No attempts at full or partial restructuring have been made. Clearly, these hotels have a centralized management structure.

HR Budgeting

In the hotels under investigation, the cost per employee is computed and then allocated to the functional departments, presuming that costs cannot be allocated to the service centers. In all hotels, the notion of treating the HRM department as a profit center does not exist.

The Compliance Role of the HRM Department

This part of the audit assessed the degree to which the HRM department has implemented the four major standards of best practice outlined in the labor relations act, the basic conditions of employment act, the employment equality act, and the occupational safety and health act. In addition to ensuring that all external rules and regulations are followed, an HR compliance practice is also responsible for ensuring that all internal requirements are followed.

It appears that all hotels under review are committed to ensuring compliance, and one of the primary responsibilities of the HRM director in all hotels is to understand the numerous state laws and regulations in order to mitigate the hotel's legal risk. In this manner, the HRM department assists the hotel in avoiding potential liabilities, penalties, and controversies that might damage its brand.

Certificates for health insurance are renewed on schedule, and personnel records are well-kept. Not all hotels utilize digital record-keeping methods. Most records are stored on paper.

Before employing candidates, medical, background, substance addiction, and criminal records checks are conducted. According to interviewees, hotels cannot afford to violate any labor law provision. Hotels appear to be strictly adhering to the legislation, but there is space to maneuver and circumvent some provisions. In certain hotels, for instance, diversity management is not properly implemented. Sometimes, conflicts of interest are disregarded. There exist grievance policies, but there is no assurance that they will be resolved in the complainant's favor. There is a policy for preventing hazards (HACCP), but employees are not adequately taught on the process. There are no mechanisms that ensure payroll fraud will never occur.

Within the confines of the law, hotels handle staff downsizing in various ways. For instance, they do not renew contracts that are about to expire. They also provide unpaid open holidays. However, there were no references to severance policies in the investigated hotels.

All hotels completely comply with the law; however, their adherence to the standard operating procedures of the parent company varies greatly.

The Service Role of the HRM Department

This section of the audit investigated the HRM department's service responsiveness. This includes the HR staff's availability and level of communication, their ability to perform HR functions and provide service dependably and accurately, their willingness to assist line/employees and provide prompt service, and their ability to empathize with and provide individualized attention to other employees.

The service role necessitates that the HRM department supply pertinent HR information. Given that the majority of hotels are completely computerized, according to respondents, all hotels have the appropriate quantity of HR personnel. They are easily accessible and responsive to employee demands. Based on an analysis of their responses, not all employees have email accounts. This raises questions about the effectiveness of communication between the HRM department and functional department personnel. It also jeopardizes the efficacy of the communication mechanism previously discussed.

Respondents reported that there are waiting rooms for prospective applicants during the recruiting process, but no maximum waiting period is specified. They claimed to have an open-door policy, but there is no limit number of days to address employee concerns. In hotels "A" and "B" run by American companies and Hotels "C" and "D" run by European companies, regret letters are not sent to individuals who did not meet the hiring requirements. When asked about the academic credentials of the HR personnel, the respondents stated that they lacked HRM certifications. They develop knowledge through involvement with the market or through individual efforts to achieve academic credentials. This indicates that there are no uniform work criteria for HR personnel at these hotels, which raises questions about the professionalism of a few employees.

The Risk Management Role of the HRM Department

Egypt's hospitality industry continues to swing from one crisis to the next, from the COVID-19 outbreak and its devastating impact on the industry to the political turbulence in the Russia-Ukraine war and its repercussions on the global economy and the worldwide lack of supplies. Add to it the growing rate of inflation and the huge decline in disposable income among residents. Experts in risk management must collaborate with HR professionals and hospitality practitioners to mitigate the people risk in hospitality facilities. This risk is intimately linked to areas of accelerating digitization, changing labor laws, health and safety, talent scarcity, and misaligned HR and business strategy.

All investigated hotels lack a risk management department and comprehensive risk assessment procedures. However, they limit risk by adhering to statutory regulations and health and safety protocols. As indicated previously, the larger unemployment rate, the increasing number of individuals employed by the industry and the industry's capacity to teach unprofessional workers to do basic tasks add to the hotels' misunderstanding of the implications of their actions.

All hotels offer employment application forms. Taxes and social insurance are paid on time. There are always unconscionable termination procedures that twist the requirements of the law to benefit the hotel, despite the fact that termination methods correspond to legal standards. Immediately following an employee's contract expiration, their connected resources are managed. However, the departure of an employee is not disclosed.

The Strategic Role of the HRM Department

There was no indication in any of the investigated hotels that the HRM department plays a strategic role in achieving the property's goals. No evidence was shown about the vertical integration of HR strategies with the overall strategies of hotels, nor was there any horizontal integration between HR sub-units or with other functional departmental strategies. In hotels managed by European companies in the resorts of Sharm Elsheikh and Marsa Alam, respondents found the phrase departmental HR strategy peculiar. To attain hotel goals, short-term objectives and daily activities are placed.

Owner Management Relationships

It appears that the era of unbreakable long-term management contracts defining the relationship between the owner and the operator has passed. Even if the hotel is partially reaching its predetermined goals, hotel owners in Egypt are replacing their operators if they fail to meet their profit margin requirements. The industry has undergone a radical transformation to solely prioritize profit and return. Even at state-owned hotels, "longer contracts that are secured for years" are no longer the norm. In the past several years, a management company that oversaw a renowned property for over 50 years has changed in Greater Cairo. This pattern suggests that the owner-operator relationship is often somewhat "tense".

Respondents stated that the owner will not intervene in any way with property management. However, this is not entirely accurate, particularly for publicly traded hotels. By default, there should be a representative of the owners who are in continual challenge of management decisions. Adding to this, there might be interference when management companies are demanding more cash from the owner for the sake of renovations. Some respondents suggested that the ownership of state of some hotel properties may ease up somehow the continual government supervision of hotel activities. However, there are no substantial confirmations of such activities.

Conclusion

In conclusion, HRM directors must engage in regular observation and continuous improvement of the hotels' policies and procedures, as well as those of the headquarters, so that hotels' operational practices are continuously enhanced. This would help hotels in surviving the fierce economic rivalry of the market, as well as preserving their competitive advantage.

References

Anand, R. (2019). Corporate governance – role of HR. *NHRD Network Journal*, *12*(4), 301–310.

Armstrong, M., & Taylor, S. (2020). *Armstrong's handbook of human resource management practice*. London: Kogan Page Publishers.

Black, J.S. (2019). *Competing for and with human capital: It is not just for HR anymore*. New York: Productivity Press.

Black, J.S., & van Esch, P. (2020). AI-enabled recruiting: What is it and how should a manager use it? *Business Horizons*, *63*(2), 215–226.

Bratton, J.G., Bratton, A., & Steele, L. (2021). *Human resource management.* London: Bloomsbury Publishing.

Busrai, A. (2019). Is corporate governance an HR responsibility? *NHRD Network Journal, 12*(4), 311–316.

Canning, A., & Hills, T. (2012). A framework for auditing HR: Strengthening the role of HR in the organisation. *Industrial and Commercial Training, 44*(3), 139–149.

Chalutz Ben-Gal, H. (2019). An ROI-based review of HR analytics: Practical implementation tools. *Personnel Review, 48*(6), 429–1448.

Choudhari, S., & Gajjar, H. (2018). Simulation modeling for manpower planning in electrical maintenance service facility. *Business Process Management Journal, 24*(1), 89–104.

Delery, J. E., & Doty, D. H. (1996). Models of theorizing in strategic human resource management: Tests of universalistic, contingency and configurational performance predictions. *Academy of Management Journal, 39*(4), 802–835.

DiClaudio, M. (2019). People analytics and the rise of HR: How data, analytics and emerging technology can transform human resources (HR) into a profit center. *Strategic HR Review, 18*(2), 42–46.

Egypt-Tourism Reform Program. (2019). Egyptian Ministry of Tourism Report. http://www.egypt.travel/media/2338/egypt-tourism-reform-program.pdf. Accessed 06.03.2023.

Falletta, S.V., & Combs, W.L. (2021). The HR analytics cycle: A seven-step process for building evidence-based and ethical HR analytics capabilities. *Journal of Work-Applied Management, 13*(1), 51–68.

Guest, D.E. (2017). Human resource management and employee well-being: Towards a new analytic framework. *Human Resource Management Journal, 27*(1), 22–38.

Heilmann, P., Forsten-Astikainen, R., & Kultalaht, S. (2020). Agile HRM practices of SMEs. *Journal of Small Business Management, 58*(6), 1291–1306.

Hooi, L.W., Liu, M.S., & Lin, J.J. (2021). Green human resource management and green organizational citizenship behavior: Do green culture and green values matter? *International Journal of Manpower, 43*(3), 763–785.

Huselid, M.A. (1995). The impact of human resource management practices on turnover, productivity, and corporate financial performance. *Academy of Management Journal, 38*(3), 635–672.

ISO 30408:2016. (2016). Human resource management – Guidelines on human governance. https://www.iso.org/standard/63492.html. Accessed 03.07.2023.

Islami, X. (2021). How to integrate organizational instruments? The mediation of HRM practices effect on organizational performance by SCM practices. *Production & Manufacturing Research, 9*(1), 206–240.

Jensen, M. C., & Meckling, W. H. (1976). Theory of the firm: Managerial behavior, agency costs and ownership structure. *Journal of Financial Economics, 3*(4), 305–360.

Kaehler, B., & Grundei, J. (2019). The concept of management: In search of a new definition. *HR governance: A theoretical introduction* (pp. 3–26). Berlin: Springer.

Auditing Human Resource Management Practices 217

Kirkpatrick, D. (1962). *Training program evaluation.* Milwaukee, USA: M. Bruce Publishers.

KPMG Report. (2019). *The future of HR 2019 – in the know or in the no – the gulf between action and inertia.* KPMG International.com.

Lewis, A.C., Cardy, R.L., & Huang, L.S. (2019). Institutional theory and HRM: A new look. *Human Resource Management Review, 29*(3), 316–335.

Makhecha, U.P., Srinivasan, V., Prabhu, G.N., & Mukherji, S. (2018). Multi-level gaps: A study of intended, actual and experienced human resource practices in a hypermarket Chain in India. *The International Journal of Human Resource Management, 29*(2), 360–398.

Mann, A., & Harter, J. (2016). The worldwide employee engagement crisis. *Gallup Business Journal, 7*(1), 1–5.

Martin, G., Farndale, E., Paauwe, J., & Stiles, P.G. (2016). Corporate governance and strategic human resource management: Four archetypes and proposals for a new approach to corporate sustainability. *European Management Journal, 34*(1), 22–35.

Martin, G., & Gollan, P.J. (2012). Corporate governance and strategic human resources management in the UK financial services sector: The case of the RBS. *The International Journal of Human Resource Management, 23*(16), 3295–3314.

Meier, O., Naccache, P., & Schier, G. (2021). Exploring the curvature of the relationship between HRM–CSR and corporate financial performance. *Journal of Business Ethics, 170,* 857–873.

Mercer report. (2003). *Why HR governance matter? Managing the HR function for superior performance.* Mercer Human Resource Consulting Report.

Ministry of Planning and Economic Development. (2021). Medium-term sustainable development third year action plan. https://mped.gov.eg/DynamicPage?id= 76&lang=en. Accessed 20.06.2023.

Mukherji, A., & Bhatnagar, J. (2022). Conceptualizing and theorizing green human resource management: A narrative review. *International Journal of Manpower,* (ahead-of-print).

Mulolli, E., Boskovska, D., & Islami, X. (2020). The competitive role of human resource management strategies on SMEs in a transitional economy. *International Journal of Multidisciplinary and Current Research, 8*(4), 521–529.

OECD Tourism Trends and Policies. (2020). 10.1787/20767773. Accessed 06.03.2023.

Ollala, F.M., & Castillo, M.S. (2005). *Human resource audit.* International Advances in Economic Research, Atlantic Economic Society.

O'Reilly, C.A., & Tushman, M.L. (2004). The ambidextrous organization. *Harvard Business Review, 82*(4), 74–83.

Peccei, R., & Van De Voorde, K. (2019). Human resource management–well-being–performance research revisited: Past, present, and future. *Human Resource Management Journal, 29*(4), 539–563.

Phillips, J., Stone, R., & Phillips, P. (2001). *The human resources scorecard – measuring the return on investment.* Waltham, USA: Butterworth Heinmann.

Phillips, J., & Phillips, P. (2016). *Handbook of training evaluation and measurement methods.* New York: Routledge.

Sacht, J. (2001). *Audit and measurement of the human resources systems and procedures at business – unit level.* Johannesburg: Workplace Performance Technologies.

The Malcolm Baldrige National Quality Award. (2020). MBNQA program, United States Department of Commerce Technology Administration, National Institute of Standards and Technology, USA.

Ulrich, D. (1996). *Human resource champions: The next agenda for adding value and delivering results.* Boston: Harvard Business Press.

Walker, J.W. (1998). Are we using the right human resource measures? *Human Resource Planning, 21*(2), 7–9.

Willis, G., Cave, S., & Kunc, M. (2018). Strategic workforce planning in healthcare: A multi-methodology approach. *European Journal of Operational Research, 267*(1), 250–263.

Wright, P.M., Gardner, T.M., Moynihan, L.M., & Allen, M.R. (2005). The relationship between HR practices and firm performance: Examining causal order. *Personnel Psychology, 58*(2), 409–446.

Wright, P.M., & Nishii, L.H. (2007). *Strategic HRM and organizational behavior: Integrating multiple levels of analysis.* CAHRS Working Paper #07-03. Ithaca, NY: Cornell University. http://digitalcommons.ilr.cornell.edu/cahrswp/468. Accessed 09.05.2017.

Wright, P.M., & Nishii, L.H. (2013). Strategic HRM and organizational behaviour: Integrating multiple levels of analysis. In J. Paauwe, D.E. Guest, & P.M. Wright (Eds.). *HRM and performance: Achievements and challenges* (pp. 97–110). Chichester, UK: John Wiley & Sons Ltd.

Yan, J., & Hu, W. (2022). Environmentally specific transformational leadership and green product development performance: The role of a green HRM system. *International Journal of Manpower, 43*(3), 639–659.

Yong, J.Y., Yusliza, M.Y., Ramayah, T., Farooq, K., & Tanveer, M.I. (2022). Accentuating the interconnection between green intellectual capital, green human resource management and sustainability. *Benchmarking: An International Journal* (ahead-of-print).

Zuma, S.K. (2018). HR governance for sustainable human resource development: Evidence from private sector of Bangladesh. *European Journal of Business and Management, 10*(12), 207–216.

12 Organization and Incentivization of Risk Management

An Agency Theory Case Study

Marta Michaelis

Introduction

Agency theory, created by Arrow (1963) and developed by Jensen and Meckling (1976), is often a tool of choice for analyzing problems of organization and incentivization in firms. Representing the firm in a formalized manner and reducing the actors to their core characteristics allow for the analysis of normative questions, free of multiple potentially disruptive environmental factors. The results derived enable qualitative recommendations for practitioners, often serving as a foundation for empirical research. Especially popular are models assuming contract linearity, exponential utility, and normal distribution of results (LEN), as they ameliorate the solvability of complex models (Spremann, 1987). Unfortunately, there exist only a few structured case studies, guiding through problem-solving, within such models (e.g., Dierkes & Ayaz, 2006). The present case study aims to broaden this scope.

The chosen exemplary problem is the organization and incentivization of risk management. Risk, a (symmetrical) effect of uncertainty on objectives, can be directed and controlled in an organization via coordinated activities (DIN e. V., 2018). The core role befits, in this context, the risk managers (RMs), whose commitment and efforts depend mostly on their contracts and position in the organizational hierarchy (Dierkes & Michaelis, 2022). Risk management influences a firm's value positively (Smithson & Simkins, 2005; Hoyt & Liebenberg, 2011), and decreases the volatility of stock prices and earnings, thus decreasing the firm's risk (Bromiley et al., 2015; Pagach & Warr, 2015; Karanja, 2017). The importance of risk management for firms is addressed by many frameworks on its design, the most important being the International Organization for Standardization (ISO) 31000:2018 and the Committee of Sponsoring Organizations of the Treadway Commission (COSO) framework, as well as legal requirements.

The role of risk in agency is widely analyzed. General discussion of trade-offs between risk and incentives in theory and empirical observations

DOI: 10.4324/9781003376583-15

220 *Marta Michaelis*

is presented by Prendergast (2002a, 2002b). Many articles focus strongly on the controllability (Demski, 1976) and design of optimal contracts with regard to risky performance measures (Baker, 2000, 2002). In this regard, monitoring as an activity, decreasing the risk of performance measures, is often addressed, with Michaelis (2021) providing a comprehensive overview, describing the difficulties with transfer of insights to risk management. Thus, many unresolved issues need to be addressed analytically, including but not restricted to organization and incentivization of risk management. The results, such as those presented by Dierkes and Michaelis (2022), are inherently complex. Assuming that the mantle of case study simplifies the approach to otherwise mathematically challenging normative questions, and using Dierkes and Michaelis (2022) as a starting point, this case study is conducted, focusing on the role of managerial risk aversion.

This case study will help readers understand the basic design of LEN models and depict risk management in this framework, compute LEN models of risk management, illustrate the results in suitable graphics, qualitatively interpret the results, and critically assess assumptions of the model and its limitations. The readers are provided with an overview of agency theory and a description of risk management as a relevant problem. Subsequently, suitable modeling is suggested and a step-by-step solution discussed, including the depiction of relevant relationships in multiple graphics. Thus, the motivational potential of managerial risk aversion for risk management is shown, and ceteris paribus preferability of the structures is addressed.

Table 12.1 gives an overview of the chapter's contributions. Such case study should be of interest to academic researchers aiming to broaden their methodological scope, students engaging in their own research projects, and practitioners interested in better understanding scientific research outcomes. The remainder of this chapter is organized as follows. First, the chapter presents the theoretical background on the LEN model of the agency theory in a hidden action situation, followed by a discussion of risk management organization in firms. Then, it lists the case study questions, which are subsequently solved and discussed. Finally, it provides a short conclusion.

Practical and Theoretical Background of the Case Study

LEN Model of Agency Theory in a Hidden Action Situation

Agency theory is a basic analytical tool for managerial problems. Originating from information economics, it deals with issues of contracting and cooperation, under conditions of information asymmetry and in the

Organization and Incentivization of Risk Management 221

Table 12.1 Overview of the core contributions of the chapter

Contributions in overview	
Methodological	The chapter provides a detailed description of an analysis of a real-world issue using an agency theoretical case study. The implemented agency theoretical model is solved step by step, enhancing the understanding of other research from this area.
Theoretical	An analysis of different organizational designs of risk management in a case study setting reveals the relevance of managers' risk aversion for:
	• Their engagement in risk management and thus for the firm's final risk • The profitability of the firm
	The motivational role of RM's risk aversion is distinguished in the stylized setting of a case study. The disappearance of this effect on the level of the RM's effort in centralization elevates the role of organizational design of risk management.
Practical	With the limitations of a case study as a research tool accounted for, it still allows for an insight into the organization of risk management in a more approachable manner than the solely theoretical results.
	For practitioners, the chapter points toward a preferability of decentralization of risk management against centralization, at least when certain conditions are met. It also distinguishes the role of managerial risk aversion.
	For students, the chapter presents a tool to better understand related literature and implement agency models in their own research.

presence of external effects (Spremann, 1987; Lambert, 2001). It has its roots in Arrow (1963), who discussed contractual relationships in the context of insurance. Based on this, Jensen and Meckling (1976) developed the theory of a firm as a complex net of contractual relationships.

In its very basic structure, the theory discusses a principal who delegates a task to an agent in a non-repeated setting. A task can broadly range from menial work to decision-making and contracting with other agents. After agreeing on the contract, the agent chooses the action on the delegated task. Then, the performance measures are observed, aiding the principal in assessing the agent's engagement, and finally the outcomes and contractual payments are realized. In this context, the agent and the principal are self-serving, effort- and often risk-averse, aiming to maximize their respective expected utilities from the contractual relationship (Sappington, 1991; Lambert, 2001).

Using agency theoretical case studies in research consists of the steps presented in Figure 12.1. First, the real-world problem is observed. Second,

222 *Marta Michaelis*

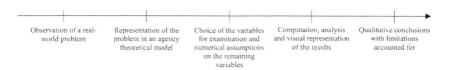

Figure 12.1 Research methodology of an agency theoretical case study.

the problem is reduced to its core characteristics and mathematically represented in an agency theoretical model. Third, these input variables must be chosen, which seem especially relevant to the problem. For all remaining input variables, plausible numerical values are assumed. Fourth, the results of the agency theoretical model are computed so that the output depends solely on the input variables, which have been chosen in the third step. The results can be analyzed through comparative statics. A visual representation further enhances their interpretability. Finally, the qualitative conclusions and recommendations are formulated, addressing the problem defined in the first step. The limitations to the results originate from the assumptions on the problem's core characteristics, model design, choice of analyzed variables and numerical assumptions.

Generally, situations discussed within the agency theory can be categorized as hidden characteristics, information, and action. The hidden characteristics situation ensues, when informational asymmetry occurs before signing the contract, so the principal cannot be sure about the agent's type and thus faces the adverse selection problem. Alternatively, the principal may face the moral hazard problem, as the agent may use for own benefit, the unobservability of effort that results from informational asymmetry before (hidden information) or after (hidden action) the effort provision (Jost, 2001; Macho-Stadler & Pérez-Castrillo, 2001; Schäfer, 2013).

The hidden action situation is the focal point of further analysis. In this case, the agent provides an unobservable effort, but its effect on the output is determined by the stand of nature, which is also unobservable. Hence, the principal cannot derive the agent's effort from observing the output, inducing moral hazard. Standardized timeline of the hidden action situation encompasses the following consecutive events: "principal offers a contract to the agent"; "agent decides about accepting the contract"; "agent provides an unobservable effort"; "nature provides an unobservable influence"; and "results and contractual payments are realized" (Macho-Stadler & Pérez-Castrillo, 2001).

Unfortunately, obtaining interpretable results and closed-form solutions in the general agency theory is inherently complex. However, certain assumptions allow a substantial simplification, namely these of a linear (L), exponential (E), normal (N) model. Concretely, it is assumed that the

Organization and Incentivization of Risk Management   223

outputs are linear to risk and efforts and contractual payments are in line with the outputs:

$$\tilde{x} = e + \tilde{\varepsilon} \tag{12.1}$$

and

$$v(\tilde{x}) = a \cdot \tilde{x} + b \tag{12.2}$$

Furthermore, the exponential utility of both parties is assumed, with constant absolute risk aversion:

$$u_P(\tilde{x}) = -\exp(-r_P \cdot \tilde{x}) \text{ and } u_A(\tilde{x}) = -\exp(-r_A \cdot \tilde{x}) \text{ with } r_P, r_A > 0 \tag{12.3}$$

Finally, the results are normally distributed (Spremann, 1987; Schäfer, 2013) through:

$$\tilde{\varepsilon} \sim N(0, \sigma^2) \tag{12.4}$$

Generally, maximizing the expected utility is the same as maximizing the certainty equivalent of an uncertain aim Θ, as:

$$E[u(\tilde{\Theta})] = u(CE(\tilde{\Theta})) \tag{12.5}$$

Given (12.1)–(12.4), the certainty equivalent can be represented directly as:

$$CE(\tilde{\Theta}) = E[\tilde{\Theta}] - 0.5 \cdot r \cdot V[\tilde{\Theta}] \tag{12.6}$$

As far as other assumptions are concerned, usually a quadratic effort cost

$$c(e) = 0.5 \cdot e^2 \tag{12.7}$$

and additive separability of the agent's utility

$$u_A(\tilde{x}, c) = u_A(\tilde{x}) - u_A(c) \tag{12.8}$$

are assumed (Spremann, 1987; Demougin & Jost, 2001).

Overall, these assumptions allow to represent the problem on a monetary level and in a simplified manner, so that for the hidden action situation, the principal faces the following maximization problem

224　*Marta Michaelis*

$$\max_a \; CE_P$$
$$s.t. \quad (PC): CE_A(e^*) \geq \bar{u},$$
$$(IC): e \in \arg\max_{e^* \in E}\{CE_A(e^*)\} \tag{12.9}$$

The agent accepts the contract only if the principal offers at least the monetary reservation in the amount of the agent's best alternative, called the participation constraint (PC). Given the contract, the agent chooses own effort in a manner maximizing own utility, denoted as incentive constraint (IC). The certainty equivalents of the principal and agent are, respectively (Spremann, 1987):

$$CE_P = E[\tilde{x} - v(\tilde{x})] - 0.5 \cdot r_P \cdot E[\tilde{x} - v(\tilde{x})] \tag{12.10}$$

$$CE_A = E[v(\tilde{x}) - c(e)] - 0.5 \cdot r_A \cdot E[v(\tilde{x}) - c(e)] \tag{12.11}$$

The analysis of the problem is usually divided in two parts. As a benchmark, it can be assumed that the effort of the agent is observable and the effort, optimal from the principal's view can be induced by forcing the contract. In this case, the principal must only account for the PC, providing the agent with the reservation utility to have the contract accepted. The problem is represented by

$$\max_a \; CE_P$$
$$s.t. \quad (PC): CE_A(e^*) \geq \bar{u} \tag{12.12}$$

In this manner, the risk is transferred between the contracting parties according to their risk aversion, optimally solving the risk-sharing problem. However, the incentive problem remains and can only be addressed by accounting for the IC, in a more complex model described in (12.9). The solution constitutes a trade-off between the risk-sharing and the incentive problem and is characterized by efficiency losses as compared to the first-best solution. In further analysis, the focus lies on analyzing the second-best solution for the risk management organization and incentivization problem, modeled in a framework of agency theory. Table 12.2 presents the overview of all the symbols from the case study.

Risk Management in the Context of the Agency

Risk management is present in most organizations (Fraser & Simkins, 2016) and is implemented as "coordinated activities to direct and control

Table 12.2 Overview of the symbols used in the case study

	Symbols		
a_i	variable incentive rate	r_i	risk aversion coefficient of i, $i \in \{B, P, R\}$
b_i	fixed base salary	$u_i, \bar{u}$	(monetary) reservation utility of i, $i \in \{B, P, R\}$
$c(\cdot)$	cost of effort function	$u(\cdot)$	utility function
CE_i	certainty equivalent of i, $i \in \{B, P, R\}$	v_i	compensation contract of i, $i \in \{B, R\}$
e	mean-increasing effort	$V[\cdot]$	variance operator
E	set of available mean-increasing efforts	x	firm's outcome
$E[\cdot]$	expected value operator	ε	environmental influence
IC_i	incentive constraint of i, $i \in \{B, R\}$	Θ	aim
m	variance-reducing effort	Π	firm's expected profit
M	set of available variance-reducing efforts	σ^2	firm's risk before risk management
$N(\cdot)$	normal distribution	$\sigma^2_{eff,j}$	firm's risk after risk management in the organizational structure j, $j \in \{c, d\}$
PC_i	participation constraint of $i, i \in \{B, R\}$		
	Sub- and superscripts		
A	agent	P	principal
B	business unit manager	R	risk manager
c	centralization	$*$	optimal
d	decentralization		

an organization with regard to risk" (DIN e. V., 2018, 3.2). In this context, risk can be seen either asymmetrically as a threat or symmetrically as a threat and an opportunity, with the second interpretation prevailing in risk management frameworks (Siegel, 2018; Lemos, 2020). Risk management is usually the responsibility of the board and thus a part of management. To adhere to risk management frameworks, either as part of legal requirements for stock listed firms or due to corporate governance, the management often delegates risk management to other players (UNECE, 2012; OECD, 2014). Pure structures of risk management encompass decentralization, when the RMs are line managers in single business units, and centralization, when RMs hold staff positions within managerial teams (Reavis, 1969; Arena et al., 2010).

Presence of risk management benefits organizations in various ways. It is a necessary strategic resource to remain competitive (Karanja, 2017), and empirical research points toward the positive influence of risk management on a firms' value (Smithson & Simkins, 2005; Hoyt & Liebenberg, 2011). It also decreases the volatility of stock prices and earnings, which could be seen as proxies for risk (Bromiley et al., 2015; Pagach & Warr, 2015; Karanja, 2017). To enjoy these benefits, however, risk management must be suitably implemented, with its "right" design depending on internal and external factors. Externally, the environment, as well as laws and regulations are of essence. Internally, the core relevance pertains to the organization's aims and risk appetite. Furthermore, the personal characteristics and attitude of an RM to risk matter, as does the manager's hierarchical position (Gordon et al., 2009; Arena et al., 2010).

Thus, many aspects must be accounted for while organizing risk management, for which recommendations grounded in empirical and analytical research are necessary. Agency theory provides a possible framework for an analysis. Modeling risk management in this framework necessitates understanding risks as variances in financial results (Arena et al., 2010). Thus, risk management is in core variance reduction, symmetrically diminishing the threat of negative and the opportunity of the positive deviation from the expected. Such variance reduction has been discussed in agency theory in the context of monitoring, where the activity of a monitor leads to better insight in the activity of the agent, and thus, leading to more effort by the agent. Especially the variance-reducing quality of the monitor's effort is of significance, as it makes performance measures less risky and thus is a more precise signal on the agent's effort (e.g., Liang et al., 2008). Hence, risk management can be seen as a special case of monitoring, focusing on the overall risk of a firm, and not only on the precision of performance measurement. The model with a variance-reducing agent is, however, not always one of risk management. First, there must be a connection between the performance measure used in a contract and the result, with perfect correlation given when the result itself is contractible for compensation schemes. Only then, as per definition, will monitoring and risk management be identical. Moreover, the RM should be modeled as a risk- and effort-averse entity, as RMs are similar to other employees and thus similar to other agents in a model. Finally, it is helpful, when the principal is modeled as risk-averse, instating an inherent interest in diminishing risk premium. Still, assuming a risk-neutral principal simplifies the model and is an acceptable assumption, given the regulatory reasons to organize risk management (Michaelis, 2021). A concrete example of modeling risk management in LEN modeling framework follows in the case study description in the Section Agency Theoretical Analysis of Risk Management in Different Organizational Structures.

Organization and Incentivization of Risk Management 227

Agency Theoretical Analysis of Risk Management in Different Organizational Structures

Case Study Description and Core Questions

Given are three contracting parties in a single-period setting. A risk-neutral board of directors representing the owner is the principal in the model, whereas two risk-averse managers act as the agents. The business unit manager (BUM) is characterized by the risk aversion r_B and engages in a productive effort e, accompanied by an effort cost of $0.5 \cdot e^2$. The RM is characterized by the risk aversion r_R and engages in risk-managing effort m, accompanied by an effort cost of $0.01 \cdot m$. The productive effort of the BUM has a mean-increasing quality, and the risk-managing effort of the RM has a variance-reducing quality. Given the assumption of the firm's risk, before risk management $\sigma^2 = 1$, the firm's outcome x can be characterized in the following way:

$$\tilde{x} = e + \tilde{\varepsilon}, \quad \tilde{\varepsilon} \sim N\left(0, \frac{1}{m}\right) \tag{12.13}$$

The firm's final risk is defined by the effective variance of the firm's outcome, after an endogenous choice of m in equilibrium:

$$\sigma^2_{eff} = \frac{1}{m} \tag{12.14}$$

The BUM and RM are offered compensation contracts, v_B and v_R, respectively:

$$v_B(\tilde{x}) = a_B \cdot \tilde{x} + b_B \tag{12.15}$$

$$v_R(\tilde{x}) = a_R \cdot \tilde{x} + b_R \tag{12.16}$$

Each contract is characterized by a base salary b as a fixed element and an incentive rate a, as a variable element contingent to the outcome of the firm. The agents choose their effort opportunistically with respect to the contracts offered and own effort aversion, which is summarized by the IC in the model. Moreover, the agents accept the contracts only if they satisfy their monetary reservation utilities $u_B = 0.1$ and $u_R = 0.1$ (PC).

The risk-neutral board is obliged to provide a risk management system and organizes it optimally with respect to the firm's expected utility. In pure form, the risk management can be organized in two ways, determined

228 *Marta Michaelis*

by the placement of the RM within the organizational hierarchy: centralization and decentralization.

In centralization, RM is more of a staff position on the highest hierarchical tier, directly employed by the board, which has the sole authority to contract. A hidden action situation in centralization of risk management encompasses the following consecutive events: "board offers contracts to BUM and RM"; "BUM and RM decide about accepting the contracts"; "BUM and RM choose and realize their efforts e, m"; "nature provides an unobservable influence"; "firm's expected profit Π, firm's risk σ_{eff}^2 and contractual payments are realized".

In decentralization, the contracting authority is delegated to the BUM, who is obliged to provide for the risk management system and does so by employing an RM, corresponding with the internal risk management system or the position of chief risk officers in single business units. A hidden action situation in decentralization of risk management encompasses the following consecutive events: "board offers a contract to BUM"; "BUM decides about accepting the contract and offers a contract to RM"; "RM decides about accepting the contract"; "BUM and RM choose and realize their efforts e, m"; "nature provides an unobservable influence"; "firm's expected profit Π, firm's risk σ_{eff}^2 and contractual payments are realized".

The analysis and comparison of both the organizational structures occur along the steps divided in the following three exercises.

Ex. 1 Optimal solutions for different organizational structures of risk management

For both the organizational structures, present the agency problem and compute the second-best results, depending on the managerial risk aversion coefficients.

1a *Centralization of risk management*
1b *Decentralization of risk management*

Ex. 2 Comparison of organizational structures

2a *Compare the second-best solutions, analytically.*
2b *Assuming $r_B = 0.2$, present the second-best results in three graphs:*

- *BUM's incentives, effort, and the expected profit depending on r_R*
- *RM's incentives and effort depending on r_R*
- *RM's effort and the final firm's risk depending on r_R*

2c *Assuming $r_R = 0.2$, present the second-best results in three graphs:*

- *BUM's incentives, effort, and the expected profit depending on r_B*

Organization and Incentivization of Risk Management   229

- RM's incentives and effort depending on r_B
- RM's effort and the final firm's risk depending on r_B

Ex. 3 Interpretation and limitations

Interpret the results of the previous exercises and discuss the preferred organizational structure with respect to managerial risk aversion. Summarize the limitations of the presented approach.

Solution to the Exercises

Ex. 1 Optimal solutions for different organizational structures of risk management

1a Centralization of risk management

I Problem representation
All parties want to maximize their expected utilities. Under the LEN assumptions, it is the same as maximization of certainty equivalents. The principal is risk-neutral, and thus strives for maximization of expected profit, defined as the expected outcome net the contractual payments to the managers. The optimization problem is solved via choice of the variable parameters of managerial contracts, under IC and PC:

$$\max_{a_B^c, a_R^c} \quad \Pi^c$$

$$s.t. \quad (PC_B): CE_B^c(e^{c,*}) \geq u_B, \qquad (PC_R): CE_R^c(m^{c,*}) \geq u_R,$$

$$(IC_B): e^c \in \arg\max_{e^{c,*} \in E}\{CE_B^c(e^{c,*})\}, \quad (IC_R): m^c \in \arg\max_{m^{c,*} \in M}\{CE_R^c(m^{c,*})\}$$

$$\tag{12.17}$$

II Computing the certainty equivalents

$$
\begin{aligned}
CE_B^c &= E[v_B(\tilde{x})] - 0.5\cdot(e^c)^2 - 0.5\cdot r_B\cdot Var[v_B(\tilde{x})] \\
&= e^c\cdot a_B + a_B\cdot E[\tilde{\varepsilon}] + b_B - 0.5\cdot(e^c)^2 - 0.5\cdot r_B\cdot a_B^2\cdot Var[\tilde{\varepsilon}] \\
&= e^c\cdot a_B + b_B - 0.5\cdot(e^c)^2 - 0.5\cdot r_B\cdot a_B^2\cdot\frac{1}{m^c}
\end{aligned}
\tag{12.18}
$$

$$
\begin{aligned}
CE_R^c &= E[v_R(\tilde{x})] - 0.01\cdot m^c - 0.5\cdot r_R\cdot Var[v_R(\tilde{x})] \\
&= e^c\cdot a_R + a_R\cdot E[\tilde{\varepsilon}] + b_R - 0.01\cdot m^c - 0.5\cdot r_R\cdot a_R^2\cdot Var[\tilde{\varepsilon}] \\
&= e^c\cdot a_R + b_R - 0.01\cdot m^c - 0.5\cdot r_R\cdot a_R^2\cdot\frac{1}{m^c}
\end{aligned}
\tag{12.19}
$$

$$CE_P^c = \Pi^c = E[\tilde{x} - v_B(\tilde{x}) - v_R(\tilde{x})] = e^c\cdot(1 - a_B - a_R) - b_B - b_R \tag{12.20}$$

230 *Marta Michaelis*

III Obtaining RM's base salary and response to incentive schemes

In equilibrium the PC binds, with rational principal granting only the necessary minimum. For RM, we obtain from (12.19):

$$CE_R^c = 0.1 \quad \Leftrightarrow \quad b_R = -\left(e^c \cdot a_R - 0.01 \cdot m^c - 0.5 \cdot r_R \cdot a_R^2 \cdot \frac{1}{m^c} - 0.1\right) \quad (12.21)$$

Furthermore, the agents have an optimal reaction to any compensation offered, and a principal can predict this reaction. According to the IC, the optimal reaction to any given contractual payment can be obtained by deriving the certainty equivalent (12.19) with respect to the effort and setting the derivative equal to zero. Without further mathematical proofs, we assume that such critical point is the optimum.

$$\frac{\partial CE_R^c}{\partial m^c} = -0.01 + 0.5 \cdot r_R \cdot a_R^2 \cdot \frac{1}{(m^c)^2} \overset{!}{=} 0 \quad \Leftrightarrow \quad m^c = 5 \cdot \sqrt{2 \cdot r_R} \cdot a_R \quad (12.22)$$

IV Obtaining BUM's base salary and response to incentive scheme

As in III, the structure of BUM's base salary and the response to the compensation scheme is derived from certainty equivalent (12.18).

$$CE_B^c = 0.1 \quad \Leftrightarrow \quad b_B = -\left(e^c \cdot a_B - 0.5 \cdot (e^c)^2 - 0.5 \cdot r_B \cdot a_B^2 \cdot \frac{1}{m^c} - 0.1\right) \quad (12.23)$$

$$\frac{\partial CE_B^c}{\partial e^c} = a_B - e^c \overset{!}{=} 0 \quad \Leftrightarrow \quad e^c = a_B \tag{12.24}$$

V Transforming the expected profit of the principal

We can depict the goal function of the principal, as depending solely on the variable incentives. For this, we first insert the base salaries computed in (12.21) and (12.23) in the expected profit, obtaining:

$$\Pi^c = e^c - 0.5 \cdot (e^c)^2 - 0.5 \cdot r_B \cdot a_B^2 \cdot \frac{1}{m^c} - 0.01 \cdot m^c - 0.5 \cdot r_R \cdot a_R^2 \cdot \frac{1}{m^c} - 0.2$$

$$\tag{12.25}$$

Then, we insert the optimal efforts derived from ICs (12.22) and (12.24), obtaining:

$$\Pi^c = a_B - 0.5 \cdot a_B^2 - 0.1 \cdot \frac{a_B^2}{a_R} \cdot \frac{r_B}{\sqrt{2 \cdot r_R}} - 0.05 \cdot \sqrt{2 \cdot r_R} \cdot a_R - 0.1 \cdot a_R \cdot \frac{r_R}{\sqrt{2 \cdot r_R}} - 0.2 \tag{12.26}$$

VI Deriving the optimal incentives

Finally, we compute the optimal variable incentives from the perspective of the principal, by deriving the expected profit (12.26) with respect to them:

$$\frac{\partial \Pi^c}{\partial a_R} = 0.1 \cdot \frac{a_B^2}{a_R^2} \cdot \frac{r_B}{\sqrt{2 \cdot r_R}} - 0.05 \cdot \sqrt{2 \cdot r_R} - 0.1 \cdot \frac{r_R}{\sqrt{2 \cdot r_R}} \overset{!}{=} 0 \quad \Leftrightarrow \quad \frac{a_B}{a_R} = \sqrt{\frac{2 \cdot r_R}{r_B}} \tag{12.27}$$

$$\frac{\partial \Pi^c}{\partial a_B} = 1 - a_B - 0.2 \cdot \frac{a_B}{a_R} \cdot \frac{r_B}{\sqrt{2 \cdot r_R}} \overset{!}{=} 0 \quad \Leftrightarrow \quad a_B = 1 - 0.2 \cdot \sqrt{r_B} \tag{12.28}$$

VII Results overview

Inserting the managerial incentives to the previously obtained results yield:

$$e^c = a_B^c = 1 - 0.2 \cdot \sqrt{r_B}, \tag{12.29}$$

$$a_R^c = \sqrt{\frac{r_B}{2 \cdot r_R}} \cdot (1 - 0.2 \cdot \sqrt{r_B}), \tag{12.30}$$

$$m^c = 5 \cdot \sqrt{2 \cdot r_R} \cdot a_R = 5 \cdot \sqrt{r_B} - r_B \tag{12.31}$$

$$\Pi^c = 0.5 \cdot (1 - 0.2 \cdot \sqrt{r_B})^2 - 0.2 = 0.5 \cdot (a_B^c)^2 - 0.2, \tag{12.32}$$

$$\sigma_{eff,c}^2 = \frac{1}{m^c} = (5 \cdot \sqrt{r_B} - r_B)^{-1} \tag{12.33}$$

232 Marta Michaelis

VIII Restrictions to the results

Logical assumptions based on the characteristic of the results may necessitate some restriction on the input factors. The core demand to avoid implausible results is that the managerial efforts are non-negative:

$$e^c \geq 0, \ m^c \geq 0 \tag{12.34}$$

This holds true as long as the incentives of the BUM are non-negative:

$$a_B^c \geq 0 \quad \Leftrightarrow \quad 1 - 0.2 \cdot \sqrt{r_B} \geq 0 \quad \Leftrightarrow \quad \sqrt{r_B} \leq 5 \quad \Leftrightarrow \quad r_B \in (0; \ 25] \tag{12.35}$$

1b Decentralization of risk management

I Problem representation

In decentralization, the principal maximizes their own expected profit, subject to IC and PC of the BUM:

$$\max_{a_B^d} \quad \Pi^d = E[\tilde{x} - v_B(\tilde{x})]$$

$$s.t. \quad (PC_B): CE_B^d(e^{d,*}) \geq u_B \tag{12.36}$$

$$\qquad (IC_B): e^d \in \arg\max_{e^{d,*} \in E}\{CE_B^d(e^{d,*})\},$$

Whereas, the BUM maximizes own expected utility, subject to the IC and PC of the RM:

$$\max_{e^d, a_R^d} \quad CE_B^d = E[v_B(\tilde{x}) - v_R(\tilde{x})] - \tfrac{1}{2}\cdot(e^d)^2 - \tfrac{1}{2}\cdot r_B\cdot Var[v_B(\tilde{x}) - v_R(\tilde{x})]$$

$$s.t. \quad (PC_R): CE_R^d(m^{d,*}) \geq u_R$$

$$\qquad (IC_R): m^d \in \arg\max_{m^{d,*} \in M}\{CE_R^d(m^{d,*})\}$$

$$\tag{12.37}$$

II Computing the certainty equivalents

$$
\begin{aligned}
CE_B^d &= E[v_B(\tilde{x}) - v_R(\tilde{x})] - 0.5\cdot(e^d)^2 - 0.5\cdot r_B\cdot Var[v_B(\tilde{x}) - v_R(\tilde{x})] \\
&= (a_B - a_R)\cdot e^d + (a_B - a_R)\cdot E[\tilde{\varepsilon}] + b_B - b_R - 0.5\cdot(e^d)^2 - 0.5\cdot r_B\cdot(a_B - a_R)^2 \\
&\quad \cdot Var[\tilde{\varepsilon}] \\
&= (a_B - a_R)\cdot e^d + b_B - b_R - 0.5\cdot(e^d)^2 - 0.5\cdot r_B\cdot(a_B - a_R)^2\cdot\tfrac{1}{m^c}
\end{aligned}
$$

$$\tag{12.38}$$

Organization and Incentivization of Risk Management 233

The certainty equivalent of the RM is defined by (12.19).

$$\Pi^d = E[\tilde{x} - v_B(\tilde{x})] = e^d \cdot (1 - a_B) - b_B \tag{12.39}$$

III Obtaining the RM's base salary and response to incentive schemes
The optimization problem of the RM does not change, thus (12.21) and (12.22) hold true.

IV Obtaining BUM's base salary and response to incentive schemes
Inserting the base salary and the RM's effort from (12.21) and (12.22) yields:

$$\begin{aligned} CE_B^d &= a_B \cdot e^d + b_B - 0.1 \cdot (2 \cdot r_R + r_B) \cdot a_R \cdot \frac{1}{\sqrt{2 \cdot r_R}} - 0.1 \\ &\quad - 0.5 \cdot (e^d)^2 - 0.1 \cdot \left(\frac{a_B^2}{a_R} - 2 \cdot a_B \right) \cdot \frac{r_B}{\sqrt{2 \cdot r_R}} \end{aligned} \tag{12.40}$$

PC of the BUM:

$$CE_B^d = 0.1 \quad \Leftrightarrow \quad b_B = - \begin{pmatrix} a_B \cdot e^d - 0.1 \cdot (2 \cdot r_R + r_B) \cdot a_R \cdot \frac{1}{\sqrt{2 \cdot r_R}} - 0.2 \\ - 0.5 \cdot (e^d)^2 - 0.1 \cdot \left(\frac{a_B^2}{a_R} - 2 \cdot a_B \right) \cdot \frac{r_B}{\sqrt{2 \cdot r_R}} \end{pmatrix} \tag{12.41}$$

We obtain the optimal response of the BUM for any given compensation scheme, in the form of own effort and incentives for RM from the IC (12.40):

$$\frac{\partial CE_B^d}{\partial e^d} = a_B - e^d \overset{!}{=} 0 \quad \Leftrightarrow \quad e^d = a_B \tag{12.42}$$

$$\frac{\partial CE_B^d}{\partial a_R} = -0.1 \cdot (2 \cdot r_R + r_B) \cdot \frac{1}{\sqrt{2 \cdot r_R}} - 0.1 \cdot \left(-\frac{a_B^2}{a_R^2} \right) \cdot \frac{r_B}{\sqrt{2 \cdot r_R}} \overset{!}{=} 0 \quad \Leftrightarrow \quad a_R = a_B$$
$$\cdot \sqrt{\frac{r_B}{2 \cdot r_R + r_B}} \tag{12.43}$$

V Transforming the expected profit of the principal
We insert the base salary of the BUM from PC (12.41)

234   *Marta Michaelis*

$$\Pi^d = e^d \cdot (1 - a_B) + a_B \cdot e^d - 0.1 \cdot (2 \cdot r_R + r_B) \cdot a_R \cdot \frac{1}{\sqrt{2 \cdot r_R}} - 0.2 - 0.5 \cdot (e^d)^2$$
$$- 0.1 \cdot \left(\frac{a_B^2}{a_R} - 2 \cdot a_B \right) \cdot \frac{r_B}{\sqrt{2 \cdot r_R}}$$

(12.44)

as well as BUM's optimal responses to the incentive scheme from (12.42) and (12.43)

$$\Pi^d = \left(1 - 0.2 \cdot \left(\sqrt{\frac{2 \cdot r_R + r_B}{r_B}} - 1 \right) \cdot \frac{r_B}{\sqrt{2 \cdot r_R}} \right) \cdot a_B - 0.2 - 0.5 \cdot a_B^2 \qquad (12.45)$$

VI Deriving the optimal incentives

Deriving (12.45) with respect to the BUM's incentives:

$$\frac{\partial \Pi^d}{\partial a_B} = \left(1 - 0.2 \cdot \left(\sqrt{\frac{2 \cdot r_R + r_B}{r_B}} - 1 \right) \cdot \frac{r_B}{\sqrt{2 \cdot r_R}} \right) - a_B \overset{!}{=} 0$$
$$\Leftrightarrow a_B = 1 - 0.2 \cdot \left(\sqrt{\frac{2 \cdot r_R + r_B}{r_B}} - 1 \right) \cdot \frac{r_B}{\sqrt{2 \cdot r_R}}$$

(12.46)

VII Results overview

Inserting the managerial incentives to the previously obtained results:

$$e^d = a_B^d = 1 - 0.2 \cdot \left(\sqrt{\frac{2 \cdot r_R + r_B}{r_B}} - 1 \right) \cdot \frac{r_B}{\sqrt{2 \cdot r_R}} \qquad (12.47)$$

$$a_R^d = a_B^d \cdot \sqrt{\frac{r_B}{2 \cdot r_R + r_B}} = \left(1 - 0.2 \cdot \left(\sqrt{\frac{2 \cdot r_R + r_B}{r_B}} - 1 \right) \cdot \frac{r_B}{\sqrt{2 \cdot r_R}} \right) \cdot \sqrt{\frac{r_B}{2 \cdot r_R + r_B}}$$

(12.48)

$$m^d = 5 \cdot \sqrt{2 \cdot r_R} \cdot a_R = 5 \cdot \left(1 - 0.2 \cdot \left(\sqrt{\frac{2 \cdot r_R + r_B}{r_B}} - 1 \right) \cdot \frac{r_B}{\sqrt{2 \cdot r_R}} \right) \cdot \sqrt{\frac{2 \cdot r_R \cdot r_B}{2 \cdot r_R + r_B}}$$

(12.49)

$$\Pi^d = 0.5 \cdot \left(1 - 0.2 \cdot \left(\sqrt{\frac{2 \cdot r_R + r_B}{r_B}} - 1\right) \cdot \frac{r_B}{\sqrt{2 \cdot r_R}}\right)^2 - 0.2 = 0.5 \cdot (a_B^d)^2 - 0.2$$

$$(12.50)$$

$$\sigma_{eff,d}^2 = \frac{1}{m^d} = 0.2 \cdot \left(1 - 0.2 \cdot \left(\sqrt{\frac{2 \cdot r_R + r_B}{r_B}} - 1\right) \cdot \frac{r_B}{\sqrt{2 \cdot r_R}}\right)^{-1} \cdot \sqrt{\frac{2 \cdot r_R + r_B}{2 \cdot r_R \cdot r_B}}$$

$$(12.51)$$

VIII Restrictions to the results

Due to interdependencies between the incentives and efforts, the managerial efforts are non-negative when:

$$a_B^d \geq 0$$

$$\Leftrightarrow 1 - 0.2 \cdot \left(\sqrt{\frac{2 \cdot r_R + r_B}{r_B}} - 1\right) \cdot \frac{r_B}{\sqrt{2 \cdot r_R}} \geq 0 \qquad (12.52)$$

$$\Leftrightarrow \sqrt{2 \cdot r_R + r_B} \cdot \sqrt{r_B} \leq 5 \cdot \sqrt{2 \cdot r_R} + r_B$$

This cannot be solved explicitly and whether it holds true, must be proved, for concrete managerial risk aversion coefficients of the second part of the case study.

Ex. 2 Comparison of organizational structures

2a *Comparisons*

I Comparing the productive incentives, effort, and expected profit

Based on (12.29) and (12.47), we examine:

$$e^d - e^c = a_B^d - a_B^c = 0.2 \cdot \sqrt{r_B} \cdot \left(1 - \sqrt{\frac{2 \cdot r_R + r_B}{2 \cdot r_R}} + \frac{\sqrt{r_B}}{\sqrt{2 \cdot r_R}}\right) \qquad (12.53)$$

As

$$1 - \sqrt{\frac{2 \cdot r_R + r_B}{2 \cdot r_R}} + \frac{\sqrt{r_B}}{\sqrt{2 \cdot r_R}} \geq 0$$

$$\Leftrightarrow \sqrt{2 \cdot r_R} + \sqrt{r_B} \geq \sqrt{2 \cdot r_R + r_B} \qquad (12.54)$$

$$\Leftrightarrow 2 \cdot r_R + 2 \cdot \sqrt{2 \cdot r_R} \cdot \sqrt{r_B} + r_B \geq 2 \cdot r_R + r_B$$

$$\Leftrightarrow 2 \cdot \sqrt{2 \cdot r_R \cdot r_B} \geq 0$$

always holds true, thus

236   *Marta Michaelis*

$$a_B^d \geq a_B^c \text{ and } e^d \geq e^c \tag{12.55}$$

For expected profit, we analyze (12.32) and (12.50):

$$\begin{aligned} \Pi^d - \Pi^c &= 0.5 \cdot (a_B^d)^2 - 2 - 0.5 \cdot (a_B^c)^2 + 2 \\ &= 0.5 \cdot (a_B^d - a_B^c) \cdot (a_B^d + a_B^c) \end{aligned} \tag{12.56}$$

From (12.55), we get the results that

$$\Pi^d \geq \Pi^c \tag{12.57}$$

II Comparing the risk-managing incentives, effort, and the firm's final risk
Analyzing the RM's incentives in (12.30) and (12.48) yields

$$\begin{aligned} a_R^d - a_R^c &= \left(1 - 0.2 \cdot \left(\sqrt{\frac{2 \cdot r_R + r_B}{r_B}} - 1\right) \cdot \frac{r_B}{\sqrt{2 \cdot r_R}}\right) \cdot \sqrt{\frac{r_B}{2 \cdot r_R + r_B}} - \frac{\sqrt{r_B} - 0.2 \cdot r_B}{\sqrt{2 \cdot r_R}} \\ &= \sqrt{\frac{r_B}{2 \cdot r_R + r_B}} + \left(0.2 \cdot \sqrt{\frac{1}{2 \cdot r_R + r_B}} \cdot r_B - 1\right) \cdot \frac{\sqrt{r_B}}{\sqrt{2 \cdot r_R}}, \end{aligned} \tag{12.58}$$

for which a nearer examination is necessary

$$\begin{aligned} &\sqrt{\frac{r_B}{2 \cdot r_R + r_B}} + \left(0.2 \cdot \sqrt{\frac{1}{2 \cdot r_R + r_B}} \cdot r_B - 1\right) \frac{\sqrt{r_B}}{\sqrt{2 \cdot r_R}} \geq 0 \\ &\Leftrightarrow \sqrt{2 \cdot r_R} + 0.2 \cdot r_B \geq \sqrt{2 \cdot r_R + r_B} \\ &\Leftrightarrow 2 \cdot r_R + 2 \cdot \sqrt{2 \cdot r_R} \cdot 0.2 \cdot r_B + 0.04 \cdot r_B^2 \geq 2 \cdot r_R + r_B \\ &\Leftrightarrow 0.04 \cdot (r_B - 25 \cdot (1 - \sqrt{2 \cdot r_R} \cdot 0.4)) \cdot r_B \geq 0 \\ &\Rightarrow r_B \geq 25 \cdot (1 - \sqrt{2 \cdot r_R} \cdot 0.4) \end{aligned} \tag{12.59}$$

resulting in

$$\begin{aligned} a_R^d &\geq a_R^c \Leftrightarrow r_B \geq 25 - 10 \cdot \sqrt{2 \cdot r_R} \\ a_R^d &\leq a_R^c \qquad \text{otherwise} \end{aligned} \tag{12.60}$$

The results transfer further to the risk-managing effort, as seen in (12.31) and (12.49)

$$m^d - m^c = 5 \cdot \sqrt{2 \cdot r_R} - 5 \cdot \sqrt{2 \cdot r_R} \cdot a_R^c = 5 \cdot \sqrt{2 \cdot r_R} \cdot (a_R^d - a_R^c)$$

$$m^d \geq m^c \quad \Leftrightarrow \quad r_B \geq 25 - 10 \cdot \sqrt{2 \cdot r_R} \qquad (12.61)$$

$$m^d \leq m^c \qquad \qquad \text{otherwise}$$

and the firm's final risk from (12.33) and (12.51)

$$\sigma_{eff,d}^2 - \sigma_{eff,c}^2 = \frac{1}{m^d} - \frac{1}{m^c} = \frac{m^c - m^d}{m^c \cdot m^d}$$

$$\sigma_{eff,d}^2 \leq \sigma_{eff,c}^2 \quad \Leftrightarrow \quad r_B \geq 25 - 10 \cdot \sqrt{2 \cdot r_R} \qquad (12.62)$$

$$\sigma_{eff,d}^2 \geq \sigma_{eff,c}^2 \qquad \text{otherwise}$$

2b Development depending on r_R

As $r_B = 0.2$ is assumed, the restriction (12.35) holds true. As for the restriction (12.52), the following is observed:

$$\sqrt{0.4 \cdot r_R + 0.04} \leq \sqrt{50 \cdot r_R} + 0.2 \quad \Leftrightarrow \quad 124 \cdot r_R + \sqrt{50 \cdot r_R} \geq 0, \qquad (12.63)$$

which always holds true. Thus, the results are given for all r_R. For better visibility, only a small interval of $r_R \in (0; 0.5]$ is depicted in Figure 12.2. It consists of three panels, depicting the results in both structures as RM's risk aversion increases. The first panel depicts the effort of the BUM and the expected outcome, higher in decentralization than in centralization, but generally almost constant and approaching each other. The second panel depicts the RM's effort in centralization at a constant level and higher than in decentralization, independent from decreasing incentives. The third panel depicts the RM's effort and firm's final risk, the latter constant in centralization and lower than the decreasing firm's risk in decentralization.

2c Development depending on r_B

As $r_R = 0.2$ is assumed, the restrictions (12.35) and (12.52) must be accounted for. The results are given up to $r_B = 25$, with this whole spectrum depicted in Figure 12.3. It consists of three panels, depicting the results in both structures as BUM's risk aversion increases. All three panels have a not-interpretable grey-layered area, in which centralization is not an acceptable structure, as it does not lead to positive utility by the board. The first panel depicts the decreasing effort of the BUM

238 *Marta Michaelis*

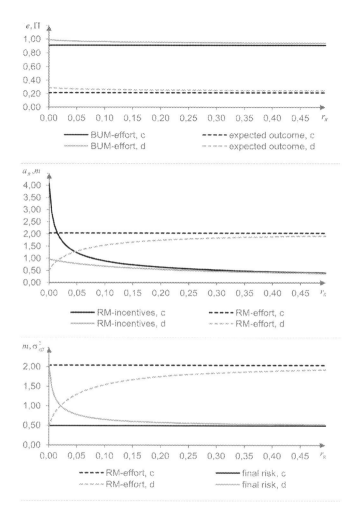

Figure 12.2 Core results in centralization and decentralization, depending on RM's risk aversion.

and the expected outcome in both structures, with stronger decrease in centralization than in decentralization. The second panel depicts the increasing incentives and effort of the RM, with the level and the increase higher in centralization than in decentralization. The third panel depicts the RM's effort and firm's final risk, the latter decreasing and lower in centralization than in decentralization.

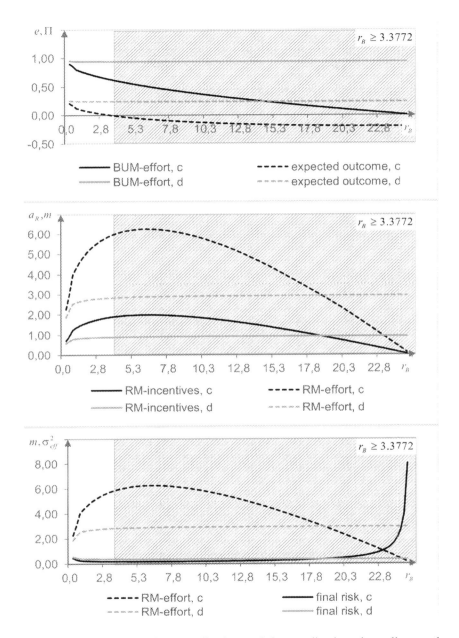

Figure 12.3 Core results in centralization and decentralization, depending on the BUM's risk aversion.

240 *Marta Michaelis*

Ex. 3 Interpretation and limitations

I Influence of r_R
An organizational design is only applicable, if it leads to a non-negative profit.

For centralization and in case of $r_B = 0.2$, it is true for all r_R, as:

$$\Pi^c \geq 0 \quad \Leftrightarrow \quad 0.5 \cdot (1 - 0.2 \cdot \sqrt{0.2})^2 - 0.2 \geq 0 \quad \Leftrightarrow \quad 0.2146 \geq 0 \quad (12.64)$$

For decentralization, the following is true:

$$\Pi^d \geq 0$$

$$\Leftrightarrow \left(1 - 0.2 \cdot \left(\sqrt{\frac{2 \cdot r_R + 0.2}{0.2}} - 1 \right) \cdot \frac{0.2}{\sqrt{2 \cdot r_R}} \right)^2 \geq 0.4$$

$$\Leftrightarrow 1 - \left(\sqrt{\frac{r_R + 0.1}{0.1}} - 1 \right) \cdot \frac{0.1}{\sqrt{r_R}} \geq 2 \cdot \sqrt{0.1} \quad \vee \quad 1 - \left(\sqrt{\frac{r_R + 0.1}{0.1}} - 1 \right) \cdot \frac{0.1}{\sqrt{r_R}} \leq -2$$

$$\cdot \sqrt{0.1}$$

$$\Leftrightarrow \sqrt{r_R} \geq -\frac{0.2 \cdot (1 - 2 \cdot \sqrt{0.1})}{(1 - 2 \cdot \sqrt{0.1})^2 - 0.1} \quad \vee \quad \sqrt{r_R} \leq -\frac{0.2 \cdot (1 - 2 \cdot \sqrt{0.1})}{(1 + 2 \cdot \sqrt{0.1})^2 - 0.1}$$

$$(12.65)$$

As the risk aversion parameter cannot be negative when risk-averse managers are assumed, the expected profit in decentralization is positive for all r_R.

Generally, the influence of a parameter on the results can be obtained by the means of comparative statics. The results are derived with respect to the parameter, in this case r_R. If the derivative is positive, the output parameter increases along with the input. However, if the derivative is negative, it is the opposite. In centralization, an increase in RM's risk aversion leads to a decrease in RM's incentives. Other results are not influenced. In decentralization, it results in a decrease of all the output parameters, except RM's effort, which increases. Detailed computations are provided in the appendix.

In centralization, an increase in the RM's risk aversion leads to a decrease in the risk management incentives, which, however, does not transfer to the risk management effort.

$$\frac{\partial m^c}{\partial r_R} = 5 \cdot \sqrt{2} \cdot \left(\frac{1}{2 \cdot \sqrt{r_R}} \cdot a_R^c + \sqrt{r_R} \cdot \frac{\partial a_R^c}{\partial r_R} \right) = 5 \cdot \sqrt{2} \cdot a_B^c \cdot \sqrt{\frac{0.1}{r_R}} \cdot \left(\frac{1}{2 \cdot \sqrt{r_R}} - \frac{1}{2 \cdot \sqrt{r_R}} \right) = 0$$

$$(12.66)$$

From (12.66), it is clear that an increase in the RM's risk aversion simultaneously leads to a decrease in the RM's incentives, negatively influencing the effort (incentive effect). However, it directly leads to an increase in this effort to the exactly same extent (risk aversion effect), so that overall, the RM's effort remains unaffected by changes in managerial risk aversion. This translates to all further results and is visible in Figure 12.2. Especially in its second panel, it is clear how the RM's incentives decrease in risk aversion, whereas the effort remains constant.

In decentralization, we can also observe the incentive and risk aversion effects, but for the given input parameters, the risk aversion effect always prevails over the incentive, so that an increase in the RM's risk aversion leads to more effort and less final risk for the firm, as seen in second and third panel of Figure 12.2. It is formally represented by:

$$\frac{\partial m^d}{\partial r_R} = 5 \cdot \sqrt{2} \cdot \left(\frac{1}{2} \cdot \sqrt{r_R} \cdot a_B^d \cdot \underbrace{\left(\frac{1}{r_R} - \frac{1}{r_R + 0.1} \right)}_{>0} + \sqrt{r_R} \cdot \underbrace{\frac{\partial a_B^d}{\partial r_R}}_{>0} \right) \cdot \sqrt{\frac{0.1}{r_R + 0.1}} > 0 \tag{12.67}$$

Still, an increase in the RM's risk aversion, from the perspective of the all contractual relationships, means an additional risk premium for the RM, that is transferred via the BUM's PC to the principal, and overall restricts the productive incentives available to the BUM, which causes the BUM's effort and firm's profit to decrease due to the RM's risk aversion, as seen in Figure 12.2.

In centralization, the only possibility to decrease risk is to induce additional risk management. In decentralization, the BUM may also use risk-sharing with the RM employed by them. This leads to a reduction in the additional risk management incentives necessary for an additional productive incentive in decentralization as compared to centralization:

$$\frac{\partial a_R^c}{\partial a_B^c} = \sqrt{\frac{0.1}{r_R}} > \sqrt{\frac{0.1}{0.1 + r_R}} = \frac{\partial a_R^d}{\partial a_B^d} \tag{12.68}$$

Thus, decentralization structurally allows the same production to be accompanied by less risk management, leading to overall higher risk, but at the same time increasing the firm's profit as compared to centralization. This result holds true for all RM's risk aversion coefficients. A risk-neutral firm is only interested in providing risk management at the level necessary for production, but not to reduce own risk premium, so

242 *Marta Michaelis*

that decentralization emerges as preferable organizational structure. Additionally, according to (12.60), for the RM's risk aversion above 3.0752, decentralization will lead to lowering the firm's risk. This is because in centralization, the principal will need to decrease the production to such an extent, that the accompanying risk management level will decrease below the level seen in decentralization.

II. Influence of r_B

For $r_R = 0.2$ and in centralization, a non-negative profit is given for certain intervals of r_B:

$$\Pi^c \geq 0 \Leftrightarrow 0.5 \cdot (1 - 0.2 \cdot \sqrt{r_B})^2 - 0.2 \geq 0$$
$$\Leftrightarrow (1 - 0.2 \cdot \sqrt{r_B})^2 \geq 0.4$$
$$\Leftrightarrow 1 - 0.2 \cdot \sqrt{r_B} \geq 2 \cdot \sqrt{0.1} \quad \vee \quad 1 - 0.2 \cdot \sqrt{r_B} \leq -2 \cdot \sqrt{0.1} \qquad (12.69)$$
$$\Leftrightarrow \sqrt{r_B} \leq \frac{1 - 2 \cdot \sqrt{0.1}}{0.2} \quad \vee \quad \sqrt{r_B} \geq \frac{1 + 2 \cdot \sqrt{0.1}}{0.2}$$
$$\Leftrightarrow r_B \leq 3.3772 \quad \vee \quad r_B \geq 66.6228$$

Moreover, due to (12.35), r_B may not exceed 25 or else negative efforts are expected. Thus, centralization is available as an organizational structure only when r_B is below 3.3772, as it generates negative expected profit afterward.

As risk aversion parameters cannot be negative when risk-averse managers are assumed, decentralization results are positive for all r_B that are permissible with respect to other restrictions.

$$\Pi^d \geq 0$$
$$\Leftrightarrow \left(1 - 0.2 \cdot \left(\sqrt{\frac{0.4 + r_B}{r_B}} - 1\right) \cdot \frac{r_B}{\sqrt{0.4}}\right)^2 \geq 0.4 \qquad (12.70)$$
$$\Leftrightarrow r_B \geq -\frac{1 - 2 \cdot \sqrt{0.1}}{2 \cdot (\sqrt{0.1} - 0.22)} \quad \vee \quad 2 \cdot (\sqrt{0.1} + 0.18) \cdot r_B \leq -\frac{12 \cdot \sqrt{0.1}}{2 \cdot (\sqrt{0.1} + 0.18)}$$

The influence of r_B on the output can be examined with comparative statics as well, with details provided in the appendix. In both structures, as the BUM's risk aversion increases, the BUM's incentives and effort, firm's expected profit and firm's final risk, decrease, whereas the RM's incentives and effort increase.

An increase in the BUM's risk aversion leads to a decrease in their incentives, effort, as well as in the firm's profit, in a typical agency result. Simultaneously, the party employing an RM (principal in centralization, BUM in decentralization) wants to incentivize additional risk management to counteract these effects. On the level of the

Organization and Incentivization of Risk Management 243

RM's incentives, we observe a decrease and an increase due to the extended incentive and extended risk aversion effect, respectively:

$$\frac{\partial a_R^c}{\partial r_B} = \underbrace{\frac{\partial a_B^c}{\partial r_B} \sqrt{\frac{r_B}{0.4}}}_{<0} + \underbrace{\frac{1}{2} \cdot a_B^c \cdot \sqrt{\frac{1}{0.4 \cdot r_B}}}_{>0} > 0 \qquad (12.71)$$

$$\frac{\partial a_R^d}{\partial r_B} = \underbrace{\frac{\partial a_B^d}{\partial r_B} \cdot \sqrt{\frac{r_B}{0.4 + r_B}}}_{<0} + \underbrace{0.2 \cdot \sqrt{\frac{1}{r_B \cdot (0.4 + r_B)^3}} \cdot a_B^d}_{>0} > 0 \qquad (12.72)$$

For the given parameters, the extended risk aversion effect over-compensates the extended incentive effect (see appendix for a proof), so that the RM's effort increases and the firm's final risk decreases, in the BUM's risk aversion. This can be seen in the interpretable area of Figure 12.3, when r_B is below the threshold identified in (12.69). The analysis of the result's development, in cases where no positive profit is generated, is without merit, as the firm would not exist.

Comparison between the structures in this case is also driven by the marginal risk management incentives, necessary for additional productive incentives:

$$\frac{\partial a_R^c}{\partial a_B^c} = \sqrt{\frac{r_B}{0.4}} > \sqrt{\frac{r_B}{0.4 + r_B}} = \frac{\partial a_R^d}{\partial a_B^d} \qquad (12.73)$$

Once more, decentralization emerges as the universally preferable organizational structure. With regard to the firm's final risk, according to (12.60) we can expect from $r_B = 18.6754$, that decentralization will lead to more risk management and thus a lower firm risk as compared to centralization. However, the comparison is not plausible, as at this point, the risk aversion of the BUM is so high that it precludes centralization as an organizational form. Therefore, from the threshold of $r_B = 3.3772$, the only profitable structure is decentralization. Thus, as long as both structures are profitable, centralization always leads to a lower final firm risk.

III. Limitations of the approach

Restricting analysis to only linear contracts is widely accepted due to tractability. Nonetheless, this assumption systematically excludes other contracting forms, which could provide better results. This is especially problematic while modeling risk management as a variance-reducing activity. However, linear incentive schemes are often used in practice, whereas non-linear ones are met with acceptance problems.

Furthermore, modeling risk management is intuitively accompanied by the assumption of risk aversion of the firm. Nevertheless, even in a case study, such assumption leads to overly complex results. Moreover, it may not be essential, as firms organize risk management, not necessarily due to their own risk aversion, but rather due to that of their employees, legal requirements, and corporate governance (UNECE, 2012; OECD, 2014).

Moreover, contracting a firm's outcome presents a limitation, as it is rarely possible in reality. Nonetheless, it constitutes a direct link between the risk of the employees and that of the whole firm. It is also important in order to avoid switching from a risk management model to a monitoring framework.

Finally, even though the results of a case study pose some interesting insights, they have no claim on generality. Deviations are expected, especially if other cost of risk management efforts were assumed. The general results are only available in the manner of analytical computation (see Dierkes & Michaelis, 2022, for those). Nonetheless, insights from the case study allow the illustration of analytical results in a more comprehensible manner.

Discussion of the Results and of the Methodology

The case study consisted of three exercises, summarized with their results and practical value in Table 12.3. In the final exercise, the results have been summarized, and the limitations of a case study approach have been highlighted. There are three contexts in which the results of this chapter can be discussed: the risk management literature, the agency theoretical literature, and case studies used for didactic purposes.

Concerning the given literature on risk management, the case study shows the expected result of risk management decreasing the firm's risk (Bromiley et al., 2015; Pagach & Warr, 2015; Karanja, 2017). The positive influence of value relevance of risk management (Smithson & Simkins, 2005; Hoyt & Liebenberg, 2011) is discussed in the context of the comparison between the organizational designs. Finally, the literature expects managerial risk aversion to affect risk management (Gordon et al., 2009; Arena et al., 2010), which is also observed in the case study results.

Only a few articles implement agency theory in the context of risk management. Dierkes and Michaelis (2022) prove the existence of (extended) risk aversion and incentive effects in a complex theoretical

Organization and Incentivization of Risk Management   245

Table 12.3 Summary of the exercises, their results, conclusions, and practical value

Ex.	Summary	Results and conclusions	Practical value
1	The agency problem is presented, and its second-best results are computed for centralization and decentralization of risk management.	Certainty equivalents and second-best solutions in two organizational structures as a foundation for the following two exercises.	Translation of a real-world problem to an agency theoretical model. Didactic support on a general understanding of the agency models.
2	The results for both structures are compared and depicted graphically.	Decentralization leads to higher expected profit than centralization. RM's risk aversion influences the RM's incentives. However, in centralization, the effect expires on the level of the incentives, whereas in decentralization it translates to all further results.	Highlighting risk aversion as a factor motivating managers to engage more in risk management or provide more incentives for such engagement. Didactic support on analysis and illustration of the analytical results.
3	The results are interpreted in the context of the methodological limitations and the original real-world problem.	The managers' risk aversion and hierarchical placement influence the firm's results in terms of profit and risk. Modeling risk management in the agency theory and the use of the case study method limit the generality of the results.	A case study is more approachable than completely theoretical studies and helps illustrate their results. Recommendation for firms to account for value relevance of managerial risk aversion and organizational design in the context of risk management. Didactic support on discerning the limitations of a methodological approach and critical review of the results.

setting. In this context, the case study emerges as a simpler approach, but without a claim on the generality of the results. The focus of agency theoretical research when risk is concerned lies on monitoring rather than on risk management, thus on the risk of the managerial performance measures rather than on the firm's risk. As the results from risk management models are usually highly complex, the case study presents a possibility to depict them more easily.

Finally, the educational aspects of this case study are important, as it is virtually the first to guide a reader through all steps of the construction, analysis, and interpretation of an agency theoretical model, at least as far as English is concerned. For German-speaking readers, a comprehensive companion piece to this chapter is the article of Dierkes and Ayaz (2006) on performance measurement in the presence of multiple activities.

Conclusion and Recommendations

Agency theory is a popular tool in managerial research. Still, the step-by-step instructions to constructing and solving the models within agency theory are hard to find in economic literature. This case study provides students, prospective researchers, and practitioners with a tool to understand the logic behind agency theory models, their derivation, and interpretation.

As an exemplary problem, the organization and incentivization of risk management is chosen, based on the analytical research of Dierkes and Michaelis (2022). The relevance of risk management for firms is widely accepted and rooted in laws, regulations, and corporate governance. Empirical research has suggested its relevance for a firm's success, but the organizational designs and incentives for RMs have only recently emerged in analytical research.

The case study shows the design of an agency's theoretical representation of a practical problem and guides the reader through its solution. It presents the tools for analysis, in the form of comparative statics and exemplary figures. Moreover, it underlines the necessity of checking for plausibility of the results before analysis and restrictions resulting from such check. Overall, the analysis of risk management in such a framework points toward preferability of decentralization of risk management and against centralization, at least when the firm implements risk management due to reasons other than actual risk aversion. Furthermore, the assumed input parameters characterize not very effort- and risk-averse managers. Even though it could reflect the preference of the employers while recruiting, these are not the characteristics of the population as a whole. Moreover, it is possible that such employees are not present in the pool of available candidates. Finally, risk aversion of an RM is shown as a factor that motivates the RM to engage in risk management, irrespective of the actual incentives for this activity.

The benefits of case study as a method, notwithstanding the limitation of this approach, must be considered. The results are not uniformly applicable

Organization and Incentivization of Risk Management 247

in practice and present only a starting point for further analytical research and discussion about the possible benefits of applying different theoretical solution in practice.

References

Arena, M., Arnaboldi, M., & Azzone, G. (2010). The Organizational Dynamics of Enterprise Risk Management. *Accounting, Organizations and Society*, *35*(7), 659–675. 10.1016/j.aos.2010.07.003

Arrow, K.J. (1963). Uncertainty and the Welfare Economics of Medical Care. *The American Economic Review*, *53*(5), 941–973. https://www.jstor.org/stable/1812044. Accessed 06.03.2023.

Baker, G. (2000). The Use of Performance Measures in Incentive Contracting. *The American Economic Review*, *90*(2), 415–420. 10.1016/j.aos.2010.07.003.10.1257/aer.90.2.415

Baker, G. (2002). Distortion and Risk in Optimal Incentive Contracts. *The Journal of Human Resources*, *37*(4), 728–751. 10.1016/j.aos.2010.07.003.10.2307/3069615

Bromiley, P., McShane, M., Nair, A., & Rustambekov, E. (2015). Enterprise Risk Management: Review, Critique and Research Directions. *Long Range Planning*, *48*(4), 265–276. 10.1016/j.lrp.2014.07.005

Demougin, D., & Jost, P.-J. (2001). Theoretische Grundlagen der Prinzipal-Agenten-Theorie. In P.-J. Jost (Ed.), *Die Prinzipal-Agenten-Theorie in der Betriebswirtschaftslehre* (pp. 45–81). Stuttgart: Schäffer-Poeschel Verlag.

Demski, J.S. (1976). Uncertainty and Evaluation Based on Controllable Performance. *Journal of Accounting Research*, *14*(2), 230–245. 10.2307/2490542

Dierkes, S., & Ayaz, M. (2006). Die Fallstudie aus der Betriebswirtschaftslehre: Performance Measurement bei mehreren Aktivitäten aus agencytheoretischer Sicht. *Das Wirtschaftsstudium*, *35*, 212–215.

Dierkes, S., & Michaelis, M. (2022). Organizational Design of Risk Management. *International Journal of Strategic Management*, *22*(1), 39–65. 10.18374/IJSM-22-1.4

DIN e. V. (Deutsches Institut für Normung e. V.) (2018). *ISO 31000:2018 Risk Management – Guidelines*.

Fraser, J.R.S., & Simkins, B.J. (2016). The Challenges of and Solutions for Implementing Enterprise Risk Management. *Business Horizons*, *59*(6), 689–698. 10.1016/j.bushor.2016.06.007

Gordon, L.A., Loeb, M.P., & Tseng, C.Y. (2009). Enterprise Risk Management and Firm Performance: A Contingency Perspective. *Journal of Accounting and Public Policy*, *28*(4), 301–327. 10.1016/j.jaccpubpol.2009.06.006

Hoyt, R.E., & Liebenberg, A.P. (2011). The Value of Enterprise Risk Management. *Journal of Risk and Insurance*, *78*(4), 795–822. 10.1111/j.1539-6975.2011.01413.x

Jensen, M.C., & Meckling, W.H. (1976). Theory of the Firm: Managerial Behavior, Agency Costs and Ownership Structure. *Journal of Financial Economics*, *3*(4), 305–360. 10.1016/0304-405X(76)90026-X

Jost, P.-J. (2001). Die Prinzipal-Agenten-Theorie im Unternehmenskontext. In P.-J. Jost (Ed.), *Die Prinzipal-Agenten-Theorie in der Betriebswirtschaftslehre* (pp. 11–43). Stuttgart: Schäffer-Poeschel Verlag.

Karanja, E. (2017). Does the Hiring of Chief Risk Officers Align with the COSO/ISO Enterprise Risk Management Frameworks? *International Journal of Accounting & Information Management, 25*(3), 274–295. 10.1108/IJAIM-04-2016-0037

Lambert, R.A. (2001). Contracting Theory and Accounting. *Journal of Accounting and Economics, 32*(1–3), 3–87. 10.1016/S0165-4101(01)00037-4

Lemos, F. (2020). On the Definition of Risk. *Journal of Risk Management in Financial Institutions, 13*(3), 266–278.

Liang, P.J., Rajan, M.V., & Ray, K. (2008). Optimal Firm Size and Monitoring in Organizations. *The Accounting Review, 83*(3), 789–822. 10.2308/accr.2008.83.3.789

Macho-Stadler, I., & Pérez-Castrillo, J.D. (2001). *An Introduction to the Economics of Information: Incentives and Contracts.* New York: Oxford University Press.

Michaelis, M. (2021). Third-Party Monitoring and Risk Management: A Literature Review. *Review of Economics, 72*(3), 229–272. 10.1515/roe-2021-0027

OECD (Organisation for Economic Co-operation and Development). (2014). *Risk Management and Corporate Governance.* Paris: OECD Publishing.

Pagach, D., & Warr, R. (2015). The Effects of Enterprise Risk Management on Firm Performance. In T. Andersen (Ed.), *The Routledge Companion to Strategic Risk Management* (pp. 381–393). London: Routledge.

Prendergast, C. (2002a). Uncertainty and Incentives. *Journal of Labor Economics, 20*(S2), 115–137. 10.1086/338676

Prendergast, C. (2002b). The Tenuous Trade-off between Risk and Incentives. *Journal of Political Economy, 110*(5), 1071–1102. 10.1086/341874

Reavis, M.W. (1969). The Corporate Risk Manager's Contribution to Profit. *The Journal of Risk and Insurance, 36*(4), 473–479. 10.2307/251307

Risk Management in Regulatory Frameworks: Towards a Better Management of Risks. (2012). UNECE (United Nations Economic Commission for Europe). https://digitallibrary.un.org/record/737834. Accessed 06.03.2023.

Sappington, D.E.M. (1991). Incentives in Principal-Agent Relationships. *Journal of Economic Perspective, 5*(2), 45–66. 10.1257/jep.5.2.45

Schäfer, U. (2013). *Performance Measurement in langfristigen Prinzipal-Agenten-Beziehungen: Möglichkeiten und Grenzen einer Analyse auf Grundlage mehrperiodiger LEN-Modelle.* Baden-Baden: Nomos.

Siegel, M. (2018). Building Resilient Organisations: Proactive Risk Management in Organisations and Their Supply Chains. *Journal of Business Continuity & Emergency Planning, 11*(4), 373–384. PMID:30670137

Smithson, C., & Simkins, B.J. (2005). Does Risk Management Add Value? A Survey of the Evidence. *Journal of Applied Corporate Finance, 17*(3), 8–17. 10.1111/j.1745-6622.2005.00042.x

Spremann, K. (1987). Agent and Principal. In G. Bamberg & K. Spremann (Eds.) *Agency Theory, Information, and Incentives* (pp. 3–37). Berlin-Heidelberg: Springer.

Appendix

Comparative statics with regard to r_R

$$\frac{\partial e^c}{\partial r_R} = \frac{\partial a_B^c}{\partial r_R} = 0$$

$$\frac{\partial e^d}{\partial r_R} = \frac{\partial a_B^d}{\partial r_R} = -\frac{0.1 \cdot \sqrt{r_R}}{2 \cdot r_R^2} \cdot \left(\sqrt{\frac{1}{0.1}} - \sqrt{\frac{1}{r_R + 0.1}} \right) \leq 0$$

$$\frac{\partial a_R^c}{\partial r_R} = \frac{\partial a_B^c}{\partial r_R} \cdot \sqrt{\frac{0.1}{r_R}} - \frac{1}{2} \cdot a_B^c \cdot \sqrt{\frac{0.1}{r_R^3}} = -\frac{1}{2} \cdot a_B^c \cdot \sqrt{\frac{0.1}{r_R^3}} \leq 0$$

$$\frac{\partial a_R^d}{\partial r_R} = \underbrace{\frac{\partial a_B^d}{\partial r_R}}_{\leq 0} \cdot \sqrt{\frac{0.1}{r_R + 0.1}} - \frac{1}{2} \cdot a_B^d \cdot \sqrt{\frac{0.1}{(r_R + 0.1)^3}} \leq 0$$

$$\begin{aligned}
\frac{\partial m^c}{\partial r_R} &= 5 \cdot \sqrt{2} \cdot \left(\frac{1}{2 \cdot \sqrt{r_R}} \cdot a_R^c + \sqrt{r_R} \cdot \frac{\partial a_R^c}{\partial r_R} \right) \\
&= 5 \cdot \sqrt{2} \cdot a_B^c \cdot \sqrt{\frac{0.1}{r_R}} \cdot \left(\frac{1}{2 \cdot \sqrt{r_R}} - \frac{1}{2 \cdot \sqrt{r_R}} \right) \\
&= 0
\end{aligned}$$

$$\begin{aligned}
\frac{\partial m^d}{\partial r_R} &= 5 \cdot \sqrt{2} \cdot \left(\frac{1}{2 \cdot \sqrt{r_R}} \cdot a_R^d + \sqrt{r_R} \cdot \frac{\partial a_R^d}{\partial r_R} \right) \\
&= 5 \cdot \sqrt{2} \cdot \left(\frac{1}{2} \cdot \sqrt{r_R} \cdot a_B^d \cdot \underbrace{\left(\frac{1}{r_R} - \frac{1}{r_R + 0.1} \right)}_{>0} + \sqrt{r_R} \cdot \underbrace{\frac{\partial a_B^d}{\partial r_R}}_{>0} \right) \cdot \sqrt{\frac{0.1}{r_R + 0.1}} > 0
\end{aligned}$$

Comparative statics with regard to r_B

$$\frac{\partial e^c}{\partial r_B} = \frac{\partial a_B^c}{\partial r_B} = -\frac{0.1}{\sqrt{r_B}} \leq 0$$

$$\frac{\partial e^d}{\partial r_B} = \frac{\partial a_B^d}{\partial r_B}$$

$$= -\left(\frac{1}{2\cdot\sqrt{0.4+r_B}}\cdot\sqrt{0.1\cdot r_B} + \sqrt{0.4+r_B}\cdot\frac{1}{2\cdot\sqrt{0.1\cdot r_B}}\cdot 0.1\right) + \sqrt{0.1}$$

$$= -\frac{\sqrt{0.1}}{2\cdot\sqrt{r_B}\cdot\sqrt{0.4+r_B}}\cdot\left(\sqrt{r_B}-\sqrt{0.4+r_B}\right)^2 \leq 0$$

$$\frac{\partial a_R^c}{\partial r_B} = \frac{\partial a_B^c}{\partial r_B}\cdot\sqrt{\frac{r_B}{0.4}} + \frac{1}{2}\cdot a_B^c\cdot\sqrt{\frac{1}{0.4\cdot r_B}}$$

$$= -\frac{0.1}{\sqrt{r_B}}\cdot\sqrt{\frac{r_B}{0.4}} + \frac{1}{2}\cdot a_B^c\cdot\sqrt{\frac{1}{0.4\cdot r_B}}$$

$$= \frac{1}{2}\cdot\left(\underbrace{a_B^c\cdot\sqrt{\frac{1}{0.4\cdot r_B}} - \sqrt{0.1}}_{\geq 0}\right)$$

For all r_B that yield positive effort, the incentives of the RM increase in the BUM's risk aversion.

$$\frac{\partial a_R^d}{\partial r_B} = \frac{\partial a_B^d}{\partial r_B}\cdot\sqrt{\frac{r_B}{0.4+r_B}} + \frac{1}{2}\cdot\sqrt{\frac{0.4+r_B}{r_B}}\cdot\frac{(0.4+r_B)-r_B}{(0.4+r_B)^2}\cdot a_B^d$$

$$= \frac{\partial a_B^d}{\partial r_B}\cdot\sqrt{\frac{r_B}{0.4+r_B}} + 0.2\cdot\sqrt{\frac{1}{r_B\cdot(0.4+r_B)^3}}\cdot a_B^d$$

$$= \left(\begin{array}{l}1 + r_B\cdot\sqrt{0.1} - 5\cdot\sqrt{0.1}\cdot\sqrt{r_B}\cdot(0.4+r_B)\cdot\sqrt{0.4+r_B} \\ +2\cdot\sqrt{0.1}\cdot r_B + 5\cdot\sqrt{0.1}\cdot r_B^2\end{array}\right)\cdot\frac{0.4\cdot\sqrt{\frac{r_B}{0.4+r_B}}}{2\cdot r_B\cdot(0.4+r_B)} \geq 0$$

It is positive, as it is a convex function without intercepts, with the term in brackets yielding:

$$(10\cdot\sqrt{0.1} - 0.3)\cdot r_B^2 + (6\cdot\sqrt{0.1} - 0.16)\cdot r_B + 1 \geq 0$$

$$\varDelta = 4.8256 - 41.92\cdot\sqrt{0.1} < 0$$

13 Embracing CSR as an Essential Part of Business

The Case of Viking by Raja Group, Cluj-Napoca

Zenovia-Cristiana Pop

Introduction

The challenge for corporate social responsibility (CSR) theorists and practitioners from various management fields, such as marketing, finance, or human resources, is to identify the current and likely future needs of stakeholders and to assess how effectively existing CSR concepts and definitions meet those needs (Jobber & Ellis-Chadwick, 2019). However, with no consensus in sight, this terminological diversity must be addressed, because it not only hinders academic research but is also too vague for successful implementation in companies. Before Davis (1967) expanded the concept of CSR to encompass institutions and businesses, Frederick (1960) and Walton (1967) stressed the role of "businessmen" who must engage in CSR instead of only focusing on the maximization of company value and the use of resources in the most efficient way, as Friedman underlined in 1970 (Prasad & Holzinger, 2013). Several aspects of CSR were incorporated into the "Pyramid of Corporate Social Responsibility" of Carroll (1991), addressing the company's economic, legal, ethical, and philanthropic obligations at the same time (Baden, 2016).

Increased awareness of a company's positive and negative political and social influence has made regulators and policymakers especially eager to monitor corporate behavior. To promote responsible use of power and curb financial malfeasance, new widespread and radical corporate governance reforms such as the Sarbanes-Oxley Act and recommendations such as Basel II have been adopted (Claydon, 2011). Companies that provide shared services have a significant impact on the CSR agenda.

Viking Part of RAJA Group – Europe's Largest Packaging Distributor

On October 19th, 2021, Office Depot Europe and Viking were acquired by the family-owned RAJA Group headquartered in Roissy near Paris, France. RAJA Group employed 4,500 people and had a turnover of

DOI: 10.4324/9781003376583-16

€1.2 billion in 2021 (RAJA Group Completes Acquisition of Viking, 2021). According to Strong (2018) when Office Depot joined with Viking Office Products in 1998, it made another breakthrough, securing the greatest market share in Europe.

As one of Europe's leading multichannel distributors of business supplies and equipment, RAJA Group has a global reach. With 26 companies in 19 countries, RAJA offers the largest range of packaging in Europe, as well as a complete range of office supplies, furniture, warehouse equipment, janitorial supplies, and retail equipment. It is the quality of its goods, the knowledge underlying its services, as well as the trusting relationships it has with its clients that make RAJA a family-run French company founded in 1954 (History of the Raja Group. Home., n.d.).

Methods

We started our research with a detailed literature review, which revealed that there are significant gaps in the literature concerning CSR activities of shared service centers (SSCs) and how they could be operationalized. In the social sciences, the in-depth case study methodology – although time consuming – fills the gap between quantitative and qualitative approaches, conveying the complexity of the focal case. In regard to validity and reliability, we followed the approach of Yin (2003) who strongly recommends using a theory-driven approach with a deep understanding of the topic of CSR and shared services under discussion, as stipulated by Garavan et al. (2008), and clearly stating the research questions. It is highly important to consider the personal experience of the researchers as well as their understanding and intuition. Sometimes, it is difficult to generalize the results on the basis of an individual case. The second stage was to select Viking by Raja Group (Office Depot Service Center, Cluj-Napoca), as a model of a successful shared-services center with a very clear profile, i.e. a set of specializations. The data were obtained through extensive content analysis (Breijer & Orij, 2022), using the rigorous qualitative analysis software MAXQDA 2022 and the Voyant toolset (Sinclair & Rockwell, 2016). We examine a dataset of media posts extending between June 2009 and February 2021 (Office Depot Viking by Raja Group Blog, n.d.), providing a more detailed understanding of the topic (Tilley & Woodthorpe, 2011), through the themes that emerged. Although the acquired data can be coded into quantitative expressions, it is not subject to statistical principles. Several reports, the company's code of conduct, brochures, websites, and published interviews with employees at various management levels were used to address the following research questions, which discussed the nature, opportunities, and challenges of SSCs while requiring effective methods for driving CSR activities.

Q1 What are the opportunities and challenges for SSCs?

Q2 What CSR practices does SSCs implement to fulfil their social responsibility?

Q3 What measures are taken by SSCs to communicate social responsibility internally (e.g., employee communication) and externally (e.g., reporting)?

During the next few paragraphs, we will examine how Viking by Raja Group in Cluj-Napoca embraced the SSC model in a way that mirrors both cross-functional opportunities and the company's commitment to CSR, providing value beyond cost savings.

Doing Business in Romania: Shared Service Center-People – the Single Most Important Asset

Romania's poor infrastructure has hampered its economic development and prevented companies from delivering original equipment manufacturer (OEM) products from well-known manufacturers, e.g., private-label products from Viking by RAJA Group, to potential customers. It is clear that poor infrastructure delivery does not enable a 24-hour service to be possible. SSCs were established by companies including Genpact or Bosch in the city of Cluj-Napoca due to the presence of several universities with multilingual education and reduced prices in this region, relative to Western Europe (Koval et al., 2016; Petrişor & Cozmiuc, 2016).

Instead of selling office supplies, the Raja Group has entered the labor market, offering attractive job opportunities at competitive wages. New jobs were created, with teams providing support in six languages with the goal of gradually expanding the finance division to a pan-European scale, reducing costs and keeping everything under one roof. An internal network connects all European branches, enabling fast, daily exchanges of sensitive, key data with customers and suppliers (Marston et al., 2011) while maintaining data security protocols to prevent data breaches, build customer relationships, and build trust between customers and suppliers.

All of the SSC's major challenges, which are constantly evolving (Knol et al., 2014; Richter & Brühl, 2017), were successfully met thanks to the steadfast commitment of all parties involved, including the local Cluj-Napoca employees. The degree of specialization simplifies how client requests are handled, thus increasing efficiency and quality. However, this option is always less realistic due to staff turnover. Like many SSCs, Viking by RAJA Group in Cluj-Napoca must find multiple ways of motivating employees. Employee retention risk should become more important to achieve better sustainable results. The costs associated with recruiting and training new employees can be significant, and the impact of losing key team members can be devastating to a company's bottom line. Employees who were hired during the phase of SSC implementation and took part in the transition process elevated the customer service to a level of standardization for which they have sometimes become overqualified.

Viking by RAJA Group (Cluj-Napoca), unlike other local companies, hires young, inexperienced employees and ensures their specialization through expert training and mentoring sessions (Office Depot Viking by Raja Group Blog, n.d.). Special attention is paid to the integration of new employees, particularly in entry-level positions strongly associated with low levels of decision-making that can lead to reduced productivity among employees (Training, 2020). The mentoring program, additionally provides new employees with specific information about a career in shared services, is an empowering experience (Office Depot Viking by Raja Group Blog, n.d.). This keeps them motivated while allowing them to get to know each other and promote teamwork.

The SSCs in Cluj-Napoca crossed new cultural boundaries with its foreign influence and value system concerning leadership styles, motivation approaches, performance appraisal systems, and organizational configurations in the context of the post-communist culture in Central and Eastern Europe. A digital time tracking system was introduced, which allows employees to know exactly how much they've worked also from home, plan their vacations in advance, and enables managers to check the holidays and working hours of their employees in different time zones. Teams are usually composed of a team leader, a process specialist, and a process assistant. The team leader understands the processes, handles all organizational aspects of the team, and is concerned with completing all tasks in a timely manner. Twice a year, employees are evaluated according to MBO (management by objectives). Each objective, quantitative or qualitative, is given a rating from 1 to 5 (1 means the employee needs to improve on the objective, 5 means the employee has done very well). The process specialist is a highly qualified employee. Each process is carried out by the process assistant in accordance with clearly defined rules and regulations. When the process assistant encounters ambiguities or more complex situations, he asks the process specialist, or ultimately the team leader, for help.

As more and more IT companies look for the same kind of worker – someone who is fluent in at least one foreign language and expects to receive a positive wage premium (Hahm & Gazzola, 2022), the demand for bilingual personnel increases, and employers must offer higher wages (Aichhorn & Puck, 2017). English is the first language in the company, followed by Romanian. Whether a company hires internally or elsewhere must be carefully considered. There are some difficulties in sourcing candidates, especially for the German markets, due to other companies looking for similar candidate profiles. However, it must also be emphasized that agreements to refrain from personnel poaching are set up with other companies of a similar nature in the Romanian market. Here, it is agreed among the companies that employees who have already been hired will not be interviewed or hired again by other similar companies (Kovács, 2021). In this way, companies avoid wage inflation in their industry and hinder job-switching in client-supplier relationships. This ensures that the company can continue to work at the same level and not worry about being understaffed.

This is not beneficial for the employee because there is no real competition in the market, and the salaries offered remain constant. This leads to significant financial savings for these companies, which are incredibly beneficial in difficult periods (Ionașcu, 2019). Such agreements are unofficial and there are no actual documents to be signed because everything is agreed in verbal form. However, this is based on rumors, and the existence of such an agreement among companies has not been established beyond doubt.

Via personnel capability development and process standardization, a worldwide competitive edge (Richter, 2021) was established. Nevertheless, employees are looking for career opportunities mainly in the same field; flexibility, workload, and autonomy are the most important criteria, along with fair compensation, that determine retention. Accordingly, we hypothesized that CSR would affect the retention of employees. The key success factor was, once again, the development of a workplace culture in SSC that gives its employees access to training, support, safe working conditions (Office Depot Viking by Raja Group Blog, n.d.), and a work-life balance that enables a healthy lifestyle.

Shared Service Centers' Need to Maintain a Strong CSR Portfolio

In a few months in May 2009, after the opening of the Cluj-Napoca office, thanks to the support of the management and with the help of ten enthusiastic employees, the Office Depot Charity Board, as a partner of United Way Romania (And then there was the Charity Board … ., 2009) was created. The CSR communication for stakeholders is web-based, as in most post-communist countries (Tetrevova et al., 2019), and can favorably influence employees and investors' impressions of the company. Commitment to personal growth and development improved during the two most important fundraising events: the Office Depot (SSC) Cluj-Napoca Charity Month in June 2009, which raised 18,000 euros for social causes; and the Shoe Box of Joy campaign in December 2009, in which a total of 320 Christmas presents were wrapped or decorated. Employees have had the opportunity to participate in fundraising activities and develop a sense of ownership and pride that leads to greater loyalty and commitment (Office Depot Viking by Raja Group, n.d.).

They were given the chance to take part in a variety of activities, including cooking, playing sports, and singing, through engagement in fun campaigns like "Great Tastes of Office Depot-Just Cook It!", "Charity Football Cup", followed by the Tennis Charity Cup in 2011, and "Charity Karaoke Party". Making different homemade foods for co-workers in exchange for donations is one inspiring employer branding, and a simple concept. Employees' identification with the SSC positively impacts on their supportive intentions (Office Depot Viking by Raja Group, n.d.).

The Office Depot Charity Board was thrilled to mark the end of the first successful year and kickstart the second year of their charity partnership with United Way with the award for "Most Creative Campaign" in Romania. Noteworthy is, "shot" by a professional, an art event, where employees attended professional photo sessions and bought their photos for a forthcoming exhibition.

Thanks to a donation of 11,000 euros from Charity for Children, the Office Depot Service Center has been able to ensure that children attending the "Every Child" and "Dumbrava" community centers in Cluj-Napoca receive a hot meal every day. Another project was to raise funds for Asociația Magic by organizing a Viking book fair, where employees sold books they owned. The SSC helped hospitals alleviate the material crisis during the COVID-19 pandemic as well as the Ukrainian refugee crisis. They also sought to enhance the well-being of the elderly in rural Romania by giving gifts and showering them with affection ("Viking – Office Depot Service Center", n.d., "Crisis in Ukraine: Solidarity Actions in Romania – Fondation RAJA-Danièle Marcovici", 2022).

In terms of equality and diversity, the SSC in Cluj-Napoca can be proud of being a non-discriminatory, family-friendly, and supportive employer that promotes equal opportunities and disability-friendly policies. As part of the Foundation's 10th anniversary celebrations, the Fondation RAJA Women's Awards were launched in 2013 and renewed in 2014, 2016 (special edition), and in 2018, to promote the foundation's actions with all its partners and to reward associations for their efforts and results. It is a reflection of the commitment they have to the well-being and continual improvement of their society (Fondation RAJA Women's Awards | Fondation RAJA-Danièle Marcovici, n.d.). The company has adopted innovative approaches that have lower environmental impact. To keep up with trends, RAJA Group developed responsible purchasing approach and eco-friendly products (RAJA and the environment | Eco-friendly packaging | Environmental, n.d.).

Compliance is taken very seriously. ISO 45001, widely accepted among stakeholders, has changed the face of international workplace safety, with health and safety hazards organized and documented (RAJA Group CSR Report, 2022). Modern slavery as is a growing social problem in developing countries, which can be addressed by implementing compliance training programs and raising awareness about human trafficking (RAJA Group CSR Report, 2022). Employees and interested parties are urged to use a confidential hotline that is independently administered to report any concerns regarding potential violations of the compliance rules and programs.

The long-term success of SSCs is supported by effective communication (Richter & Brühl, 2017). Our exploratory study suggests that the need for socially responsible corporate communications has increased significantly in recent decades, as have stakeholder expectations. CSR Report (2022) that the company acts as socially responsible as possible and, at the same time, fosters good customer and supplier relations. The analysis of all published non-English interviews with employees at different management levels, sharing their experiences within SSCs (Cluj-Napoca), extending between June 2009 and February 2021 (Office Depot Viking by Raja Group Blog, n.d.), emphasized the relevance of the team either in their own development as individuals or in achieving the company's goals. Therefore, we can conclude that the cornerstone for all of company's business decisions and behaviors – i.e., the code of conduct, which outlines the company's key principles of integrity, accountability, innovation, teamwork, and respect has been internalized. In other words, the value of teamwork is particularly well communicated to all employees and across all company departments.

It is suggested by the employees at different management levels that many CSR activities help foster an "us" mentality, allowing collaborative work tasks to become the main focus of the group and be performed more efficiently. Because each individual feels accepted and focuses on the task of the group, they are more truthful, helpful, and content. No member of the team is less or more important than another. So, a common shared understanding, where teams are constantly and quickly forming and changing, is essential.

People, sustainability, and climate are the three main pillars of the company's CSR Policy, which encapsulates its CSR attitude (Vision and Values, 2012; RAJA Group CSR Report 2022). According to the results of content analysis, people is the second theme. Perhaps even more important is the ability to get the right people in the right job and at the right time together and work.

The SSC from Cluj-Napoca strives to create an ethical work environment: "things are done by the book", with employees sharing "same values" with talented and motivated employees, supporting and encouraging an environment fostering "the connection with people coming from different countries

258   *Zenovia-Cristiana Pop*

and cultures"; continuous development through learning, embodied in "keep going, keep learning, keep trying" (Office Depot Viking by Raja Group Blog, n.d.). Every employee shares responsibility for creating a productive work environment characterized by motivation, trust, and respect.

To retain employees, the SSC must adopt procedures that follow those of the rest of the industry. The employees referred to the workplace "home", implying they are excited by what they are doing and the environment they are working in – "home" refers to a place you love or where your loved ones are, describing organizational identification and organizational pride (John et al., 2017) and a sense of belonging and a greater purpose they feel they are working toward. CSR activities are identified as beneficial for the employees, mentioning the fact that they gained trust in themselves and realized that they could do something different from their role, explicitly mentioning CSR activities such as gathering "funds for charity organizations" or taking part "in charity events" (Office Depot Viking by Raja Group Blog, n.d.). Therefore, while the findings suggest that CSR events are fun learning experiences, we believe that the company should be able to create CSR programs that are tailored to each employee's skillset and interests as a way to also boost morale and build a stronger sense of community. Favorable group dynamics is helpful for this endeavor.

From the responses of employees working in this SSC, four concepts emerged through the thematic analysis: tolerance, personal development, workplace, and career. Expressions such as "move away from stereotypes" or do not "put people in categories" suggested tolerance. They are aware of their own biases and preconceived notions and actively work to overcome them. Future success will depend heavily on tolerance in particular because it fosters teamwork and is essential to successful collaboration and product development (Office Depot Viking by Raja Group Blog, n.d.).

In regard to their personal development, interviewees made the following observations: they became "more mature", "independent", more attentive to details, more flexible, and patient, more kind to people but with a "cool head", "focused and engaged with the company", pushing personal limits. The company uncovered important life skill gaps in their personal development, and employees have begun to gradually close those gaps while being clearly encouraged to overcome obstacles (Office Depot Viking by Raja Group Blog, n.d.).

However, the interviewees also described their workplace as "home", "my home away from home", or "my second school", "my place for growth". The verbal descriptors of career seen as a road or a journey are "not short or easy", "nice and fruitful", "challenging and rewarding", suggesting the simultaneous existence of two opposed and conflicting attitudes and emotions (Office Depot Viking by Raja Group Blog, n.d.).

Embracing CSR as an Essential Part of Business 259

To improve and to proactively coordinate its portfolio of CSR activities, the main barrier SSCs faces is the insufficient knowledge about the concept of CSR at the societal level of Romania. Whether these gaps are a result of the lack of comprehensive studies or of insufficient development of a corporate culture based on moral values or the lack of public support and involvement in the promotion and application of CSR, remains to be seen.

Conclusion

Our findings suggest that a robust growth of the shared services and outsourcing industry mainly in Central and Eastern Europe, with Poland in the leading role (The Shared Services & Outsourcing Network, 2016) and the global COVID-19 pandemic has put pressure on companies to find new solutions to increase transparency in workflows and to improve process quality and efficiency at reduced costs (Richter & Brühl, 2020). In addition, companies have taken several steps to prevent and address unethical conduct and become more purpose-driven in a market that is sometimes challenged by low prices.

With many of these SSCs operating internationally in various time zones, the demand for multilingualism is very high. SSCs must present themselves in an attractive way, offering special incentives (bonuses in the form of lump sums) or extra services to attract new employees. As a result, branding must be visible locally.

Although the pandemic has increased employee loyalty, the number of company leavers is a major drawback in terms of opportunities for SSCs, who must rely on high employee productivity. Particularly when faced with continuous cost pressures, only administrative e-linking will enable SSCs to focus on operational activities, motivating employees and assuring them that they make a difference and can add value to the SSCs projects while being on the payroll. Graduates joining a company early in their career can lead to a personnel deficit and work excess, requiring SSCs to constantly hire and train new employees, increasing expenses and time consumption.

Looking at other sources of career paths (Rothwell et al., 2011) within SSCs' leading-edge talent management practices (Koval et al., 2016; Zainee & Puteh, 2020) can help achieve desired organizational transformation. Seeking and keeping an eye on high-performing employees who are primarily in charge of creating and retaining knowledge should be one of HR's top priorities. Therefore, more creative training and seminars on automation solutions for different processes to improve the knowledge and skills of employees are the preferred approach (Meinel et al., 2019) for ongoing work on an application. Tackling labor quality besides looking into tailoring services or customizing is also vital. We suggest focusing on cross-department work-shadowing, so that each team member understands the tasks that the other team members are performing. As noted by Farndale et al. (2009), work rotation can also be used by employees to pick up new skills and develop a greater interest in their jobs something that is extremely important. Similarly, it would be interesting to provide greater freedom to employees in SSCs to choose their benefits.

Employees that perform the same tasks on a daily basis feel demotivated. Time-intensive, repetitive, and previously manually performed tasks ought to be automated (Howcroft & Richardson, 2012). Thanks to further process optimization through high level of automation and the accelerated use of new technologies, synergistic effects can be realized. Furthermore, as underlined by Figueiredo and Pinto (2020), compliance regulations are easily met, and scalable processes suitable for the use of intelligent ERP systems and Robotic Process Automation (RPA) can also be developed. It will still take several years before the full potential through automation becomes visible as high investments in technologies and experts are required.

After taking into consideration the security and stability of the institutional, legal, and political environment, SSCs are on their right track to evolving into so-called digital expert service centers, ensuring the right mix of both technical and recently digital capabilities and very diverse language skills, at still relatively low labor costs.

The ability to use data to articulate more than one position on a topic has been quite an achievement as an aid to overcome the impact of the pandemic and the financial crisis. There are numerous challenges associated with data entry. Therefore, although you can have the right approach, if the information used is incorrect, then you cannot analyze the data later. Accordingly, major multinational players use data that can either empower or manipulate regularly, to handle customer support, finance, and HR and recruitment operations. Due to the lack of available and/or reliable data from the government and private institutions in many Central and European countries for shared service industries, finding a pattern and a meaningful connection might be quite difficult.

Although the SSC is a concept that has been evolving for a couple of years now, people should not be taken out of the equation because the future is still all about people, as in the above presented success story. Fulfilling the need for employees' autonomy, the need for competence, and the need for relatedness within the workplace leads to higher employee satisfaction, engagement, and performance, and in turn reduces the risk of employee fluctuation and burnout. The HR department must look into CSR activities in a more holistic way because people are the value added in creating a required customer experience and, as our findings reveal, the SSC is regarded by employees as part of their extended selves, generating positive effects on their satisfaction and retention intention. The motivations that lead people to become involved in CSR activities are complex and usually result from a mixture of altruistic and self-centered motives.

Some employees stated that the CSR practices are integrated into the SSC and ultimately linked to their well-being as it contributes to their agility in shared procedures and provides support in maintaining the capacity of attendance of the different stakeholders. The company goes beyond talking about certain social issues and becomes part of a solution.

There is room for improvement in learning how to promote and inform both internal and external stakeholders. Promoting its CSR practices via its website and blog and other social media channels is an effective way to let the public know for what the company stands for. Still, these are company-controlled sources of CSR information dissemination to stakeholders, and our findings show moderate levels of CSR commitment by employees. Therefore, those responsible for creating and managing digital CSR communication strategies should not rely on the use of only these channels for encouraging engagement in new CSR activities that would have a positive impact on the motivation of their employees and the SSC's reputation by addressing issues within their communities – CSR must become a multi-stakeholder effort.

References

Aichhorn, N., & Puck, J. (2017). Bridging the language gap in multinational companies: Language strategies and the notion of company-speak. *Journal of World Business, 52*(3), 386–403.

And then there was the charity board … Office Depot Viking by Raja Group. (2009, June 1). Retrieved September 25, 2022, from https://officedepot-career.ro/and-then-there-was-the-charity-board/

Baden, D. (2016). A reconstruction of Carroll's pyramid of corporate social responsibility for the 21st century. *International Journal of Corporate Social Responsibility, 1*(1), 1–15.

Breijer, R., & Orij, R.P. (2022). The comparability of non-financial information: An exploration of the impact of the Non-Financial Reporting Directive (NFRD, 2014/95/EU). *Accounting in Europe, 19*(2), 332–361.

Carroll, A.B. (1991). The pyramid of corporate social responsibility: Toward the moral management of organizational stakeholders. *Business Horizons, 34*(4), 39–48.

Claydon, J. (2011). A new direction for CSR: The shortcomings of previous CSR models and the rationale for a new model. *Social Responsibility Journal, 7*(3), 405–420.

Crisis in Ukraine: Solidarity Actions in Romania – Fondation RAJA-Danièle Marcovici. (2022, October 22). Retrieved from https://www.fondation-raja-marcovici.com/en/uncategorized/crisis-in-ukraine-solidarity-actions-in-romania.html

Davis, K. (1967). Understanding the social responsibility puzzle: What does the businessman owe to society? *Business Horizons, 10*, 45–50.

Farndale, E., Paauwe, J., & Hoeksema, L. (2009). In-sourcing HR: Shared service centres in the Netherlands. *International Journal of Human Resource Management, 20*(3), 544–561.

Figueiredo, A.S., & Pinto, L.H. (2020). Robotizing shared service centres: Key challenges and outcomes. *Journal of Service Theory and Practice, 31*(1), 157–178.

Fondation RAJA Women's Awards | Fondation RAJA-Danièle Marcovici. (n.d.). Retrieved September 18, from Fondation RAJA-Danièle Marcovici. https://www.fondation-raja-marcovici.com/en/the-foundation/fondation-raja-womens-awards.html

Frederick, W.C. (1960). The growing concern over business responsibility. *California Management Review, 2*(4), 54–61.

Garavan, T.N., Wilson, J.P., Cross, C., Carbery, R., Sieben, I., de Grip, A., & Heaton, N. (2008). Mapping the context and practice of training, development and HRD in European call centres. *Journal of European Industrial Training, 32*(8/9), 612–728.

Hahm, S., & Gazzola, M. (2022). The value of foreign language skills in the German labor market. *Labour Economics, 76*, 102150.

History of the Raja Group. Home. (n.d.). Retrieved October 13, 2022, from https://www.raja-group.com/en/our-group/history-raja-group

Howcroft, D., & Richardson, H. (2012). The back office goes global: Exploring connections and contradictions in shared service centres. *Work, Employment and Society, 26*(1), 111–127.

Ionașcu, D. (2019, October 8). E-mailul care dovedește că Renault s-a înțeles cu subcontractorii săi să nu-și ia angajații reciproc. Libertatea. Retrieved November 25, 2022, from https://www.libertatea.ro/stiri/dovada-cartelului-salariilor-mici-email-ul-care-tradeaza-intelegerea-dintre-renault-si-subcontractorii-sai-2760972

Jobber, D., & Ellis-Chadwick, F. (2019). *Principles and practice of marketing.* McGraw Hill.

John, A., Qadeer, F., Shahzadi, G., & Jia, F. (2017). Corporate social responsibility and employee's desire: A social influence perspective. *The Service Industries Journal, 37*(13-14), 819–832.

Knol, A., Janssen, M., & Sol, H. (2014). A taxonomy of management challenges for developing shared services arrangements. *European Management Journal, 32*(1), 91–103.

Kovács, I. (2021, February 24). Moving between employers who don't recruit from each other? [web log]. Retrieved September 18, 2022, from https://workplace.stackexchange.com/questions/169856/moving-between-employers-who-dont-recruit-from-each-other

Koval, O., Nabareseh, S., Klimek, P., & Chromjaková, F. (2016). Demographic preferences towards careers in shared service centers: A factor analysis. *Journal of Business Research, 69*(11), 4798–4803.

Marston, S., Li, Z., Bandyopadhyay, S., Zhang, J., & Ghalsasi, A. (2011). Cloud computing – the business perspective. *Decision Support Systems, 51*(1), 176–189.

Meinel, M., Wagner, T.F., Baccarella, C.V., & Voigt, K.I. (2019). Exploring the effects of creativity training on creative performance and creative self-efficacy: Evidence from a longitudinal study. *The Journal of Creative Behavior, 53*(4), 546–558.

Office Depot Viking by Raja Group. (n.d.). Office Depot Viking by Raja Group. Retrieved September 13, 2022, from https://officedepot-career.ro/ro/

Office Depot Viking by Raja Group Blog. (n.d.). Retrieved September 13, 2022, from https://officedepot-career.ro/category/blog-ro/

Petrişor, I., & Cozmiuc, D. (2016). Specific models for Romanian companies – finance shared services. *Procedia-Social and Behavioral Sciences, 221*, 159–165.

Prasad, A., & Holzinger, I. (2013). Seeing through smoke and mirrors: A critical analysis of marketing CSR. *Journal of Business Research, 66*(10), 1915–1921.

RAJA and the environment | Eco-friendly packaging | Environmental. (n.d.). Retrieved September 18, 2022, from https://www.rajapack.co.uk/environment/ecological-commitment

RAJA Group Completes Acquisition of Viking. (2021). Retrieved June 16, 2023, from https://www.raja-group.com/en/our-news/raja-group-completes-acquisition-viking

RAJA Group CSR Report 2022. (2022) Retrieved September 18, 2022, from https://raja.scene7.com/is/content/Raja/PDF/ENG_RAJAGroup_CSR_Report_2022.pdf

Reinhold, R. (2021, August 16). RAJA Group completes acquisition of Viking. Raja. Retrieved August 22, 2022, from https://www.raja-group.com/en/our-news/raja-group-completes-acquisition-viking

Richter, P. (2021). Shared services: Configurations, dynamics and performance. *Baltic Journal of Management, 16*(4), 501–518.

Richter, P.C., & Brühl, R. (2017). Shared service center research: A review of the past, present, and future. *European Management Journal, 35*(1), 26–38.

Richter, P.C., & Brühl, R. (2020). Ahead of the game: Antecedents for the success of shared service centers. *European Management Journal, 38*(3), 477–488.

Rothwell, A.T., Herbert, I.P., & Seal, W. (2011). Shared service centers and professional employability. *Journal of Vocational Behavior, 79*(1), 241–252.

Sinclair, S., & Rockwell, G. (2016). Voyant tools. Retrieved September 25, 2022, from http://voyant-tools.org/

Strong, J.S. (2018). Staples: Strategic evolution and decline in retailing. *Journal of Business Strategy, 39*(3), 9–16.

Tetrevova, L., Patak, M., & Kyrylenko, I. (2019). Web-based CSR communication in post-communist countries. *Applied Economics Letters, 26*(10), 866–871.

The Shared Services & Outsourcing Network. (2016, May 31). Poland still leads CEE shared services (but for how long?). *The Shared Services & Outsourcing Network.* Retrieved September 25, 2022, from http://www.ssonetwork.com/sourcing-modelsstrategy/columns/poland-still-leads-cee-shared-services-although-ro

Tilley, L., & Woodthorpe, K. (2011). Is it the end for anonymity as we know it? A critical examination of the ethical principle of anonymity in the context of 21st century demands on the qualitative researcher. *Qualitative Research, 11*(2), 197–212.

Training. Office Depot Viking by Raja Group. (2020, October 14). Retrieved September 18, 2022, from https://officedepot-career.ro/training/

Viking – Office Depot Service Center. (n.d.). Retrieved September 15, 2022, from https://www.facebook.com/VikingOfficeDepotRomania/

Vision and values. (2012, September 26). Office Depot Viking by Raja Group. Retrieved September 15, 2022, from https://officedepot-career.ro/values/

Walton, C. (1967). *Corporate social responsibilities*. Wadsworth.

Yin, R.K. (2003). *Case study research: Design and methods* (3rd ed.). SAGE Publications.

Zainee, I.A., & Puteh, F. (2020). Corporate social responsibility impact on talent retention among Generation Y. *Revista de Gestão, 27*(4), 369–392.

Index

Note: *Italicized* and **bold** page numbers refer to figures and tables.

ABC Chemists Union 187
ABC Industry Forum 187
ABC Metalworkers' Union 186, 187
ABIHPEC (Associação Brasileira da Indústria de Higiene Pessoal, Perfumaria e Cosméticos) 188
Abriko, A. 182, 184
Abugabah, A. 106, 107
Acar, O.A. 65
AC Milan Football (Soccer) Team: blockchain technology, use of 159–170; brief history of 164–165
adaptive project framework (APF) 108
ADEGABC *see* Around the Greater ABC Economic Development Agency (ADEGABC)
Adenuga, K.I. 145
Agbo, C.C. 162
Agencia de Desenvolvimento do Grande ABC 187
Agenzia Sviluppo Nord Milano (ASNM) 186
Aggelidis, V.P. 144
agile project management (APM) 108
Agur, C. 163
Ahumada, L. 27
Aichhorn, N. 254
Aidar, G. 188
Ajzen, I. 144
Alawadhi, M. 145
Albania 4
Albrecht, S. 29–30
Albrecht, U.V. 142
Alegre, H. 118

Algozzine, B. 69
Alon, I. 159
Alpar, A. 107
Amadu, L. 145, 146, **148**
ambient and guerilla marketing communication 66–67
"Ambient Marketing Creative Skills Development" Course 70–71
Anagnostopoulos, C. 161
Anand, R. 198
Anau, R.V. 186
Ang, S.H. 64
Ante, L. 163
APF *see* adaptive project framework (APF)
APL (Local Productive Arrangement) Project 186
APM *see* agile project management (APM)
Arbuckle, J. 32
Arena, M. 225, 226, 244
Armstrong, K. 89, 99
Armstrong, M. 195
Arnott, D. 122
Around the Greater ABC Economic Development Agency (ADEGABC) 178
Arrow, K.J. 219, 221
Arslan, Z. 49
Ashby, W. 107
ASNM *see Agenzia Sviluppo Nord Milano* (ASNM)
Association for the Development of Tolima 24
auditing human resource management

266   *Index*

practices 193–215; complications in 199–200; contemporary perception 195; employee relations 210–211; employee retention 209; employee reward management 211; employee training 207–209; evolution of 195–199, *197*; gap in literature 200; HR audit 203; HR budgeting 212; HRM department *see* HRM department; methodology 200–203; off-boarding 207; on-boarding 207; organizational development 212; owner management relationships 215; performance monitoring 209–210; personnel management 207; recruitment 204–205; selection 205–207; succession planning 209; theory of the firm 200; workforce planning 203–204

augmented reality, in medical training of patient referrals 137–154; applications 141–143; calibration results 150–151, **151**, *152*; case study 147, 149–150, *149*; children 139–141, *140*, *141*; launching 140–141; matching patients to appropriate hospital 139; recommendations 154; research framework and hypotheses 145–147, *147*, **148–149**; scheduling 139–140; technological background 138–145; technology acceptance model 143–145, *144*

Australia: in-service teacher training 47
Austria 4
AXELOS Ltd. 108
Ayaz, M. 219, 246
Azhari, A.G. 66

Baack, D.W.
Babiloni, F. 3
Bacon, T. 28
Baden, D. 251
Baker, G. 220
Bakker, A. 29, **31**
Balyer, A. 46

Barry, J.A. 120
Bartlett, M.S. 150
Bashar, M.A. 138
Basoglu, N.A. 145, 146, **148**, **149**, 153
Basupi, I. 120
Baumgartner, H. 145, **148**
Belschak, F. 29
Bernabéu Brotóns, E. 65
Bessant, J. 85
BG-1103 4–10; innovations in effectiveness and research achievements, impact of 16–19, *17*, **19**
Bhatnagar, J. 195
Bio-psycho-social approach 66
Black, J.S. 205, 206
blockchain technology in sports sector, use of 159–170; case study 164–168; methods 164
Bogucki, J. 89
Bohanec, M. 119, 121, 122, 124, 125, 127
Borštnar, M. 43
Bosnia and Herzegovina 4
Boumans, N. 29
Bourgault M. 85
Bradley, P. 141
Brandão, K. 188
Bratton, J.G. 29, 195
Brazilian Chemical Industry Association (Abiquim) 187
Breijer, R. 252
Bresciani, L.P. 184–186
Briz-Ponce, L. 144
Bromiley, P. 219, 226, 244
Brown, M. 27, **31**
Brühl, R. 253, 257, 259
Bruno, R.R. 141
Bui, D.T. 142
Bulgaria 4
Bulut, D. 69
Burland, J.P. 160
Burneske, G.W. 88, 89
Burns, J. 27
Busrai, A. 198

CAD *see* Computer Aided Design (CAD)
Canning, A. 199
Capuava Refinery (Recap) 187
Carenzo, L. 142

Carlos, L.P. 161
Carroll, A.B. 251
Castillo, M.S. 198
CEEPUS *see* Central European Exchange Program for University Studies (CEEPUS)
Center of Industries of the State of São Paulo (Ciesp) 187
Centers, D.P. 161
Central Europe 3
Central European Exchange Program for University Studies (CEEPUS) 3–4; BG-1103 4–10, 16–19, *17*, **19**; CEEPUS IV incubator 4; cooperation with business partners 15–16; coordinator's tour 10–11; development, limitations of 19–20; event-based approach 5–10; innovative flexible course, implementation of 5–10; involvement in International Weeks 6–8; joint doctoral program with innovative network-wide joint co-tutorship and co-supervision 11–13; Summer/Winter/Doctoral schools or academia 6; Workshops or Special sessions at International Conferences 8–10, **9**
Cervone, R. 188
Ceylan, V.K. 49
Chalutz Ben-Gal, H. 195
Chametzky, B. 110
Chankong, V. 119
Chatzipanagiotou, P. 60
Chatzoglou, P.D. 144
Chatzoudes, D. 30
Chen, J. 162
Chen, R. 161
Chen, Y.W. 138, 139
Cherchi, C. 118, 120
Chesbrough, H. 112
Cheung, C.K. 65
Cho, H. **148**
Choudhari, S. 204
Choudhary, H. 64
Ciaian, P. 161
Ciampa, K. 58, 59
Ciulla, J. 28

Claydon, J. 251
Cohen, J. 118
Cole, T.R. 65
Combs, W.L. 195
committed employee 29–30
Committee of Sponsoring Organizations of the Treadway Commission (COSO) 219
Computer Aided Design (CAD) 89
Conceição, J.J. da
Constructive Technology Assessment 105
Contreras, F. 27
Cooper, R.G. 86
Cordella, A. 106
corporate social responsibility (CSR) 251–261; methods 252–253
Corporation for Human Development of Ibagué 24
COSO *see* Committee of Sponsoring Organizations of the Treadway Commission (COSO)
COST 3, 18
Cova, B. 68
Cova, V. 68
COVID-19 159, 162, 187, 194
Cox, A. 162
Cozzens, S. 105
crativity: research sample 70
Creaco, E. 118
creativity 64–77; analysis and results interpretation 71–74, *72*, **73**; development of 65–66; limits of 74–76; methodological framework and methods 69–70; research problem and hypotheses 68–69
Creswell, J.D. 69
Creswell, J.W. 69
Critical Theory of Technology 105
Croatia 4
cryptocurrencies 161–163
Csikszentmihalyi, M. 145
CSR *see* corporate social responsibility (CSR)
Curran, V.R. 137
Czech Republic 3, 4

Dacey, J.S. 66, 71
Damşa, C. 59
Daniel, C. 186

268   Index

Datta, A. 162
Datta, R. 143
Davidson, N.P. 161
Davis, F.D. 143, 145, 146, **148**, **149**
Davis, K. 251
Daymon, Ch. 75
decision support systems (DSS) 122
De Feo, G. 121
De Franco, F. 32
De Gisi, S. 121
De la Peña, C. 65
Delery, J. E. 195, 196
DeLone & McLean (D&M) model 107
Demir, E. 164
Demircioðlu Diren, D. 46
Demougin, D. 223
Demski, J.S. 220
Den Hartog, D. 29
Denmark: in-service teacher training 47
design science research 122–123
DeSouza Fleith, D. 75
DEX methodology 122, 124
Dhanvanth, S. 160
Díaz, C. 30
DiClaudio, M. 195
Dierkes, S. 219, 220, 244, 246
digital transformation: definition of 43;
   in education *see* digital
   transformation, in education;
   inevitability 44; irreversibility
   43; main elements of 43–45, *44*,
   45; systematic approach to 44;
   uncertainty 44
digital transformation, in education
   43–60; components of 46–47;
   data collection and analysis
   49–50; motivation 56–58, **57**;
   participants 50, **50**; scope and
   content 50–53, **51**; teachers'
   competencies 55–56, **55**;
   technical and design features
   53–55
D&M *see* DeLone & McLean (D&M)
   model
Doty, D. H. 195, 196
Doyle, J.P. 161
DSS *see* decision support systems (DSS)
Du, C. 88, 98
Duarte, M.L. 142
Dvir, D. 92
Dyer, J.S. 121

Edwards, R. 110
Edwards, W. 121
effective leadership 23, 26, 28, 29, 31,
   34, 38; *see also* leadership
   effectiveness
Egypt: Central Agency for Public
   Mobilization and Statistics
   193–194; hospitality and tourism
   industry 193–215
Eisenbeiss, S. 28
Ekvall, G. 71
electromagnetic compatibility (EMC)
   88–99
Ellis-Chadwick, F. 251
EMC *see* electromagnetic
   compatibility (EMC)
employee: relations 210–211; retention
   209; reward management 211;
   training 207–209; well-being 29
ERASMUS + 3, 20
Erdem, H.H. 46
Ernest, P. 60
Eroglu, K. 88, 99
ethical leadership: contributions 39; data
   collection 32; data triangulation
   32, 34–35; demographic aspects
   35; hypotheses testing 36–37, **36**,
   37; limitations of 39–40;
   literature review 26–30; mean
   scores 35–36; measures in factor
   analysis 31–32, **31**; practical
   implications 38; qualitative
   research measurement tool 34;
   reliability 32, **33**; researching
   technique 34; research
   methodology 30–35; research
   model *30*; samples 34; secondary
   data collection 34–35; validity
   32, **33**
EU Directive EMC 2014/30/EU 88
Europe 3
European Commission 110
event-based approach 5–10
event marketing and marketing
   communication 67–68
extended reality (XR) 137
extreme project management model
   (xPM/MPx) 108

Fabrigar, L. 32
Falletta, S.V. 195

Fan, L. 120
Fanning, K. 161
Fan Tokens 159, 162–164, 170
Farndale, E. 260
Fergusson, C. 160
Ferreira, J.J. 159
Ferreira, P. 188
Ferrer, J. 28
Fertak, B. 66
Fichnová, K. 65, 66
Figueiredo, A.S. 260
Fiorito, S.S. **148**
Fischbein, E. 110
Fishbein, M. 144
Fishburn, P. 119
Flyvbjerge, B. 67, 69
Fortunato, J. 162
France: in-service training seminars 47
Francis, D. 85
Fraser, J.R.S. 224
Frederick, W.C. 251
French, S. 121
Fülöp, J. 119

Gajjar, H. 204
Gallagher, T.L. 58, 59
Gao, X.-R. 65
Garavan, T.N. 252
Garcia-Garcia, B. 159
García-Peñalvo, F.J. 144
Garrett, J.J. 64
Gary, T. 69
Gazzola, M. 254
Gefen, D. **148**
Gehlbach, R.D. 71
Geladeira, Claudinho da 188
Germany: in-service training
    seminars 47
Gerup, J. 142
Girginov, V. 160
Glaser, B. 111
global value chains (GVCs) 177
Glover, J.G. 65
GLT see Goal-Line Technology (GLT)
    system
Goal-Line Technology (GLT)
    system 160
Goebert, C. 160
Gökalp, E. 43
Gollan, P.J. 198
good leadership 28

Goodrich, D. 88, 99
Gordon, L.A. 226, 244
Gorman, C. 145
GOTCHA program 66, 68, 70,
    72–74, 76
Great ABC Region, Brazil: "Pacto pela
    Industria" 177–191; Regional
    Pact 188–190; socioeconomic
    indicators 178–184, **179**,
    180–181, **183**
Greater ABC Economic Development
    Agency 184–187, 190, 191
grounded theory 111
Grundei, J. 198
Gu, X. 65
Guaiquirima, C. 28
Guest, D.E. 195
Gündoğdu, K. 49
Gündüz, Y. 47
Gündüzalp, S. 47
Gunnarsdottir, M.J. 118
GVCs see global value chains (GVCs)
Gyensare, M. 29

Hahm, S. 254
Haimes, Y. 119
Hammerschmidt, J. 159
Hancock, D.R. 69
Hansen, S. 29
Harter, J. 195
Harvard Kennedy School 105
Haselhuhn, M.P. 65
Heffernan, T. 3
Heilmann, P. 194
Heinrichs, W.L. 142
Hendl, J. 75
Hester, P.T. 121, 123
Hevner, A.R. 122–124, 128
Hills, T. 199
HMCDM see hybrid MCDM
    (HMCDM)
Hofmeister, C. 58
Hoghughi, M. 139
Holden, R.J. 143
Holicza, P. 3
Holistic-Oriented Approach to
    Stimulating Creative
    Competences 66, *67*, 70–71
Holland, J. 110
Holloway, I. 75
Holzinger, I. 251

270 *Index*

Hooi, L.W. 1095
Hoque, S.F. 120
Horizon 2020 3
Horta, E. 23, 28
Horzum, M.B. 46
Hou, H.T. 60
Howcroft, D. 260
Hoyt, R.E. 219, 226, 244
HR audit 203
HR budgeting 212
HRM department: compliance role of 212–213; role of 203; service role of 213–214; strategic role of 214–215
Hu, W. 195
Huang, H.M. 153
Huang, L.S. 198
Huang, T.K. 143
Huang, Y.C. 145, **148**
Hungary 3–5
Hurajová, A. 75
Huselid, M.A. 195
hybrid MCDM (HMCDM) 119, 120, 123, 127, 128, 131
hybrid project management model 108

Iannacci, F. 106
Ibagué University: background of 23–26; ethical leadership 23–40; High Quality Accreditation 24; Institutional Development Project 25; leadership effectiveness 23–40; "Necessary University, The" 25; organizational structure 24–26, 25
ICT see Information and Communication Technology (ICT)
IMA-NET 6, 10, 12, 20; e-management, innovative platform for 13–15, 13
Information and Communication Technology (ICT) 87, 104, 108
information system (IS) 103–116, 122; definition of 106; in project management 103–116; quality of 106–107; research 106; theoretical background 104–108
"Informe de Autoevaluación con fines

de Acreditación Institucional" 24
Intermunicipal Consortium Greater ABC 187
International Organization for Standardization (ISO): ISO 21502:2020 108; ISO 30408:2016 198; ISO 31000:2018 219
Ionaşcu, D. 255
IS see information system (IS)
Islami, X. 194
ISO see International Organization for Standardization (ISO)

Jang, J. 144
Japan: in-service training seminars 47
Jensen, M.C. 200, 219, 221
Jobber, D. 251
John, A. 258
Johnston, D. 3
Jonsta, Z. 3
Jost, P.-J. 222, 223
Jung, I. 60
Júnior, J.A. 187
Jurčová, M. 69, 72

Kabak, O. 120, 122
Kaehler, B. 198
Kahn, K.B. 85
Kaiser, H.F. 150
Kamen, J.F. 66
Kapelan, Z. 120
Karanja, E. 219, 225, 226, 244
Karni, R. 121
Karoğlu, A.K. 46, 48
Karpova, E. 76
Karsh, B.T. 143
Katsarou, E. 60
Kaufman, J.C. 64
Keeney, R.L. 119, 121, 124
Keizer, J.A. 85
Keller, R.B. 88
Khan, S.N. 162
Khun, T.: *Structure of Scientific Revolutions, The* 105
Kim, M. 107
Kitagawa, H. 188
Klaus, S. 3
Klemenc-Ketis, Z. 142
Klinker, K. 145

Knol, A. 253
Kolios, A. 119
Kontić, B. 121
Kořan, M. 69
Korkmaz, İ. 47
Kosovo 5
Kostelidou, K. 3
Kovács, I. 255
Koval, O. 253, 259
Kraus, S. 159
Krause, M. 119
Kuechler, W. 122
Kwok, A.O.J. 162

labor absenteeism 30
Lai, C.M. 144
Lambert, R.A. 221
Lampis, A. 182
Landeweerd, J. 29
Latchem, C. 60
Latif, Z. 188
Laudon, J. 106
Laudon, K. 106
leader behavior 28
leadership: effective 23, 26, 28, 29, 31, 34, 38; effectiveness *see* leadership effectiveness; ethical *see* ethical leadership; good 28; transactional 27; transformational 26, 27
leadership effectiveness: contributions 39; data collection 32; data triangulation 32, 34–35; demographic aspects 35; hypotheses testing 36–37, **36**, *37*; limitations of 39–40; literature review 26–30; mean scores 35–36; measures in factor analysis 31–32, **31**; practical implications 38; qualitative research measurement tool 34; reliability 32, **33**; researching technique 34; research methodology 30–35; research model *30*; samples 34; secondary data collection 34–35; validity 32, **33**; *see also* effective leadership
Lee, J. 146, **148**, 153
Lee, W. M. 161
Lee Ludvigsen, J.A. 160

Lehiste, P. 59
Lemos, F. 225
LEN model 219, 220; of agency theory in hidden action situation 220–224, *222*, **225**
Lennon, K.H. 66, 71
Leung, A.K.Y. 76
Levin, A. 138, 139
Lewis, A.C. 198
Liang, P.J. 226
Liebenberg, A.P. 219, 226, 244
Liguori, E. 159
Lin, T.C. 60
Lipušček, I. 120, 121
Lorenzen-Huber, L. 65
Lucas, B. 64

Ma, H-H. 76
Macho-Stadler, I. 222
Macrometrópole of São Paulo (MMP) 182, 184
Mahraz, M.-I. 43
Majumdar, B. 163
Makhecha, U.P. 199
Malcolm Baldrige National Quality Award 202
Mandrusov, V. 88, 99
Mann, A. 195
Mao, C. 88, 98
Mardani, A. 120
Marie, K.J. 118
Marie Skłodowska-Curie Actions (MSCA) 3
Marino, C. 188
Marinova, G. 4, 6, 13, 14, 19
marketing communication: ambient and guerilla 66–67; event marketing and 67–68
Marquis, D.G. 85
Marston, S. 253
Martin, G. 198
Martinez, V. 43
MAUT methodology 122, 124
Maxwell, J. 28
Mayo, E. 75
MCDM *see* Multi-Criteria Decision Methodologies (MCDM)
Mc. Farland, L. 28
McSweeney, M.J. 159
Meckling, W.H. 200, 219, 221
Megale, A. 188

272   Index

Meier, O. 195
Meinel, M. 74, 259
Menaia, J. 118, 120
Merritt, G.M. 101
Methodist University: Observatory of Economics 178
Meyer, J. **31**
Michaelis, M. 219, 220, 226, 244, 246
Mikuláš, P. 66
MMP *see* Macrometrópole of São Paulo (MMP)
Moldova 4, 5
Mondello, M. 162
MonkeyLeagu 167–169
Montenegro 5
Montrose, M.I. 88, 99
Morakanyane, R. 43
Moran, J. 137
Moravčíková, E. 68
Morceiro, P.C. 182
Mostert, N. 64, 65
MSCA *see* Marie Skłodowska-Curie Actions (MSCA)
Mugo, D.G. 138
Mukherji, A. 195
Mulolli, E. 194
Multi-Criteria Decision Methodologies (MCDM): comparison of 118–132; design science research 122–123; model development 124–125, *125*, *126*; previous research 120–121; project evaluation 127–131, **128–130**, *130*; recommendations for 132; research aims 119; selection of 123–124; theoretical background of 119–120; utility function 125–127
Munzer, B.W. 142
Myers, S. 85

Nadini, M. 163
Naha, S. 163
Naman, V. 162
Naraine, M.L. 162
National Accreditation Council (Colombia) 24; design 87–90
National Association of Motor Vehicle Manufacturers (Anfavea) 187
National Association of the Industry of Components for Motor Vehicles (Sindipeças) 187

National Institute of Standards and Technology 202
National Taiwan University Children's Hospital (NTUCH) 138
NBA Top Shot 163
Negreiros, I. 182, 184
New Product Development (NPD): data analysis 95–100; data collection 91–95; in electronics industry, testing and certification of 85–101; methodology 86–87; preparation of 90–91; research plan 86–87
NFTs *see* Non-Fungible Tokens (NFTs)
Nickel, O. 68
Nicola, M. 159
Nishii, L.H. 199
Non-Fungible Tokens (NFTs) 159, 162–170
North Macedonia 5
Nowak, B. 119
Nowak, M. 119
NPD *see* New Product Development (NPD)
NTUCH *see* National Taiwan University Children's Hospital (NTUCH)
Nufer, G. 68
Nuti, S. 138

off-boarding 207
Office Depot Europe 251
Oliveira, M. 187–188
Ollala, F.M. 198
Olsson, G. 120
on-boarding 207
OneFootball 168
O'Reilly, C.A. 198
organizational development 212
Orij, R.P. 252
Osborn, A.F. 71
owner management relationships 215
Öz, Ö. 46
Ozdemir-Gungor, D. 145
Özerbaş, M.A. 49

Pagach, D. 219, 226
Park, J. 142
Parlak, B. 46
Parnell, D. 159

Index 273

Patton, M.Q. 69
Paz, A. 28
Peccei, R. 195
Pérez-Castrillo, J.D. 222
performance monitoring 209–210
Perry, A. 76
personnel management 207
Pervan, G. 122
Petersen-Wagner, R. 160
Petrişor, I. 253
Petrobras 187
Petrochemical Pole 187
Phillips, J. 196
Pichot, N. 64
Pilz, M. 58
Pinto, L.H. 260
PMLC *see* project management life
    cycle (PMLC) model
Poland 4, 5
Prasad, A. 251
Prendergast, C. 220
PRINCE2 "Projects in a Controlled
    Environment" 108
project management, information
    system in 103–116; attitude
    toward software 114;
    recommendations 115–116;
    research aims 109; research
    methodology 109–110; results
    110–114; training of employees
    114; usage and types 113; work
    organization 111–113
Project Management Institute, Inc.:
    PMBOK®Guide 108
project management life cycle (PMLC)
    model 108
Pucihar, A. 43
Puck, J. 254
Puteh, F. 259

Qian, T.Y. 160
Quijada, G. 28

Rai, S.L. 107
Raiffa, H. 119
Rajasekaran, A.S. 161
Ratcliffe, J. 139, 140
Ratten, V. 159
Rauschnabel, P.A. 150, 153
R Core Team Software 37
Reavis, M.W. 225

recruitment 204–205, 205–207
Reinartz, W. 64
Reinhold, R.
Reis, C.F.B. 177, 178, 182
return on investment (ROI) 196
Rezende, R. 188
Richardson, H. 260
Richter, P. 253, 255, 257, 259
Rip, A. 105
risk management: in agency 224–226;
    agency theoretical analysis of
    227–246, *238*, *239*, **245**;
    organization and incentivization
    of 219–247, **221**, 249–250;
    recommendations for 246–247
Ritter, S.M. 64, 65
Robinson, B. 60
Rockwell, G. 252
Rodic, B. 110, 114
Rodríguez, V. 23, 28
Rogers, C.R. 71
ROI *see* return on investment (ROI)
Rolnik, R. 185
Romania 4, 5; doing business in
    253–255
Rosenblatt, E. 65
Rothwell, A.T. 259
Rothwell, R. 85
Rozman, Č. 121
Ruan, D. 120, 122
Runco, M.A. 64

Sacht, J. 197, 198
Saffert, P. 64
Sagnier, C. 153
Sandoval, C. 34
Santo André Foundation 188
Sappington, D.E.M. 221
Šavrič, J. 110, 114
Scanlon, C. 161
Schäfer, U. 222, 223
Schaufeli, W. 29, **31**
Scheck, H. 3
Scott, G. 66
SDGs *see* Sustainable Development
    Goals (SDGs)
SDSN network (UN Sustainable
    Development Solution
    Network) 182
Seijo, C. 28
Selltiz, C. 34

274 Index

SEM *see* Structural Equation
Modeling (SEM)
Şener, G. 47
Serbia 5
Serin, M.K. 47
Serra, Rio Grande da 188
Shamay-Tsoory, S.G. 71
shared service centers (SSCs) 252–255;
CSR portfolio, maintaining
255–259
Shared Services & Outsourcing
Network, The 259
Shenhar, A.J. 92
Shrivastava, R. 85
Sicotte, H. 85
Siegel, M. 225
Siemens, G. 58
Sierpina, M. 65
Silva, A. Oliveira da 187, 189
Simkins, B.J. 219, 224, 226, 244
Simonton, D.K. 76
Şimşek, H. 49
Sinclair, S. 252
Sindusfarma (Sindicato da Indústria de
Produtos Farmacêuticos) 188
Singh, A. 162
Sistenich, F. 68
Slovakia 4, 5
Slovenia 5
Smart Contracts 162
SMA *see* social media addiction (SMA)
Smith, P.G. 101
Smithson, C. 219, 226, 244
social labor 24
social media addiction (SMA) 145, 146
socio-technical systems design
(STSD) 105
Sola, E. 65
Solodukhova, O.G. 64
Sołtysik-Piorunkiewicz, A. 65
Solvay, R. 188
Somekh, N. 185
Sorantin, E. 3, 4
Sorare 167
Soviet Union 4
Spitz, J. 161
sports sector: broadcasting 160–161; use
of blockchain technology in
159–170; video assistance
160–161; wearables 160–161
Spremann, K. 219, 221, 223, 224

SSCs *see* shared service centers (SSCs)
Stake, R.E. 34
Stanek, S. 65
Steenkamp, J.B.E. 145, **148**
Sternberg, R.J. 69
Straub, D.W. **148**
Straus, S.G. 138
Strauss, A. 111
Štrbová, E. 68
Strong, J.S. 252
Structural Equation Modeling (SEM)
36, **36**
STS (Science, Technology & Society)
103–105
STSD *see* socio-technical systems design
(STSD)
Stylsvig, C. 168–169
Su, S.P. 144
succession planning 209
Sustainable Development Goals
(SDGs) **180–181**, 182, 189, 191
Světlík, J. 66
Swathi, B. 30
Switzerland: in-service teacher
training 47
Szobiova, E. 66

TAM *see* technology acceptance
model (TAM)
Tang, K.S. 154
Tang, L. 59
Taşkıran, A. 45
Task-Technology Fit (TTF) model 107
Taylor, S. 195
Teacher Information Network (TIN),
Turkey: digital transformation
in education 43–60; scope and
content of 50–53, **51**
teachers' competencies 55–56, **55**
TEACH platform 60
Technological Pedagogical Content
Knowledge (TPACK) 59
technology acceptance model (TAM)
107, 138, 143–146, *144*
Teichert, R. 43
Tekin, H. 49
Tekin, H.H. 49
Teknofest 48
Temizyürek, D.D.F. 46
Tetrevova, L. 255
theory of the firm 200

Index 275

Theriou, G. 30
Till, B.D. 64
Tilley, L. 252
TIN *see* Teacher Information Network (TIN), Turkey
Titko, J. 44
Tola, K. 6, 13, 14
Torrance, E.P. 65, 69, 72
Torrance test of creative thinking (TTCT) 69, 70, *72*
TPACK *see* Technological Pedagogical Content Knowledge (TPACK)
TPM *see* traditional project management (TPM)
traditional project management (TPM) 108
transactional leadership 27
transformational leadership 26, 27
TTCT *see* Torrance test of creative thinking (TTCT)
TTF *see* Task-Technology Fit (TTF) model
Turkey: "81 Cyber Heroes in 81 Cities" 47; "Deneyap Technology Workshops" 47; "Design-Skill Workshops" 47; digital transformation, in education 43–60; Digital Turkey Roadmap of the Ministry of Industry and Technology 48; Education Information Network (EBA – Eğitim Bilişim Ağı) 47; Foundation of Türkiye Technology Team 48; Human-Education Infrastructure Development and Qualified Workforce Training policies 48; MEB Information System (MEBBİS) 48; Ministry of Technology and Industry of Türkiye 48; Movement for Increasing Opportunities and Improving Technology (FATİH – Fırsatları Arttırma ve Teknolojiyi İyileştirme Hareketi) 47; Teacher Information Network (TIN) 43–60; Teaching Profession Law 49; "Teknofest" event 48
Tushman, M.L. 198

Uçak, S. 46
Ulrich, D. 197
United Nations' Security Council: Resolution 1244 4
University Corporation of Ibagué, Coruniversitaria 23–24
University of Creative Communication, Prague 66
Ünlü, O.N. 46
USA: in-service teacher training 37
Uymaz, A.O. 153
Uymaz, P. 153

Vaishnavi, V.K. 122
Vallejo, R. 32
Vally, Z. 75
Van De Voorde, K. 195
van Esch, P. 205, 206
VAR *see* Video Assistant Referee (VAR)
Velasquez, M. 121, 123
Venckuté, M. 65
Verina, N. 44
Video Assistant Referee (VAR) 160–161
video game 91–93, 96–97
Viking by RAJA Group, Cluj-Napoca 251–263
Vinterová, K. 65
virtual reality (VR) 137–138; applications in medical rraining 141–143
Volpi, C. 187
Von Winterfeldt, D. 121
VR *see* virtual reality (VR)

Wake, N. 143
Walker, J.W. 196
Walton, C. 251
Wang, Y. 145, **148**, 153
Warr, R. 219, 226
water management investment project 118–132
Weber, M. 27
Wegener, D. 32
Weinberg, P. 68
Welker, R.B. 107
"wicked" problem 122
Wilczek, P. 66
Williams, T. 88, 99
Willis, G. 204
Winand, M. 160

276   Index

Winkler, C. 159
Winkler-Schwartz, A. 137
Winner, E. 65
wire breaking strength tester 93–95,
    97–98
Woodthorpe, K. 252
workforce planning 203–204
Wright, P.M. 195, 199
Wuller, H. 137
Wysocki, K.R. 107–108

xPM/MPx *see* extreme project
    management model (xPM/MPx)
XR *see* extended reality (XR)

Yan, J. 195
Yavuz, M. 144
Yazici, E.B. 49
Yazıcı, Ö. 47
Yıldırım, A. 49

Yıldız, E.P. 45
Yin, R.K. 69, 75, 86, 91, 95, 100,
    164, 252
Yinanç, A. 45, 46
Yong, J.Y. 195
Yu, S. 162
Yuwono, T. 88, 98, 99

Zainee, I.A. 259
Zaleznik, A. 28
Zanakis, S.H. 121
Zanger, C. 68
Zaucha, T. 163
Zavadskas, E.K. 119, 120
Zelina, M. 65, 66, 71
Zglinski, J. 161
Zhu, E. 138
Žnidaršič, M. 121
Zuma, S.K. 198

Printed in the United States
by Baker & Taylor Publisher Services